Letts study aids

Revise Economics

A complete revision course for O level and CSE

Keith West BSc (Econ), MEd

Head of Economics, Matthew Humberstone School, Cleethorpes

Charles Letts & Co Ltd
London, Edinburgh & New York

D1334984

First published 1985
by Charles Letts & Co Ltd
Diary House, Borough Road, London SE1 1DW

Design: Ben Sands and Anne Davison
Illustrations: Peter McClure
Editor: John Bishop

ISBN 0 85097 632 4

Printed by Charles Letts (Scotland) Limited

Preface

Economics is a fairly new examination subject. Some old-fashioned schools still do not have Economics courses. Thus, not all examination boards have Economics examinations. For instance at Certificate of Secondary Education (CSE) level, there are only three boards currently offering Mode 1, as most boards offer Mode 3. However, the Certificate of Extended Education (CEE), which is like a sixth form CSE, has spawned many Economics courses (Mode 3) which include the subject matter of this book, at this level. The 17+ examination, which will replace CEE, will undoubtedly feature many Economics courses which will probably be of the Mode 1 type. The level of this book makes it appropriate for CSE, CEE, 16+, 17+ and O-level students.

There are several different examination titles which embrace Economics content. At O level and Mode 1 CSE the most common titles are Economics, and Social Economics. In addition, Economics is sometimes an optional part of a multidisciplinary social science examination *e.g.* Government, Economics, Commerce. Furthermore, Economics is sometimes combined with another subject in an integrated course, particularly at CSE level.

Clearly a straight Economics course will utilize more of this book than the other interdisciplinary courses. The syllabus analysis in Part I will show you which topics are covered by the different O and CSE Mode 1 syllabuses.

This book has been written primarily to prepare candidates for O-level and CSE examinations in Economics. It should also prove useful as a preparation for 16+ (and 17+ when it is introduced) Business Studies and Professional examinations which contain Economics. As an experienced teacher and examiner I have written this book to show students the standards and skills required at this level by the different examination boards. It assumes some familiarity with the subject which two years study should give. Thus, it is not a course textbook, but a **Revision Guide**. For this reason, there are **Self-test units** for each chapter. There is also a section containing recent **Essay questions**. For both these sections, answer guidelines (rather than model answers) have been provided. The answer hints are my sole responsibility and have not been provided or approved by the boards concerned.

I acknowledge with thanks the permission given to me by the examination boards, whose questions I have used:

AEB	: Associated Examining Board for the General Certificate of Education
Cambridge	: University of Cambridge Local Examinations Syndicate
JMB	: Joint Matriculation Board
Oxford	: Oxford Delegacy of Local Examinations
London	: University of London University Entrance and School Examination Council
Welsh	: Welsh Joint Education Committee
London REB	: London Regional Examinations Board

I am also grateful to the Trustee Savings Bank for permission to reproduce one of their cheques, cheque guarantee cards and credit cards on pages 63–4.

I have endeavoured to use questions which are as up-to-date as possible from those available. Some questions feature the marks per part in brackets. This guidance varies between boards, as do the total marks per essay question. The statistics, adapted from several HMSO publications, were also the latest available at the time of writing.

I wish to express my special thanks to David Sowden for his perceptive comments and thoughtful mnemonics. He contributed the major part of Units 4, 16 and 17 and substantial sections in 13 and 15. He also prepared many Self-test questions and suggested some of the essay guidelines for these Units.

I also want to thank Dorothy Hollinshead for her typing in the face of close deadlines at short notice. The staff at Charles Letts & Co., too, have been most interested, supportive and considerate. Mainly though, I am most grateful to my wife, Chris, for her help, enthusiasm, patience and typing (again!)

The shortcomings, which I expect fellow teachers to identify, are entirely my own.

K. C. West

Contents

Part I

Introduction and guide to using this book

Organization of the book

This book has been designed for O-level, SCE and CSE level candidates. It is not a substitute for a textbook, but a comprehensive revision guide, based on examination experience. Each part in the book has a clear and specific function. The most important part is **Core Units 1–20** (Part II).

The main syllabus topics, which are given for each board in the syllabus analysis in Part I, form chapters called **'Units'**. Within each unit there is a subdivision into **Sections** representing the most important areas of knowledge and understanding. At the beginning of each Unit each section is starred according to its usefulness for revision:

  *** must be known thoroughly
   ** often examined
    * necessary background reading

Throughout each unit **Mnemonics** are used to aid memory. For instance in Unit 5, external economies of scale can be remembered by **'LICE'** which stands for Labour, Information, Concentration and Education.

Within each section the main points are in **bold type** for emphasis. This is done particularly where there is an introduction, *e.g.* 5.1, in which the key points of 'productive', 'paid employment' and 'indirect' have been emphasized in this way.

Towards the end of each unit, other important **linked topics** are listed. The revision of these topics is very important as they provide supplementary knowledge which helps in understanding the topic given. Also, these linked topics are sometimes combined with the main unit in examination questions. For instance, an analysis of questions shows that the topic **Money** is often linked, and thus best revised, with **Banking** and **Inflation**. Thus, if you do not wish to (or do not have the time to) revise all of this book, related units should be chosen for study. The linked topics section, in all units except 19 and 20, gives guidance on which units 'go together'. This organization is based on the theory of the structured approach.

The structured approach

Research on cognition by Reed shows that information is better recalled if it is presented in an **organizational framework**. A framework makes retrieval systematic.

This book contains a **Core Units** chapter of twenty units, (Part II), containing the necessary information relating to O/CSE Economics. It is followed by **Self-test questions and answers**, (Part III) which covers each of the twenty units in turn. Part IV, **Essay questions and answers**, gives examples of recent examination board questions for students to attempt and provides guidelines to the answers. It, too, is organized so that the questions relating to one unit are kept together.

In Part II, **Core Units 1–20**, which is the bulk of the book, the **same structure** is repeated across units. This shows you the way in which information needs to be stored and retrieved. The different details in each unit are designed to make the material as different as possible. This should encourage separate stores of information to be developed.

Evidence shows that pupils learn hierarchical information quickly and have considerable difficulty in learning the same information when it is presented in a random manner. Thus a **hierarchical** structure, as in this book, enables the search of memory to be structured and material to be recalled more efficiently.

The study of how people retrieve information reveals that they are likely to group from **two to five items together**. Groups of this size form a hierarchy. This has been borne in mind in the organization of material under headings.

There are usually three or four subheadings within each section. Most of the mnemonics feature four or five ideas within a subheading. There are often several key words, which are emphasized, within a mnemonic.

For instance, **Unit 5.6 Large-scale production** is structured as follows:

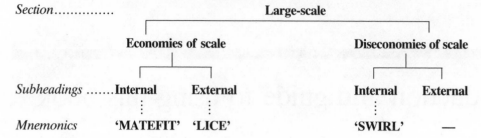

Section...............   **Large-scale**

    Economies of scale   **Diseconomies of scale**

Subheadings ....**Internal**   **External**   **Internal**   **External**

Mnemonics   **'MATEFIT'**   **'LICE'**   **'SWIRL'**   —

Learning and remembering

When we **learn** we use our senses in the following proportions:

75% sight ⎫
13% hearing ⎬ relevant to this subject
6% touch ⎫
3% smell ⎬ irrelevant to this subject
3% taste ⎭

Thus, seeing the printed page and hearing about the subject are vitally important.

It is also reckoned, by the British Audio-Visual Association, that we **remember** –

80% of what we say
50% of what we see and hear
30% of what we see
20% of what we hear
10% of what we read

Clearly, reading information **on its own** is a poor way to remember. However, combined with **saying** the information, it is very effective.

You should try to **read** and **say aloud** what you revise. You therefore need to study in isolation. You are likely to distract or annoy other people if you study with them around. Also, by being on your own, you are less likely to be interrupted, and more likely to learn effectively.

Revision

Revision is an important part of effective studying. As O-level and CSE examinations are the culmination of two years' school work there is plenty of information which needs to be learnt. This makes thorough and well-organized revision most important. I would recommend a **minimum of fifteen hours** revision in the period before your Economics examination. This should enable you to cover sufficient syllabus topics to give you a fair choice of questions on the normal essay-dominated examination paper.

A **programme** of revision is thus clearly needed. It is usually advisable to have a schedule of revision covering **all** of your examinations. Once you know the dates of your examinations you should work out when you are going to revise for each one, bearing in mind the **quantity of revision** needed. For some subjects, such as English Language, a lot of revision is not required, whilst for others, such as Economics, it is! You should have a rough idea of how much revision is needed for each subject and the total amount of time available for revision. Build a couple of blank days into your schedule for emergencies. By **Easter** you should have all this information and be able to devise your programme of revision.

The length of your revision programme depends partly on when your examinations are timetabled. You should start at least two weeks before your first examination. If most of your exams are bunched together at the start of the examination period then more time (say three weeks) will be needed for revision before the start. In general, the period of **intensive** revision and examinations will be about one **month**.

You need to ask yourself 'Is it **worth** devoting one month out of a lifetime to revision in order to obtain "good" exam results?' If you are not sure that the answer is **'Yes'** then bear in mind the following:

1 A month is just ⅑₀₀th of a lifetime. It is not much to give up, as there is a lot at stake.

2 You will undoubtedly gain higher grades by revising than by not revising and thus better qualifications. In the long run those with better qualifications earn more and have a more satisfying life!

3 You will gain respect from friends and teachers.

4 You may well prove certain teachers wrong – there's an incentive!

5 You will prove to yourself that you have self-discipline *i.e.* you can make sacrifices.

6 A proper revision schedule allows some relaxation anyway.

The **order** in which you revise is important. Try to arrange your revision schedule so that you revise for a subject in the last few days before you take that examination. If that is not possible, and you have two subjects being examined on the same day, then make your least familiar subject the last one you revise. Similarly, the order in which you revise the topics of a subject is important. Topics with which you are least familiar/happy should be revised towards the end of your schedule and quickly reviewed right at the end of your revision programme.

The **use** made of revision time is important. It is not a case of just sitting down and reading a book for two hours! Your revision timetable needs structuring. Effective revision requires:

Organization and planning We have already outlined the pre-study planning needed and the priorities which need to be set. In addition, you should plan how to use your revision time. Psychologists reckon that **thirty minutes revision**, followed by a **ten minute break**, up to a maximum of **two hours at a time**, is the most effective. This should be done in a quiet place at home or school (*e.g* library).

Maintaining motivation A revision schedule should have clear **objectives** and immediate built-in **rewards**, as well as the long-term prospects of better examination results. For instance, you should set yourself a target, *e.g.* learn Unit 5 in a two-hour revision session and score 15/20 on the self-test. If this is achieved, reward yourself *e.g.* listen to your favourite LP for twenty minutes.

Motivation can be maintained by using techniques to stop mind-wandering. For instance, occasional **physical movement** such as getting up and pacing the room and talking aloud often break the monotony of continued study. Many experts suggest revisions at **different times of day** each day and frequent **change of subject**, as well as targets and rewards to stimulate interest and prevent boredom.

Learning the notes There are several possible methods of learning which could be employed. There is no one definitive method, but some are more accredited than others. You could:

1 Make notes from a unit and then read and re-read the notes.

2 Learn key words and sentences/definitions off by heart.

3 Read a unit several times and then test yourself by writing out/saying out loud the main points.

Whichever method is used, the memory needs to be trained and you should make the best use of the resources at your disposal. This book should be a most useful resource!

A simple memory-training technique, which has been referred to already, is the **'work-test-rest'** routine. The test element is particularly important because it tells you how effective your revising has been. If, after a period of learning, you can write out the main points from memory accurately (when checked against the book or notes), both immediately and days later, then you have developed an effective technique. Another aid to memory is the **mnemonic**. These have been used extensively in this book as a type of shorthand to help remember several main points.

The P.Q. 4R method

This study method incorporates many of the general points made above. It was developed by E. L. Thomas and H. A. Robinson in 1972. It has been loosely used by the author in the preparation of this book and can be applied to revising from this book as follows:

P = Preview You should survey the syllabus review in Part I to discover which units you need to cover for your examination, because the syllabuses vary between examination boards. Then, in each unit, you should see which topics are covered. The unit subheadings are listed at the start of each unit, *e.g.*

5	**Production**	
5.1	Introduction	*
5.2	Types of production	**
5.3	Factors of production	**
5.4	Division of labour/specialization	***
5.5	Costs of production	***
5.6	Large-scale production	***
5.7	Growth of firms	***
5.8	Small firms	***
5.9	Linked topics	***

The asterisks * stress the relative importance of the parts.

Q = Questions This method advises asking yourself questions about the sections. This may involve transforming the subheadings into questions. For instance 5.4. What is the Division of labour? What are its advantages/disadvantages?

4R = Read, Reflect, Recite, Review.

Read – Read through the text answering the questions to yourself as you go along.

Reflect – This means try to understand the text and think of examples (in this book plenty are given). You should also relate the material learned to other knowledge. In this book some cross-referencing is done by the section 'Links with other topics' at the end of each unit.

Recite – Try to recall what you have read (and spoken – see above, **Learning and remembering**). If you cannot recall the information, re-read the text.

Review – Go through the unit again, after a break. In the review you should recall the main points and answer the questions. At this stage you could use the Self-test and/or Essay Questions.

Revision also involves **examination preparation generally**. Probably your teacher will have organized revision tests during the year, a mock examination, and a review of major topics. Although many frown upon 'question spotting', certain topics are fairly predictable at O level and your teacher should have made you wise to them. He/she may even have several **'bankers'** for you to concentrate upon. However, do not rely on just such topics, although obviously devote time to them.

In your revision at school, you will probably have practised writing 'against the clock' *i.e.* **test essays**. If not, you should do so as part of your revision. This book can help. In the Essays section it provides on average four old examination questions per unit. After learning a unit, you could tackle the first question for half an hour; then read the answer section where the main points which were needed in the answer are outlined. If you are genuinely pleased with the answer which you have written then pass on to another unit. Be particularly careful to 'know' your **examples**. You do not want to have to think them up during the actual examination.

The final general aspect to revision is **coping with stress**. You need to be able to manage stress. For some casual people it is less of a problem than for most students. A properly-devised revision schedule should help allay stress somewhat. It should **balance study** and **other activities**. Thus, if you divide your daily revision time into four two-hour periods, then leave one of these periods free. This can be used for thorough relaxation, going out, or watching television – *i.e.* a break from studying. Furthermore, if you are getting behind with a unit you could push over into one of these free periods if it means you take pressure off yourself and become less worried about completing all of the necessary revision. If, generally, you are finding that units are taking longer to revise than expected, adjust your revision programme. In devising a programme of revision, at the start of this section, I suggested allowing a couple of blank days for an emergency – getting behind is one such emergency!

In your periods of relaxation it might occasionally be worth meeting friends who are doing similar revision. Discussion with them can be reassuring and common problems can be examined, even if they are not resolved. Whatever you do, do **not** give up.

To pass examinations you need to be:

1 **Honest** – *i.e.* don't kid yourself when you sit reading that you are learning.

2 **Realistic** – *i.e.* don't skimp through a topic in ten minutes, looking at the headings – and hope to remember it.

3 **Self-disciplined** – *i.e.* don't shelve your revision work because a friend calls or television looks interesting or you fancy a walk in the sun!

Table of analysis of examination syllabuses	AEB Econ. Principles	AEB Social Econ.	Cambridge	JMB Govt. Econ. Comm.	London Univ.	N. Ireland	Oxford	Scottish	Welsh	E. Anglia	London Reb.	Southern
Level	O	O	O	O	O	O	O	O	O	CSE	CSE	CSE
Economic Ideas												
1.2 Roles		●								●		
1.3 Concepts	●	●	●	●	●	●		●			●	●
1.4 Economic problem		●	●	●		●		●	●		●	
Economic Systems												
2.2 Capitalist	●	●	●	●		●		●			●	
2.3 Collectivist	●	●	●	●		●		●			●	
2.4 Mixed	●	●	●	●		●	●	●			●	
2.5 Subsistence	●	●	●	●		●		●			●	
Business Units												
3.1 Public & private sector	●	●	●	●	●	●		●		●		●
3.2 Public corps/Nat. Ind.	●	●	●	●	●	●		●		●	●	
3.3 Companies	●	●	●	●	●	●		●		●	●	
3.4 Partnerships	●	●	●	●	●	●		●		●	●	
3.5 Sole traders	●	●	●	●	●	●		●		●	●	
3.6 Co-operatives	●	●	●	●	●	●		●		●		
3.7 Finance				●						●		
3.8 Shares		●	●		●			●		●		
Demand and supply												
4.2 Demand	●		●	●	●	●	●		●			●
4.3 Supply	●		●	●	●	●	●		●			●
4.4 Price	●		●	●	●	●	●	●	●			●
4.5 Elasticity	●		●		●	●	●					●
Production												
5.2 Types	●	●	●			●	●	●				●
5.3 Factors	●		●		●	●		●	●		●	●
5.4 Div. of labour/specialistn.	●	●	●	●		●	●	●	●	●	●	●
5.5 Costs			●	●	●	●	●	●				
5.6 Large scale	●	●	●	●	●	●	●				●	
5.7 Growth of firms	●		●	●	●	●	●					
5.8 Small firms	●			●	●	●	●					
Location of Industry												
6.2 Factors	●	●	●	●	●		●	●	●	●	●	●
6.3 Regional problems	●	●	●		●		●	●	●	●		●
6.4 Regional policies	●	●	●	●	●		●	●	●	●		●
6.5 Steel					●			●	●	●		
6.6 North Sea Oil					●			●	●	●		
Markets												
7.1 Introduction		●					●	●				●
7.2 Perfect competition		●	●				●	●				●
7.3 Monopoly		●	●				●	●			●	●
7.4 Government & monopoly		●	●				●					
7.5 Imperfect competition		●	●				●					
Money												
8.2 Definition	●	●	●	●	●	●	●	●	●			●
8.3 Functions	●	●	●	●	●	●	●	●	●	●	●	●
8.4 Qualities	●		●	●	●	●	●	●	●			
8.5 Historical development	●	●	●	●	●		●	●	●	●		
8.6 Measurement		●										
Inflation												
9.2 Definition	●	●	●	●	●	●	●	●				●
9.3 Types	●	●	●	●	●	●	●	●		●		●
9.4 Measurement	●		●	●	●	●	●	●				●
9.5 Method of calculation			●	●	●	●		●			●	●
9.6 Effects	●	●	●	●	●	●	●	●				
9.7 Causes	●	●	●	●	●	●	●	●				
9.8 Control & policies	●	●	●	●	●	●	●	●				

Table of analysis of examination syllabuses — *continued*	AEB Econ. Principles	AEB Social Econ.	Cambridge	JMB Govt. Econ. Comm.	London Univ.	N. Ireland	Oxford	Scottish	Welsh	E. Anglia	London Reb.	Southern
Level	O	O	O	O	O	O	O	O	O	CSE	CSE	CSE
Banking												
10.2 Types	●	●	●	●	●	●	●	●				●
10.3 Commercial banks	●	●	●	●	●	●	●	●		●	●	●
10.4 Balance sheet			●	●	●	●		●				
10.5 Credit creation	●		●	●	●	●	●	●			●	●
10.6 Money Market	●		●	●				●	●			●
10.7 Bank of England	●		●	●	●	●	●	●	●	●	●	●
10.8 Monetary control	●		●	●		●	●	●				
Saving												
11.2 Borrowers	●	●				●		●	●	●	●	●
11.3 Savings institutions	●	●				●		●	●	●	●	●
11.4 Stock exchange		●	●		●			●	●	●	●	
11.5 Personal savings	●	●								●		●
Population												
12.1 Growth		●	●	●	●		●	●	●		●	●
12.2 Size		●	●	●	●		●	●	●		●	●
12.3 Structure		●	●	●	●		●	●	●		●	●
12.4 Mobility of labour		●	●	●	●		●	●	●		●	●
12.5 World population					●		●					●
Wages and trade unions												
13.2 Means of payment		●	●	●		●			●	●	●	●
13.3 Demand for labour		●	●	●		●						
13.4 Supply of labour		●	●	●		●						
13.5 Wage differentials		●	●	●		●						
13.6 Incomes policy		●						●			●	
13.7 TU–aims, functions, types		●	●	●	●			●	●	●	●	●
13.8 TU–organization, methods		●	●	●	●			●	●	●	●	●
13.9 Govt. & Indust. relations		●	●	●	●			●	●			●
13.10 TUC & CBI		●	●	●				●			●	●
National Income and std. of living												
14.1 Circular flow	●		●	●		●	●	●				
14.2 Measurement	●		●	●			●	●			●	●
14.3 Use of N.I. statistics		●	●	●			●	●			●	●
14.4 Economic growth	●			●	●	●		●				●
Public finance												
15.1 Public expenditure		●	●		●	●			●	●	●	●
15.2 Taxation–aims, principles	●	●	●	●	●	●	●		●	●	●	●
15.3 Taxation–types	●	●	●	●	●	●	●		●	●	●	●
15.4 Taxes on income, expenditure & capital	●	●	●	●	●	●	●		●	●	●	●
15.5 Incidence					●							
15.6 Budget & PSBR	●	●				●			●		●	
15.7 National debt	●									●		
Unemployment												
16.2 Characteristics		●	●	●			●	●			●	●
16.3 Costs		●	●	●			●	●				●
16.4 Measurement		●	●	●			●	●				●
16.5 Types		●	●	●			●	●			●	●
16.6 Causes		●	●	●			●	●				●
16.7 Policies	●	●	●	●			●	●			●	
Trade												
17.1 Advantages	●	●	●	●	●	●	●	●	●	●	●	●
17.2 Patterns of UK trade	●			●	●		●	●	●			●
17.3 Terms of trade	●	●	●	●	●		●		●			
17.4 Government control	●	●	●	●	●		●	●	●		●	●
17.5 Methods of protection	●	●	●	●	●		●	●	●		●	●
17.6 Int. economic organizations		●									●	●
17.7 EEC		●			●			●		●	●	●

Table of analysis of examination syllabuses — *continued*

	AEB Econ. Principles	AEB Social Econ.	Cambridge	JMB Govt. Econ. Comm.	London Univ.	N. Ireland	Oxford	Scottish	Welsh	E. Anglia	London Reb.	Southern
Level	O	O	O	O	O	O	O	O	O	CSE	CSE	CSE
Balance of payments												
18.1 B. of P. accounts	●	●	●	●	●		●	●	●	●	●	●
18.2 Problems	●	●	●	●	●		●	●	●	●	●	●
18.3 Policies	●	●	●	●	●		●	●	●	●	●	●
18.4 Exchange rates												
18.5 IMF								●				●
Government Policy												
19.1 Objectives	●	●	●			●		●			●	●
19.2 Limitations	●	●	●			●		●			●	●
19.3 Methods			●	●		●		●			●	●
19.4 Problems & policies	●	●	●			●		●			●	●
19.5 Local government	●	●								●	●	●
Consumption and distribution												
20.2 Distribution			●		●			●		●	●	
20.3 Wholesalers				●				●		●	●	
20.4 Retailers				●				●		●	●	
20.5 Advertising		●						●		●	●	
20.6 Marketing								●				
20.7 Consumer protection		●								●	●	
20.8 Credit		●								●	●	

'Two paper' boards

Board	Level	Paper title	Paper 1			Paper 2			
			Time	%	Type of question	Time	%	Questions Type	Number
Cambridge	O	Economics	1 hr	30	Simple completion and multiple choice	2 hr	70	Essay	4
Scottish	O	Economics	1 hr	40		1¾ hr	60	Essay	3
AEB	O	Economic principles	¾ hr	30	Multiple choice	2¼ hr	70	Essay	1 compulsory; 3 from 7
JMB	O	Govt. Econs., commerce (Econ. option)	½ hr	20	Multiple choice	2 hr	80	Essay	1 compulsory; 3 from 6
AEB		Social economics	1¾ hr	50	Simple completion data interpretation	2 hr	50	Essay	4 from 5

'One paper' boards

Board	Paper title	Paper number	Time	Parts
Oxford	O Economics	2840	2½ hours	5 from 14 essays
Welsh	O Economics	0112	2½ hours	5 from 11 essays
London	O Economics	120	2½ hours	A–compulsory: multiple choice (10%) data (30%) B–3 from 7 essays (60%)
N. Ireland	O Economics		2½ hours	A–2 out of 3 (40%) B–3 from 6 essays (60%)
Southern	CSE Economics		2½ hours	A–compulsory, short answer B–5 from 10 essays
E. Anglia	CSE Soc. Econ.		2½ hours	A–short answer } 85% +15% Teacher B–essays } Assessment
London REB	CSE Elements		2½ hours	A–simple completion C–2 essays B–data D–1 essay or optional project

Examining Boards: Addresses

General Certificate of Education – Ordinary Level (GCE)

AEB
Associated Examining Board
Stag Hill House, Stag Hill, Guildford, Surrey

Cambridge
University of Cambridge Local Examinations Syndicate
Syndicate Buildings, 17 Harvey Road, Cambridge CB1 2EU

JMB
Joint Matriculation Board
Manchester M15 6EU

London
University of London, School Examinations Department
Stewart House, 32 Russell Square, London WC1B 5DN

NIEC
Northern Ireland Schools GCE Examinations Council
Beechill House, 42 Beechill Road, Belfast BT8 4RS

Oxford
Oxford Delegacy of Local Examinations
Ewert Place, Summertown, Oxford OX2 7BX

O and C
Oxford and Cambridge Schools Examination Board
10 Trumpington Street, Cambridge; *and* Elsfield Way, Oxford OX2 8EP

SUJB
Southern Universities' Joint Board for School Examinations
Cotham Road, Bristol BS6 6DD

WJEC
Welsh Joint Education Committee
245 Western Avenue, Cardiff CF5 2YX

Certificate of Secondary Education

ALSEB
Associated Lancashire Schools Examining Board
77 Whitworth Street, Manchester M1 6HA

EAEB
East Anglian Examinations Board
The Lindens, Lexden Road, Colchester, Essex CO3 3RL

EMREB
East Midland Regional Examinations Board
Robins Wood House, Robins Wood Road, Apsley, Nottingham NG8 3RL

LREB
London Regional Examinations Board
(*formerly:* MREB Middlesex Regional Examinations Board)
Lyon House, 104 Wandsworth High Street, London SW18 4LF

NIEB
Northern Ireland CSE Examinations Board
Beechill House, 42 Beechill Road, Belfast BT8 4RS

NREB
North Regional Examinations Board
Wheatfield Road, Westerhope, Newcastle upon Tyne NE5 5JZ

NWREB
North West Regional Examinations Board
Orbit House, Albert Street, Eccles, Manchester M30 0WL

SEREB
South East Regional Examinations Board
Beloe House, 2–4 Mount Ephraim Road, Royal Tunbridge Wells, Kent TN1 1EU

SREB
Southern Regional Examinations Board
53 London Road, Southampton SO9 4YI

SWEB
South Western Examinations Board
23–29 Marsh Street, Bristol BS1 4BP

WJEC
Welsh Joint Education Committee
245 Western Avenue, Cardiff CF5 2YX

WMEB
West Midland Examination Board
Norfolk House, Smallbrook Queensway, Birmingham B5 4NJ

*WYLREB**
West Yorkshire and Lindsey Regional Examining Board
Scarsdale House, 136 Derbyshire Lane, Sheffield S8 8SE

*YREB**
Yorkshire Regional Examinations Board
31–33 Springfield Avenue, Harrogate, North Yorkshire HG1 2HW

*Yorkshire and Humberside Regional Examinations Board, at the *YREB* address, now embraces *WYLREB* and *YREB*

Part II Core units 1–20

1 Economics ideas and concepts

In this Unit, many economics terms are used. It is assumed that you know what they mean from your study so far.

1.1 Introduction

Economics is about making the best use of 'things'. These things are usually referred to as **'resources'** which may be human, natural or man-made. For instance, the **Population** of a region (see Unit 12) is one major resource. These resources are used to make goods and provide services in order to satisfy people's needs and wants. **Thus Economics is about the creation and distribution of wealth**.

Goods and services are produced, distributed and consumed in various ways which differ between **economic systems**. These systems are examined in Unit 2, and the main aspects of **production** are outlined in Unit 5. The specific features of the British mixed economy which students need to know are in **Business units** (Unit 3). O-level and CSE Economics syllabuses concentrate on production and consumption in the main, whereas Commerce examines distribution and the aids to trade in detail. However, the elements of **distribution** which most touch on economics, and are questioned by some boards, are considered in Unit 20.

Resources, goods and services usually have a price which is determined by **market forces** (see Unit 7). The goods which are sold in markets are valued using **money**, which is featured in Unit 8. Changes in the value of money are examined in Unit 9 under the heading of **Inflation**. Some products and services are freely available *e.g.* wild raspberries, a walk on the moors. In order to pay for goods and services and to utilize free amenities, decisions have to be made involving utility, choice, income and wealth.

The usefulness and satisfaction gained from a good or service needs to be assessed. This is its utility. The more useful a good is, the higher the **demand** for it is likely to be. The concept of demand is examined in Unit 4. However, we cannot do and have everything we want because we lack time and money. This **scarcity** means that we have to make choices between alternatives. The cost of an alternative which is given up in order to gain the utility of the chosen good is known as **opportunity cost**. These concepts are further considered in Unit 1.3.

1.2 Roles

The use made of resources may vary, from different viewpoints. People have roles in society as consumers, producers and citizens.

All people are **consumers** – they buy goods and services and they make economic decisions. They choose how to allocate their resources of time and money in order to maximize satisfaction. Their decisions affect other people in society.

Most people act as **producers**. They contribute their labour to the production of goods and services when they are employed. A person's capacity to produce depends on his skills, abilities and interests. The income received enables money to be spent on consumption.

All members of society are **citizens**. Although their involvement in political decision-making varies enormously, people have certain economic rights which politicians can influence. For instance, increased taxation reduces an individual's ability to spend his income as he likes. The economic environment is determined by decisions made by elected politicians *e.g.* the laws on consumer protection, the spending plans of nationalized industries.

1.3 Underlying economic concepts

These main concepts are summarized below. The 14–16 Economics Education Project identified them as crucial to the understanding of economics at this level. They can be remembered by the word 'SCOCIE', based on the initials of the concepts.

1 Scarcity and Choice

As **resources are scarce**, **choices** are continually being made. Consumers choose which wants to satisfy, producers choose which resource combinations to use and citizens choose (indirectly) how they want society to develop. (See Unit 1.4.)

2 Opportunity Cost

When **choices** are made, **alternatives are given up**. Consumers forego certain wants, producers relinquish other methods of production, and citizens (in a democracy) accept policies with which they disagree. Thus the opportunity cost of spending £2 to watch a football match is anything else that could be done with £2 during the period of time involved. Governments, as well as individuals, are always involved in opportunity cost decisions because their funds are so extensive and their responsibilities are so wide.

Opportunity cost does not necessarily involve money as the alternatives may be free. For instance, **time** could be spent sunbathing or weeding, neither of which costs money to do. Generally, the opportunity cost of a decision is the alternative wants which remain unsatisfied.

3 Interdependence

In modern economies people **specialize** in education, training and employment. This enables increased total production and more for each person. This system forces dependence on others *e.g.* a school teacher needs to buy the goods from a grocer and the services of a plumber because he cannot provide them for himself. Thus he earns the income to pay for them by his specialization.

International trade (Unit 17) increases interdependence between economies and the **Balance of payments** (Unit 18) indicates the extent of the dependence.

4 Efficiency

When making decisions consumers, producers and citizens are interested in obtaining the most effective resource utilization in solving the scarcity problem. However, their interests differ, as a benefit to one group may be a cost to another *e.g.* price controls imposed by a government may benefit consumers (through lower prices) but appal producers (who, for example, cannot raise prices to maintain profits).

1.4 The economic problem

In theory the basic economic problem is how to use the available resources in a community to meet the existing needs of society. The **resources** are usually **limited** (or finite). All countries have land, raw materials, people and capital but their quality and quantity vary significantly. For instance Britain has insufficient land (245 000 sq km) to meet its food needs but a large and enterprising population (56 m). In contrast Tanzania has a plentiful supply of land (945 000 sq km) but a relatively small population (16 m). However, Tanzania's average income per head is £100 and Britain's is £4500.

On the other hand, **needs and wants are infinite** (unlimited). The basic needs of food, clothing and shelter are fulfilled for most people living in the developed countries of the world. With the improvements in the standard of living people's demands and expectations have accelerated *e.g.* families want two of most luxuries (*e.g.* colour TV) instead of one, so wants are outstripping needs.

In **underdeveloped** countries basic needs are often rarely met, although occasionally the luxurious wants of the rich few are satisfied *e.g.* expensive racehorse purchases of Arab oil sheiks. The GDP per capital of Tanzania indicates that its capacity to produce goods and services is very restricted and thus the average standard of living is low.

As all wants cannot be met, choices have to be made in allocating the resources. In making these choices, decisions about production have to be made:

1 For whom to produce?
2 What to produce?
3 Where to produce?
4 How to produce?

1 For whom to produce?

This depends on the type of economic system (see Unit 2). The type of economic system used in allocation of resources will be determined by the **political structure** of the society. For instance, the USSR, which is a communist state, has a centrally planned economy in which the government decides the purpose of production. In theory, production is organized for the equal benefit of all society, rather than for a particularly privileged or wealthy group.

2 What to produce?

The goods and services produced will be dependent on the first decision. For instance in 1929 in the USSR, Stalin decided that production should be concentrated on capital goods to further future economic development and national defence. This meant that the consumer goods section was neglected. Thus the people's immediate needs were partly sacrificed for the overall benefit of society and the indirect benefit of future generations.

In a market economy, those with most income and wealth will usually heavily influence what is produced. For instance in the USA ostentatious luxury services, such as doggie funerals, abound because the rich are prepared to pay for them. Thus income and prices determine what is produced.

3 Where to produce?

In theory, goods and services are produced where the **average cost** of production per unit is lowest. The factors influencing location are outlined in Unit 6. In a command economy the State dictates where goods are made and what services are provided. However, in a mixed economy, the 'best' location is not always chosen, because of government policies, government regulations and inefficient decisions made by firms.

4 How to produce?

The factors of production need to be combined in the most **efficient** way to produce lowest average cost. The quantities of labour and capital will vary between products, *e.g.* oil production is capital intensive whereas the postal service is labour intensive. Mechanization will be introduced, in theory, if the average cost of production can be lowered as a result.

In the real world, economic decision-making may mean that some resources are not used, or are underutilized. For instance, the factor labour may be left unemployed in market and mixed economies whereas in a centrally planned economy labour is sometimes employed without regard to its output.

Production possibilities

The basic concepts (1.3) all feature in the economic problem. The problem of 'what to produce' and also 'how much to produce' can be illustrated through a production possibility curve. This curve, shown in Figure 1.1, indicates the possible combinations of goods which can be produced if resources are fully utilized.

In Figure 1.1 we assume a simple peace-loving economy with no trade and the potential to produce just two goods. Vegetables represent a consumer good and fertilizers represent a capital good.

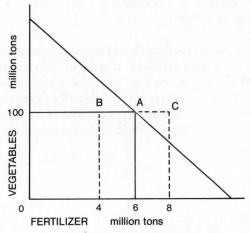

Fig. 1.1 Production possibility curve

At point A, 100m tons of vegetables and 6m tons of fertilizer are produced. Above A on the curve, more vegetables can be produced but at the expense of fewer fertilizers. Thus the **opportunity cost** of more vegetables is less fertilizer. Conversely, below A on the curve more fertilizer will be combined with fewer vegetables.

However, the combination of 8m tons of fertilizer and 100m tons of vegetables (Point C) cannot be reached as there are insufficient resources. This **scarcity** means that a **choice** has to be made between the quantity of each product required. Point C can only be achieved by economic growth, which makes more resources available.

If production is at B on the curve, it indicates **inefficiency** *i.e.* the existing resources are not being fully utilized. Fewer fertilizers (4m tons) are being produced at B than at A, although the volume of vegetables is maintained (100m tons).

1.5 Links with other topics

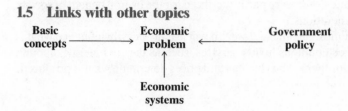

2 Economic systems

2.1	Introduction	*
2.2	Capitalist	***
2.3	Collective	***
2.4	Mixed	***
2.5	Subsistence	*
2.6	Linked topics	

2.1 Introduction

Economic systems are divided into three main types – capitalist, collective and mixed. A fourth category, subsistence, which does not apply in the modern world, is also included. In addition the term **'black economy'** has been developed for illegal activity in both collectivist and mixed economies. This **unofficial trading** occurs in order to satisfy the consumer and the producer and avoid payment to the government. It takes the form of:

1 Payments in kind *e.g.* one man mends another's plumbing leak in return for having his lawnmower repaired. Neither man records the income (and this avoids paying VAT if they are self-employed).

2 'barrow jobs' – these are jobs done at cheap prices with no documents involved so that expenditure tax (VAT) is not declared and the income is not officially recorded. This saves the producer paying extra income tax. A good example is hairdressing. It has been estimated that the value of the 'black economy' in Britain is £15 billion per year.

The advantages and disadvantages of the **different economic systems** depend to some extent on a person's **viewpoint**. It is worth bearing in mind that political and economic ideas intermingle. For instance, a Socialist would see an uneven distribution of wealth as a disadvantage whereas a Conservative might not. Also, the economic performance of a system may be measured in many ways, *i.e.* per capital income, volume of output, environmental conservation, the 'quality of life'. The measure chosen will probably indicate a personal value judgement.

2.2 Capitalist

Also known as **Free Market**

1 Features

In this type of economy there is **no government interference** in economic activity. Resources are allocated on the basis of **price**. The **private individuals** who own resources sell them to the **highest**

bidders who organize production to make **maximum profits**. The goods and services produced are sold to consumers at market prices which are determined by demand and supply.

The sellers of successful products make a profit and the buyers are satisfied. Rising demand for a good leads to increased output by the supplier in order to gain higher profits. This increases the demand for land, labour, and capital resources. It assumes they are **adaptable** and **perfectly mobile** in their use. Conversely, unprofitable goods are no longer produced, as resources are transferred into profitable ventures. In addition, this system assumes that consumers have **perfect knowledge** of the goods and services on the market. This helps to make the consumer sovereign – **he** decides what is supplied, by his spending.

2 Advantages

(a) Efficiency – as unsuccessful producers go out of business, it is argued that they must cut every corner and employ every cost-cutting device in order to sell at the lowest possible price. Such cut-throat **competition** keeps producers on their toes and stimulates **innovation** in selling and production techniques. These new ideas make such an economy **dynamic**.

(b) Economic freedom for the individual is maximized – he can dispose of his income how he wishes without having to pay taxes to the government. He can sell his labour/skills to any employer and buy whatever goods and services he wants. He is not restricted by government regulations.

(c) Incentives – employers and employees have the incentive of the possibility of unlimited wealth if they work hard.

Disadvantages

(a) Excessive luxuries – production may be organized to meet the needs of those with plenty of money, as producers can probably make larger profits from the manufacture of luxury products. As a consequence basic services may be neglected.

(b) Externalities such as pollution may occur because producers in maximizing profits only consider their own private costs and not the social costs of their activity.

(c) Public goods may not be produced. Certain public services such as defence are only effectively provided on a national basis and so without a government they would not be operated. Instead private armies might be developed and political factors would override economic ones. The price mechanism is not well equipped to provide certain goods whose benefits can not be attributed to individual users.

(d) Wealth distribution – as political power is dependent on income and wealth in this system, an uneven distribution of resources is particularly unfair. The rich have more economic freedom than the poor and more 'votes' (money) in how the system develops.

(e) Social hardship – during times of rapid change, many people will suffer as demand for their labour falls. This may have social and political effects, such as **poverty** and **militancy** respectively. The lack of government involvement means that the relief of poverty is only done voluntarily by charities. Furthermore as there is no government to set basic standards, consumers may be **exploited** through unsafe, unhealthy and misleading trading.

(f) Wasteful competition – this may arise when firms strive to increase sales against their rivals *e.g.* the early British railway companies often duplicated services between towns, which wasted resources from the point of view of national interest. Alternatively, monopolies and cartels may replace competition thereby leading to higher prices and poorer-quality goods as well as unethical trading. (see Unit 7).

Britain during the **Industrial Revolution** was a clear example of these features. Those with wealth and education (which had to be bought), who were the landowners and merchants developed the nation's resources and utilized new inventions, such as the steam engine. Costs were cut through the development of the factory system and gigantic profits were made. British trade expanded and economic society changed dramatically. However, because there was little government involvement, the consequences for many were undesirable – unemployment, particularly for agricultural labourers, slum housing, lack of sanitation for city dwellers, appalling working conditions and exploitation for many factory labourers. Reformers such as Shaftesbury and Chadwick and voluntary charities tried to fill the gap which was later occupied by the government. The initial government response to stay outside the market place was known as a *laissez-faire* approach. It could be argued that the few profited at the expense of the many.

The **USA** is usually given as an example of modern capitalist society. However, in practice the State and Federal Governments do get involved in providing some basic services. Nevertheless, the extremes of poverty and wealth indicate that there is little redistribution of income by the government. In reality, the USA is a mixed economy with a larger per cent of the private sector than most economies.

2.3 Collectivist

Also known as **Planned**. Sometimes termed **Command** when referring to practice in modern world.

1 Features

In this economy, **everything** is decided by the **government**. All the basic production questions (see Unit 1) are made by the central government as it **controls the resources** on behalf of the people. The politics of the society have determined its economic system. Communist political theory requires State control.

Thus land is used as the government decides and workers are allocated to jobs most suited to their skills. Labour tends to be very **specialized** and geographically mobile, for instance sixty per cent of all doctors in the USSR are women who have been selected on ability from an early age and not allowed to fritter their skills away. Production schedules are devised in the light of **long-term** plans. These plans are based on the government's assessment of the consumers' needs. There is little scope for individualism. **Prices are fixed** by the government. In theory, profits are returned to the people indirectly through lower prices, better services and investment in social capital. The resource of labour is paid **almost equally**.

Less international trading takes place than in capitalist economies, mainly for political reasons. The command economies prefer to be fairly **self sufficient**, fearing infiltration and foreign economic pressure. However, in recent years, China has opened up itself to Western goods *e.g.* Cherry Valley of Lincolnshire sell Peking ducks in Peking! Similarly, the USSR has become increasingly dependent on USA grain and surplus EEC agricultural produce.

2 Advantages

(a) Economies of scale can be acquired by this organization of production (see Unit 5.6). Wasteful competition will be eliminated and natural monopolies (see Unit 3.2) placed under State control.

(b) Basic needs of most of the population can be met, rather than production being geared to the demands of the rich few.

(c) Full utilization of resources is obtained by state control and planning. Full employment is maintained and economic growth can be planned, as resources can be allocated towards capital goods and away from current consumption.

3 Disadvantages

(a) Lack of personal freedom – people do not get the chance to choose their career but have to accept the job which the government allocates to them.

(b) A large bureaucracy of planners and administrators is needed to operate the system. Production and consumption are matched through government planning machinery, but **choice** is limited to the production which the government authorizes. Bureaucrats who are publicly responsible make decisions but they do not take risks as entrepreneurs do. It can be argued that there is **inefficient** use of resources when price does not determine their allocation.

(c) Few incentives arise in the production process because people are directed into jobs and prices are fixed. This might mean that production per head is not as high as it might be. In addition, actual demand may be different from planned demand leading to shortages and surpluses. This reduces consumer satisfaction and leads to a 'black economy'.

In practice, the **USSR**, which is usually given as the best example of a planned economy, operates a mixed economy. Ninety-five per cent of activity is State controlled but there is a developing private sector. People are allowed to own their own property, such as holiday homes, but the private ownership of the **means of production**, including land, is forbidden by law. These assets and savings could be passed on. Thus a large gap between rich and poor has developed. The tax rate is not very progressive, so a well-off factory manager earning £400 a month maintains his differential over the factory worker on a minimum wage of £45. The result is that a **privileged elite** of about 250 000, composed of party officials, diplomats, armed services personnel and professional people have a much higher standard of living than the majority of the population. In addition, the elite have many **perks** such as special shops selling cheap imported luxuries, holiday villas, 'the thirteenth month' salary.

2.4 Mixed

As the name suggests this economy is a mixture of capitalist and collectivist.

1 Features

There is a **public sector** controlled by the government which provides many public and merit goods and a **private sector**, in which individuals risk capital in producing goods and commercial services. In the public sector, **profit** is not the main motive, unlike the **private sector**. The amount of mixture of public and private is determined by the **government**. Thus it varies between countries and within one country over time. For instance in Britain, Labour Party governments prefer a large public sector whereas Conservative Party governments **denationalize** and privatize to reduce the size of the public sector. In a mixed economy the public sector usually provides:

(a) Public goods and services
These give benefits which everybody obtains but which can not be charged for on an individual basis because of their individuality, *e.g.* national defence. No entrepreneur would provide them because consumers could refuse to pay their share and yet still benefit. Instead the government collects the money through taxes and pays for the services provided.

(b) Merit goods
These are 'free' on the basis of need, *e.g.* education is 'zero priced' in the State sector.

(c) Uneconomic goods and services which the private sector is unwilling to supply, *e.g.* coal, railways.
    When these goods and services make a loss, this is made up by government **subsidies**. In a capitalist system all 'loss-makers' would go out of business to the detriment of many consumers.

(d) Transfer payments *e.g.* income for certain non-earners, such as grants for students and pensions for widows. The money to pay for these incomes comes out of taxation revenue.
    In addition, the government also **regulates the private sector** directly and indirectly, through legislation, fiscal policy and monetary policy. Occasionally there are **mixed enterprises** in a mixed economy. In these enterprises the public and private sectors join together to form companies for trading purposes *e.g.* Gas Corporation and Amoco to obtain gas from oilfields.
    Both the USA and the USSR appear to be becoming **more mixed** and less rigid. In Britain the non-market sector of the economy accounts for forty per cent of GDP and thirty per cent of employment.

2 Advantages

It is usually argued that this system obtains the **best of both worlds**. Necessary public services are provided and most goods are competitively marketed. Producers have the incentive to work and save, even though the government intervenes through fiscal policy to change income levels. Consumers receive basic services, a large measure of economic freedom and plenty of choice. Citizens have some influence over the use of national resources. (see 2.2 Advantages of capitalist system, and 2.3 Advantages of collectivist system.)

3 Disadvantages

Again the disadvantages of the capitalist (2.2) and collectivist systems (2.3) may be said to apply in certain circumstances. For instance, the removal of the profit motive from some industries, such as steel, which are taken into public ownership, might mean **lower efficiency** and less innovation. However, alternatively, the existence of government control in other industries, *e.g.* British aircraft production with its *Concorde*, may lead to **greater innovation** and higher efficiency.

2.5 Subsistence

1 Features

This old system of economics organization does **not apply** to economic systems today, although some small groups of people and individuals may practise a subsistence 'way of life'. **Before trade** took place, some communities were organized to meet just their **own basic needs**. Each person performed a task, or tasks, of benefit to the community and the produce of their labours was **pooled**, so there was enough for everybody. The group was often based on a tribe. The system required trust and co-operation. Often money was not used. Production was just enough to meet consumption. For instance, people planted seeds to grow food to give them energy to plant seeds, and so on. They did not create a surplus – they were trapped in subsistence.
    With improvements in world communications, these communities became less isolated, and trade began. In order to trade they needed to produce a surplus, which they did by specialization; in this way, they escaped from the subsistence trap.

2 Advantages

The people fulfilled their basic consumption needs and lived a simple, uncomplicated life. It was free from the competitiveness of modern living.

3 Disadvantages

These heavily outweighed the advantages and led to the decline of the subsistence economy. In this economy, there was **little choice** and little progress. Economic activity was irregular and resources tended to be underutilized, *e.g.* if a person took two hours to perform his/her job, then he/she might use the remainder of the time in leisure. Thus, the economy tended to **stagnate**. In addition, the growth of the population made the organization of work and distribution of produce **complicated**.

2.6   Links with other topics

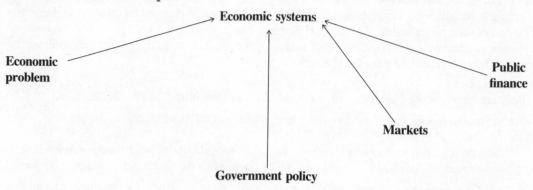

---

3 Business units

3.1   Private and public sector

The public sector refers to business organizations which are set up and controlled by **central government** and **local government**. The largest and best-known type are the public corporations, which are popularly called 'nationalized industries', *e.g.* British Rail.

The private sector is made up of business units set up by **individuals** and **groups** of people. There are a variety of types – sole traders, partnerships, companies and co-operatives. They are subject to various laws laid down by governments. However, the distinction between the public and private sectors is not clear at all. British governments have bought shares (equity) in the private sector companies, and made loans to them to maintain their viability, *e.g.* British Leyland. Such organizations have been termed **'mixed enterprises'**.

The Industrial Re-organisation Corporation 1966–70 and National Enterprise Board 1974–79 sponsored **State involvement** in the private sector under successive Labour governments, *e.g.* IRC created ICL (International Computers Ltd.). In contrast, Conservative governments have sold off parts of the public sector, *e.g.* British Rail sold off Thomas Cook to the Midland Bank. Also they have reduced their holdings in mixed enterprises, *e.g.* British Petroleum went from 49% to 33% under government control by the sale of shares to the private sector. This policy of **privatization** aims to increase the size of private sector and encourage individual economic activity.

Reasons for privatization

1 To reduce the need for state **finance** (taxes) to pay off losses.

2 To encourage **competition** in some sectors where at present there is a monopoly, *e.g.* British Telecom.

3 To reduce **trade union** power – **private firms are less likely to give in to industrial action seeking big pay increases**.

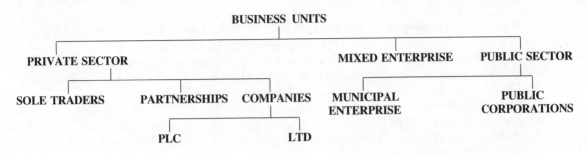

Fig. 3.1 Different types of business

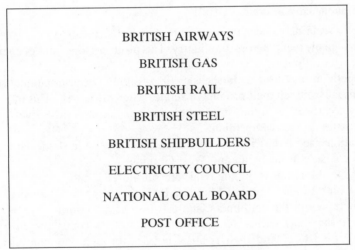

Fig. 3.2 Large public corporations

3.2   Public corporations and nationalized industries

Public corporations and nationalized industries are not exactly the same. Some public corporations such as the Bank of England, and regional water authorities are not classed as nationalized industries because:

1 They do not sell goods and services.

2 They do not derive their revenue directly from their consumers.

However, the major nationalized industries which are also **public corporations** have the following characteristics:

1 They were created by **Act of Parliament** with specific organization and functions.

2 General public control is under a **Minister** responsible to Parliament.

3 Assets are **publicly** owned.

4 Daily management is by a **Board**, appointed by a Secretary of State (Minister) and under a limited degree of government control.

5 They are not required to make a **profit**.

Reasons for public corporations   'WEE' and 'SUDS'

Natural monopolies should be controlled by the State to:

1 Avoid **Wasteful** Duplication – for example, more resources would be used if two postmen from rival organizations competed to deliver the post. It would be unlikely that the service would be any better and the price any cheaper. In the past, rival railway companies provided alternative services to many towns. Since nationalization, this no longer occurs and there is less duplication.

2 Achieve **Economies** of scale – for example, British Steel's huge complexes enable most of the technical benefits of large-scale production to be achieved. This tends to lower costs per unit than would otherwise be the case.

3 Prevent Consumer **Exploitation** – for example, nearly all houses require electricity. If this service were not provided by the Electricity Council and publicly controlled, very high prices could be charged to consumers who would have no option but to pay.

Part of the private sector has been nationalized in order to:

4 Provide **Sufficient** Capital for large-scale development *e.g. Concorde* would not have been developed if British Aerospace had not been created and government money had not been available.

5 To provide an **Uneconomic** Service *e.g.* British Rail operates trains on routes on which it makes a loss; but it provides a necessary service for many small towns and villages.

6 To prolong the life of a **Declining** Industry in order to protect employment – in the shipbuilding industry uneconomic and inefficient yards have been kept open in order to maintain employment in already depressed areas and to minimize social misery.

7 To control industries of **Strategic** Importance, *e.g.* atomic power is in public ownership. Nuclear weapons are in the hands of the government rather than ordinary individuals!

These are the main **economic** arguments for public corporations. There is also the political argument that 'ownership of the means of production and distribution' is power and this should be under State control. Some in the Labour Party take this view, although a majority support the mixed economy and thus favour a larger public sector than the Conservative Party want.

Disadvantages of public corporations   'DIPPI'

1 Diseconomies of scale may occur in large units. For instance, some industries are difficult to control as they have many plants across the country. This produces long lines of communication and often little check over output.

2 Lack of competition may lead to **Inefficiency**. This occurs because nationalized industries as monopolies can usually still sell their product or service when prices rise. This may mean that costs are not as closely controlled as in industries where firms face competitive rivals. However, some nationalized industries do face **competition**:

(a) from other nationalized industries *e.g.* coal v. gas, electric, oil in domestic fuel supply.

(b) from imports *e.g.* steel from Japan and West Germany.

This competition may be unfair if trading rivals are subsidized.

3 Little **Public** Control either through Minister, Parliament or Consultative Committee, all of whom supposedly represent the consumers' interests (see next section).

4 Political Interference may occur. As nationalized industries contribute over 10% of GDP, governments have tried to extend their political policies through nationalized industries. Price increases by British Steel have been stopped and investment spending by gas authorities has been hindered in order to set an example on inflation and public spending respectively. By such actions the government hoped that private enterprise might follow suit. Thus long-term planning by nationalized industries has been disrupted as governments seek to meet short-term political objectives.

Control over public corporations

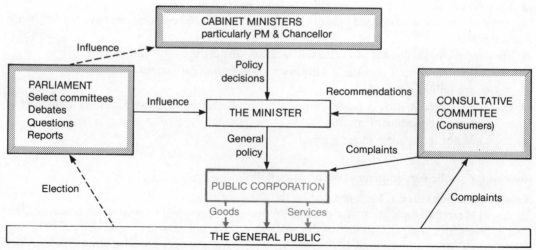

Fig. 3.3 Control of public corporations

1 The Cabinet The Cabinet as a whole may decide policy regarding a public corporation. This will bind the particular Minister who is responsible, whether he agrees or not. Thus uneconomic coal pits have been kept open against the Minister's and Board's advice.

2 The Minister – each public corporation is under the general supervision of a Government Minister, who may appoint the Chairman of the Board and other members. For instance in 1983 Norman Siddall's contract as Chairman of NCB ended and the Conservative Government appointed Ian McGregor, former Chairman of British Steel. The Minister may give the board guidance on general policy. However, the board is responsible for daily matters and internal policy.

The Minister also negotiates on behalf of his industry with the Chancellor of the Exchequer when seeking finance for development. On other occasions he may defend the industry in answer to MPs' questions and during debates.

3 MPs – MPs, as individuals, can obtain information and exert a little indirect influence over the policies of public corporations. A group of MPs in a Select Committee may pry deeply into an industry's affairs, and through their criticisms bring about changes.

4 Consultative Committees – these semi-official public bodies collect complaints from the general public who use the goods and services produced by public corporations. They also suggest improvements.

Finance for public corporations

The income to meet current expenditure usually comes from the sale of goods/services and from government subsidies.

The income for capital is borrowed from the Treasury, which lays down a **rate** of **return** which should be obtained. Each year the total amount borrowed from the Treasury is calculated – this is known as the **external financing limit**.

Municipal enterprise

District and County Councils provide goods and services for public consumption in local communities. For instance, local transport is mainly provided by municipal authorities and is usually **subsidized**. Some councils have diversified into the building sector and other trades and actually compete with the private sector.

The control of municipal enterprise by the public is again very indirect. However, it is less complicated with councillors on committees taking the responsibility for decisions and being made accountable at local elections.

3.3 Companies

Characteristics

1 Limited liability. Before 1862, few companies were formed because the risks of loss were too great. Unlimited liability meant that people starting up a business might lose all their personal assets if the business failed. Nowadays, a shareholder's liability in a business is limited to the amount of his original share subscription. Unfortunately, this law is often used unscrupulously. The most famous bankrupt, William Stern, who owed £142m, arranged to put his house and possessions beyond the reach of his creditors when his property empire crashed in 1974.

2 Legal entity. A company is a separate 'being' in law. It is distinct from its shareholders. As such, a company can sue, be sued, enter into legal contracts, own property and continue its separate existence, unaffected, for example, by such events as the death of any of its shareholders.

3 Registration and submission of documents. A company has to register with the Department of Trade and supply:

(a) Memorandum of Association. This outlines important information for **outsiders** such as the title of the company, its registered address, the amount of authorized capital and the type of trade which it is in.

(b) Articles of Association. This document lays down the rules and regulations governing the **internal** organization of the company *e.g.* powers of directors.

In addition a company needs to keep proper books of account by law. These may be inspected by the Inland Revenue and Customs and Excise department.

4 Directors elected by shareholders at AGM The Board of Directors decide company policy and the Managing Director is there to carry it out. The Annual General Meeting declares the **dividend** for ordinary shareholders, outlines the company **performance** over the last year, and presents the **Balance Sheet**.

Directors usually control elections, from which their powers are derived, when no large shareholder dominates. Usually meetings support the **existing management** while the company is profitable and often the AGM lasts half an hour. Vacancies on the Board are often filled by **nominees of the Board** and ratified at AGM. Shareholders have very little power in practice, although in theory they can change the Articles of Association, sanction dividends and confirm the choice of auditors.

1980 Companies Act

This Act amended company law and distinguished two main types of company: public limited companies (PLC) and limited companies (Ltd. Co.) There are two major differences:

1 PLC – this suffix must follow the title of a company whose shares are quoted on the Stock Exchange. This covers the companies previously called public limited company.

2 Ltd Co. – this suffix is used with companies whose shares are not freely transferable on the Stock Exchange. These companies were formerly known as 'private limited companies'.

	Issued ordinary shares (m)	Equity market value (m)	Sales (m)	Profit 1981 (m)	UK Employees	Shareholders
British Petroleum	1817	5268	31 399	2432	41 700	276 376
General Electric	549	4516	3462	476	157 000	155 000
Shell*	1105	4198	21 897	2341	12 800	362 000
Marks & Spencer	1313	2049	1872	.181	44 646	243 121
ICI	598	1879	6581	335	74 700	450 837

*Royal Dutch Shell. British-owned subsidiary

Fig. 3.4 The five largest UK companies (March 1982)

Advantages of PLC

PLC such as Bass-Charrington, Watneys have advantages which can be remembered by the word **'ALES'**.

1 Access to capital through the Stock Exchange (rights issues) and the Money Market makes expansion easy. In addition, shareholders can easily sell shares without depriving companies of long-term capital.

2 Limited Liability increases risk-taking and enterprise.

3 Economies of scale can be obtained, leading to lower costs per unit.

4 Specialists can be employed. The suppliers of capital (shareholders) are separated from the managers of capital. Thus, people can invest in chemicals without knowing about them and trust the experts to use their capital wisely.

Disadvantages of PLC

These can be remembered by mnemonic: **'DISAD'** appropriately for disadvantages.

1 Diseconomies of scale may occur – see Unit 5.

2 Interests of the management may be different from those of the shareholders. In most PLC there are thousands of shareholders who are not united and only meet at the AGM. Thus the management's aims usually prevail. For instance, the management may want maximum sales/bigger market share, whilst the owners want a large return on their investment. However, increasingly, **directors hold shares** in the companies which they manage and this may make their interests closer to the interests of shareholders.

3 Small groups of shareholders may dominate a company. Often the **institutional investors**, such as insurance company and pension funds, may wield great influence over company policy *e.g.* West Midlands County Council own 1m out of 364 m shares in BAT. Clearly, shareholders with just small holdings lack the influence and expertise to have much effect. However, occasionally an AGM hits the headlines – in 1982 a few shareholders critical of Rio Tinto Zinc's operations in Namibia and Australia disrupted the meeting and the police were called! Usually, though, the Chairman rushes through the formalities and the AGM is a public relations exercise in keeping shareholders happy.

4 Accounts have to be submitted annually to the Dept. of Trade – however, companies are often years behind!

5 Documentation is expensive and extensive. Since 1980, all companies except those trading under the name of the owner, need to disclose their identity on their stationery and in their business premises. Companies no longer provide a cloak of anonymity.

Limited companies (private limited company)

These are generally smaller in size, but more numerous. They are not quoted on the Stock Exchange, but they must file annual accounts with the Registrar of Companies. They are usually family businesses which have been made into companies to gain the advantages of limited liability. The best example is Littlewoods – the retail variety chain store.

Advantages of limited company

1 Some privacy retained in a family organization
2 Limited liability
3 Continuity maintained
4 General benefits, such as flexibility, specialization, which accrue to small firms. See Units 5.7 and 5.8.

Disadvantages of limited company

1 Limited amount of capital
2 Transfer of shares not easy as the consent of other shareholders is needed and private buyers need to be found, and the Stock Exchange cannot be used
3 Vulnerable to changes in demand, as often specialist companies

3.4 Partnerships

Characteristics

The main headings – **1**, **2**, and **3** – can be remembered by the word '**DUO**'

1 Deed of partnership is signed by the partners. The decision of one partner then binds the other partners. The **partnership deed** (agreement) usually gives details of:

Amount of capital contributed by each partner
Share of profits/losses to each partner
Salary to each partner
Type of trade engaged in
Arrangements for dissolution of partnership
Number of partners and name of partnership

If no written agreement is made, the 1890 Partnership Act has laid down the following **guidelines**:

Loans to receive 5% interest
Equal division of profits
No salary for partners
No interest on capital

So the **DUO** includes **AS STAN** and **LENN**

2 Unlimited liability – this means that the partner's own personal assets may have to be used to pay any debts. However, the **1907 Act allowed limited** partnerships. In these the general partners have unlimited liability and sleeping partners have limited liability. General partners usually receive fees whereas sleeping partners get a return from the profits.

3 Ownership – between two and twenty people may create, own and control a partnership *e.g.* estate agents. In the cases of solicitors and accountants, more than twenty partners are allowed.

Advantages of partnerships

1 Easy and cheap to set up.
2 More capital available than sole trader, as more providers.
3 Specialization among partners *e.g.* solicitors specialize in divorce, conveyancing, wills.
4 Small enough to maintain good employer-employee relations and good consumer-producer relations.
5 Worries shared between partners eases the mental load.

Disadvantages of partnerships

1 Unlimited liability for some/all partners.

2 Size may be limited by lack of capital.

3 Personal differences can cause problems in the running of the business. Partners need to agree and trust each other, otherwise management becomes difficult.

4 Dissolution of the partnership, when one partner dies, may cause loss of goodwill, reputation and contacts.

3.5 Sole traders

There are approximately **1½ million** self-employed people in Britain. They mainly provide **specialist** services and crafts *e.g.* plumbing, printing, hairdressing, window cleaning. These people may work entirely on their own or employ a few workers. In either case, they are **totally responsible** for all decisions made, they control their own business and they have unlimited liability. The sole proprietor takes all the risks and receives all the profits.

Advantages

1 Flexible and efficient because of personal control.

2 Good relations with employees as frequent contact and working together.

3 Easy and cheap to set up – no documentation needed except VAT registration if turnover exceeds £18 700.

4 The owner is his own boss and thus has considerable freedom in his work. He also has the incentive to succeed as all profits accrue to him.

Disadvantages

1 Very risky, because of unlimited liability.

2 Lack of continuity – holidays, illness and death may mean that the business ceases to operate. Temporary closures may lead to a loss of trade and stability.

3 Shortage of capital which may inhibit expansion. Borrowing is often difficult and expensive because of the individual's lack of contacts, assets and reputation.

3.6 Co-operatives

The aim of the other private sector organizations is to make a profit for the owners/shareholders. However, the initial aim of the original co-ops in Britain was to break even and **return any profits** back to the customers. There are two types of co-operatives:

1 **Producer co-operatives** – groups of workers who provide the capital and jointly run the business of making goods. Only a few workers co-operatives have been set up in Britain and these have been mainly **'buy-outs'** by workers. For instance, when the Meridan Motorcycle Co. went into receivership, most of the workers used their redundancy pay to buy the company's assets and re-establish the business – this venture eventually failed. In Israel, the **kibbutzim** (collective farms) are very numerous and economically successful. Most producer co-operatives operate through committees of workers and **elected** managers who make decisions.

2 **Consumer co-operatives** – The best known co-operative of consumers is the **Co-op Retail Society** (CRS). It originated in 1844 with the **Rochdale Pioneers**. This group of twenty-eight weavers put their money together to open a retail store, because they disliked being exploited by existing shops which sold poor quality goods and charged expensive credit. They bought goods from their own shop and distributed the profits according to how much they had spent. This method of redistribution through a **dividend** per £1 spent was a basic principle of the Co-operative movement up to the 1960s.

Co-operative Wholesale Society (CWS)

This was set up in 1863 to buy in bulk for the CRS. It provides **70%** of their needs such as packaged food, household goods and electrical equipment. It owns **133 factories** which produce for CRS and other retailers. In addition, it is the nation's biggest **farmer**, producing one third of all liquid milk, biggest **undertaker** and biggest **transport fleet** manager. The sales of £2 billion in 1982 also made it the biggest wholesaler in Europe.

Decline of Co-op Retail Societies

Between 1950–1975, CRS % share of the grocery market fell from 20% to 13%, although it has slightly recovered since (to 15%). The reasons for its decline were:

1 Heavy dependence on **food sales** (75% of total, compared to 60% in Tesco) where the profit margins are low and the sales fairly stable.

2 Small-sized stores giving little scope for expansion.

3 Location of shops in decaying urban areas and underpopulated rural areas.

4 Lack of centralization – as most co-ops value their local status and independence, there was little bulk buying to gain economies of scale.

This decline began with the development of **supermarkets** and **family motoring**. The result has been many closures and society amalgamations, as well as the ending of dividend payments. The number of co-operatives has fallen from 932 in 1958 to 160 in 1983. The existing CRS are mainly in the **North of England** and they sell **15% of food** bought in Britain. Their market share has recovered a little because mergers have taken place to create a viable size of shop and a new go-ahead **image** has been presented.

However, in many **rural areas**, uneconomic co-ops still operate and provide a service to the community. They are **subsidized**: often CWS does not charge transport costs of delivery to CRS in outlying areas. Falling profits have meant no dividends, less capital and less incentive for people to buy from co-operatives.

Common characteristics

1 Ownership – co-ops are owned by their shareholders. Any purchaser can become a **shareholder** for **£1 minimum**. The shares receive a fixed rate of interest, which is usually low.

2 Aims – co-ops have **broader objectives** than most businesses and have diversified into many areas. The Co-op movement has a bank, insurance society and has MPs who represent its interests. It is not narrowly profit-orientated but has political and social aims.

3 Control – CRS are run by **Boards of Management**, which are **elected**. Every shareholder has one vote, irrespective of the amount of shares he/she holds. Thus a £1 shareholder has the same power as a £1000 shareholder. This is very different from public companies – see Unit 3.3. Interestingly the CWS is controlled by the CRS on the basis of their purchases rather than one vote per member!

4 Capital – the deposits of members, which receive interest, can be used to finance expansion. In addition, co-ops borrow like public companies from the banking sector.

Advantages of Co-ops 'CELT'

1 Customers get profits
2 Economies of scale through bulk buying from CWS
3 Limited liability
4 Tax on profits is lower because co-ops are classed as friendly societies

Disadvantages 'BO'

1 Board of management is part-time – the members are chosen on the basis of popularity rather than business expertise
2 Old fashioned, low quality image

3.7 Finance

Sources of finance for **Sole Traders** and **Partnerships**

1 Personal **savings** and loans from friends/relations.
2 Bank loans and overdrafts.
3 Trade credit – *i.e.* receiving goods ready to sell before paying for them, usually one month.
4 Hire purchase – capital assets such as machines can be bought in this way.
5 Leasing – use of equipment/vehicles without having to pay the capital cost.
6 Profits ploughed back into the business.
      For **private companies** (Ltd). $(1 \rightarrow 6+)$
7 Shares sold privately.
      For **public limited companies** (PLC) $(1 \rightarrow 7+)$
8 Shares sold to general public through merchant banks and stock exchange (see Units 10 + 11)
9 Investors in Industry – this body is independent of the Government, being funded by the clearing banks (85%) and Bank of England (15%). It is subdivided into:
(a) Industrial and Commercial Finance Corp. which provide **long term** finance for **small to medium sized firms**; they give between £5000 and £3m per firm. By 1983, 4000 firms had received £480m between them. This sort of finance enabled the development of the hovercraft.
(b) Head Office Division (formerly the bulk of Finance Corporation for Industry) provides

medium-term finance for **larger** firms. In 1980, forty-five companies received £300m between them. It provides loan finance up to £35m and equity capital up to £5m.

(c) Shipping and Energy Division In shipping they provide finance for the purchase and leasing of ships whilst in energy they have provided equity and loan finance for UK oil exploration and production. Altogether in these two areas it has invested £175m.

10 Government bodies

(a) National Enterprise Board 1974 set up by the Labour Government to provide loans and equity capital for British firms. The NEB was an expanded version of 1967 Industrial Re-organization Corporation, which promoted restructuring of industries. In 1979 it was put under the British Technology Group, run by Dept. of Trade, and parts were sold back to the private sector.

(b) Welsh Development Agency – similar to NEB.

(c) Scottish Development Agency – similar to NEB.

(d) Council for Small Industries in Rural Areas (COSIRA) also gives money to firms in rural areas for development.

11 Government grants

Certain firms may be given specific amounts in rare circumstances *e.g.* Rolls-Royce 1971; ICL 1982.

3.8   Shares

A shareholder **owns** part of a company. He takes a **risk** in putting up his capital but he does have **limited liability**.

Nominal and market value

The nominal value of a share is the price paid when it was **first issued**. The market value is the price which can be obtained when the share is **sold**, usually on the Stock Exchange. Large companies will have thousands of individual shareholders *e.g.* ICI has ½m shareholders with the largest being the Prudential Assurance Co., with just 3% of total shares.

Ordinary (equity) shares

These shares pay a **dividend**, twice yearly. The dividend received **varies** from year to year, and is decided by the board of directors in the light of profits made. The owner of equity shares has **voting rights** at the AGM; thus he can influence how the company is run.

Anyone owning more than **9.0%** of a company's equity has to inform the Dept. of Trade. To avoid this, shareholders not wishing to reveal their influence often 'warehouse' their shares with relatives, so that their influence does not become apparent.

The Diamond Commission on the distribution of income and wealth in the UK showed the pattern of ordinary share ownership – Figure 3.5.

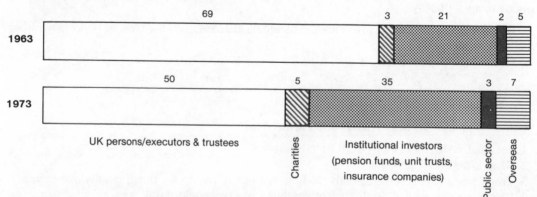

Fig. 3.5 Ordinary share ownership in the UK

Preference shares

These shares give the holders first call on the company profits. The shareholders receive a dividend which is a **fixed** % of the **nominal** value of the share. Preference shareholders have no rights in the control of the company's activities.

Some issues are **cumulative**. If the dividend is not paid in one year because of low profits or losses, then the amount owed is carried forward to the next year. It will be paid (hopefully) when the company is more successful.

Debentures

These are not shares. They are **loans**, for which the holders receive a **fixed** rate of interest. This is paid

before the profits are calculated. If a company fails to pay interest on debentures, the debenture holders can force it into bankruptcy. Thus, debenture holders get paid before shareholders. They do not have any voting rights.

Authorized, Issued and Fully-Paid Capital

A company's share capital is not all raised at once. There are three stages:
  1 **Authorized share capital**: **total** share capital of company laid down in its Articles of Association *e.g.* 200 000 × £1 shares
  2 **Issued** – the amount that shareholders have subscribed so far *e.g.* 50 000 × £1 shares.
  3 **Fully paid** – all the current issue has been paid *e.g.* all 50 000 have been paid.

New issues

A company may issue some new shares in order to raise more capital *e.g.* 1983 Tottenham F.C. (Spurs) raised £2.9m. Although existing shares are bought and sold in the Stock Exchange, new issues are sold by Issuing Houses (merchant banks) who often underwrite the amount *i.e.* promise to buy any shares not taken up (see Unit 11.2).

3.9 Links with other topics

Stock Exchange ⎯⎯⎯⎯→ **Business units** ←⎯⎯⎯⎯ **Markets**

4 Demand and supply

4.1	Introduction	*
4.2	Demand	***
4.3	Supply	***
4.4	Price	***
4.5	Elasticity	***
4.6	Linked topics	***

4.1 Introduction

In Unit 2 we noted how scarce resources are allocated by **The Price Mechanism**. It is therefore of vital importance for economists to be able to explain how prices are determined.
  'Market prices are determined by the interaction of Supply and Demand'
  Throughout this unit relationships have been simplified. The reader must remember that in the real world economic relationships are generally much more complicated.

4.2 Demand

Definition: 'The amount consumers are willing and able to purchase at any given price.'
  Demand needs to be **'effective'** *i.e.* backed by necessary money. The **individual** demands of people are added together to form the **market** demand. This is illustrated in Figure 4.1

The demand schedule for LPs per week (millions)

Price £	Quantity demanded
2	12
3	10
4	8
5	6
6	4
7	2

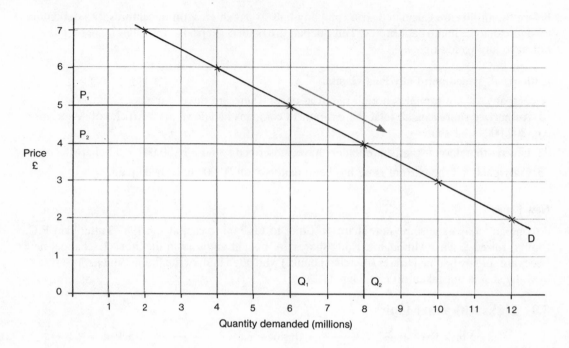

Fig. 4.1 Extension of demand

The Demand Curve shows the same information as the Demand Schedule but in a graphic form. As the price of LPs rises the 'amount consumers are willing and able to purchase' falls. For instance at £6, 4 million LPs are bought but at £3, 10 million LPs are bought. Thus there is an inverse relationship between **Price** and **Quantity Demanded** for most normal goods.

Contractions and extensions of demand

Extensions and contractions of demand result from **Price** changes only. It is **assumed** that other things, such as conditions of demand below, are held constant. As we can see in Figure 4.1, when price falls from P_1 to P_2 the quantity demand rises from Q_1 to Q_2. This is an extension of demand. Conversely when price rises from P_2 to P_1 the quantity demanded falls from Q_2 to Q_1. This is a contraction of demand.

Conditions of demand

It is clear that demand depends upon many factors – not merely price. These are known as the underlying conditions of demand. They can be remembered by the word **'CIST'**.

1 Complements

Many goods are in joint demand *e.g.* cars and petrol. It is clear that changes in the price of cars will affect not only the demand for cars but also the demand for petrol, as the two go together. Generally, if the price of a complementary good increases then the demand for the jointly-demanded good is likely to fall. Thus if price of petrol rises, demand for cars falls.

2 Income

If you were to receive an increase in income (*e.g.* from a Saturday job) you would be in a position to increase your demand for LPs even if the price remained unaltered. It is clear that changes in the level of income are likely to have a considerable impact on demand. Furthermore changes in the distribution of income will also affect market, though not individual, demand. For example, if income tax becomes more progressive (see Unit 15.3) the demand for luxuries may fall and the demand for normal goods may increase.

3 Substitutes

Many products have a number of close substitutes or goods which may be consumed instead. For example, many people would be largely indifferent as to whether they eat cabbage or cauliflower for dinner. Hence if the price of cauliflower suddenly rose, consumers are very likely to buy cabbage instead. Thus when the price of a substitute good rises, demand for the original good increases too.

4 Tastes and fashions

This will obviously be a major factor affecting the demand for certain products. Many people would not be 'seen dead' in last year's style of clothes no matter how cheap they are now. Tastes can be influenced by advertising. Thus over the past decade demand for lager has risen while the demand for bitter has fallen.

Graphic representation of changes in the conditions of demand

A demand curve shows only the effects on quantity demanded of changes in price. To demonstrate the effects of changes in the conditions of demand it is necessary to shift the entire demand curve. A new demand schedule has occurred.

Price £	Quantity demanded (D_2)
2	14
3	12
4	10
5	8
6	6
7	4

Figure 4.2 Increase in demand

After an increase in income existing consumers will be able to afford more LPs and new customers will enter the market. Hence at each price the quantity demanded has risen (*e.g.* at £6, 6m LPs are bought now instead of 4m). A new curve (D_2) is thus parallel and to the right of the original curve. Always remember to include an arrow showing the direction of change.

A decrease in demand may have been caused by:

1 An increase in the price of **Complements**.

2 A reduction in the level of **Income** perhaps caused by a lower level of taxation or increased wages or both.

3 A reduction in the price of **Substitute** goods.

4 An adverse change in **Taste or fashion**.

These can be remembered by '**CIST**'.

4.3 Supply

Definition 'The amount producers are willing to offer for sale at any given price'.

As with demand, price is a major influence on quantity supplied. As price rises new supplies enter the market attracted by potentially higher profits and existing firms are tempted to increase production. Thus:

Supply Schedule
–LPs per week (millions)

Price £	Quantity supplied
2	2
3	4
4	6
5	8
6	10
7	12

This market supply schedule is a combination of the supplies offered onto the market by all the individual producers.

In Figure 4.3 as price rises from P_1 to P_2 so Quantity Supplied rises from Q_1 to Q_2. Vice versa when price falls.

1 Contractions/extensions of supply

Figure 4.3 shows the extension of supply. This occurs when producers increase supply as the **price** rises. It shows a movement **along** a curve and it assumes that conditions of supply remain unchanged.

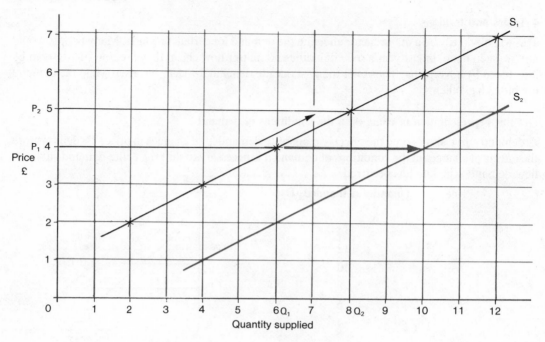

Fig. 4.3 Increase in supply and extension of supply

2 Conditions of supply

There are a number of conditions of supply which may change and produce a new supply curve. These can be remembered by the word **'COPING'**.

(a) Costs

This item refers to the cost to the firm of paying the Factors of Production. (see Unit 5.5) If a firm has to pay more for its raw materials etc., it will require a higher selling price in order to maintain its normal profit at existing output levels.

(b) Other prices

The impact of other prices depends on the relationship between the good being supplied and other goods:

(i) **Unrelated goods** – if the price of ice cream rises it will not induce BL to switch its Longbridge lines to the production of Raspberry Ripple!

(ii) **Goods in competitive supply** – however, many firms are capable of switching production at relatively short notice and will do so if higher profits can be obtained. For instance a market gardener of peas is likely to react to high carrot prices by planting more carrots and less peas next season.

(iii) **Goods in joint supply** – the production of one good leads to production of another so farmers raise more cows, which will also increase the output of leather even though its price has remained unchanged.

(c) Innovations

We live in an age where rapid technological change is the norm. Thus firms are often able to use technological change to produce goods much more cheaply *e.g.* the use of robots and computers.

(d) Government policy

Here we are particularly concerned with the effects of **Indirect taxation** and **Subsidies** upon the supply curve. For instance an increase in VAT means that suppliers will wish to produce less at existing prices and so the supply curve will shift to the left. In contrast a subsidy acts to reduce costs
and so the supply curve shifts to the right and more is supplied at existing prices.

Graphic representation of changes in the conditions of supply

As with demand, the supply curve shows only the effects on changes in price upon quantity supplied. To demonstrate the effects of changes in the conditions of demand it is necessary to shift
the entire supply curve. (See Figure 4.3)

An increase in Supply shifts the Supply to the right. This may have been caused by:
'COPING'

1 A reduction in Factor Cost   3 A technological breakthrough
2 A fall in the price of other related goods   4 A government subsidy.

4.4 Price

Definition

'Price is determined by the interaction of Supply and Demand'

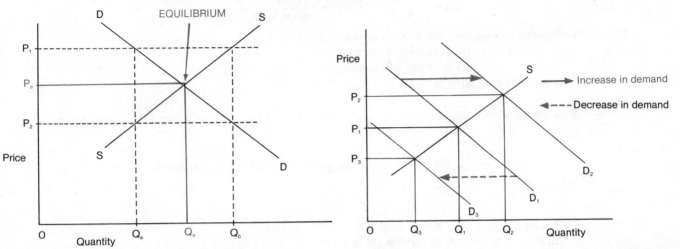

Fig. 4.4 Equilibrium price and quantity

Fig. 4.5 The effects of changes in the conditions of demand

Equilibrium is defined as 'The position from which there is no tendency to change'

In Figure 4.4 at Price P_1, Demand is OQa while Supply is OQb thus indicating an **Excess supply**. In this situation suppliers, as in the January or Summer Sales, will lower their prices to eliminate this excess supply. Thus at all prices above P_e there will be excess supply and a tendency for price to fall, until demand and supply are equal at the equilibrium price.

At P_2 there is clearly an **Excess demand** thus at all prices below P_e buyers will bid up prices in order to obtain goods which are in short supply *e.g.* sugar. At P_e there is neither a tendency for price to rise nor to fall, thus P_e represents equilibrium price.

The effect of a change in conditions of demand:

In Figure 4.5 we can see that following an increase in demand $(D_1 \rightarrow D_2)$ both equilibrium price $(P_1 \rightarrow P_2)$ and quantity $(Q_1 \rightarrow Q_2)$ will rise. Conversely when demand falls $(D_1 \rightarrow D_3)$ so too will equilibrium price $(P_1 \rightarrow P_3)$ and quantity $(Q_1 \rightarrow Q_3)$.

Effects of a change in conditions of supply

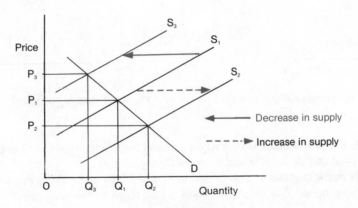

Fig. 4.6 The effects of changes in the conditions of supply

In Figure 4.6 as supply increases $(S_1 \rightarrow S_2)$ equilibrium price falls $(P_1 \rightarrow P_2)$ but equilibrium quantity rises $(Q_1 \rightarrow Q_2)$. Similarly when supply falls $(S_1 \rightarrow S_3)$ equilibrium price rises $(P_1 \rightarrow P_3)$ but equilibrium quantity falls $(Q_1 \rightarrow Q_3)$.

4.5 Elasticity

The **shape** of a demand curve is known as its elasticity. It tells us 'by how much demand will change in response to price changes.'

Definition

Elasticity is defined as 'The responsiveness of supply/demand to a given change in price'

1 Measurement of price elasticity of demand

Elasticity is measured by the **Co-efficient of elasticity** $\Sigma D/\Sigma S$

$$\Sigma D = \frac{\% \ QD}{\% \ P} = \frac{\text{percentage change in qty demanded}}{\text{percentage change in price.}}$$

Calculation can be: (a) over a range of prices
                     (b) at one point on a curve
                     (c) over the whole curve

It is normally calculated between two prices.

Examples If a **price increase** from £5 to £6 brings about a fall from 6m to 4m LPs demanded per week, then $\Sigma D = \dfrac{-33\frac{1}{3}}{+20} = -1\frac{2}{3}$

Note that the same data gives a different result if a **price fall** is considered.

Then $\Sigma D = \dfrac{+50\%}{-16\frac{2}{3}} = -3.6$

In calculating Ed the minus symbol is usually ignored.

In these two cases the D curve is **relatively elastic**, indicating that demand is very responsive to price changes. The Ed formula gives a value between 1 and ∞ (infinity)

Conversely, the quantity demanded may be very **unresponsive** to price changes. For instance, when price of LPs fell from £3 to £2 quantity demand increased from 10m to 12m.

$$\Sigma D = \frac{\% \ QD}{\% \ P} = \frac{+20}{-33\frac{1}{3}} = 0.6$$

In this latter case Σ_D is less than 1 which indicates relatively inelastic demand. Elasticities between 0 and 1 show **relatively** inelastic demand.

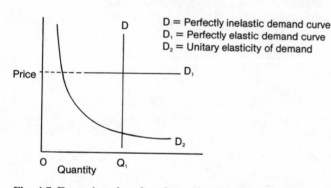

D = Perfectly inelastic demand curve
D₁ = Perfectly elastic demand curve
D₂ = Unitary elasticity of demand

Fig. 4.7 Examples of perfect demand curve elasticities

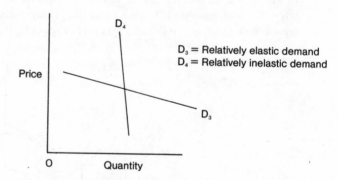

D₃ = Relatively elastic demand
D₄ = Relatively inelastic demand

Fig. 4.8 Examples of relative demand curve elasticities

Perfectly inelastic demand occurs when demand remains constant at Q irrespective of price. In this case $\Sigma_D = 0$ and demand is said to be perfectly inelastic.

Perfectly elastic demand is represented in Figure 4.7 by curve D_1 as at any price above P_1 demand falls to zero hence $\Sigma_D = X$ and demand is said to be perfectly elastic.

Unitary elasticity is a special case where % $\triangle$ QD = % $\triangle$ P at all price/output levels along D_2 hence $\Sigma_D = 1$ and demand is said to have unit elasticity. In this situation Total Revenue $[P \times Q]$ will be unchanged following a price change. A demand curve with a constant unit elasticity is called a **rectangular hyperbola**.

The above curves are all theoretical special cases and we should expect to find most cases where demand is either **relatively elastic (D_3) or relatively inelastic (D_4)**.

Straight line demand curves

It is important to note that elasticity will vary along the length of any straight line demand curve. As the quantity demanded increases, the curve becomes more inelastic. See Figure 4.9.

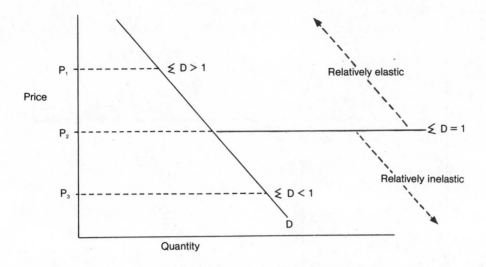

Fig. 4.9 A demand curve of varying elasticity

2 Factors influencing (price) elasticity of demand

These can be remembered by the word 'THIS'

(a) Time
In the short term consumers may not fully appreciate possible alternatives and thus continue to purchase certain goods following a price rise. However, in the longer period they will become more aware of other possibilities. Therefore, *ceteris paribus*, demand is more elastic in the long run.

(b) Habit
Quite often we purchase goods automatically without, perhaps, being fully aware of the price which we are paying *e.g.* newspapers, milk. Thus goods which are habitually bought are more likely to be in inelastic demand. Furthermore some products have an **addictive** effect *e.g.* cigarettes. The nicotine addict will continue to burn away his/her money almost regardless of price.

(c) Income
Some goods constitute only a small proportion of consumers' income *e.g.* matches. In this case even a 100% rise in the price of matches can be quite easily absorbed since most consumers spend only a tiny fraction of their income upon matches. Demand is thus likely to be inelastic. Compare this with how you think consumers would react to a doubling of car prices.

(d) Substitutes
Possibly the single most important factor is the closeness and availability of substitutes. For example, petrol has no genuinely effective freely available substitutes. Thus motorists have little option but to keep on buying it. However, faced with a rise in the price of cabbage the consumer has a wide range of more or less acceptable substitutes to choose from. Thus the demand for petrol is inelastic while the demand for cabbage tends to be elastic. In general the more substitutes and the closer the substitutes the more elastic the demand

3 Measurement of elasticity of supply

The co-efficient of elasticity of supply is defined as

$$\Sigma S = \frac{\% \ QS}{\% \ P} = \frac{\text{Proportionate change in Qty Supplied}}{\text{Proportionate change in Price}}$$

When (a) $\Sigma s > 1$ Supply is said to be Elastic
   (b) $\Sigma s < 1$ Supply is said to be Inelastic
   (c) $\Sigma s = 1$ Supply is said to have Unit elasticity.

A Perfectly Inelastic Supply Curve has $\Sigma s = 0$ and is illustrated in Figure 4.10. Supply does not respond to price changes at all. Unlike perfectly inelastic demand, $\Sigma s = 0$ may be observed in many real world cases during the **short run**. Consider a farmer, once he/she has planted the seed the eventual harvest will depend upon climatic conditions and changes in price will have no effect at all upon supply. In the long run, however, we would expect farmers to adjust the pattern of their crops in the light of price fluctuations.

Perfectly Elastic Supply is shown by S_2 in Figure 4.10 its $\Sigma s = \propto$ i.e. if price falls below P_2 then producers will be willing to offer nothing for sale at all. Unlike perfectly inelastic supply, $\Sigma s = \propto$ is a purely theoretical concept.

We can see that any straight line Supply Curve through the origin will have a constant Σs of 1.

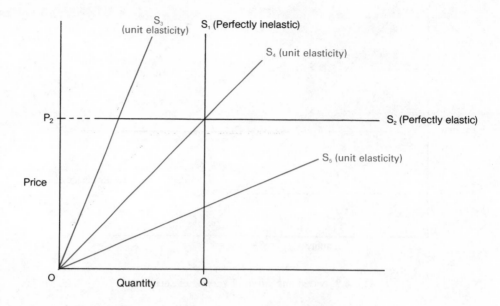

Fig. 4.10 Different supply curves

4 Factors affecting elasticity of supply

(a) Time

In most manufacturing industry production plans can be altered relatively quickly, bearing in mind that contracts for purchases of raw materials etc., are often binding for around six months. However, in agriculture the eventual size of the harvest, once the seeds are planted, depends upon climatic conditions. Current market prices will have no effect upon crop yields at all. It takes seven years for a newly-planted rubber tree to yield its sap, hence we can see that in many cases supply is likely to be more inelastic in the short run. Generally, the elasticity of supply increases over time.

(b) Factors of production

Manufacturers can only respond to increased prices if the extra factors of production are freely available. If however, the factors of production are unavailable or available only at an increased cost, then firms may be less inclined to respond to rising prices by increasing output. Thus supply will tend to be more inelastic.

Uses of elasticity

A knowledge of real world elasticities will be vitally important to both **government and industry**. The former is able to raise revenue by taxing goods with an inelastic demand (see Unit 15). The latter will use their market research to enable them to evaluate the likely effects of any changes in the price of their products. Thus helping them to maximize their profits.

5 Income elasticity of demand

This concept shows the responsiveness of demand to changes in income. It is calculated by $\frac{\% \text{ change in demand.}}{\% \text{ change in income.}}$ For example if income increased by 10% and demand for LPs grew by 8%

then Y.Ed (income elasticity of demand) $= \dfrac{+\ 8}{10} = \dfrac{+\ 4}{5}$

As the Y.Ed is between 0 and 1 the good would be considered as normal.

In cases where demand increases more than income, the Y.Ed will exceed 1. This would indicate a **luxury** such as expensive consumer durables, or meals out. Conversely, the demand for **inferior** goods will tend to fall as income rises. Thus Y.Ed will be a minus value for wash leathers as better-off people will pay for window cleaners' services.

4.6   Links with other topics

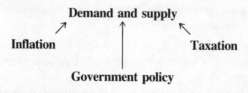

5 Production

5.1 Introduction

The making of goods and the providing of services is known as production. Today a decreasing number of people actually create/manufacture articles and more are employed in the service sector. Those providing services ensure that wants are met and goods are sold in the form, at the time, and when and where they are required. A dentist is just as **'productive'** in economic terms as a farmer, as both fulfil needs and get paid for doing so. (See Figure 5.1) Thus **any paid employment** which arises from the supply of raw materials to the consumption of a good/service may be considered as 'productive'.

Direct production refers to a worker supplying his own needs, *i.e.* self sufficiency, subsistence farming. In modern society nearly all production is **indirect** with people producing goods and services for others.

5.2 Types of production

There are three types of production. The percentage of the working population employed in each type is shown in Figure 5.1.

1 Primary

Extraction of raw materials from the earth's surface *e.g.* coal-mining. This sector is providing less employment because machinery is replacing manpower. Traditional British industries such as **fishing** are declining because of increased competition, although **North Sea oil** and **gas** are providing new jobs.

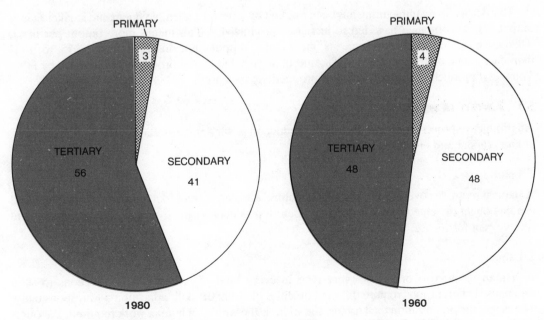

Fig. 5.1 % of working population in different types of production

2 Secondary

Conversion of raw materials **into finished products** *e.g.* manufacturing **tweed skirts**. Again, British manufacturing now employs fewer people. This is because capital is substituted for labour, and Japanese, American and European competition is taking away some traditional British trade. See De-industrialization below.

3 Tertiary

Provision of services for people. These services are essentially of two types:

(a) Commercial services – a charge is made and the provider of the service seeks to make a **profit** *e.g.* an estate agent charges a fee for selling a house, a car mechanic mends a vehicle. This type of service is **increasing** as people have more leisure time and their standard of living is improving. Thus **luxury services** such as eating out at restaurants and playing golf, are becoming more numerous.

(b) Social Services – these services are provided **free** or subsidized at a **cheap rate**, because the government thinks it is desirable. They are not given in order to make a profit, but in order to meet a need. Examples are dental treatment, provided free to people under sixteen and subsidized for adults, and the work of **school teachers**. Services such as these have increased because the government wants certain minimum standards to be met and the public are demanding that much more should be provided. For instance, an ageing population produces a need for more social services, such as meals on wheels.

Before the Industrial Revolution, most of Britain's population was employed in agriculture (primary production). As Britain has become wealthier through the growth of the economy, the structure of industry and commercial life has changed. Then, in each sector, more jobs involve **brain power** and fewer need muscle power. For instance, in the steel industry between 1950 and 1970 total employment increased but the number of process (manual) workers was nearly halved.

De-industrialization

This term refers generally to the **fall in manufacturing output** and the consequent closure of factories. The decline in British manufacturing has occurred since 1950, when manufacturing produced 37% of national income, and it has intensified since 1979 – (see Figure 5.2)

Year	Manufacturing % share of national income	Oil and gas % share of national income
1975	28.3	0
1979	27.2	3.4
1982	23.3	6.2

Source: *Lloyds Bank Economic Bulletin*. March 1983

Fig. 5.2 Shares of national income for manufacturing 1975–82

This decline in manufacturing has been marked by large falls in employment and smaller falls in output. These combined have led to **increased productivity**. This means more output per head, whereas increased production means more total output. For instance from 1975 to 1982 manufacturing employment fell by 19%, output by 10% **but** labour productivity increased by 11%. Thus total production (output) fell, but productivity increased.

5.3   Factors of production

All productive processes require factors of production in varying proportions. The factors are land, labour, capital and enterprise.

1 Land

A **natural** resource covering all 'free gifts of nature' *e.g.* earth, trees, flat land, sea, rivers etc. Land can be bought or rented, but it is necessary before production can be started. The owners of land receive **rent** for its use.

2 Labour

A **human** resource – workers of every type in every kind of activity – from surgeons to shop assistants. Different jobs require **different qualities** of strength, skill, education and responsibility. The bigger the organization then usually the wider is the variety of human work required. Labour is **'owned' by individuals** who sell it to firms, and receive wages/salaries in return.

Factor of production	Examples: Farmer	Engineering Co.	Dentist
LAND	Fields	Factory site	Surgery premises
LABOUR	Farm labourer	Different types of worker	Receptionist
CAPITAL	Tractor	Machinery	Chair & equipment
ENTERPRISE	Planning crop rotation	Organizing production & selling	Choosing place to set up

Fig. 5.3 Examples of factors of production

3 Capital

Capital is a **man-made** resource, for example machinery, a lorry, or a robot. It is used to **make consumer goods** and services. Without capital, there would be no production. Usually capital and labour are combined. Capital **lasts a long time** but eventually needs replacing. When its value declines with age, it is said to be 'depreciating'. Some industries are labelled as 'capital-intensive' in that they have few labour costs and rely heavily on automated machinery *e.g.* the chemical industry. The money borrowed to provide capital is paid **interest**.

4 Enterprise

Another **human** resource. This factor refers to the organizing, planning and risk-taking by the owner of a business. He receives **profit** for his work, and is called the **entrepreneur**. However, in modern economies large businesses are seldom owned by one person; instead they are owned by many shareholders and controlled by a Board of Directors–(see Unit 3.3).

Not all enterprises aim to make a profit. Charities such as Oxfam aim to cover their basic costs and give the surplus away. Some nationalized industries operate in order to provide a service rather than to make a profit.

5.4   Division of labour/specialization

Even in a subsistence economy (see Unit 2) people specialized. For instance one person farmed while another collected wood, and so on. This specialization was **by product**. As the scale of production expanded the division of labour occurred on a finer scale. People specialize **by process**, *i.e.* they make part of a product–for example fish is caught, filleted, packed and sold by different people. Today most **consumer durables** are produced on a large scale by the joint efforts of thousands of workers.

Specialization occurs at various levels in a modern society–individual, factory, firm, industry. **All workers are specialists**.

For instance, the individual may have a specialized job *e.g.* paint spraying in a factory which concentrates on one aspect of production *e.g.* car body assembly. This factory may be part of a large firm which sells different makes of car in the vehicle industry. The vehicle industry includes the production of bicycles, motor bikes, buses, lorries and vans as well as cars. Throughout this industry the division of labour operates with different workers working separately and each producing something which contributes to the production of the final product.

1 Advantages to a firm of the division of labour — 'POST ME'

(a) Practice makes perfect–the repetition of a task improves worker expertise.

(b) Output increases as more is produced per man.

(c) Savings in training and time occur because workers need less instruction if they are only performing part of a job or operating just one machine.

(d) Tools/equipment–each worker does not need a complete set of tools because he is only performing part of the output, unlike a traditional craftsman.

(e) Machinery can be used more often. Such mechanization leads to faster and cheaper output.

(f) Efficiency will probably be increased if piece rate can be used to reward individual workers. The use of piecework is facilitated by mass production and specialization.

2 Disadvantages to a firm — 'DIMS'

(a) Dislocation of production can easily occur because of the interdependence of the specialists. One problem such as absence, faulty workmanship, or a strike, may stop the whole production process.

(b) Industrial action is more likely.

(c) Motivation of workforce may be reduced when individuals perform a single monotonous task. They may become dissatisfied with their jobs and alienated from their employers.

(d) Size of market limits the division of labour. If the market is small then there is less scope for specialization.

3 Advantages to individuals

(a) The increased production and reduced cost per unit have led to a general improvement in the standard of living.

(b) Individual workers can concentrate on the jobs for which they are best suited. Thus a man interested in motor repairs may become a mechanic and not worry about food, clothing and housing production as these jobs are performed by others.

4 Disadvantages to individuals as consumers

(a) Standardized products are made, leading to less choice.

(b) Loss of individual craftsmanship may lead to lower quality products being made, *e.g.* machine-knitted and hand-knitted jumpers.

5.5 Costs of production

1 Fixed and variable costs

Fixed costs are costs which **do not change with the level of production** *e.g.* the rent of premises is paid usually months in advance whether a dentist treats one patient a day or fifty per day.

Variable costs **change with** the amount of **production** *e.g.* the amount of filling used by a dentist is dependent on the number and type of patients treated.

In Economics, the definition of the **short run** is determined by fixed costs. The short run is defined as a period of **time in which at least one cost of production is fixed**. Thus, the short run varies between firms and industries *e.g.* in manufacturing it is probably about nine months *i.e.* the period of time needed to change the use of a piece of land, which is the most immobile factor of production. A decision in principle would be followed by drawings, planning applications and buildings before the new use could be operational. In the **long run all costs** are considered to be **variable**.

2 Average and marginal cost

(a) Total cost = all current costs of production (fixed and variable) added together.

(b) Average cost = total cost divided by total number of units of output.

(c) Marginal cost = extra cost of increasing output by **one** unit.

Average costs often fall as production increases, because fixed costs are spread over more units of output. The point of **lowest average cost** is called the **Optimum** output. This is the point of **maximum efficiency**. The average cost curve is normally U-shaped in the short run.

Marginal cost falls faster than average cost and **rises faster than average cost**. The marginal cost curve crosses the average cost curve at the lowest point of average cost. (See Figure 5.4)

Output	Fixed costs	Variable costs	Total cost	Average cost	Marginal cost
5	30	10	40	8	8
10	30	40	70	7	6
15	30	60	90	6	4
20	30	70	100	5	2
25	30	120	150	6	10
30	30	180	210	7	12

3 Average and marginal revenue

In practice a firm's **total revenue** is its income over a period of time. It is usually composed of sales but may also include government grants and subsidies.

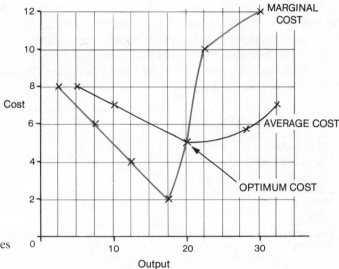

Fig. 5.4 Cost schedule and cost curves

In economic theory, we assume that total revenue is just from **sales** and that all **goods are sold at the same price**.

Thus total revenue = sales + price.

Average revenue = total revenue divided by number of units sold.

Marginal revenue = extra revenue obtained from the sale of one more unit.

4 Profit

Generally, and simply, a profit arises when **total revenue exceeds total costs**. Alternatively, if total costs are greater than total revenue a loss occurs.

Normal profit

Total costs include normal profit which is considered as a **cost** of production. In theory, this is the amount of profit which an entrepreneur needs, to stay in a particular industry. Normal profit is the **least profit** which an entrepreneur is prepared to make and **stay** in that industry.

Normal profit is the reward for organization and risk-taking earned by the factor 'enterprise'. Any profits earned above normal profit are an extra reward for the entrepreneur's success in an industry and they are termed **'abnormal profit'**.

In practice, there is usually not just one profit from the sale of a good, but several. By the time a consumer buys a product from a shop, profits may have been made by the manufacturer, distributor and seller. All these entrepreneurs calculate **profit margins** *i.e.* they add a percentage to purchase price which they have paid, before they resell the good.

Profit maximization

In Economics it is assumed that firms seek maximum profit or minimum loss. The position of maximum profit is where **marginal cost equals marginal revenue with marginal cost rising** *i.e.* the extra cost of producing one more unit equals the extra revenue received from selling it.

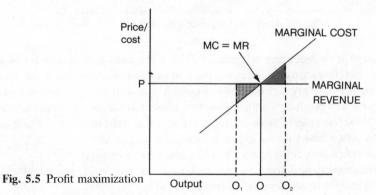

Fig. 5.5 Profit maximization

In Figure 5.5, MC = MR at price P and output O. If one less unit is produced – O1 – then some profit is being given up (the black shaded area). Alternatively, if O2 is produced then a loss is incurred on the output of that unit (red area) as marginal cost is greater than marginal revenue.

Often a business will remain in operation for a short time even if making a loss. It might consider the loss to be temporary and be prepared to sustain the loss. If it is a public company it might maintain its dividend by using profits retained from earlier years.

If a firm's **losses** are **less** than its **fixed costs** then it is better to continue production, because the financial sacrifice is lower. This is illustrated in Figure 5.6 when total revenue changes with the fluctuations in price of a product.

Total revenue £	21 m	26 m	19 m
Fixed costs	2 m	2 m	2 m
Variable costs	20 m	20 m	20 m
Total cost	22 m	22 m	22 m
Profit + Loss −	−1 m	+4 m	−3 m
Production decision	Continue as loss less than fixed cost	Continue as profit	Possibly cease as loss greater than fixed costs

Fig. 5.6 Profit/loss and production decisions

5.6   Large scale production

In the past, before the Industrial Revolution, production was on a small scale. As **transport was undeveloped**, **markets** were **local** and not very large. Each village had its own specialist craftsmen and goods were often custom built. The main traders in villages and towns were **sole traders** and **partnerships**. The population of UK was fairly small.

The development of the **factory** system requiring water, and later steam power, led to manufacturing on a larger scale. Even then the manager was usually the owner (**entrepreneur**) and knew all his employees. As transport became more rapid and communications improved, **markets** became **larger** and firms grew in size. In addition, the advances made in agriculture and health led to a rapid increase in population size which also extended the size of the market. As large factories could produce much more at lower average cost than individual craftsmen, small enterprises either went out of business or were swallowed up by large firms. This process of **merger**, or conglomeration, has speeded up in the twentieth century and now many companies are **international** *e.g.* Royal Dutch Shell. Consequently, the average size of firm has increased considerably.

Output	Total cost	Average cost
0	200	0
1	300	300
2	320	160
3	333	111
4	340	85
5	345	69
50	400	8
51	510	10
52	572	11
60	840	14

Fig. 5.7 Costs and scale of production

Operating on a large scale has many **advantages**. These are known as **economies of scale**. By producing large quantities, firms are able to reduce the cost per unit. The fixed costs are spread over a greater quantity of units and so average cost falls – Figure 5.7, output 1 to 50. Thus, it costs £8 each to make 50, but £111 each to produce 3 units. However, after 50 units, average cost begins to rise. Thus beyond 50 units **diseconomies of scale** operate. These are certain handicaps which occur and raise the costs of production when a firm expands beyond a certain size.

Economies and diseconomies are of two types – internal and external:
Internal – **specific advantages to one firm** which arise because of the way it operates.
External – general advantages to **all firms** in an industry.

1 Internal economies of scale

These can be remembered by the mnemonic **'MATE FIT'**

(a) Managerial – in most firms, as production increases, management and supervision do not need to increase at the same rate. Thus one managing director can probably control a company with 100 employees as easily as 400. Furthermore, a large firm can use many specialists, whereas in a small firm people have to be more general, undertaking several tasks. The manager of a small firm might actually work on the machines, deal with complaints, solve industrial disputes and carry out the paperwork. He may be a 'jack of all trades' and master of none. However, in many cases, the owner-manager may be a successful and efficient co-ordinator. In the large firm the use of specialists brings about the advantages of the **division of labour** (see 5.4)

(b) Technical – larger-scale operations may make use of **advanced machinery**. Some machines are only worth using at a **minimum level of output** which may be beyond the capacity of a small firm *e.g.* it is no good using a computer to calculate the wages of three employees but for 1000 it becomes viable. Also, resources can be used for **research and development** in large organizations because the cost is easily absorbed as a small part of the total cost. Such research may bring about improved processes and development of **new products** *e.g.* plastics from chemicals.

Large-scale production enables **fuller utilization of capital** equipment and **lower average cost**. For instance, a small furniture store may use its delivery van only two days per week whereas a large departmental store has its delivery van operating every day.

The production line of a mass-produced consumer durable, such as a TV set, motor car, is the epitome of internal technical economy. It enables **time** and **cost savings**.

(c) Financial – large organizations are usually well known and this often makes it easier for them to **borrow** money from commercial banks than businesses such as Fred's Café. A large company may also obtain a **preferential rate of interest** (lower) on its borrowing, because it has many valuable assets and a **reputation** for reliability.

(d) Trading – these advantages cover several areas:
 (i) Purchasing – large organizations often gain discounts for bulk buying *e.g.* large regular order may gain 25% off price, thereby reducing unit cost. Occasionally, the bulk buyer can dictate type of product and quality to be supplied. Marks & Spencer do this with their suppliers. One large order is more convenient and less costly in administration for the supplier than several small ones.
 (ii) Selling – large firms can spread advertising and other marketing costs over a large number of units *e.g.* in winter 1983 Tottenham F.C. spent £100 000 on a series of **adverts** to attract families to watch football. The **cost of this spread over** their average 30 000 attendance was little per head. However, Halifax Town could not have afforded such advertising with just 2000 spectators normally.
 (iii) Diversifying – instead of selling just one product, large firms may produce **several products for different markets**. Thus, if one product makes a loss, the profits on others will carry it. When Shell had a tough time selling petrol and other oil products in America it diversified into growing carrots, oranges and lemons! The extent of ICI's diversification is shown in Figure 5.8.

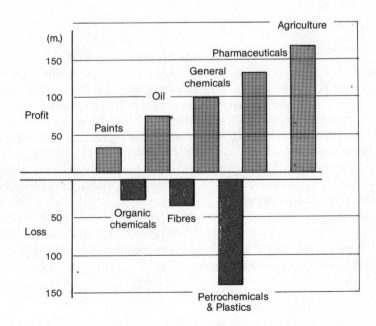

Fig. 5.8 ICI trading profits (1982) by product

2 External economies of scale – remember by — 'LICE'

(a) Labour – a pool of skilled labour may develop in an area where many firms are concentrated (*e.g* white-collar computer workers in Silicon Glen, Scotland). This helps to reduce a firm's training costs and probably makes recruitment easier.

(b) Information – this may be shared by firms in an industry, particularly against foreign competition. They may combine resources into research facilities or use computers on a time-sharing basis.

(c) Concentration – often the firms in an industry are localized in a region. A concentrated industry may benefit by attracting specialist suppliers of raw materials, components and services. BL cars at Solihull rely on local suppliers of radiators, petrol tanks, door hinges, hand brakes and so on, within a 50-mile radius. As these suppliers have a regular local bulk buyer they too can benefit from internal economies of scale.

(d) Education and training – specialist facilities are provided within most industries to develop the knowledge and skills of the manpower. Industrial Training Boards provide many general needs, although small firms receive a better return because of their smaller outlay. Specialized requirements may be met locally *e.g.* Grimsby Tech. College refrigeration technology is specifically geared to frozen fish and food industry.

3 Internal diseconomies of scale – 'SWIRL'

(a) Standardization of product – this often results with the mass production technique being used. This **lack of individualism** may reduce customer choice and increase customer neglect. Each item may not be as well made as the equivalent would be by an individual craftsman *e.g.* pottery. Furthermore, standardized products on production lines may **not** be **able** to adapt to **changing trends** very quickly.

(b) Waste may be undetected, unless there is thorough supervision (which is costly). Materials may be **misused**, **lost** or **stolen** or machinery may be underutilized; both of which increase the costs of production. Manpower may be wasted too. A firm may be overmanned, employing staff who are not really needed. As a result some of the advantages of large-scale production may be lost.

(c) Impersonal behaviour – the lack of a **personal touch** may lose sales for a big firm. In addition, it may be difficult in a large hierarchy to **get hold** of the people responsible for decisions.

(d) Red Tape – memos from one department to several may be needed to explain any decision made. This involves **people, time and cost** in perhaps unnecessary communication rather than production. Co-ordination may be complicated. For instance the accountant may want to cut costs but the marketing executive may seek increased advertising expenditure in order to raise sales.

(e) Labour relations in large organizations tend to be more difficult to manage, particularly if several trade unions are involved. Trade unions may be well **organized** and more **militant**, thus industrial **unrest** may result.

4 External diseconomies of scale

The main external diseconomy to firms in an industry arises out of **shortages** which may occur. Scarcity of labour or resources may lead to competition by firms which will up the **costs** of production *e.g.* high fees paid to qualified divers by North Sea oil companies.

There may be diseconomies to a local community where firms are concentrated. Land prices may escalate, pollution may arise and traffic problems may occur. However, these **social costs** do not directly affect the firm, although they may indirectly suffer through inability to attract workers, and bad publicity. The **decline** of a heavily concentrated industry will affect the whole economy of the area *e.g.* N. East depression in 1980 as coal, steel and shipbuilding have all declined, giving much higher than average unemployment.

The diseconomies of scale may outweigh the economies of scale. For instance, Watney became the second biggest brewer in Britain in the 1960's through takeovers but in 1972 it was taken over by Grand Metropolitan hotels. However, in 1976, it was broken up into regional companies because of its decline in performance, over fifteen years.

5.7 Growth of firms

In the private sector, most firms start from small beginnings. Some expand and swallow up other small firms whilst others continue to remain small. Firms grow through internal expansion and integration.

1 Internal expansion

A firm may expand from within by producing and selling more of its existing products or by extending its product range. These moves may result from:

        (a) Growing market   *e.g.* jeans
        (b) New markets   *e.g.* video machines
        (c) Technical improvements *e.g.* automatic washer

Successful firms usually feature **enterprising management**, a devoted **workforce**, available **finance** and **unused capacity** in the growth period. The rate of growth is usually limited by the speed with which research and development, management and selling teams can be developed. The life cycle of a growing firm is illustrated in Figure 5.9.

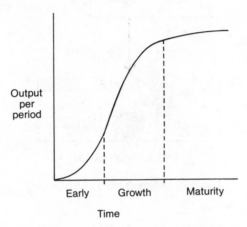

Fig. 5.9 Life cycle of a growing firm

2 Integration

This is the process of **firms joining together** through either:

(a) Merger – The amalgamation of 2+ firms to form one organization *e.g.* Cadbury – Schweppes. Usually the shareholders in the old firms got shares in the new firm in agreed proportions. The Monopolies Commission vets large mergers (+£15m).

(b) Takeover – the acquisition of shares in one company by another. The takeover price is usually in excess of the market price of the shares. It is financed by cash, or shares in the company which is taking over, or both. It is different from a merger in that the directors of the target company may oppose the bid *e.g.* Lonrho for House of Fraser 1982 – 84.

3 Types of integration

(a) Horizontal – firms join together in **same industry** and at **same stage** of production *e.g.* National Westminster formed from the Westminster and the National Provincial banks. Thus a good is produced by one large company rather than two. For example, in Figure 5.10, the Four Fish Finger producer takes over another firm making fish fingers, the Five Fish Finger factory.

Reasons/advantages

  (i) larger production unit →**economies of scale**
 (ii) reduced competition leads to more control over market and **greater market share**. The integration may be defensive against imports.

    This type of integration accounted for most of nineteenth-century mergers. It is most common today at the **retail stage** *e.g.* W. H. Smith. Occasionally, **demergers** occur when part of a large company is sold off *e.g.* House of Fraser do not wish to sell off Harrods, the largest of its 100-plus department stores, although this has been demanded by prominent shareholders.

(b) Vertical – One firm **controls different stages** of production, which might otherwise be independent. Thus in Figure 5.10 if the Four Fish Finger producer buys out a trawler owner it will have its own source of raw materials, rather than having to buy them from a supplier. It may of course still buy from other suppliers *e.g.* Ross Group have their own fleet of trawlers.

This type of integration may be:

(i) backwards when the producer purchases stages of production **towards the source of raw materials,** *e.g.* above

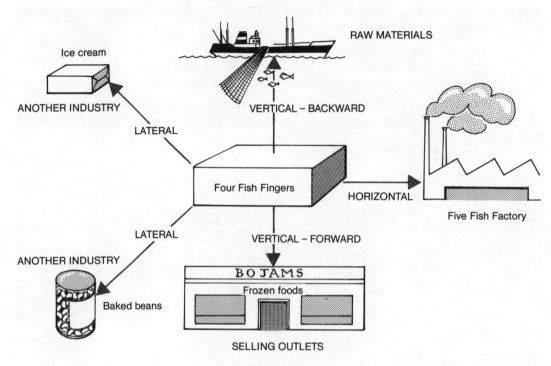

Fig. 5.10 Different types of integration

(ii) forwards when the producer purchases stages **towards the market** *e.g.* in Figure 5.10 the Four Fish Finger company has acquired a shop through which it can sell its goods.

Reasons

(a) **increased efficiency** and lower costs between various stages of production by eliminating delivery costs and middlemen profits.

(b) **safeguard sources of supply**/outlets – control of own sources probably enables more flexible production.

(c) **increase barriers to entry**, thereby making it more difficult for competitors.

(d) **improve research by co-ordination** between stages of production.

(e) **better access** to markets.

(f) **fuller use of by-products** *e.g.* ammonia and slag from blast furnaces enables diversification.

A nationalized industry, such as NCB is a good example of total vertical integration. British Leyland can be given as an example of failed integration.

(c) lateral/conglomerate/diversified – the expansion of an existing firm into an **unrelated industry** with which it was previously not connected *e.g.* BP into eel farming. The integration may occur as a result of research findings.

Reasons

(i) **To increase profits in long run**. If a firm is in a declining industry it may seek profits elsewhere as a precaution, *e.g.* British Match Corporation made 75% of all matches in Britain but diversified into packaging and printing. This enabled risks to be spread and a wider range of products to be sold.

(ii) **To make better use of assets/resources**. Economies in common activities such as accounting, outlets and exporting could be achieved. For instance, Cadbury-Schweppes merger enabled chocolate and soft drinks to be sold through some retail shops, thereby reducing distribution and selling costs.

The **failure** of lateral integration indicates **diseconomies of scale**. This sometimes occurs through management loyalty to former companies, and squabbles, in the new set up.

5.8   Small firms

Definition – this varies considerably. The 1971 Bolton Committee laid down a variety of cut-off levels, based on **employment** and for **turnover**. It restricted its analysis to firms **run by owners** and having **miniscule market share**. For example:

200 employees in manufacturing

£50 000 turnover in retailing (£200 000 at today's prices) were maximum limits for 'small'. Thus most **hotels, pubs** and **farms** are small firms: as are hauliers with less than five lorries. If the **self employed** are included, then there are about 3 million small firms in Britain.

Development There are fewer small firms in Britain than in most other countries. They are a declining breed with a falling share of national output. There is a **low birth rate** and a **low death rate** *i.e.* relatively few bankruptcies. Thus the average life expectancy is twenty-two years (compared to USA – seven years).

1 Strengths 'FIT'

(a) Flexibility – small firms, particularly self employed, can adapt readily to **customers' needs** *e.g.* working unsociable hours in order to fulfil a contract; designing products to meet individual requirements. They provide a **personal service** and often fulfil needs which large firms neglect.

(b) Industrial relations – the boss of a small firm tends to have a wide **general knowledge** of his good/service and through working with his few employees he may have a **friendly** relationship with them. This should make morale high and industrial action low.

(c) Transport costs – usually small firms have a local market, thus transport costs are fairly low. Furthermore in remote areas, the high transport costs to larger firms reduce their interest in the market and perhaps guarantee a local monopoly for a small firm.

2 Weaknesses 'STEAM'

These weaknesses cause 2000 liquidations per year:

(a) Susceptibility – if a single product supplier, a sharp change in demand may spell disaster *e.g.* Rolls-Royce 1971 collapse at Derby had ripple effects throughout local economy as local firms, such as window cleaners, were heavily dependent on one big contract and they 'went bust'.

(b) Taxation – high **income tax** rates are a disincentive to effort while tax reliefs on pensions, national savings, etc, channel funds to institutions who are less able/interested in the small firm sector. However, many **tax reliefs**, such as three year start-up losses being offset against previous tax payments, can be claimed (assuming the small firm owner uses an accountant!)

(c) Expensive finance – small businessmen face a tougher life than large companies' directors because **loans are more expensive** and security requirements are higher. Furthermore, they are less well informed and lack the **prestige and status** of their corporate rivals. However, in recent years the major clearing banks have started small business advisory services which may have helped a little.

(d) Administration – accounting, disclosure of information, and **filling forms** weigh relatively more heavily on the owner-manager. For instance, the introduction of VAT created a major problem for many small businesses as more extensive records needed to be kept. Similarly, the Employment Protection Acts have increased Government regulation of their activities.

(e) Management defects – often there is little forward **planning**, no **budgeting**, and nepotism (promotion of relatives) which make the business unstable. Many have new ideas but lack capital.

3 Limitations on small firms growth

These may 'SAP' its strength.

(a) Size of market – this keeps many small firms small. A market can be limited by:

 (i) supply of raw materials *e.g.* a diamond cutter
 (ii) demand *e.g.* valet usually employed by high income groups
(iii) transport costs *e.g.* small-scale caterers
(iv) perishable product *e.g.* flower sellers.

(b) Available capital

Small businesses rely heavily, especially when opening, on loans from family and friends and their own savings. These sources are known as borrowing from **'Aunt Agatha'** and they have become more difficult to get in recent years. A lack of finance can also limit expansion. See Unit 3.7. The main sources of finance for small firms are compared with those available to big public companies in Figure 5.11. Undistributed profits dominate in both.

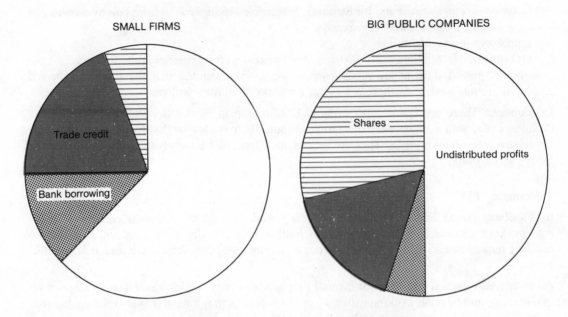

SMALL FIRMS

BIG PUBLIC COMPANIES

Trade credit

Bank borrowing

Shares

Undistributed profits

Fig. 5.11 Sources of finance for small and big firms

(c) Personal preference – the owners of small firms often do not want the headaches and problems of expansion, and so choose not to expand.

4 Government help – 1981 Budget

This introduced several new schemes to aid small firms in overcoming basic weaknesses.

(a) Business Start Up Scheme – to encourage outside investors to provide equity capital of between £1000 – £20 000 in a new firm for up to five years. In return, the Government gives the investor his marginal rate of income tax in tax relief.

(b) Loan Guarantee Scheme – the Government guarantees to financial institutions 80% of loan on new loans up to £75 000.

(c) Preferential Corporation Tax – small firms pay 40% (as opposed to 52%) with profits of less than £90 000. This reduces the tax burden and leaves more undistributed profit for expansion.

(d) Capital Transfer Tax – increased exemptions and the raising of threshold to £55 000 has made it easier for people to pass their businesses on intact to their children.

(e) 1980 Employment Act – this made small firms exempt from certain requirements *e.g.* maternity reinstatement, uniform dismissal procedures.

5 Value of small firms – 'ICEES'

(a) Innovation – small firms seem more likely to develop new techniques than bigger firms.

(b) Competition – the existence of many firms in an industry may lead to more competition and lower prices. This is particularly the case in retailing.

(c) Employment – jobs are created by small firms as they tend to be labour-intensive.

(d) Efficiency – as small firms seem to have better labour relations and exercise closer supervision over their employees, it is often argued that they are more efficient than larger enterprises.

(e) 'Seedbed' function – small firms, like seeds, may develop into industrial giants *e.g.* a man selling hot dogs in street gradually builds food chain empire.

5.9   Links with other topics

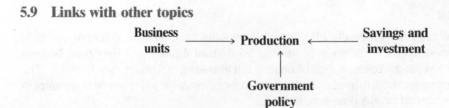

Business units → Production ← Savings and investment

↑

Government policy

6 Location of industry

6.1 Background

The location of industry really refers to the location of **factories and offices** rather than whole industries. Whole industries do not suddenly start, but individual firms do. We are mainly concerned with the location of the **firms** which compose an industry. Even within firms though, there may be factories and offices around the country for different reasons *e.g.* Laporte Industries main plant is on the Humber, most of its subsidiary factories are near the coast, but its head office is in London. However, often a **large proportion of an industry** is concentrated in one geographical **area** *e.g.* car-making in West Midlands, whisky distilling in S. Scotland.

The individual location decisions will generally be determined by **profit** calculations in the private sector. Alternatively, a public corporation may locate a new plant in an area of high unemployment for **political** and **social** reasons.

The factors determining location **vary between industries and sectors**. For instance, new firms providing a service usually begin in the area where the owner lives, to have access to customers. New branches of existing firms often radiate out into other nearby towns in the region to make control easier.

The employment trend towards the Tertiary Sector and the decline of primary and secondary production (see Unit 5.2) have dramatically changed the importance of various location factors. In the past, **geographical factors**, such as available supplies of water, determined where some firms would site. Entrepreneurs often had no **choice**.

However, modern industry is footloose (not tied to a certain location by dependence on one source of power), as the sources of power are more varied and widely available. The costs of several available sites may be similar so a modern firm may be able to choose from several possible locations. These two trends have meant that modern industries are **more dispersed** and **less concentrated** than in the past. Highly concentrated industries derived peculiar advantages from locating in specific areas, *e.g.* water supplies for Lancashire textiles, and were manufacturers in the main. The new dispersed industries relate to the service sector and require large populations to provide a market.

6.2 Factors influencing location 'PANTS GLEEM'

1 Power

Access to power was influential during the Industrial Revolution when steam power was needed. **Steam** was generated from **coal** and so many firms were located near coal mines. As coal was bulky and costly to move, it was more economical to locate near the source of power than to transport the coal to a factory. This factor was crucial in iron and steel production. However, as **electricity and gas** have been developed, **nationwide supplies** have been created through national grids. Thus power as a locating influence has declined, as shown by the many abandoned water mills and the fact that coal is now imported.

2 Natural Advantages

In each case below there is a natural advantage, followed by an industry to which it applies and an example.

Soil – agriculture *e.g.* Lincolnshire
Deep water harbour – shipbuilding *e.g* Tyneside
Sea – fishing *e.g.* Aberdeen
Climate – cotton *e.g.* Lancashire – damp climate
Rock structure – oil *e.g.* Wytch Farm, Dorset
Forest – timber *e.g.* Kielder Forest

Tidal estuary – chemicals waste disposal *e.g.* Humber
Water – nuclear power *e.g.* Windscale, Cumbria
Water – brewing *e.g.* Burton upon Trent
Flat land – motor vehicle assembly *e.g.* Midlands

3 Transport/communications

Transport takes many forms and each can be a crucial cost as below:

(a) Road – access to motorways is increasingly important. Industrial estates have developed alongside motorway interchanges.

(b) Rail – more important in past when rail was the main means of freight transport. With the reduction in rail network and increased cost, it has declined as a locating factor. However, many large companies such as Fords, Dagenham, have their own lines, sidings and stock.

(c) Sea – firms relying on imported raw materials are often located near deep water ports *e.g.* oil refining at Immingham.

(d) Air – speed is essential for fashion goods such as Dior dresses. Generally, a good transport system increases the attractiveness of an area as it enables **speedy delivery** of raw materials and finished products. Firms have moved out of city centres to the suburbs and **outlying districts** to avoid the congestion which may develop. In addition, the land for factory building may be cheaper outside towns.

4 Supplies of raw materials, components and water

Access to raw materials was vital to the old extractive industries *e.g.* quarrying next to a quarry! This was so that impure waste was not transported, being quickly and easily dumped. Today, fish products are made by firms located at fishing ports so that the offal can be disposed of locally, without undue cost.

Generally, if the essential raw materials are bulky and costly to move and involve a lot of waste, firms are attracted to the source of the raw materials *e.g.* canned peas alongside farming areas. In contrast, if **weight is gained** in production then firms will tend to **locate near its market** *e.g.* lemonade near towns/cities.

Many consumer durables are dependent on component parts, which have to be **assembled**. The suppliers of components tend to be found near the car makers. Thus, a new car plant might need to be located in the same area to take advantage of this.

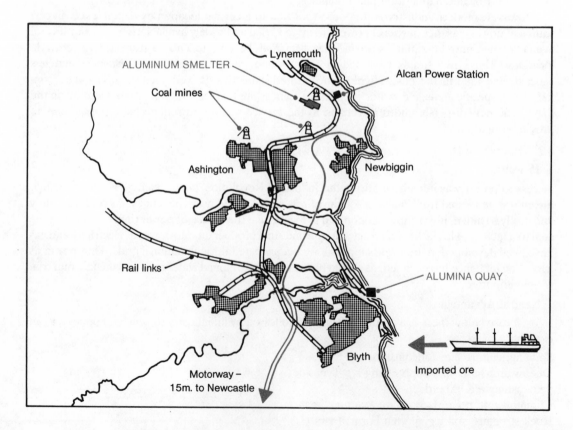

Fig. 6.1 Pull of raw materials and power in manufacturing

A large supply of **water** is needed in the production of goods such as steel and chemicals. Thus, the raw material may influence where a factory is sited.

The **pull of raw materials has declined** with improvements in transport. The extension of the motorway system and competitive haulage industry have reduced transport costs as a % of total cost. Figure 6.1 shows the importance of raw materials, transport, water and power to aluminium smelting at Lynemouth.

5 Government policy

Since the 1930s, successive governments have tried to influence the location of firms. They have occasionally interfered for non-economic reasons, but **supplied economic incentives** such as rent-free buildings and grants. The Aluminium smelter in Figure 6.1 attracted a 40% grant being in a development area. Also, by using the coal from local coalfields, it kept pits open which otherwise might have been closed. This slowed down **unemployment** in the area. Such policies artificially distort costs, and may persuade firms to locate in a place which otherwise might not be economic.

The Government has set **examples** by locating some of its offices in seemingly uneconomic locations *e.g.* Giro centre at Bootle, DVLC at Swansea. In 1982, the Government refused extra funds to ICL unless it located the next part of its development programme in Mid-Wales. In 1983-4 the Government spent **£750m on regional aid**. In addition, it has created Special Development Areas and Enterprise Zones to attract firms to areas of high unemployment and banned location in areas of natural beauty and historic significance.

6 Labour

Available and appropriately-skilled labour is necessary for all firms. As labour is not very mobile, quantities of labour with certain characteristics often occur in certain areas *e.g.* textile workers in Nottingham, blast furnacemen in S. Yorkshire. **Cheap**, often **female, labour may attract** firms to areas of high unemployment *e.g.* clothing manufacturing.

Conversely, certain types of labour may be a **disincentive** to prospective employers. The **absenteeism** and **strike** records on Merseyside have been cited as reasons why some firms have been reluctant to establish themselves there despite Government grants. The lack of an **assembly line tradition** led to increased labour costs/unit at Bathgate.

7 External Economies

When the firms of an industry are concentrated in one area, the area tends to adapt to its special needs, as explained in Unit 5.6. These economies of **concentration** give a cost advantage to a firm setting up and so pull firms to certain locations *e.g.* prestige of Sheffield Steel and the specialist training facilities encourage cutlery firms to locate there.

8 Markets

The products of many **new industries** (*e.g.* cookers) and the **service sector** (*e.g.* hairdressing, insurance brokers) need access to their customers. Thus, they seek locations near centres of population, which the producers of perishables and retailers have always sought.

Similarly, where the **cost of transporting the finished product is high**, a firm will tend to locate near its market *e.g.* bread and lemonade. As London and the South East is the biggest market in the UK, it pulls new firms into its region. This is despite government attempts to hinder the pull because of the congestion and overcrowding which it partly causes.

6.3 Regional problems

Different regions of UK suffer from contrasting problems:

1 High unemployment *e.g.* N. Ireland and Scotland. Fig. 6.2 shows that there has been little change in the **traditional pattern**, whereby unemployment rates in Scotland and North are well above the national average while the South East and East Anglia are well below it. However, the W. Midlands, which is normally below average, rose above the national average partly as a result of the decline of engineering and motor car production in 1980s.

The staple industries such as **coal and shipbuilding** which were flourishing in the nineteenth and early twentieth centuries have **declined** and not been replaced by modern growth sectors which are attracted by markets. Their decline has created localized unemployment *e.g.* specific towns with +20% unemployment for years. Such unemployment is a waste of resources. Also it creates income inequalities between regions with certain areas being less prosperous.

2 Congestion and overcrowding *e.g.* London and S. East. The pull of the market has worsened these problems by creating miles of urban sprawl and inadequate recreational space. The problems cause

Region	Year % Unemployed			
	1971	*1976*	*1979*	*1981*
North	5.7	7.5	8.7	15.3
Yorks/Humberside	3.8	5.5	5.7	12.3
E. Midlands	2.9	4.7	4.6	10.2
E. Anglia	3.2	4.8	4.5	9.2
S. East	2.0	4.2	3.7	8.1
S. West	3.3	6.4	5.7	10.0
W. Midlands	2.9	5.8	5.5	13.7
N. West	3.9	6.9	7.1	13.9
Wales	4.4	7.3	7.9	14.8
Scotland	5.8	7.0	8.0	13.8
N. Ireland	7.9	10.0	11.3	18.4
UK Average	3.5	5.7	5.7	11.4

Fig. 6.2 Unemployment rates by standard region 1971–81

economic inefficiency as time and money are added to journeys by traffic holdups. Public facilities are overstretched and social problems created.

In contrast in the areas of falling population, social services, transport and other local facilities may be **under-utilized**. Thus, the best use of resources is not achieved.

 3 Inner city decay *e.g.* London, Birmingham, Manchester. In many large cities, such as these, there are areas containing run-down housing, disused industrial property, empty shops and boarded-up houses. The problems created are **social**, but they have **economic side effects** *e.g.* increased **vandalism** raises insurance premiums on the shops of remaining traders, whilst the need for public expenditure on policing and renewal may raise rates.

Since 1945 **'the regional problem'** has been focused on trying to narrow the unemployment difference between regions. The regional problem has been seen in terms of an **imbalance** between the standard regions. This imbalance has been in terms not only of unemployment, but also of earnings and social capital. In 1975, the Government began to take a broader perspective and devised a more general industrial policy (see Unit 19).

6.4 Regional policies

1 Alternative approaches

(a) Free market – in which firms make their own decisions on the choice of location, **without government guidance**. In theory they might take advantage of high unemployment in order to reduce wage rates and thereby lower costs relative to other potential sites. However, in practice, national collective bargaining prevents this, whilst unemployment benefit may act as a deterrent to unskilled unemployed seeking lower-paid jobs. It also assumes that firms seek **lowest cost location**, which many do not.

This approach only looks at private costs and benefits (*i.e.* to the firm). The social costs of high unemployment, reflected in such things as juvenile delinquency, increased crime and depression, are neglected. They clearly have an economic dimension *e.g.* cost of control, detection, cure, etc.

The defenders of the free market argue that restrictions on location may deter firms from building at all. Furthermore, governments give **benefits** which are **short term** and so in the long term some sites become uneconomic, if they are chosen for short-term reasons, then in the long term the resources may be wasted.

(b) Government intervention – Government tries to influence location policies of firms. It has concentrated on attempts to reduce unemployment differences. A few measures have been introduced to combat congestion. Since 1979, regional aid has been reduced because the Conservative Government believe in less Government interference in economic decision making.

The two basic methods used are:

 (i) move work to the workers – capital mobility
 (ii) move workers to the work – labour mobility

In summary, it is clear that in practice, the debate centres around the **extent of intervention** rather than 'to intervene or not to intervene'.

2 Government policies

(a) Regional unemployment

 (i) Capital mobility – over the years the Government has created Assisted Areas, which are currently of three types:

Development Areas – large areas of high unemployment with declining basic industries.
Special Development Areas – high and persistent unemployment blackspots within the development areas.
Intermediate Areas – areas where unemployment is increasing and there is little prospect of economic growth.

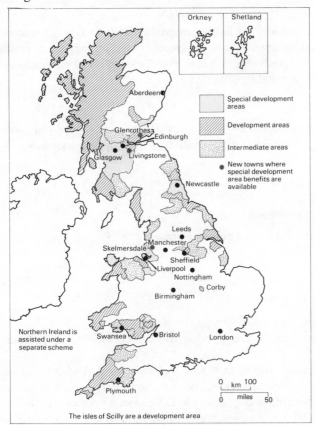

Fig. 6.3 Assisted areas since 1.8.82

Firms setting up in these areas receive **incentives** such as:

(a) grants towards cost of machinery, buildings, factories. *(b)* factory rents on favourable terms *(c)* grants and subsidies towards employing/training workers *(d)* tax allowances on plant and machinery

The current rates of grant are given in Figure 6.4

> **15%** grant on new buildings
> rent-free period if buildings ceased
> **15%** grant on new plant, machinery & equipment
> **100%** tax allowance on new plant, machinery & equipment
> **75%** tax allowance on building costs
> Assistance with training costs

Fig. 6.4 Development Area assistance January 1984

The incentives cost about £750m annually. They act as **external economies** to an area. Furthermore, the extension of the motorway system has improved the facilities which some areas can offer. Many local authorities were given money by central government to improve their areas by making them look more attractive *e.g.* clearance of derelict land, landscaping slag heaps and building industrial estates.

The Government has also tried to **deter** movement to prosperous areas. **Industrial Development Certificates** (IDC) were needed before certain building could be erected, as well as normal planning permission. Currently, factories exceeding **5000 sq ft in London** need an IDC. These certificates were **not** needed in Development Areas in order to encourage expanding firms to locate there. Similarly, between 1965-79 Office Development Permits were required in S. East and Midlands.

(ii) **Labour mobility** – the encouraging of workers to move from areas of high unemployment to areas of low unemployment received little financial support. **Grants of £600** were given to workers who moved and **council housing** was made easily available. If this geographical mobility had been successful, it would have made congestion worse.

Generally, **occupational** rather than geographical mobility (see Unit 12) has been encouraged by generous payments to workers who retrain on Government schemes at Government centres. Government policies have been classed into **'sticks'** and **'carrots'**; sticks being deterrents such as IDCS, and carrots being incentives such as grants.

(b) Congestion

New Towns – since 1946, more than 30 new towns have been established in Britain. They were set up to attract people out of overcrowded old towns into newly created ones. Towns such as Washington (near Newcastle), Skelmersdale (Liverpool) and Milton Keynes (serving London) were planned to contain **housing and work** there by stimulating growth.

(c) Urban decay

Enterprise Zones – created 1981 to encourage business development and selected run down inner city areas. These zones would be a focal point for growth. The advantages given were:

(i) free rates
(ii) no industrial training board payments
(iii) 100% tax allowance on building costs
(iv) simplified planning and VAT procedures

Local authorities have also spent funds on attracting industry.

3 The results of regional policy

Assessment of regional policy is difficult because:

(a) We cannot tell what would have happened without the policies.
(b) Not all the jobs created were 'new', many being perhaps diverted from other areas where firms might have been located.

The costs can be roughly calculated. £600m in 1983-4. It has been worked out that **each job** created cost at least **£35 000**. The Government has to spend more on welfare services in areas of high unemployment. The younger members of the community in Development Areas tend to **migrate** to find employment. Despite all the public money used, the **unemployment is still** worse in the Assisted Areas and the gap with the prosperous areas is not closing – see Figure 6.2.

The benefits have been in some new jobs and a slowing down of industrial decline in a more humane way perhaps. New **foreign** investment has been attracted by the incentives available, and Britain's place in the EEC. For instance, **Japanese investment** in Wales (seven factories providing 3000 jobs) has been used as a base for expansion into Europe. Exports from Japan directly would be subject to tariffs, but from within Britain, their cars and motorbikes are not taxed on entry.

The EEC has also helped in another way, through its Regional Development Fund. This gives **'disfavoured'** industrial and regional **grants** of up to 40% of the capital cost of investment. For instance, it gave £600 000 towards £6m Glendevon water treatment and dam project in Scotland.

6.5 Steel industry

1 Location

Nineteenth century Britain led the world in steel production, but today it is behind the USA, the USSR, Japan and West Germany.

The major steel plants are found:

(a) on/near coastal coalfields *e.g.* N.E. England
(b) near iron ore fields *e.g.* Scunthorpe
(c) on inland coalfields *e.g.* S. Yorkshire

They are situated near their sources of supply because of the waste involved in production. Originally, they used low grade British iron ore and local **coal**. Steel also needed **water** and **limestone** as a flux. It was used in the manufacture of ships, bridges, mining equipment and other heavy engineering. However, new plants require **high grade** ore. This is now largely **imported** from Liberia, Venezuela and Sweden on giant tankers. This changed source of supply gave the plants situated near deep water ports a big advantage. The older, inland works were phased out as they were less economic, having to bear the extra transport costs of imported ore. The production of steel is now concentrated into **single plants**, with all the processes from purifying raw materials to loading finished products existing in one integrated steel works.

2 Organization

Up to 1951, the steel industry consisted of private and public limited companies. However, in 1951, the Labour Government nationalized it. It was denationalized in 1953 (by Conservatives) and renationalized in 1967 (by Labour), although some private steel makers remain.

BSC expanded up to 1973, but now, faced with falling demand, concentrates its production in five plants – Port Talbot, Llanwern, Scunthorpe, Teeside, Ravenscraig (Motherwell). The two plants in S. Wales, which concentrate on sheet steel for the car industry in Midlands, are the most important.

3 Prospects

The steel industry in Britain is in **decline**. Its output has dropped from 28m tonnes in 1976 to 13m tonnes in 1982. The reasons for the **fall in demand** have been:

(a) decline of the older industries which they supplied *e.g.* shipbuilding, mining.

(b) decline of new British industries which they supplied *e.g.* cars.

(c) development of plastic and other synthetic products as substitutes.

(d) intense competition from subsidized rivals *e.g.* W. Germany and Japan have aided their industries and guaranteed contracts.

The consequences of the decline have been more redundancies (workforce reduced by a third in five years) and increased losses for BSC and private sector suppliers. BSC has a financial target set by government to 'break even after depreciation and interest', but since 1976-7 it has lost over £400m per annum, on average. The private sector has also fared badly and been forced into mergers and sell-offs to BSC. For instance, Round Oak is partially owned by BSC now, whilst GKN and BSC are working together in many ways.

Industrial restructuring has occurred because of:

1 declining markets
2 overcapacity
3 overlaps in production – see Figure 6.5.

This restructuring has mainly seen BSC working capital combined with private sector assets. Occasionally, the Government, more directly through Dept. of Industry and European Coal and Steel Community, has made grants to enable investment and rationalization. In 1983, BSC employed just 78 000 men and made £386m loss, both of which were half of 1980 figures.

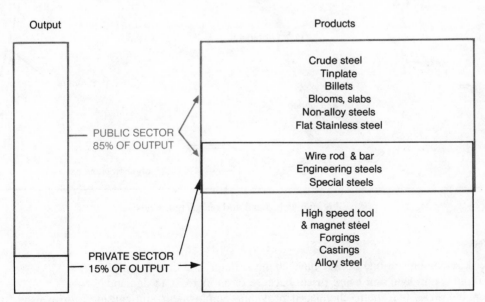

Fig. 6.5 British steel industry – products and ownership

6.6 North Sea Oil at Peterhead

1 Needs

Before 1973, Peterhead was a small, unimportant fishing port, outside the main N. Scotland transport network. See Figure 6.6. However, the discovery and development of gas and oil dramatically changed its lifestyle. These industries needed:

(a) back up bases which were accessible and located in safe and sheltered harbours. These bases needed to supply:

  (i) equipment ranging from platforms down to spanners.
 (ii) office accommodation for white collar staff.
(iii) food, drink and other basic needs for workers on rigs.
 (iv) services such as hotels, taxis and aircraft for all staff working there temporarily.

(b) facilities for processing oil and gas:

  (i) pipeline terminal for storage and distribution
 (ii) industrial sites for immediate use of the liquids *e.g.* power station, ammonia plant, gas conversion, petro-chemicals.

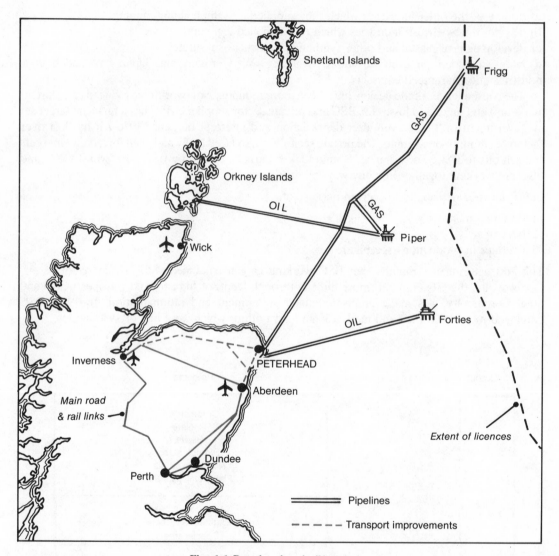

Fig. 6.6 Peterhead and oil/gas industries

2 Effects

These developments in one decade have changed Peterhead dramatically:

(a) a rapid rise in **land and house prices** because of an increase in demand

(b) new industries (*e.g.* petro-chemicals) providing employment and causing a drift away from traditional fishing and whisky activities

(c) a large, short term **cash boost** to the local economy caused by demand from new industries and their workers

(d) local opposition because of the disruption to the old lifestyle, fears of spillage and concern over the disposal of waste

6.7   Links with other topics

Government policy ─────────→ **Location of industry**

7 Markets

7.1 Introduction

'A market is **where goods and services are bought and sold**'. This need not be an actual place, although most markets can be located. For instance, the market for second hand shares is the Stock Exchange in London. The main requirement for a market is that buyers and sellers can **communicate** – this may be done by telex, letter or word of mouth.

The term market is used in many ways in Economics:

1 Retail market – people normally mean **stalls** from which goods are sold to the **final consumer**. Most towns have **traditional** market **days** in which itinerant traders sell their products.

2 Wholesale markets – in the chain of distribution (Unit 20) manufacturers sell to retailers through wholesalers. Their function is to **buy** the manufactured goods and raw materials and **distribute** them to shopkeepers. Most wholesale markets are in regional centres such as Sheffield, Birmingham, Manchester or in the national centre at London *e.g.* Covent Garden (fruit and vegetables).

3 Product markets – in Economics, a market refers to the trade in a particular product when it is **made**.

4 Factor markets – the **factors of production** (land, labour, capital, enterprise) are sold to buyers who wish to make goods and provide services. Their demand is said to be **derived** from the demand for the final product *e.g.* oil companies seek more divers if demand for oil increases.

5 Geographical markets – this refers to the **size** of the market in terms of potential customers. For instance, the market for 'self pick' strawberries is limited by the distance people are prepared to travel and the price difference between self picking and buying from a shop. As the sale of many raw materials *e.g* silver and primary products such as cocoa is world-wide, these would be classified as international. In between local and international markets, there will be regional and national markets.

6 Commodity markets – the trade in basic raw materials and foods is centred in London *e.g.* cotton, tea exchanges. The goods can be bought immediately at the prevailing price (spot) determined by demand and supply or at a future date at an agreed price. The latter system was developed to protect traders from price changes over time.

7 Free market or market ecomony – in Unit 2, the market or capitalistic economy was outlined. In it there was resource allocation and price determination as a result of **competition** between buyers and sellers. In contrast, in a collectivist economy there is usually a small range of goods, and prices are fixed by the State. Between these two extremes, most economies operate as mixed economies. In practice, the conditions under which trading takes place vary enormously. The main market structures are Perfect Competition, Monopoly and Imperfect Competition.

7.2 Perfect Competition

This structure describes an **imaginary** situation in which no one buyer and no one seller can determine the market price and each has perfect knowledge of market conditions. It is characterized by:

1 A large number of sellers Each seller provides just a small share of the total and this makes him unable to influence market price.

2 Perfect information Each buyer has complete knowledge of the market. Such information means that no seller can raise his price as he will lose all his customers, assuming that they are rational.

3 Freedom of entry into the market If firms in a market are making large profits (abnormal), more entrepreneurs will be attracted into the industry. It is assumed in perfect competition that entry is easy and that there are no restrictions on entry (Unit 7.3).

4 Homogeneous products All goods are identical and cannot be distinguished apart. Any differences between products would make competition less than perfect.

5 Many buyers Each consumer buys only a small proportion of the total goods available and thus cannot influence market price by their own actions.

6 No government interference

7 Perfect mobility of goods/factors throughout the market. This assumes no transport and no training costs.

These assumptions were made when demand and supply were discussed in Unit 4.

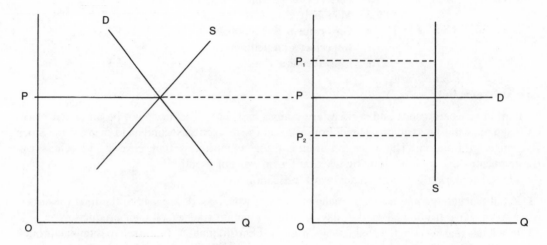

Fig. 7.1 Market price–perfect competition   Fig. 7.2 Individual firm's demand and supply in perfect competition

The demand and supply diagram in Figure 7.1 shows market demand intersecting with market supply at **market** price P. Although the market demand curve is downward sloping left to right, the **individual** firm faces a **perfectly elastic** Demand curve as illustrated in Figure 7.2. This is because each firm has to accept the market price and sell just at that price. If a firm tries to sell at P_1, it will price itself out of the market. It will get **no sales** as people will buy cheaper substitutes which they know about.

Conversely, if a firm tries to sell at P_2 it will **not make normal profit** because its supply is inelastic in the short run. The only effect of this price cutting will be to reduce total revenue.

In perfect competition, **market price = average revenue** – this is because all units of production are sold at the same price. For the same reason **average revenue = marginal revenue**.

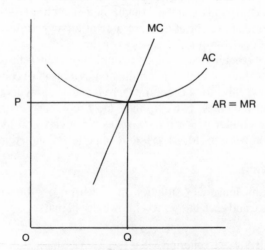

Fig. 7.3 Firm's output in perfect competition

When costs and revenue are combined, in Figure 7.3, it can be seen that for **marginal cost** to equal marginal revenue (profit maximization–Unit 5.5), **average revenue** must also **equal average cost**. Thus, in perfect competition, the firm produces output where AC=MC = AR=MR. It sells OQ at OP and makes normal profit. This position produces **normal profit** because normal profit is included within average cost (see Unit 5.5).

The firm's production in perfect competition will be at the **optimum** (lowest AC)–*i.e.* greatest efficiency.

For a short period of time, **abnormal profit** might be earned in perfect competition as in Figure 7.4. However, **new firms would enter the industry**. This would lower prices probably until P_1 occurred and just normal profit was made.

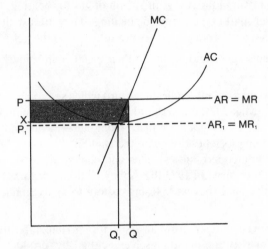

Fig. 7.4 Effect of new firms entering perfect competition

Perfect Competition in the market economy

The general advantages and disadvantages of capitalism apply to perfect competition. In addition, there are some **specific advantages** to perfect competition:

1 No excessive profits are made because higher prices lead to no sales. In the long run there are new entrants and normal profits obtained (see Figure 7.4).

2 Production is at lowest average cost in the long run. This produces efficiency. Inefficient firms cannot sell at the market price and so will be forced out of the industry.

Specific disadvantages to perfect competition

1 Small scale production means less scope for economies of scale, thus higher costs than in other market structures perhaps.

2 As all **products are the same**, there is no incentive for research and development in a market and less consumer choice.

7.3 Monopoly

A monopoly occurs when the **supply of a product is controlled by one firm**. It is very rare in practice. In a **pure** monopoly, the one firm has no competitors and the good has no close substitutes. The government has a wider definition of monopoly in Britain. Its definition is 'where **a quarter of an industry** is controlled by one firm'. This means that the market structures of oligopoly and duopoly come within the supervision of monopoly.

A duopoly is two firms controlling an industry.

An oligopoly is a few large firms controlling an industry.

Causes of monopoly 'LAST'

1 Legal protection–some monopolies are granted by law. Investors get patents (*e.g.* cats' eyes) which allow only them to make something. On a larger scale, NCB has the sole right to extract coal in UK, although it does allow others to mine under licence from it. Furthermore, it cannot stop people collecting coal washed up on the beach.

2 Avoid wastage of resources–some industries are considered to be unsuitable for competition *e.g.* gas, electricity. Competition would lead to duplication of resources. (See Unit 3.2.)

3 Supply restrictions–geological and geographical features may mean that some minerals *e.g.* gold, diamonds, are only found in a few parts of the world. Within an area, a local monopoly, *e.g.* village shop, may develop where transport costs limit the size of the market.

4 Takeovers – one firm may emerge victorious from a competitive situation through technical efficiency and superior marketing strategy *e.g.* London Brick Co. However the Stock Exchange panel may examine proposed takeovers.

Forms of monopoly

1 Nationalized industries (see Unit 3.2) These are legal monopolies created by the **State**. Although having a monopoly in their own industry *e.g.* provision of gas for heating, they may be competing with one another in a wider market *e.g.* domestic heating. They are usually allowed because they operate in the **public interest** and profits in theory are returned to the people through lower taxes.

2 Cartels – a **group of firms** agree and arrange to **act together** in a market. They either restrict supply or fix prices.

(a) In theory, the cartel sets up a **selling syndicate** (group) which sells on behalf of the members. The best example of this is the Milk Marketing Board which acts for farmers in UK.
(b) In **practice**, the term 'cartel' covers **loose price fixing agreements and market shareouts**. For instance the 'Big Five' building societies dominate the Building Societies Association, which meets regularly. They agree recommended interest rates and change them simultaneously with ninety days notice being given of a change. In 1983 the Abbey National departed from this, as did some other societies subsequently, since they were losing custom to many smaller societies who did not adhere to the cartel.

3 Trade Associations – firms in industry form an association to **look after their interests**. They may agree to **share out the market** among themselves, either by product or geographical area. Alternatively, they might decide a **common price**, thereby avoiding the cost of unnecessary advertising and subsidizing unprofitable parts of the market. Both would lead to greater profits. Such restrictive practices are now scrutinized by Government (see Unit 7.4).

Characteristics

As the **monopolist's output = industry's output**, he faces a downward sloping demand curve. He is not tied to accepting the market price like a firm in Perfect Competition. He has a choice:

1 He can **fix price** and **make supply elastic** at that price and let quantity demanded determine the quantity sold.

2 He can **fix quantity sold**, thereby **making supply inelastic** and let quantity demanded determine the price.

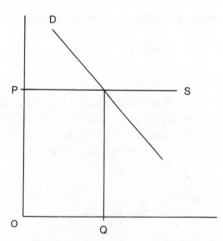

Fig. 7.5 Monopolist – fixing price

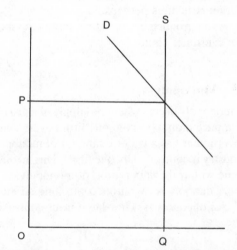

Fig. 7.6 Monopolist – fixing quantity

The monopolist can only sell more by reducing price, because demand slopes downwards. This means that MR does not equal AR. MR is less than AR as illustrated in Figure 7.7.

However, monopolist still produces where MC = MR, so in Figure 7.7 he supplies OQ at market price P (we are assuming S inelastic). The cost of producing OQ is OC (where AC crosses S line). PC is **abnormal profit**, on each unit sold. A situation like this can persist in the long run because new firms cannot enter the industry.

Specific advantages 'WERE'

1 Wasteful competition is reduced.

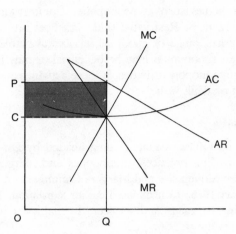

Fig. 7.7 Monopolist – output

2 Economies of scale – this enables production at lower average cost than several small competing firms.
3 Research and development can be undertaken as there is a secure market.
4 Excess capacity is avoided.

Disadvantages

1 High prices may be maintained to keep abnormal profits in the long run.
2 Lack of competition may lead to lower quality goods.
3 Optimum production not obtained (not best use of resources) because production not at lowest average cost, unlike Perfect Competition.

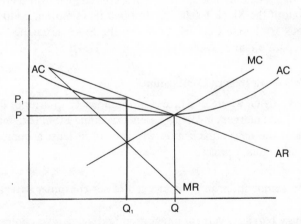

Fig. 7.8 Monopoly + perfect competition – efficiency

In Perfect Competition the market price would be where AC = AR, where MC = MR too, *i.e.* in Figure 7.8 price P, quantity Q.

However, in monopoly as MR is lower than AR, the market price is different P_1 Q_1. Thus production at Q_1 is **not at the optimum** *i.e.* most efficient, lowest cost output. Thus best use of the resources is not obtained. A monopolist will produce there, as it is **maximum profit** which motivates him. However, this diagram assumes that the average costs of a monopolist are similar to those of a firm in perfect competition. This may not be the case as a monopolist can benefit from economies of scale and thereby lower costs.

7.4 Government and monopoly

Government control may be:

Direct
1 Breaking up a monopoly, by making it illegal *e.g.* USA policy of trust busting.
2 Nationalization *e.g.* British National Oil Corp., Gas.
3 Supervision of activities of public corporations which are regularly accountable to a Minister and Parliament.

Indirect

4 Establishing independent bodies such as Monopolies Commission to **investigate/report on** monopolies and restrictive practices. Restrictive trade practices are agreements between firms which limit competition in price, range of goods or services available within an industry. This approach recognizes that some monopolies may be beneficial or only harmful in part.

5 Setting up a **court** to judge monopoly activities. If these activities are deemed to be against the public interest then they can be dealt with.

Summary of major legislation

Fair Trading Act 1973 – set up Office of Fair Trading headed by Director General. It protects consumers against **harmful** trading practices, monopolies and mergers. The 1948 Monopolies Commission was renamed the **Monopolies and Mergers Commission** in 1965.

Restrictive Trade Practices Act 1976 – Consolidated earlier legislation. It covers the regulation of **restrictive agreements** relating to **goods** and **services**. It enables a judicial investigation by a Restrictive Practices Court, set up in 1956.

Resale Prices Act 1976 – this brought together earlier legislation. It prohibits **collective** and **individual** resale price maintenance for goods (*i.e.* manufacturer telling shops what price to sell goods for, or else they would not supply them).

Competition Act 1980 – it supersedes Price Commission (set up 1977 with power to freeze prices while investigating price rises) and established a new **'competition reference'** procedure. The Director General (OFT) investigates any **anti-competitive** activity. This is anything likely to restrict, distort, or prevent competition. The Director General publishes a report and then either:

1 negotiates a **voluntary** undertaking with the firm to drop the practice within **two months**, or:

2 refers it to **Monopolies and Mergers Commission** within a **six month** deadline. If the MMC decides that the activity is 'against the public interest', then the **Dept. of Trade can prohibit it**. In addition, the Dept. of Trade can refer nationalized industries and other bodies to the Monopolies Commission for examination of their **efficiency, costs and service**. He can ask Director General (OFT) to investigate cases of 'major public concern'.

In 1983, the Dept. of Trade bargained with the Stock Exchange over its restrictive practices. It agreed not to investigate if the Stock Exchange dropped its minimum commissions and brought outsiders onto the Stock Exchange Council. In return the Stock Exchange was allowed to keep jobbers and brokers separate (single capacity) – (see Unit 11.4).

The work of Monopolies and Mergers Commission

This commission can investigate where one firm controls at least a quarter of the market (originally this 'rule' was one-third) and mergers involving assets exceeding £15m (originally £5m). It can also look into mergers where the new organization will control at least a quarter of market. It **can prohibit** acquisitions and regulate prices.

Aims

1 It seeks to promote competition, in particular it stresses **consumer sovereignty, efficiency** and **reward to enterprise**.

2 It opposes most **entry barriers**, vertical integration and aggressive competition.

3 It acts as a deterrent against misuse of **monopoly power**. However, it does recognize the benefits of **economies of scale**. It also supports **abnormal profits** as a reward for research, development and the risk of investment.

Powers

1 It can impose sanctions *e.g.* Hoffman Le Roche ordered to repay £3m to NHS; Unilever and Proctor and Gamble were told to reduce prices by 40% in 1975.

2 It can prevent mergers *e.g.* Imperial Tobacco who make Golden Wonder and Smiths Crisps.

Work of Restrictive Practices Court

It enforces the 1976 Act. This act requires:

The registration of all agreements under which **2+** persons support restrictions relating to the **price of goods, the conditions, quantities, processes or areas and persons supplied**.

It operates on the principle of **guilty till proven innocent**. It assumes all restrictive practices are against the public interest unless satisfying one of the **eight gateways**. These gateways or exceptions include:

1 Avoiding local unemployment

2 Promoting exports

3 Satisfying public interest
Any restrictive practice not registered is illegal

Achievements

1 Less than 1% of all registered agreements have been found to be illegal – nearly all of the guilty ones were for price fixing.
2 Cartels have been swept away *e.g.* Ready Mix Concrete.
but
1 Price wars often follow the Court's decisions. These may benefit the consumer in the short term. However, in the long run, if the winner dominates the industry, then the consumer may suffer.
2 Recommended prices have been developed and many unofficial, informal arrangements still operate.

7.5 Imperfect competition

Sometimes called Monopolistic Competition

Between the extremes of pure monopoly and perfect competition, there are **several market structures** collectively known as Imperfect Competition (or Monopolistic Competition). They are:

Monopolistic – **many firms** **very competitive**	**but** market limitations and information restrictions
Oligopoly – a few firms **Duopoly** – two firms	tendency to collusion and monopoly behaviour

Examples Monopolistic – furniture making — largest five firms = 25% of market
Oligopoly – canned beer — largest five firms = 80% of market
Duopoly – household detergents — largest two firms = 90% of market

The % of the market supplied by five largest firms is usually called the concentration ratio. It has increased for nearly every industry in Britain in the last twenty-five years.

Monopolistic Competition – the market is characterized by:

1 Price cutting *e.g.* ZX81 computers – £100 → £69 → £49 → £39 – inside two years, in response to competition from Spectrum, Tandy, Dragon, Vic 20, Electron, Oric.
1 Non-price competition *e.g.* free offers, holidays etc.
3 Packaging and advertising – these are often 20% of total costs.
4 Consumer services often provided *e.g.* 'interest-free credit'. The idea of such behaviour is to create brand loyalty.

Oligopoly and Duopoly – the temptation and the ability to co-operate have produced **less aggressive marketing**. For instance one firm might take the lead on raising prices which others follow *e.g.* petrol prices.

The behaviour of firms in these markets has occasionally been seen by the Monopolies Commission to be **'not in the public interest'**. This has been because of higher profits, inefficiency and prevention of new entrants.

7.6 Links with other topics

Government policy → Markets ← Economic systems
↑
Price mechanism

8 Money

8.1 Introduction

Today, money can be obtained legally by:

1 Working for it *e.g.* a week's wages.
2 Gaining an income for letting someone use your assets *e.g.* rent for a flat.
3 Being paid by the State *e.g.* Supplementary Benefit.
4 Receiving a gift *e.g.* £5 for birthday.
5 Borrowing, *e.g.* a bank loan.

The last is repayable with interest, but 1–4 usually involve no further expense. These four sources of income enable a person to buy goods and services (consumption) and save money (savings).

8.2 Definition

'Money is anything that is **acceptable** to its users in an economic system.'

As most economic systems operate through trade, because people are not self sufficient, the money has to facilitate the exchange of goods/services. These goods and services need to be valued and money is the measure which does that. Any profits made might wish to be saved for future use, thus money needs to keep its value.

It is often said that **'money is what money does'**. This means that anything can be used as money as long as it performs certain key functions.

8.3 Functions

There are four main functions of money. They can be remembered by the word **'SUMS'**

1 Store of value When people receive money the amount not spent is saved. People expect their savings to maintain their value for when they wish to spend them. Thus money should be capable of holding its value through time, so that the buying of goods in the future by savers does not put them at a disadvantage.

In the past, people hoarded gold because it kept its value. Clearly if inflation is rapid, the value of savings falls and money does not function efficiently as a store of value. This occurred in Britain in 1978 when the annual rate of inflation exceeded 25%. Thus within one year the real value of £100 of savings was reduced by 25%.

2 Unit of account This is sometimes referred to as a **'measure of value'**. It means that all goods and services are valued in common units (*e.g.* £ and pence) which people accept and understand. This enables the easy comparison of products *e.g.* £10 skirt = 20 × 50p blocks of chocolate. It also avoids the disadvantages of barter (see Unit 8.5). The unit of account used for calculations need not actually exist. It can be hypothetical *e.g.* EEC 'green pound' has been created for agricultural payments.

3 Medium of exchange This function means that the money is acceptable to the seller when the buyer pays for the good bought. Thus money enables exchange/trade to take place and barter is no longer needed. (See Unit 8.5).

In a modern society a worker is paid wages in money (rather than goods) and this enables him to spend when and where he wants. Furthermore, the benefits of specialization can occur because surpluses can be sold.

4 Standard for deferred payments Deferred means 'postponed'. Money allows for goods to be obtained one day and paid for on another day, or over a period of time, in an acceptable way. Thus it enables credit to be given to buyers and reassures sellers that they will receive the expected amount, valued in money, later. Credit thereby encourages trade. Thus, a car bought on hire purchase will involve the buyer in monthly repayments of money to the garage owner/HP company.

In the past when goods were paid for 'in kind'–by performing a service or receiving food/lodging–the payment was open to dispute, *e.g.* an itinerant gardener weeds a lord's lawn in return for his food/lodging for a week: how much food is he entitled to, what nature should his lodgings take?

8.4 Qualities

In order to perform the above functions, anything used as money needs to possess certain desirable properties. These characteristics can be remembered by the phrase **'ADDS UP'**.

1 Acceptability This key quality means that people are prepared to accept something as money. Thus the Yap Islanders in the South Seas used to make payments in giant stone cartwheels which were kept under water. They facilitated the Store of Value function better than the other functions!

2 Durability Money needs to be long-lasting, particularly in order to remain as a store of value and standard for deferred payment. Thus perishables are no good as money. It is probably because of this that people keep new crisp notes and spend old tatty ones.

3 Divisibility The money used has to be capable of being divided into units, so that small amounts can be paid exactly. Thus, we have £1 which divides into 50p, 20p, 10p, 5p, 2p and 1p pieces. The development of cheques is making this quality less important, but it will remain whilst 40% of the adult population do not have bank current accounts.

4 Stability The maintenance of value over time is important for money to keep its store of value function, so that trust is maintained. If a currency loses its stable value then the economic system goes haywire. For instance, the hyperinflation of Germany in 1920's led to wages being paid twice per day and money being quickly spent because its value was rapidly declining.

5 Uniformity If money is of variable quality then people may be wary of certain types of money. For instance in 1983, people were reluctant to hold £1 coins and preferred £1 notes. In the past coins with more precious metal in them were retained and others spent. Thus, today, all 10p pieces are indentical in shape, size, weight and content and this facilitates all functions of money except the store of value idea. Uniformity aids easy recognition of money.

6 Portability Money needs to be easily carried around so that it can be exchanged for goods/services as required. In the past when workers were paid in tokens, which could only be redeemed at factory shops, they had no freedom of choice and were easily exploited. This was known as the truck system. Today cheques give a consumer flexibility and increased choice, because they are easy to transport and generally acceptable.

8.5 Historical development

1 Barter

Primitive communities in the past managed without money. Tribes produced just enough for themselves. Skills and abilities were pooled and production was amicably shared out. Some tribes in the Amazon jungle still operate in this way today.

However, as simple economic systems advanced through specialization and the division of labour (see Unit 5.2) groups and individuals often produced a surplus. This surplus was traded for the surpluses of other groups. Initially the trading was by barter–the **swopping of goods** or direct exchange. One tribe might have a surplus of apples which it could exchange for another tribes' surplus cow. There were three main problems with barter, which can be remembered by the word **'RID'**. You could say that barter was got **rid** of–because of its deficiencies! For example:

(a) Rate of exchange Primitive traders had to agree how many apples were worth one cow. This involved haggling and dispute over the value of the swopped goods. It made trade difficult. Today, sellers fix prices and the consumer either accepts that price or does not buy–usually it is 'take it or leave it' which makes trade much easier and less time-consuming.

(b) Indivisibility of goods Some goods, such as apples, were capable of division into small quantities whereas others such as cows were only useful as a whole unit. As a cow could not be divided without losing its value, the person swopping it could not make an exchange if the other person offered only a small quantity of his surplus such as a few apples. Thus, there was no flexibility in the bargaining when large indivisible goods were involved.

(c) Double coincidence of wants If the trader with apples wanted a cow then there was a possibility of exchange. However, finding someone who wanted what you had, and who was prepared to offer in exchange what you wanted, was not easy. Thus one person's wants had to equal another person's needs, and vice versa, at the same time. This made obtaining the right combination of goods and services very difficult and time-consuming.

2 Early forms of money

(a) Goods (or **commodities**) As the scale of trade developed, an easier method of exchange was needed within communities, goods with some intrinsic value to the people were used. Such goods were usually chosen because of their acceptability and stability of value. However, some goods, such as salt, cattle and tobacco, suffered from the disadvantage of variable quality and perishability.

The early American settlers in Virginia used tobacco as money for 200 years up to the mid-nineteenth century. However, as the bales were cumbersome and people paid in the worst quality tobacco, public warehouses were provided to weigh, grade and certificate set quantities.

If trade in the communities using such goods was limited, the function of this money was as a Store of Value. However, if it was perishable then its primary function would be as a medium of exchange.

(b) Rare objects Some systems developed rare objects as money. Cowrie shells and dog's teeth, which were easily divisible into convenient units, were graded into proper monetary systems. Although useful as a means of exchange this form of money lacked homogeneity and was susceptible to sharp fluctuations in value, as the market could be disturbed by new finds. For instance, in the Admiralty Islands, dogs teeth were rare until Western traders flooded the market with some imported from China, and created inflation!

(c) Precious metals These came into use because their properties overcame the weaknesses associated with earlier forms of money. As gold and silver were attractive in appearance, fairly rare and non-deteriorating, they were readily acceptable. In addition, being portable and divisible into different standard sizes and weights, they facilitated exchange and acted as a clear unit of account. The general shortage of such metals meant that their value was maintained over time, enabling them to perform as a Store of Value also. A further advantage of gold was that it was acceptable in most countries and this encouraged international trade.

3 Paper money

The popularity of gold gradually reduced its usefulness as money. Its supply did not expand quickly enough to meet its demand. Furthermore, because gold was precious it was liable to theft. Thus people holding gold often left it for safe keeping with **goldsmiths**. They received a receipt, for the gold deposit, which they took back in order to collect the gold when it was needed.

(a) Bank notes The use of these goldsmith's receipts developed into bank notes, through several stages:

Stage 1, X deposits £30 gold with a goldsmith and gets a receipt back, with which he can recover his gold. If he only wants a part of gold then it is weighed out, etc,. and he gets a new receipt for the quantity of gold remaining.

Stage 2, X takes £30 gold and gets 3 × £10 receipts, if he needs £10 gold he just takes one receipt–this slightly simplifies matters.

Stage 3, X deposits £30 gold – he needs £10 gold to pay trader Y. As trader Y uses the same goldsmith and accepts his receipts, he is prepared to accept a receipt given by X knowing that G has the gold. Such receipts were acceptable as money as they promised 'to pay the bearer on demand the sum of ....' Y collected the gold from G.

Stage 4 Many traders such as X, Y, Z accept the goldsmith's receipts and use them to buy goods/services from other traders who know that they can redeem the gold if necessary or 'spend' the receipt. Thus the gold remained with the goldsmith and the receipts circulated, like bank notes, as money. It was only necessary to move gold about if transactions occurred between two people who did not use/trust the same goldsmith.

However, as much gold was left idle in the goldsmith's vaults because few receipts were redeemed, goldsmiths put the gold to use. They made loans to people by issuing notes for which they did not have gold backing. They charged a rate of interest for this service. Thus the goldsmiths were:

 (i) Creating money by giving credit
 (ii) Earning profits by charging interest
(iii) Taking risks by judging the credit worthiness of borrowers.

These functions are similar to those of modern **banks**. During the Industrial Revolution many goldsmiths were tempted into overlending, because of the profitability. They lent more money than their gold holdings and could not redeem receipts. This caused financial crises. Thus **the 1844 Bank**

Charter Act gave the Bank of England the sole right of note-issue. Joint-stock banks, the successors of the goldsmiths, could not issue new notes. This Act also introduced the **Fiduciary Issue** which enabled the Bank of England (only) to issue bank notes without full gold backing. This issue has rapidly increased from the initial £14 m with inflation to £10 000 b. It is not possible nowadays to go to a bank and ask for the gold equivalent (about 1/300 oz) of £1 note.

(b) Cheques In the early days of banks, some traders requested their 'bank' to pay a named sum to a particular person on a certain day. This was convenient, safe and saved the trader time. Such written instructions were the forerunner of today's cheque (see Figure 8.1.).

In 1882 the Bill of Exchange Act defined a cheque as a bill of exchange drawn on a banker payable on demand. The main advantages of cheques as money are:

(i) Convenience – easy portability, divisible.
(ii) Time saving – avoids frequent withdrawals from bank.
(iii) Generally acceptable, if accompanied with a cheque guarantee card, although not legal tender.

Fig. 8.1 A typical cheque

Legal tender This is money that a creditor has to accept in settlement of a debt. For instance, £s are legal up to any amount, but 10p coins can only be used up to £5 limit (*i.e.* 50 × 10p coins).

Cheque guarantee card A small plastic card issued by a bank to those with cheque books (Figure 8.2). These cards, which make cheques acceptable to most retailers, were introduced in 1966. The initial limit on the amount guaranteed by the Bank was £30. The current limit of £50 has been in force since 1977. The banks do not wish to raise the limit because most customers (not just an élite as originally) have these cards and fraud is costly to them.

Fig. 8.2 A typical cheque guarantee card

Coins These are still an important form of money – for students and those purchasing goods under £5. They are produced by the Royal Mint. They are 'token money', as the face value of the coin (*e.g.* 20p) is worth more than the intrinsic value (value of metal in it *i.e.* 2p). With inflation, there has been an increased demand for higher denomination coins and notes. In 1983 the £1 coin was introduced. This will gradually replace the £1 note.

(c) Credit cards The development of credit has enabled people to 'buy' goods without using money. Informal credit ('on tick', 'on the slate') at the local shop still operates, but credit cards are now widespread. These enable the user to buy goods from a shop, if it participates in a credit card scheme, and instruct the shop to obtain a sum of money from the buyer's account. The transaction is completed by the buyer giving his credit card number and signing a standard slip of paper for the shopkeeper. The credit card company guarantees the money to the shopkeeper and in return takes a small % of the amount spent. Credit is the main form of money used to buy consumer durables.

Three types of credit card can be classified:

(i) **Bank customers** The banks have led the way by issuing Barclaycard (now VISA) and Access to their favoured customers. These two plastic cards account for 90% of credit business. The main advantages and disadvantages to the **Customer** are:

Advantages	*Disadvantages*
(a) Wide range of outlets	*(a)* Established good credit record needed
(b) Buy now, pay later	*(b)* Interest charged, if repayment not made within the specified time (usually 3 weeks)
(c) Easier and safe shopping	*(c)* Minimum age 18 usually

(ii) **Businessmen** Less common and more exclusive are credit cards for businessmen *e.g.* American Express, Diners Club. Generally, these give more days interest-free credit and a lower rate of interest **but** their use is more restrictive and they apply more to services than to goods.

(iii) **Retailers' customers** Most department stores and some other retailers issue their own cards which are often called 'credit cards', although some are more accurately classified as 'budget accounts' because they require regular repayment and are limited to one store or group of stores. The rate of interest charged varies enormously, whilst bank credit cards' interest rates fall within a fairly narrow competitive range. A typical credit card is shown in Figure 8.3.

A major drawback from the point of view of credit card companies is the increasing amount of fraud. In 1984, Access, Barclaycard, American Express and Diners Club lost £15m through fraud. It is reckoned that on average a credit card is stolen every five minutes in Britain today.

Fig. 8.3 A typical credit card

8.6 Measurement of money

The total volume of money in the economy is important. Clearly, if the quantity of money in the system increases, and production is constant, this will cause inflation and the value of money will fall. However, **'what is money?'** is the subject to some dispute and there are several official definitions. The different measures are distinguished by their **'liquidity'**, that is, how quickly they can be used to buy goods/services. Figure 8.4 illustrates the differences.

Fig. 8.4 Components of main money measures

MI = notes and coins and private sector sight (current account) deposits. This narrow money stock has components which function both as a store of value and a medium of exchange.

M3 = cash and current account holdings and deposit account balances, in the private sector. M3 = 10% cash, 30% current account and 60% deposit account.

This is a broader definition of the quantity of money in the system. However, as the distinction between current accounts and deposit accounts is becoming less clear cut, the usefulness of M1 is diminishing.

PSL1 = Private Sector Liquidity. It includes the private sector share of M3 and holdings of Treasury bills, deposits with local authorities, and other money market short-dated assets.

PSL2 = PSL1 and easily accessible savings, such as building society deposits and trustee savings bank balances.

M1 is the most liquid but smallest volume measure, whereas PSL2 is the least liquid but largest size. Many people treat **building society deposits** as 'money', mainly because they are a store of value. For instance, usually £250 can be withdrawn in cash without notice being given. However, **credit cards**, which are a means of exchange but not a store of value, are not included in any of the definitions.

In operating economic policies, the government often utilizes a **monetary target**. M3 has often been chosen and governments have tried to influence its growth. However, M3 has increased much faster than the other monetary aggregates. The growth has also been above the Government's targets, *e.g.* in 1980-81 M3 increased by 18.3% despite a 7-11% planned target. It has been claimed that when a measure of money is officially adopted and control is attempted, the measure loses its meaning. This occurs because the banks often seek to maintain their profits, even if this means thwarting government credit restrictions.

In October 1983 the Government discarded M3 as its main monetary target. They replaced it with **Mo**. This consists almost entirely of **notes and coins**. It has been chosen as it **should** indicate **changes in demand** in the economy. For instance, more cash in circulation (Mo increase) means more demand for goods and services, and the increased possibility of inflation.

However, the increased use and acceptance of plastic credit cards rather than cash may make Mo a less effective measure of demand.

8.7 Links with other topics

Banking ⟶ Money ⟵ Inflation

9 Inflation

9.1	**Introduction**	*
9.2	**Definition**	***
9.3	**Types**	**
9.4	**Measurement**	**
9.5	**Method of calculation**	***
9.6	**Effects of inflation**	**
9.7	**Causes**	***
9.8	**Control and policies**	***
9.9	**Linked topics**	***

9.1 Recent history

Since 1970, inflation has become a major economic problem in Britain and most other developed countries (see Figure 9.1). The annual rate of price increase started rising above the acceptable 1960s average of 4% and reached a peak of 24.2% in 1975. Thus, the main priority of the Conservative Government elected in 1979, and re-elected in 1983, was to reduce inflation.

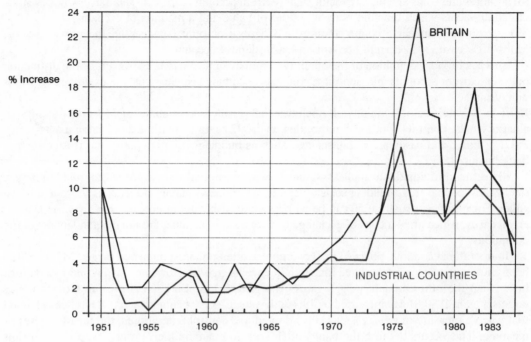

Fig. 9.1 Inflation in Britain and elsewhere

9.2 Definition

'A persistent general increase in prices'

The result of this tendency for prices to rise is that the value of money falls. The rising prices of goods and services mean that the **cost of living** has increased. If people's incomes do not improve, then they become worse off. When this happens we say that **real income has fallen**, as the same income purchases less. Thus, an increase in the cost of living will lead to a **fall in the standard of living**, if other things remain unchanged.

9.3 Types

Many different types of inflation have been described. However, the most common today and therefore the most important are:

 1 Creeping – a 'low' inflation rate which lasts for many years. This occurred in **Britain** and other industrialized countries in the 1960s and 1970s, with each trough being higher than the previous ones – as shown in the diagram. The figure given for the annual % increase in this type of inflation has been revised upward over the years. 'Low' is now considered to be less than 10%, whereas in the 1960s text books described it as 2-3%!

 2 Strato – a **'high'** but fluctuating inflation rate. It is a characteristic of **developing** economies, with rates of over 100% common in bad years. South American countries are particularly prone to this type of inflation, partly because of their authoritarian government policies.

 3 Hyper – **short-lived** and unusually **high** rates of inflation *i.e.* 1000% per annum; *e.g.* Israel 1984. Such astronomical rates are often caused by gross economic mismanagement and/or political crises. These may occur anywhere, but the best example was **Weimar Germany in 1923** when prices rose daily and people lost faith in the currency. The history books quote the famous example of a person putting down a basket of money and having the basket stolen and the money left! In times of hyper-inflation, barter returns, as money ceases to function as a means of exchange and store of value.

9.4 Measurement

Inflation cannot be measured exactly, as its impact varies between people, places and times. For **example:**

 1 Different people buy **different goods** – if the price of cheese doubles and price of jam remains unchanged, then people eating cheese sandwiches are affected more by inflation than people eating jam sandwiches.

2 The price of goods in **big towns** may be lower than in remote village areas, thus people living in towns suffer less from inflation.

3 In the **summer** months the price of fresh fruit and vegetables is much lower than in the winter and thus inflation in food is relatively slower. The official figures can only be **estimates** because of such variations as these. They are **averages** which are calculated **monthly** and aggregated for yearly figures. There are several indices with the main one being the **Retail Price Index** (RPI). An index number provides a statistical method of measuring the average % change in the price of a set of **related goods and services** over a period of time. This is usually calculated from a **base year** of 100.

Usefulness of RPI

1 Information is needed for government policy-making – the monthly movement of RPI can indicate the performance of a government's policies and enable more accurate forecasts of future trends. The Treasury estimates of inflation are 3% out on average!

2 General indication of the cost of living is given by the RPI. This is often used by trade unions as a guide when making wage claims. It is also useful to businessmen when they are assessing future economic prospects.

3 Certain government benefits are determined by the RPI. Pension increases are now index linked by law and so the RPI provides a standard measure.

Characteristics of RPI 'WEBB'

1 Weights are allocated to goods and services according to the proportion of family income spent upon them. In Figure 9.2, the weight for food has declined since 1966, whilst one new general category, meals out, has been introduced. The weights are adjusted each January and changes reflect modifications to the spending pattern of the average family.

	1966	1974	1979
Food	298	232	214
Alcoholic drink	67	82	82
Tobacco	77	46	40
Housing	113	108	124
Fuel & light	64	53	59
Durables	57	70	69
Clothing & footwear	91	89	84
Transport	116	149	151
Misc. goods	61	71	74
Services	56	52	62
Meals out	0	48	41
	1000	1000	1000

Fig. 9.2 Retail Price Index weights

2 Exclusions are made for pensioners and household heads earning at least twice the national average. This is done to maintain the 'average' approach to expenditure. Similarly, certain payments which are variable or non-measurable services (*e.g.* insurance premiums) are excluded.

3 A **Basket of Goods** is chosen. In 1914, when the price index began, it measured the changing price of necessities. Since 1945 it has been extended to include the bulk of consumer spending. A **representative** sample of goods is obtained from the Family Expenditure Survey and data is collected for them. **Consistency** is maintained by reviewing the same quality of good each time; each month 200 people collect information on over 500 goods, covering each of the 11 categories in the index.

4 A **Base Year** is selected. January 1962 was a new base year, as was January 1974. Typical years are chosen so that inflation is not measured from an unreliable base. For instance, 1973 would have been a poor year for revision of RPI because of the dramatic quadrupling of oil prices which was occurring at the time.

9.5 Method of calculation

The calculation of RPI can be explained simply by assuming that the index covers a **basket** of just three items – chips, coke and cigarettes. Each is weighted according to its relative importance in the family budget.

Item	Price	Weight	P. & Wt.
Chips	100	50	5000
Coke	100	10	1000
Cigarettes	100	40	4000
		100	10 000

Base year

$$\frac{10\ 000}{100} = 100$$

Fig. 9.3 RPI example – base year

If 50% of the budget is spent on chips, 10% on coke and 40% on cigarettes, then the weights are as in the base year table (Figure 9.3). Each item's initial price is represented by 100 in the price column of the index.

Item	Price	Weight	P. & Wt.
Chips	120	50	6000
Coke	140	10	1400
Cigarettes	110	40	4400
		100	11 800

Next year

$$\frac{11\ 800}{100} = 118$$

Fig. 9.4 RPI example – next year

In Figure 9.4, the prices of chips have increased by 20%, coke by 40% and cigarettes by 10%. The index number, which is an average, shows an increase of 18%.

Item	Price	Weight	P. & Wt.
Chips	120	40	4800
Coke	154	10	1540
Cigarettes	132	50	6600
		100	12 940

Following year

$$\frac{12\ 940}{100} = 129.4$$

Fig. 9.5 RPI example – following year

Figure 9.5 shows the following year in which both spending patterns and prices have changed. People have spent less on chips (weight falls to 40) and 10% more on cigarettes (weight rises to 50). The price of chips remained unchanged (120) whereas the price of coke rose by 10% (140 + 14 (10% of 140)). The Government increased VAT on cigarettes causing a 28% price rise and raising its index price to 132 (110 + 22). Overall, although the price index rose to 129.4, prices increased less quickly compared to the previous year (9.7% *i.e.* $\frac{11.4}{118}$ as opposed to 18% – *i.e.* $\frac{18}{100}$)

Problems of measurement 'CRABS'

1 Changes in the nature of the goods and services used in the index may occur, although the weights and price remain the same. For instance, a ¼lb. bar of chocolate may contain less cocoa and more water, and so perhaps it becomes of lower quality. Thus comparisons become more difficult and less clear cut over time, as products change.

2 The **Range of households** to include in the survey will influence the weights. As patterns of expenditure depend on income, then different income groups have different baskets. For instance, if food prices rise rapidly, then pensioners, who spend a higher proportion of their income on food than average, will suffer more than the RPI indicates. Thus changes in RPI do not affect all groups equally.

3 Averages are used – in practice few people fall into this category and thus RPI is too simple and too general.

4 A **Base** year soon gets out-of-date and unrealistic. For instance, the new base year of 1974 was 100 in the index, yet by April 1982, the index read 319.7 and with 10% inflation would be leaping +30 points in the index.

5 Spending patterns change rapidly and so the weights and items need frequent revision. Factors such as:

(a) Changes in taste *e.g.* less spending on haircuts by men.

(b) New products *e.g.* video boom in 1980s.

(c) Increased income – less spending on necessities, more spending on luxury services *e.g.* meals out.

9.6 Effects of inflation

The impact of inflation is illustrated in Figure 9.6

Item	1976	1983 (Sept)	% increase
Denim jeans	£9.70	£17.00	75
Colour TV	£274	£350	28
20 cigarettes	£0.46	£1.11	141
Retail Price Index	£156.00	£339.5	117.5
Average male weekly earnings	£65	£140	115.4

Fig. 9.6 Inflation – selected examples

The mnemonic **'BIRDS'** can be used to remember the effects of inflation:

1 Business confidence

Fluctuating rates of inflation make it difficult for entrepreneurs to **predict** the economic future and accurately calculate the returns on their investment in new plant and machinery. They may fear Government action which may depress demand and thereby reduce likely sales. Less investment usually means more unemployment. A high rate of inflation requires them to seek higher profits or else they will lose in real terms. If high profits do not seem likely then businessmen may cease production and put money into less risky ventures, such as Gilts.

2 International competitiveness

If the prices of exports are rising faster than competitors' goods, then a nation's trade will probably suffer unless the goods are inelastic in demand. Britain's world market share in manufactured goods has slumped, partly for this reason.

Alternatively, imports may be relatively cheaper than home-produced goods *e.g.* consumer durables in a modern kitchen in Figure 9.7. Such imports mean:
(a) Less trade for British firms and so less production and likely unemployment.
(b) The balance of trade (on just goods) is in deficit.

Percentage sales of imported consumer goods

Kitchen equipment
Toasters 61%
Fridge/freezers 69%
Washing machines 45%
Dishwashers 99%
Cookers 21%

Other electrical goods
Clocks 61%
Portable radios 96%

Fig. 9.7 Inflation and imports in the kitchen

3 Redistribution of income

Those people on **fixed** incomes or incomes not keeping pace with inflation (*e.g.* unemployed) will become relatively worse off as their purchasing power falls. Increases in food prices and rent tend to hit poorer families most, because they spend a higher proportion of their income on such necessities. Thus income in **real terms** is redistributed from poor to rich.

Some groups, often those in strong and successful trade unions (*e.g.* miners), gain real wage increases whilst others such as teachers and bus drivers, which are weak and poorly mobilized, lose out.

Deflation

Inflation is frequently followed by economic depression when a government takes measures to curb rising prices. However, the deflation does not feature falling prices (at least in nominal terms) but **lower output** and **fewer jobs**. Prices are 'sticky' downwards, in that the main costs of production, particularly wages, are difficult to reduce, as people have come to expect rising wages and rising prices.

5 Savings

With inflation, the value of savings falls. This is compensated for by the interest given by financial institutions. However, if the rate of inflation is higher than the rate of interest received, savers are losing in **real terms**.

Conversely, borrowers paying a rate of interest below the level of inflation will gain, as the money which they repay is worth less than the amount borrowed. In these conditions, increases in demand for credit could lead to excess demand in the economy and further fuel inflation. Thus, generally, inflation discourages saving and encourages borrowing.

9.7 Causes of inflation

Although British inflation has moved up and down with the other industrialized countries, it has tended to be 50% higher on average (see Figure 9.1). The two main causes of inflation are known as 'demand pull' and 'cost push'.

1 Demand pull

Generally, this is caused by excess purchasing power – too much money chasing too few goods. Thus increases in demand **pull up** prices, as supply is fairly constant.

Supply may be unable to expand, to meet the increased demand, because of lack of capacity – insufficient space, inadequate machinery, shortage of trained labour. Generally, in the economy, a low level of unemployment indicates supply as being near its maximum.

Increases in demand may be created by:

(a) Increases in the supply of money Monetarist economists believe that increases in money supply lead to price increases after 18 months. The money available can expand through:

 (i) The commercial banks issuing **more credit** to consumers and businessmen and thereby raising aggregate demand in the economy as a whole *e.g.* 1972–73 relaxation of credit control by government.

 (ii) The government running (or increasing) a **budget deficit** where spending exceeds income and money is pumped into the economy. If the deficit is covered by borrowing from abroad, then it is likely to be more inflationary. When the government borrows from domestic sources it may reduce the banks' capacity to create credit and so money supply may remain largely unchanged.

(b) A balance of payments surplus A current account surplus can lead to increased spending power in the domestic economy. Britain has rarely suffered from this, but West German inflation 1980–82 was accentuated by its export earnings.

(c) Tax reductions These occur through:

 (i) Lower basic rates of income tax

 (ii) Increased personal allowances

(iii) Reduced national insurance contributions

They all reduce the Government's tax revenue and increase individual spending power.

Demand pull inflation serves to increase demand for particular goods. For instance, tax rebates often stimulate the purchase of consumer durables. The demand for dishwashers shifts to the right in

Figure 9.8 and price rises to P_1.

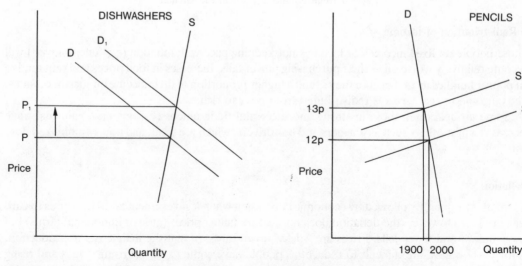

Fig. 9.8 The effect of demand pull inflation on a good   **Fig. 9.9** The effect of cost push inflation on a good

2 Cost push

An increase in costs, not matched by similar higher production, which results in price rises is known as 'cost push inflation'. As producers set their prices in markets, they may decide to maintain profits and so **pass on** rising costs by raising their prices.

For example, a pencil sells for 12p, which is made up of 3p manufacturer's profit, 5p cost of production, 3p cost of distribution, 1p VAT. If production costs rise by 20% (an extra 1p) then in order to **maintain** his 3p **profit**, the manufacturer needs to sell the pencil for 13p. However, this price rise will usually lead to a fall in quantity demanded, as in Figure 9.9.

Thus:

(a) Manufacturer's **total profit has fallen** from 6000p (2000 × 3p) to 5700p (1900 × 3p).

(b) Manufacturer's **profit percentage mark-up** has fallen from 33% $\left(\frac{3p}{9p} \ i.e. \ \frac{profit}{costs} \right)$ to 30% $\left(\frac{3p}{10} \right)$

The factors which produce increased costs are:

(a) **Imported raw materials** These may arise because of world **shortages**, particularly in the case of primary products like cocoa and sugar where the weather may devastate supply. Furthermore, the depreciation of the exchange rate (falling pound) serves to make imports more expensive and this may raise the cost of imports. Britain's **open** economy, which imports 30% of GDP, and dependence on international trade, make her particularly vulnerable to this type of inflation. For instance, the quadrupling of **oil prices** in 1973 sent large shockwaves throughout the western world, forcing up prices because of industry's reliance on oil for power.

(b) **Domestic costs** The main factor here is **wages**. Their impact varies between industries. In labour intensive sevices *e.g.* Post Office, as wages account for 70% of total cost, wage increases will probably be passed on in higher prices. Conversely, in **capital intensive** industries, such as petrochemicals, wage costs may be less than 10% and less important than interest rate and fuel price changes. In these industries, high wage increases could be fairly easily absorbed. It is often argued that the increased power and greater militancy of **trade unions** in the 1970s forced employers to concede unrealistically high wage demands. These wage rises were then passed on in the form of higher prices because of the **monopolistic power** of the producers in many markets.

(c) **Poor productivity** If wage increases are matched by productivity improvements, the cost per unit of output does not necessarily rise. However, output per man has risen only slowly in the UK compared with the other major industrialized countries. This reflects low levels of investment, badly directed investment, a lack of modernization, old fashioned working practices and lack of labour mobility.

(d) **Profiteering** Some Marxists argue that businessmen who exploit labour anyway, raise their profits (which are a cost of production and thus added into the selling price) and cause inflation. In theory, this assumes that the demand for products is relatively **inelastic**, otherwise consumers would buy substitutes. In practice there is little evidence for this view as the 'real profits' of British industry have fallen during the last twenty years.

3 A combination of demand pull and cost push

As many factors in Economics are **interdependent**, the two main causes are likely to be intertwined and interacting. For example, increased raw material prices may cause the price of consumer goods to rise. This cost push may provoke wage increases (further cost push) to maintain living standards or increased borrowing (demand pull) by businessmen to finance production.

Alternatively, making credit available to businessmen by an expansionary monetary policy (demand pull) may enable them to give in more easily to large wage demands (cost push). In particular, when there is a boom, firms may accept rapidly rising costs in order to supply the market profitably. Thus workers threatening strike action in pursuit of a wage claim, may obtain high wage rises because the extra cost to the manufacturer of the claim is less than the extra profit obtained by selling the product in an expanding market (opportunity cost!).

9.8 Control and policies

In modern economic society, inflation is **influenced** rather than controlled. It is certainly not within the government's capacity to cure it.

Restraints on government

Success for the government in the area of inflation control may have detrimental **side effects**, because economic policies do not operate in isolation *e.g.* lowering inflation may increase unemployment which may have social and political consequences. Furthermore, the **time period** involved is significant. There may be short-term hardships for society to bear in return for the long-term benefits.

Essentially the government needs to take a view on the cause of inflation, and choose suitable measures for that type. However, in practice, there is **not one cause** and as such the two broad theories may be intermingled.

Policies Thus the possible policies proposed need to be qualified:

1 Reducing demand

(a) Limit increases in the supply of money by:

  (i) **Curbing the banks'** ability to create credit – this can be done by a tight monetary policy (calling in special deposits, sales of gilts). However, the banks may thwart such policy as providing credit is profitable to them. If the credit limitation is successful, through high interest rates, this may lead to less consumer expenditure, lower production and more bankruptcies, which in turn increase unemployment.

 (ii) **Reducing the budget deficit** or generating a budget surplus – a contraction in government spending will lead to less money in the economy via lower consumption and investment. But the policy means fewer public services thereby reducing the general standard of living, as well as probably redundancies in the public sector.

(b) Obtaining a Balance of Payments balance or deficit – extra imports and government expenditure abroad take money out of the domestic economy and thus reduce the inflationary pressure. However, this may bring about a Balance of Payments crisis. A falling £ makes imports more expensive and may encourage cost push inflation.

(c) Increased taxation – higher tax rates and lower allowances will increase government revenue and take more funds out of the economy, thus reducing **consumption** potential. Similarly, higher national insurance contributions raise revenue and cut spending. However, these measures may have **disincentive** effects on production and through lower consumption they serve to increase unemployment. As real incomes are cut, it may also lead to higher wage claims.

2 Limiting costs

(a) Cost of imports reduced by appreciating £. This is only indirectly under the influence of the Bank of England, although sensible and acceptable government policies can create confidence in the currency.

In addition, the development of import substitutes and the discovery of raw materials (*e.g.* North Sea oil) can operate to minimize imported inflation.

(b) Production costs could be subsidized to minimize their impact. The British Steel industry has complained that its international rivals are subsidized, thereby putting it at a competitive disadvantage. Certainly industrial electricity prices are subsidized in Germany.

(c) Wage costs could be lowered/wage increases slowed down. The usual ways proposed for doing this are:

  (i) **Incomes policy** – the statutory control of incomes has been used in Britain in 1967, 1972 and 1975. It usually lays down an upper limit to wage settlements and thereby inhibits trade union bargaining. (See Unit 13.6.)

 (ii) **Reduction of trade union power** – the ability of many trade unionists to obtain wage increases above the level of inflation increased considerably in the 1970s. The increased use of the strike weapon and the development of the closed shop, combined with the unwillingness of successive governments to let unemployment increase, strengthened trade union bargaining power. The Conservative Government of 1979 decided by legislation on picketing and strike ballots to curb this power. In addition, their deflationary policies led to moderation of wage claims as workers began to fear unemployment and accept low wage offers.

(d) Raising productivity Costs can be reduced if production is maintained with a smaller work-force or greater production is obtained with the same workers. Clearly, technological investment and production incentives can generate improvements. There was a spurt in British productivity in 1981–82 as labour was shed faster than output fell. British Steel, for instance, in certain plants, raised productivity by +40% in one year.

9.9 Links with other topics

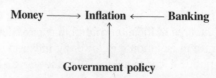

10 Banking

10.1 Introduction

Until 1979 there was no law to prevent any institution calling itself a 'bank', if it **accepted deposits and lent money**. The 1979 **Banking Act** classified all banking institutions into either:

1 **'recognized banks'** such as Midland, Lloyds. This group contains three catagories of bank – British, overseas and consortium (a bank set up by several other banks and including at least one overseas member);

or

2 **'licensed deposit takers'** such as the 'Baptist Union Corporation' which can no longer use the word 'bank' in its name.

10.2 Types of bank

1 Commercial banks

These are the main clearing banks which have High St. premises. They all take deposits from the general public and because of this direct relationship, they are sometimes called **'retail'** banks. They are **public limited companies** (see Unit 3.3) who aim to make a profit, *e.g.* Midland averages £400m per annum. The main commercial banks in Britain, which were initially called joint-stock banks, are the 'Big Four' – Barclays, Lloyds, Midland and National Westminister, and Coutts, and Williams & Glyn's.

2 Merchant banks

These are banking brokers who bring together lenders and borrowers of large sums of money. They operate in a **high risk** area and handle very large sums of money daily through their **international** transactions. They advise companies on money management, arrange short-term finance and accept/negotiate bills of exchange. They are thus **wholesalers** of money. Many of the merchant banks are **privately owned** *e.g.* Rothschilds, and trade on their reputation and family name. Others are subsidiaries of the Commercial banks *e.g.* Samuel Montagu (Midland). Seventeen merchant banks are known as **Accepting Houses**.

3 Savings banks

These banks are defined by their main function – savings. However, organizations like Trustee Savings Bank are **diversifying** into lending etc.

4 National Girobank

The Government created this bank in 1968. It is based on the network of **Post Offices** around the country. It operates like the other Commercial banks and is increasingly **competing** with them in services provided.

5 Discount Houses

Although these bodies do not have 'bank' in their title, they operate like banks. They borrow from the Commercial banks with very **short-term loans** (often overnight) and **lend for up to three months** (by buying Treasury Bills). They make a profit on the difference in interest rates paid and charged.

Their skill lies in anticipating market trends. There are just ten discount houses left in Britain. No such institution exists in other countries. They survive because they are **specialist** and **convenient**. In addition, they protect the **Commercial banks** from the effects of sudden interest rate changes.

10.3 Commercial banks

Functions – these can be remembered by **'CAST'**, if you are angling for the answer!

1 Customer services

The banks provide numerous services which are given detailed coverage in most Commerce books. They are listed below together with the customers for whom they were designed.

Type of customer	Specific services
Most current account holders	standing order, direct debit, bank giro credit, cheque guarantee cards, cash dispensers, credit cards
Reputable current account holders	credit cards
Anyone	budget accounts, savings accounts, deposit accounts
Any account holder	advice on insurance, investment, legal matters, references
Owner occupiers	mortgages
Travellers	foreign exchange, travellers cheques
Businessmen	night safe, bills of exchange, certificates of deposit, small firm advisory service, references, tax and legal advice.

11 million people have current accounts and deposit accounts
16 million people have just current accounts
3 million people have just deposit accounts
25 million have building society accounts

2 Advancing money

Banks lend to personal customers and businesses through loans and overdrafts usually for short and medium periods of time.

(a) Loans – a formal means of borrowing usually over a **set period** of time at **fixed rate** of interest with **regular** (monthly) payments. The customer completes an **application form** for the Bank Manager. He needs to state the reason for wanting the loan, the amount and the time involved. He will have to give personal particulars of income, previous credit record, other existing credit commitments and character references. Banks look for customers to 'share the risk' by providing a proportion of funds from their savings *e.g.* 25% on a motor bike. If it is a large loan, the bank may seek **collateral** (a valuable asset to be left in bank's possession which can be sold to repay the loan if the borrower defaults on payment). Usually the customer has a separate loan account which he repays and his current account is credited with the total amount lent.

(b) Overdrafts – informal borrowing, usually for a very **short period** of time, mainly used by traders. The bank agrees to let the trader spend more from his current account than he has in it. Thus his account is said to be overdrawn *i.e.* **'in the red'**. For instance, businesses often have to pay for goods before they are sold, and so need temporary finance to tide them over. An approved overdraft arrangement is a very **flexible** form of borrowing and firms may have overdrafts for years. **Interest** is charged on a **daily** basis on the actual amount overdrawn. Overdrafts are usually cheaper than loans for borrowing, but the rate of interest charged varies with the risk involved *e.g.* new customers will pay more than established, reputable customers.

3 Safeguarding money

Originally goldsmiths (see Unit 8.5) performed this function. Today, money is held in either a **deposit** account or a **current** account. The main differences between these accounts are summarized below.

Characterisic	Current account	Deposit account
General function	transactions	savings
Frequency of use	regular	occasional
Services	cheque book monthly statements standing orders direct debits credit cards	statements twice a year
Withdrawals	no notice needed	7 days notice for large sums
Gain/loss	charges quarterly	interest received twice per year
Minimum age	16	–
Average balance	£400	£800

Increasingly, the differences are becoming less clear-cut as some banks do not charge when current accounts fall beneath £100, whilst others pay out interest on certain current account balances.

4 Transferring money

The banks move **cash** between branches to meet needs. For instance, a branch near to a market may well be a net receiver of cash when takings are paid in, whilst a branch on a housing estate may face more withdrawals than deposits. Thus, within a bank, cash needs to be transferred to where it is required.

In operating the clearing system, the banks transfer money, but in the form of cheques. Cheques today are written on printed forms issued by the banks. Clearing occurs in three ways:

(a) Within a branch

A writes a cheque to B. Both have accounts at same branch. On the day when B pays the cheque into the branch, B's account is credited and A's account is debited.

(b) Within a bank

A has an account at Hay Street branch and gives a cheque to C, who has an account at Sea Street branch of the same bank. C pays the cheque into his branch and his account is credited. The cheque is sent with other cheques drawn on different branches to the bank's **Head Office**. There, the cheques are sorted into the branches of origin and returned to them. Thus, **two days later**, A's branch will receive his cheque from Head Office and then debit his account.

(c) Between different banks

A banks with Midland and pays a cheque to D whose account is at a Lloyds branch. This is illustrated in Figure 10.1. The process usually takes **3 to 4 working days**.

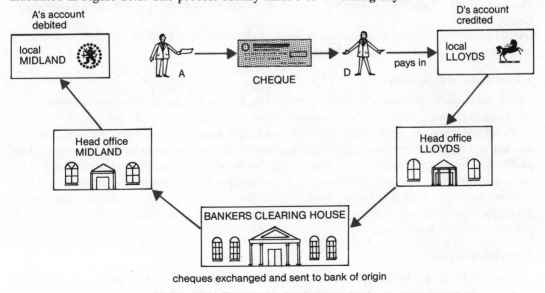

cheques exchanged and sent to bank of origin

Fig. 10.1 Cheque clearing between banks

The transfer between accounts is more complicated when two different banks are involved. At daily clearing, each bank totals up its accounts with every other bank. For instance, if the Midland has cheques worth £50m drawn on Lloyds and Lloyds has cheques worth £40m drawn on the Midland; then Lloyds owe Midland £10m. However, they do not pay each other directly. Each has an account at the Bank of England and so £10m is deducted from Lloyds account and £10m is added to the Midland balance at the Bank of England.

10.4 Balance sheet

1 Liabilities and assets

Liabilities are what the banks **owe**. Thus, all **deposits** at bank are liabilities because the bank has to provide money when customers wish to withdraw either in cash or by cheque.

Assets are the ways in which the bank has used the deposits. Some deposits are **retained in cash**, but most have been **lent to individuals, companies and the government**. In deciding how much to keep in cash and how much to lend, the banks are guided by the principles of liquidity and profitability.

Liabilities		Assets				
Deposits	50	Cash in tills	1	} cash ratio		
		Balance at B. of E.	2		reserve assets	liquid
		Money at call	3			
		Treasury bills	3			
		Special deposits	5			
		Investments	9		illiquid	
		Advances	27			
	50		50			

Fig. 10.2 Bank liabilities/assets

(a) Cash in tills – notes/coins needed for everyday transactions.
(b) Balance at Bank of England – each bank has a deposit at B of E which enables clearing debts to be settled (see Unit 10.3).
(c) Money at call – overnight lending to Discount Houses which can be quickly recalled at short notice.
(d) Treasury bills – 91 day loans to the government.
(e) Special Deposits – the B of E, at the government's instigation, often requires banks to leave a fixed % of funds with them. It is not classed as a liquid asset and cannot be used.
(f) Investments – longer-term lending *e.g.* government stocks in £100 blocks for up to 25 years called 'gilts' (see Unit 11.)
(g) Advances – loans and overdrafts (see Unit 10.3).
Cash Ratio – the % of assets needed to be kept in cash and balances to meet immediate customer requirements.
Liquid assets – those redeemable within one year.
Reserve assets – between 1971 and 81 the banks were supposed to maintain a reserve assets ratio. This was 12½% of eligible liabilities (*i.e.* most deposits) and consisted of the most liquid assets, except cash.
Illiquid assets – those assets which cannot be quickly turned into cash because of longer-term lending or 'frozen' (*i.e.* special deposits) at Bank of England.

2 Profitability and liquidity

Liquid assets can be most easily transformed into **cash**. Thus money in the till is the most liquid asset. Alternatively, a loan which will be redeemed in five years time is very illiquid.

Profitable assets are those which earn the banks most **interest**. Thus, loans are very profitable and money kept on the premises gains no return at all. Therefore, the **most liquid** assets are the **least profitable**. The most profitable are the least liquid. The banks have to strike a balance between these two requirements on their balance sheet. Their customers desire ready cash (*i.e.* liquidity) yet their shareholders seek high dividends (from profitability). The banks may increase liquidity of investments by spreading their maturity dates out *i.e.* a 20-year loan matures 1986, a 15-year loan matures 1987 and so on.

3 Interest and profits

As most banks are **public limited companies** they aim to make a profit for their shareholders. One way of doing this is through charging interest on **loans and overdrafts**.

The banks have a **base rate** to which they link the interest paid on deposits (*e.g.* base rate −3%) and the amount charged to borrowers (*e.g.* base rate +2% at least). The rates charged/given **vary** with the period of time involved and the status of the customer. Thus, if base rate is 9%, then the interest paid may be 6% and the interest charged at least 11%, depending on the credit-worthiness of the customer. This gives at least a 5% (11−6) **profit margin**. In addition, as a lot of money on deposit at the bank is in (non-interest bearing) current accounts, the profit margin may be a lot higher (*i.e.* 11−0 = 11%).

Generally, when interest rates are high, the banks make larger profits because this margin on current account becomes higher. For this reason, in 1981, the Chancellor of the Exchequer imposed a 'windfall' profits tax on the major banks for just one year. In that year, the interest rates had been 17%. It did also help him to raise finance for the Government (see Units 19 and 15).

10.5 Credit creation

Theory – In order to explain simply how banks create credit, several **assumptions** have to be made: just one bank and a 10% cash ratio. This means that any money lent will be spent and returned to the

Liabilities	Assets
Stage (a) £1000 (deposit)	£1000 (cash)
Stage (b) £1000 (deposit)	£1000 (cash)
£9000 (current)	£9000 (loan)

Fig. 10.3 Simple credit creation

one bank. The bank needs to keep 10% of its assets in cash. For example, a person deposits £1000 in cash. Another customer seeks a £9000 loan.

The bank, knowing that only 10% of its assets need to be in cash (£1000) to meet regular withdrawals, can raise their assets to £10 000 by granting a loan of £9000. In Figure 10.3 Stage b, the bank's liabilities are £1000 in deposit account and £9000 in current account. Thus there has been an expansion in bank deposits (deposit + current account) which is a **multiple of liquid reserves** (*i.e.* cash ratio) held by the bank. The multiple is 9 times (9000 to 1000). This can be shown in diagrammatic form (Figure 10.4).

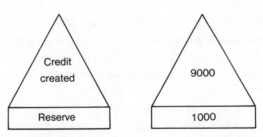

Fig. 10.4 Credit pyramid with 10% cash ratio

Practice. There are many banks who differ in their ability to attract customers. The daily differences in settling the balances when cheques are cleared are fairly small and so their liquidity cash positions do not fluctuate much. There is a much looser link between liquid assets and liabilities created. Furthermore, there are other financial institutions, such as building societies, competing for deposits.

Limitations on credit creation
1 Demand for cash by customers fluctuates.
2 Government policy (see Unit 10.8)
3 Money is moved around by Institutional investors (see Unit 11.2) to gain the benefit of a higher rate of interest when rates change. They move their funds in and out of the various savings institutions.

10.6 Money market

The money market refers to the institutions which deal in **lending money** for **short periods** of time, up to **three months**. The lending is through Bills of Exchange for companies and Treasury bills for the Government.

1 Bills of Exchange and Commercial Bills

On these, a trader promises to pay a sum of money (in return for goods received) on a certain date to a seller. The seller can sell the bill for cash to someone who will 'discount' it. **Discounting** means that a bank buys a bill (say £1000) for less than its face value (*e.g.* £950), knowing that it will receive the face value at a later date from the buyer who has promised to pay. Thus, the purchaser of the goods gets the goods immediately and 'accepts' them. Accepting means that the buyer gets his bank (for a small fee) to promise to pay the bill on his behalf when it matures (is due for payment). The seller of the goods gets paid immediately. The bank pays him, less their discount. This bank knows that the buyer's bank will pay them on the set (maturity) date, because the bill has been accepted. So each bank earns commission for what is effectively lending.

2 Treasury bills

These are short-term loans to the Government. In return for a sum of money now (say £4800) the Government promises to pay the lender £5000 in 91 days. Thus, the Government gets **91 days credit at a cost**. The buyers of these bills are Discount Houses and Merchant Banks (see Unit 10.2). They make a profit (pay £4800, receive £5000) which is calculated as a **rate of interest**. The rate of discount is the rate of interest. In this example, $\frac{200}{4800}$ for 3 months (roughly 4%), approximately 16% per annum.

Each Friday the Discount Houses **tender** (offer) to buy Treasury bills. If the tender price is low, then the rate of interest paid by Government is high and Discount Houses make bigger profit.

10.7 Bank of England

It is the **central bank** and exercises general control over the banking system. It was founded in 1694 as a private institution, but it has always been subject to government influence. In **1946** it was formally **nationalized**. It has two main departments: the **issue** department which deals with note issue and the **banking** department which deals with the banking sector. There are a small number of private individual accounts there, too.

Functions 'BINGOES'

1 Banker's Bank – all banks and other financial institutions (Discount Houses, Merchant Banks) keep **deposits** at the Bank of England. They are used in **clearing** to make payments between each other (see Unit 10.3). They are also used for making payments to the government. These balances form part of a bank's liquid assets and can be used to influence their lending policies (see 10.8).

2 Issue of Notes – The 1844 Bank Charter Act paved the way for the Bank of England to have the **sole right** of note issue in England and Wales. The Bank of England prints and releases notes and coin from the Issue Department to the Clearing Banks as necessary. There are **seasonal fluctuations** *e.g.* Xmas, Summer holidays.

3 Government accounts – The Bank of England acts as Banker to the Government in the same way as the Commercial Banks service customers. It holds the Government's balances. In so doing, it **(a)** pays out for government **expenditure** and receives in **taxation**, **(b)** manages the **National Debt** (see Unit 15) by issuing government stocks, paying interest and redeeming securities as they mature. As part of this function, Treasury bills are issued to raise short-term finance for expenditure because tax income is irregular. It mainly comes in towards the end of the financial year.

4 Operating Monetary Policy – The Bank of England assists the Government in trying to control the economy. The Bank of England can influence **lending** and **interest rates**. Generally, in times of inflation, it tries to force up rates and discourage spending. The weapons for achieving these policies are outlined in 10.8.

5 External functions. The Exchange Equilization account is operated by the Bank of England. This account contains Britain's gold and foreign currency reserves. It also services IMF loans.

6 Supervising the monetary system. The Bank of England aims to maintain a **stable and public confidence** in its efficiency. Thus in 1975, when several 'fringe banks' looked like collapsing, it organized a 'lifeboat' scheme to save them. The main clearing banks and the Bank of England lent funds to the secondary banks in trouble. This action showed the Bank of England as a **'lender of last resort'**. It also plays this part in its dealings with Discount Houses on a more frequent basis. Discount Houses may have to quickly repay the Commercial Banks and so need to borrow to do so (because they 'borrow short and lend long'). If no other source is available the Bank of England will step in and lend the money, but at a penal (higher than market) rate of interest.

10.8 Monetary control

Much of the discussion around monetary policy relates to two basic economic problems:

Inflation and **unemployment** (see Units 9 and 16). It has been argued that by reducing the supply of money (credit included) in the economy, inflation could be reduced. Alternatively, by raising the supply of money, unemployment could be lowered (through more spending).

The Government can affect the **quantity** of money in the economy and the **cost** of borrowing money (*i.e.* rate of interest). In trying to change the quantity of money, the Government will try to control the creation of credit. It will seek to increase credit to expand money supply and thus stimulate spending in order to lower unemployment. With the same aim the Government might seek to **lower interest rates**, thus making borrowing easier.

Government influences

The monetary weapons available and the techniques used have varied greatly since 1951. The mnemonic **'OARS'** is appropriate because they have given the Government little power in steering the banks in the troubled waters of the economy!

1 Open market operations

The Bank of England buys and sells Treasury bills and other government securities in the money market. If the Government wishes to **stimulate spending** it will get the **Bank of England to buy stocks**. The following process takes place:

(a) Sellers of stock receive cheques from the Bank of England
(b) Thus banks' balances at the Bank of England increase (as their customers, the sellers, have gained income)
(c) This gives each bank more liquid assets which enables the banks to expand credit (*i.e.* lend to borrowers who will spend the money). Thus the credit pyramid would have a wider base and larger top. (see Figure 10.5.)

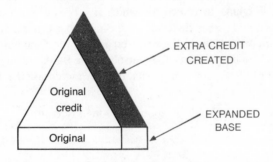

Fig. 10.5 Cost pyramid expanded with govt. buying of stock

In curtailing spending, the reverse process may be less effective. Would-be borrowers who cannot obtain credit from banks may go elsewhere. These other **financial institutions**, such as HP Finance Companies, are **not under the direct control of the Government**. Thus they could expand lending when the Government wanted it limiting.

2 Assets ratio

Post-war -8% cash ratio
1951–71 –28% liquid assets ratio
1971–81 –12½% reserve assets ratio
1981 –**monetary base** or modified cash ratio

In theory, if the reserve assets ratio of the credit pyramid is altered, the shape and size of the pyramid is altered. Thus in Figure 10.6, less credit is created (7000) than in Figure 10.4

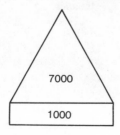

Fig. 10.6 Credit pyramid with 12½% reserve assets ratio

In practice, governments have not regularly changed the assets ratio as a monetary weapon. On average in 1971–81 the commercial banks kept 13½% of the assets in the necessary reserve form and this prevented small changes being effective. These %s were used to make open market operations effective, but they did not work in 1971–81 because banks kept at least 13% as reserve assets. Thus, usually open market and interest rates changed at the same time. The Bank of England bought stocks and interest rates fell, leading to more credit creation. The failure in practice of the assets ratio, open market operations and interest rate changes led the Conservative Government to try a new system – the monetary base. For the first time the **'monetary sector'**, not just the banks, were included. The banks have to keep **½% of their eligible liabilities** in a non-interest bearing account at Bank of England. This is in addition to their normal liquid assets.

It is not yet clear how this system will operate (Jan. 1984) because the Government keeps intervening, despite their belief in competition and government withdrawal from the market.

3 Rates of interest

Postwar to 1971 – bank rate
1971–1981   – minimum lending rate
BR and MLR were the rate at which the Bank of England would lend to Discount Houses, as a lender of last resort. It was fixed weekly at ½% above the Treasury bill rate, thereby following interest rates in the market. However, on occasions the Government did depart from this practice.

Importantly, **other interest rates** (such as bank base rate) were fixed from bank rate/minimum lending rate. Thus, if Government increased MLR, then other interest rates in the economy rose *e.g.* loans. This discouraged borrowing and reduced the money supply.

In August 1981, MLR was suspended, as the Government did not want to 'lead' the market. However, in practice it still interferes.

4 Special deposits

These were introduced in 1960 to restrict bank lending. Each bank had to keep a **specified % of deposits at the Bank of England** in return for which it received interest. However, the special deposits did not count as liquid assets. So a call for special deposits meant cash was given up and so loans had to be recalled in order to keep the required assets ratio. The banks got round this though by keeping more than 28% in liquid assets. Conversely, if the Bank of England wishes to encourage lending, it releases some of these captive deposits, thereby increasing the banks' liquid assets. This allows the banks to create more credit.

There are two other less important weapons of monetary control:

5 Funding

This describes government action of selling more long-dated stock and fewer (short) Treasury bills. This leads to banks holding a small % of liquid assets and thus having less potential to create credit.

6 Directives

The Bank of England may **advise** banks about specific things. For instance, they might ask banks to lend less to the personal customer and more to businessmen and exporters. Usually, the Bank of England's advice is accepted by the commercial banks and so an order (directive) is not needed. In practice, these weapons have been largely ineffective. Hence the introduction of the **monetary base**. However, it is too soon to say how effective this change has been.

10.9 Links with other topics

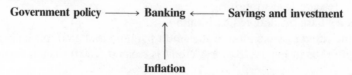

11 Savings and investment

11.1 Introduction

In Unit 10 we examined the Money Market where short-term loans are obtained. In this unit we turn to the **Capital Market**. This is the market for **large long-term** borrowers, particularly the Government, local authorities and large companies. The funds for lending often come from institutions which attract and accumulate the funds of many small savers.

Investment has two meanings:

1 Buying capital goods *e.g.* machinery to make consumer goods.

2 Buying 'claims for money' *e.g.* putting money in a bank, buying shares in PLC, making deposits in a building society. These may be 'investments' in the sense that they may give extra income, but they are normally called savings.

In Economics, **Investment is capital formation**

11.2 Borrowers

1 **Companies** – mainly PLC. They take loans from savers occasionally but rely heavily on bank borrowing and undistributed profit (see Figure 5.11). If a particularly large capital project needs financing a PLC may make a new issue of shares, *e.g.* Saatchi and Saatchi raised £26m in 1982.

New companies seeking to become PLC (with shares quoted on the Stock Exchange) mainly make **new issues** of shares. They get the services of an experienced merchant bank (see Unit 10.2) to advise them on timing and method of issue. In doing so, it acts as an Issuing House. There are five methods of issuing shares available. They can be remembered by **'POP IT'**.

(a) Prospectus This gives detailed information about the nature of the business, its financial position and an application form for the shares at a given price. If the view of the investing public is favourable then the shares will be sold.

(b) Offer for sale This is similar to a Prospectus, except that it is all done by the Issuing House who promise to take up any shares not sold.

(c) Placing All the shares are taken up by a few large investors, which is arranged by a merchant bank.

(d) Issue to existing shareholders This is known as a **'Rights issue'**. It enables existing shareholders to buy new shares in proportion to their holdings of old shares, *e.g.* 5 old shares = 1 new share plus 20p.

(e) Tender This is similar to issue by prospectus except that offers are invited above a minimum price. When all the bids have been received the shares are issued at the highest price which enables all of the shares to be taken up.

2 **The Government** As well as issuing Treasury bills in the Money Market (see Unit 10.6), the government's broker sells **gilt-edged securities** *e.g.* 1993 Treasury Loan 13¾% Stocks. This means that a loan to the Treasury paying 13¾% interest each year will be repaid in 1993. These can be either **fixed or variable yield**. Occasionally, variable yield stocks may be 'indexed' to the rate of inflation. The bonds are sold in **£100 units** by the government in two different ways:

(a) Tap. Stocks are offered for sale at **specified price** and yield (interest). If they are not all bought, then the government sells them off gradually, as they are demanded. Thus, eventually the government gets the **price** it wants.

(b) Tender. Government decides to sell a **particular quantity** of bonds on a certain day and invites offers. It then sells the bonds to the **highest bidders**. The government gets the quantity sold that it wants.

The amount borrowed by the government to finance public expenditure (see Unit 15) adds to the National Debt.

3 **Local authorities** In order to finance expensive capital projects, many councils issue bonds. They tend to offer attractive rates of interest. They borrow over short-medium term in the £1000 to

£10 000 range, usually from private individuals and institutional investors (below). In 1983 the total local authority debt from borrowing was £43 billion.

11.3 Savings institutions

Most of these institutions are large suppliers of funds to the capital market. They buy Government Stock and subscribe to new issues. In general, they seek, like banks, to earn more from **lending** than they pay out to savers.

The institutions 1 to 4 are private sector profit seekers, 5 is private sector non-profit-making (trustee status) and 6 is public sector non-profit-making. The banks were dealt with in Unit 10.2.

1 Insurance companies They collect 'sums of money called premiums from people who take out insurance policies'. This money is invested in a portfolio (range) of paper assets, each earning **interest**. Insurance companies make their profit from wise investment rather than from underwriting risks (where the claims paid usually exceed the premiums income). The **Prudential** is one of the biggest investors in the stock market.

2 Investment trusts These PLC **buy shares** in other businesses. They manage these investments by switching between profit uses. In effect, they are expert speculators in finance. Their funds come from people buying their shares as new issues, usually plus £1000. The Scottish Provident offer six investment funds and a mixed fund.

3 Unit trusts These trusts attract **small savers** who buy units of a stated value in a trust, often by answering a **newspaper advertisement**. The trusts specialize in certain sectors of the stock market and spread their investments for safety. They are fairly flexible and allow units to be redeemed for cash easily. *e.g.* Kleinwort Benson.

4 Pension funds Most workers contribute to private pension schemes, which top up the State pension. The funds are managed by boards of trustees who invest in a wide range of assets, from government stock to oil paintings. The aim is to obtain as big a return on the savings as possible. The National Union of Miners (NUM) pension fund holds £15 billion assets.

5 Building societies They are **mutual institutions** owned by their members (depositors and borrowers), each of whom has one vote at the AGM. They are not intended to be profit makers because of their **Friendly Society** status, although they do make 'surpluses'.

The Chief Registrar of Friendly Societies checks building societies by vetting their **annual accounts** and regulating their activities. For instance, in 1984 the New Cross Building Society was shut, although members' deposits and loans were fully guaranteed to maintain general confidence in building societies.

Since 1970 they have rapidly expanded and now hold £70 billion of personal savings, with half of all adults holding a building society account. They offer **savings accounts** to lenders.

Since 1975 the building societies have offered high-paying instant-access accounts and attracted large investors. However, by offering instant liquidity they may become vulnerable when sums of money are shifted. At present building societies are supposed to keep a **2½ reserve ratio**.

Home loans are given to borrowers. 78% of their assets are in **mortgages**, which are usually plus 20-year loans. The funds are provided by the deposits of the savers. The **rates of interest** offered vary over time and between different types of saving accounts. For instance, regular savers obtain higher returns. In addition, in Britain the saving with building societies is encouraged by the government as the interest received is tax paid by the society.

Building society	Assets (£bm)	Shareholders (m)	Borrowers (m)	Number of Branches
Halifax	14.1	6.5	1.1	577
Abbey Nat.	12.1	7.8	0.9	674
Nationwide	6.4	3.1	0.5	513
Leeds Perm.	4.2	2.1	0.4	453

Fig. 11.1 Top four building societies 1983

Between 1980-1983 the main clearing banks began to compete with building societies in providing mortgages. The building societies retaliated by increasing their **financial services** *e.g.* Leicester began cheque clearing and issuing credit cards, as well as withdrawals/deposits through the Post Office. Future developments are uncertain. Figure 11.1 details the four largest building societies.

6 Government savings schemes

Trustee Savings Banks are government supervised and non-profit-making. They are no longer simply savings institutions as they provide current accounts and participate in the Clearing House. They are designed for private individuals, charities and trade union funds rather than companies.

Savings Certificates of various types are issued by the government usually to raise finance for itself. They vary in rates of interest, terms and redemption dates.

National Savings Banks are government operated. They accept deposits in ordinary and investment accounts, which they invest in Government Stock.

11.4 Stock Exchange

1 People

The main Stock Exchange is in London but there are also regional exchanges. They are controlled by their members who elect a **council of 47 members**. This council tries to ensure that the 4000 members stick to the rules; it fixes entry fees, it vets new members; it approves new issues and investigates suspected malpractices.

All members have to pay 1000 guineas nomination, 1000 guineas in entry fee and 215 guineas yearly subscriptions. They have to become Stockbrokers or (Stock) jobbers. They cannot be both, which is known as dual capacity. Most firms are **partnerships** and have **unlimited liability**.

Stockbrokers deal directly with the **general public**. They follow a client's instructions and charge a **commission** for their service in buying/selling shares from jobbers. They give advice to their customers, based on their knowledge and experience of the stock market. There are about a hundred stockbroking firms now, compared with three hundred, twenty years ago. The brokers Cazenove act for Midland Bank.

Jobbers hold shares in the same way as **wholesalers** store goods. They buy/sell in order to make a profit, called the **'jobbers turn'**. Generally, they try to sell at prices higher than they buy for in order to make this profit. Jobbers tend to **specialize** in a narrow range of markets. Their work involves more risk than stockbroking as they may be left with shares that they cannot sell except at a loss.

Stocks and Shares
Ordinary Shares
Preference Shares } (see Unit 3.8)
Gilt-edged Stock

These shareholders receive **dividends**, usually calculated as a % of the nominal price of the share (*i.e.* original issue price) *e.g.* £10 Share, 60p dividend = 6%. However, the share may have been £15 on the stock market so in fact it yields less than 6% *i.e.* $= \frac{60p}{£15} = 4\%$. Its **yield** $= \frac{\text{dividend}}{\text{market prices}}$.

2 Procedure

When shares/stocks are bought or sold, certain steps are involved in the transaction:
You wish to buy **1000 ordinary shares** in Rentokil, and so contact a **stockbroker**. This may be done through your bank manager. He will get his contact on the floor to approach **jobbers** in the chemicals market. He will ask several jobbers to **quote their prices** for 'Rentokil ordinary'. For instance, 107-112, 108½-112½, 109-114 may be given. As the broker is buying on your behalf he wants the **lowest selling price** quoted by the jobbers. In this case, 112 would be chosen (112½, 114 more expensive) and the broker would return to the jobber saying 'I buy 1000'.

Both the stockbroker and jobber make a note of the transaction, called the **'bargain'**. This agreement is binding, in accordance with the Stock Exchange motto **'My word is my bond'**. 20 000 bargains are made per day, averaging £50 000 each.

Fig. 11.2 Cost of share buying (June 1983)

Expenses	500 at £1	1500 at £1
Broker's commission	15.00	24.75
Stamp duty 2%	10.00	30.00
Contract stamp	0.10	0.60
VAT	2.25	3.72
	27.35	59.07

The broker informs you (the client) of the purchase and you have to pay at the end of the **account**, a two-week period into which the financial year is divided. The broker will give you a **contract note** which lists the price paid, commission and date for payment.

4 Savings and investment

3 Prices

The stock market is usually claimed to be a **perfectly competitive** market because there are many buyers and sellers with excellent knowledge and rapid reactions to price changes. Check Unit 7.2 for the features of Perfect Competition.

Share prices are published daily. They reflect changes in demand and supply. For instance, jobbers will **'mark down'** prices of shares for which they have a plentiful supply. However, the prices in practice are caused by many wider, often non-economic, considerations:

(a) Company prospects They may be enhanced by:
 (i) Likely takeover by bigger company.
 (ii) Beneficial government policies *e.g.* increased spending by Department of Transport will probably help Wimpey Shares.
 (iii) Optimistic statement by company chairman.
 (iv) Political stability *e.g.* the ending of a war or political crisis in a part of the world where a company's trade has been disrupted.

(b) Company performances Reduced profits, or lower profits than expected, together with low dividends are likely to cause a fall in demand for the share and thus a share price drop.

(c) General economic trends Optimism about economy and government policies may stimulate confidence in share buying. Thus most shares may increase in value.

(d) Political factors Wars, crises and elections tend to depress prices generally because of the uncertainty created.

These factors may shift the demand for a share, as in Figure 11.3.

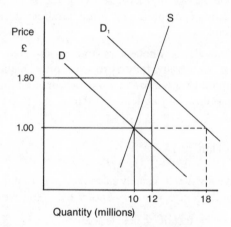

Fig. 11.3 Application of demand theory to share price changes

In this diagram, supply (S) is relatively inelastic. This means that some but not a lot of extra shares will be put on the market if the price rises. Many potential sellers may not know of the price increase and some jobbers holding shares may wish to keep their shares (perhaps expecting further price rises).

Demand is drawn as relatively elastic. The reason being that a small change in price may make a share much less attractive, as speculators work on tight profit margins and knowledge is nearly perfect. The shift to D1 is caused by anything improving company prospects/performance. At £1 per share the demand increases from 10 to 18m. However, only another 2 million are made available for sale and so the quantity supplied expands to 12 million. The excess demand cannot be satisfied and so the market price is bid up to £1.80, at which point demand = supply.

4 Speculators

Many stock exchange investors want a **regular income** through dividends. Others, though, seek a quick profit by anticipating changes in share prices. They want **capital gains**, from selling at a higher price than buying the shares.

(a) Bulls People who **buy** expecting **prices to rise** before they have to pay for them.

(b) Bears Speculators who **sell** expecting **prices to fall**, usually within one period of account. This is so that they can buy back the same shares but at a lower price.

(c) Stags Investors who **buy** new issues anticipating a price rise in oversubscribed shares *e.g.* in 1982 Amersham was sold off by the Government. 250 000 people applied for shares and 65 000 were successful. Once issued, the market price shot up and most of the 65 000 sold off their shares at a big profit. In November, 1983 there were just 7717 shareholders, with the bulk of the shares in the hands of the big pension and insurance funds.

5 Functions 'MINGS'

(a) Market for **second-hand** securities. The Stock Exchange brings together buyers and sellers. It enables sellers to obtain **liquidity** and buyers to get paper assets.

(b) Indicator of **business** prospects. It is said that the Stock Exchange acts as a barometer of business confidence. This can be seen to some extent in the changes of the **Financial Times** (FT) Index. This measures **changes in share price** of the top 30 shares, such as Allied Brewery, BP, etc. There is also an All Share Index which is based on 750 share prices. This is calculated slightly differently but it moves in same direction as FT Index.

It is the **relative change** in the index, not its absolute level, which is **important**. For instance an index number of 300 could mean different things. If it had reached 300 from 200 in a month then it would indicate **business confidence** growing. However, if it had fallen to 300 from 400 it would show pessimistic prospects in the market. Thus changes in FT Index indicate the health of the economy, to some extent.

The movement of share prices in a **specific sector**, say chemicals, may show depression or expansion in that part of the economy. In indicating expanding areas, it points to areas where funds might be channelled.

(c) New issues are **supervised**. New public companies need Stock Exchange approval for their accounts, prospectus etc. The fact that new issues can be **resold** on the Stock Exchange makes individuals and institutions more willing to take up new issues. They have a seal of approval and the chance to regain liquidity by selling the shares.

(d) Government funds are obtained on the stock market. The government sells bonds/stocks to acquire finance for its spending on defence, education etc. The sales of **gilt-edged** securities account for **80%** of the turnover on the Stock Exchange.

(e) Savings can be 'invested' on the Stock Exchange. Individual savings eventually find their way onto the stock market. It gives pension funds and insurance companies another profitable source for their funds in which they are protected (to some extent) by the supervision of the Stock Exchange Council.

7 Criticisms of the Stock Exchange

(a) Short-term profit is more important to speculators than productive investment
Many 'investors' are interested in **capital gains** rather than dividends from profits. Thus shares may be bought for reasons which do not help the economy. For instance, companies have been taken over so that the **assets could be sold off** ('stripped'). This meant that production ceased and unemployment resulted. Similarly, investment funds may be channelled into empty property, as happened in 1973 when bank lending expanded.

(b) The supervision of companies is weak
Shady activities such as false accounting, non-submission of accounts and **insider trading** occur and sometimes go unpunished. The **voluntary code** of the Stock Exchange is ignored by some company directors who trade in their company's shares, using their privileged knowledge to maximize capital gains and minimize capital losses. The Stock Exchange Council does not include outsiders and is a very weak policeman. In contrast, America's Securities and Exchange Commission can issue injunctions and take cash from companies if they misbehave.

(c) It is an inaccurate barometer
The FT Index was increased to record levels in 1983. However, Britain with three million unemployed, falling manufacturing production and worsening trade was in a **depression**!

(d) It allows restrictive practices
The two main ones are **minimum commission** rates being fixed, which hinders competition, and the **single capacity** of brokers and jobbers, which prevents efficient amalgamations. In August 1983, the Stock Exchange Chairman agreed with the Minister of Trade to dismantle minimum commissions by December 1986 (but single capacity was to remain).

(e) The average person in the street cannot participate He cannot hope to have sufficient 'spare funds' to run the risk of share ownership.

(f) It is a gambling club The Stock Exchange was described by Tony Benn as a 'capitalist casino', where rich people bet on share price movements.

11.5 Personal savings

People save for different reasons and in different places. However, they are all **giving up immediate use** of their money, and thus consumer satisfaction, in order **to obtain** a **future benefit**.

The government encourages personal savings for three main reasons:

1 It provides funds for **investment**.
2 It saves the government from having to provide some support for families when they fall on hard

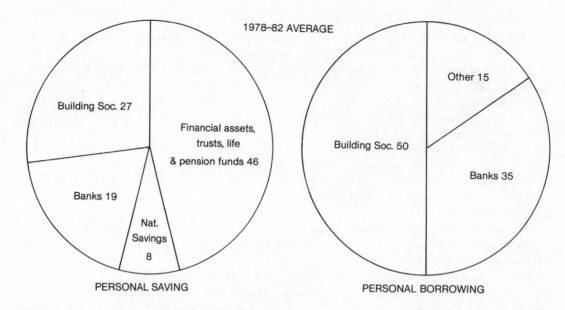

Fig. 11.4 Personal saving and borrowing

times. For instance, some State benefits *e.g.* home help, are not subsidized if a person has savings of more than £1200. Thus, indirectly, personal savings **reduce Government spending** a little.

3 It is thought to encourage the right **attitude to thrift** and self discipline. Planned, regular saving means going without current consumption; it teaches people certain values such as self sacrifice. This may indirectly limit pressure on the government if it does not fulfil its economic promises.

General factors influencing how you save – 'MURT'

1 How much **Money** you have *e.g.* small savers cannot use the Stock Market as £500 minimum is usually needed, in practice.

2 What you want to **Use** it for. Savings can be used to obtain a regular income, through interest and dividends obtained, or a lump sum at the end of a period of time. This sum may be quickly obtained through share speculation or eventually paid when a set period loan is agreed.

3 How willing you are to take a **Risk**. Some savings institutions *e.g.* banks, are much safer than others.

4 How much **Tax** you pay. If the income from savings is taxed then its net value is reduced *e.g.* bank deposits. However, saving in some institutions, *e.g.* building societies, is tax paid. Thus non-taxpayers such as most children and pensioners are better off saving outside building societies.

Specific factors influencing saving – 'STILE'

1 Safety Most savings institutions are directly or indirectly government backed and thus reliable.

2 Tax liability The tax position varies between institutions and individuals. For instance, the Clearing Banks interest is subject to tax but not all receivers of interest earn enough to pay tax *e.g.* students, pensioners.

Institution	Type of account	Interest
Building Society	Ordinary	7¼% tax paid = 10.36 gross
	Term	7¾–9% tax paid = 11.07–12.86
	Subscription	8¼–9% tax paid = 11.79–12.86
Clearing banks	Deposit	5½% taxable
Finance house		9½–10% taxable
Local authority	Yearling	9¾% taxable
	1–2 years	10½% taxable
	3–5 years	11⅛% taxable
National Girobank		6% taxable
National Savings	Ordinary up to £500	3% tax free
	Ordinary + £500	6%; £70 interest tax free
	Investment	11% taxable
	Income bond	11½% taxable

Fig. 11.5 Saving accounts and returns (Oct. 1983)

3 Interest The rate of interest earned varies between savings institutions as illustrated in Figure 11.5 on the previous page.

4 Liquidity The speed with which savings can be turned into cash may be significant. For instance, the withdrawal of £500 from a bank account is much easier than redeeming a local authority loan which may be committed for two years.

5 Easiness The convenience of paying in and taking out money is important. The Post Office which administers National Savings has the advantage over banks and building societies in having more branches. The building societies have a slight advantage over the banks through Saturday opening and longer hours.

Places to save in Short Term

These give **immediate liquidity without penalty:**

1 **Commercial banks** ⎫ All safe
2 **National savings** ⎬ All convenent
3 **Building societies** ⎭ Building societies give best net interest

Places to save in Medium Term

These give **maximum benefit** over a period of **up to seven years**:

1 **Government Savings Certificates/Bonds** ⎫ All safe and all convenient to buy.
2 **Local Authority Loans** ⎪ Liquidity varies as in 2 and 4 you
3 **Save As You Earn** ⎬ cannot withdraw but in 1 and 3 you
4 **Building Societies Term Shares** ⎪ can, with loss of interest/bonuses.
 ⎪ Interest varies but 3 pays best interest in
 ⎭ times of high inflation.

Places to save in Long Term

These give **maximum benefit** over a period of **over seven years**:

1 Unit trusts They are fairly safe as authorized by the Department of Trade and supervised, but the return cannot be predicted and there is the possibility of loss if units are sold at wrong time. It is a risky 'investment' as the units are linked to share prices. The earnings are taxable.

2 Life assurance Very safe and convenient. However, liquidity is gained at a high cost. Endowment policies guarantee a sum of money which is not liable to tax.

3 Government stocks Safe, convenient and unexciting. Regular interest and a guaranteed capital gain on redemption.

4 Gold coins Very risky as there are rapid fluctuations in the price of gold to which their value is linked. Cannot predict.

Other means of saving

1 Property particularly **housing**. Very lucrative as:
(a) Tax relief on monthly mortgage interest payments up to £30 000.
(b) Asset increases in value (antiques, paintings and wine are saved for the same reason).
(c) No capital gains tax on sale.
(d) Mortgage repayments fall in real terms with inflation.

2 Premium Bonds £5-£10 000 Very safe but no interest, although a gambler's chance of a big prize.

3 Commodities such as cocoa, silver, potatoes can be bought and sold often without putting up the full amount (10% of purchase price needed). Very risky and very specialized.

11.6 Links with other topics

12 Population

12.1 British population growth

Population provides **labour** in a country and it is a source of **demand** for the goods and services which labour produces. Thus changes in the size and composition of the population have important economic effects. These changes need to be handled so that a nation continues to make the best use of its **resources**.

In all types of economy, awareness of population change is important because it affects demand and supply. For instance, an increase in population requires more educational facilities, and so resources will need to be allocated into school building. In the long run, this increase brings about an expansion of the workforce which will need to be employed. Similarly a change in the structure of the population, with total population remaining constant, will influence demand and supply patterns. For example, more old people and fewer young ones (an ageing population) necessitates more retirement homes and fewer nurseries. Again, resources need to be reallocated from one sector to another. Such changes require **planning** to get the most efficient use of resources. Planning depends on accurate information. Hence every ten years, the government conducts a **census** (since 1801).

1981 Census

Completion of the census form is compulsory and refusal can be subject to a £50 fine. After the 1971 census, 324 people were convicted and fined. The 1981 census cost £40m and was briefer than 1971 version. There were 21 questions requiring box-ticking, such as:

Accommodation – do you live –

- [ ] in a caravan
- [ ] in any other mobile or temporary structure
- [ ] in a flat/maisonette
- [ ] in a permanent building with entrance from outside the building

This question was followed with enquiries about the number of rooms, tenure, amenities and vehicles.

Population information on date of birth, sex, address, was sought, together with the person's whereabouts on 5/6 April, their job, employment status, journey to work and qualifications. From census data, and that collected regularly on births and deaths, population trends can be projected and plans undertaken.

Usage of census

1 Housing – calculation of present and future needs from size and age of families.
2 Social capital – government grants to local authorities and NHS provision depend on number and needs of people in different areas.
3 Transfer incomes – government future spending on pensions and other allowances can be worked out from the information on families, marital status etc.
4 Planning – the census will show changes in the workforce and the information can be used to plan offices, shops, public transport and leisure services.

Brief history of UK population growth

The history of Britain's population can be divided into three periods:
1 Pre-1801 very slow growth – there were **very high birth rates** and **very high death rates**, thus

Year	Population (m)	Birth rate	Death rate
1066	1 (estimate)	—	—
1701	6 (estimate)	—	—
1801	12	37	27
1851	22	35	23
1901	38	25	15
1951	50	16	13
1983	56	12.8	11.7
2001	58 (projection)	—	—

Fig. 12.1 UK population growth

cancelling each other out. Life expectancy was low. The eighteenth-century increase resulted from **better food, clothing and living standards** caused by the agrarian and industrial revolutions.

  2 **19th Century – fast growth** – the high birth rate remained constant but the **death rates fell** markedly. This produced a natural rate of increase, such that the population tripled in 100 years. The main factors causing the fall in death rate were **better sanitation**, prompted by government regulations, improvements in **medical knowledge** and techniques and greater awareness of public and private **hygiene**.

  3 **20th Century – rapidly declining rate of growth** – the general trend has been a declining birth rate, with occasional sharp increases. For instance, the 1901 birth rate of 25 per 1000 has declined to 12.8 in 1983, but there have been occasional peaks *e.g.* 21 in 1947 and 20 in 1964.

This **declining birth rate** has been caused by:

(a) New and cheaper methods of **birth control** have been developed. In addition, birth control is now more socially acceptable and popular. Also, people are better informed.

(b) Children have become more of an **economic liability** than an asset. The ending of child labour, compulsory education and the raising of the school-leaving age have all made large families more expensive to maintain.

(c) The desire for **higher living standards** has made many couples defer child bearing until they have major material possessions *e.g.* cars, videos, foreign holidays etc. Providing for children means less for such luxuries and so the birth rate has fallen.

(d) The **emancipation of women**, particularly since the 1960s, has meant fewer women in the home and more at work. The traditional women's role as a mother now faces competition from career aspirations. This makes women less likely to want children. Furthermore, the extra income from female employment enables a higher standard of living for a couple, which they may be reluctant to give up in order to have children.

  The **death rate** has fallen a little in the twentieth century. It has been **fairly stable** for the last thirty years although the causes of death have changed. Heart attacks, cancer and suicide which are associated with modern living styles, have replaced the old killers such as perinatal and infant mortality, tuberculosis and pneumonia.

12.2 Size

Factors affecting population size:

  1 **Birth rate** (fertility rate): ratio of total live births to the total population, usually expressed in 'births per 1000 of total population' per annum.

The birth rate is influenced by:

(a) Number of women of child-bearing age (16-45) in the population.

(b) Number of children born per woman.

These two influences are determined by other factors, remembered by **'MALE'**

(a) Marrying age If people marry later in life then there are likely to be fewer children reared. Thus a lower average age of marriage will raise the birth rate, other things being equal.

(b) Attitudes to marriage and family size. The declining importance of religion and the increased emancipation of women have made marriage and large families less popular. For instance, in some Catholic countries, such as the Irish Republic, where the contraceptive pill is banned, the birth rate is much higher than Britain. The desire for a better standard of living has meant an average of fewer children per family. Such factors affect the willingness of women of child-bearing age to have children.

(c) Law A minimum age of 16 for marrying means that most children are born to women of between 18 and 30 who are married. The social custom of children being born to married women means that changes in the age of marriage could influence the birth rate. Similarly, the accessibility of abortion and birth control, both of which the government may manipulate, can influence the number of live births. In China, because of the massive population, the government tries to restrict families to not more than one child.

(d) Education If people are better informed about the costs and duties of parenthood, it is likely that the birth rate will fall. Sex education in schools has indirectly contributed to the falling birth rate in the 1970s and early 1980s.

2 Death rate (mortality rate): ratio of total deaths to total population, usually expressed in 'deaths per 1000 of total population per annum'. The death rate is influenced by:

(a) Health standards If many basic services, such as refuse collection, water purification and efficient sewerage disposal are provided, then death from infectious disease can be reduced. Such improvements in late nineteenth century accounted for the dramatic drop in the death rate. They came about as the government took a more active role in society's welfare and enforced minimum standards by law.

(b) Medical advances New discoveries, drugs and inventions have enabled increases in life expectancy. The development of anaesthetics, antiseptics and radium in the nineteenth century and penicillin and sulphonamides in the twentieth century, significantly reduced the death rate. The average life expectancy is now seventy-four.

(c) Food, clothing and housing With the improvements in nutrition and self care, the general standard of living of the population has improved. This is shown in the earlier maturity of children and the higher average height of the population. Thus the natural death rate in Britain is low and a further substantial decline is unlikely.

3 Migration The difference between the number of people leaving a country (emigration) and the number entering (immigration). If immigration exceeds emigration, then a nations' population increases.

This factor has been of little importance in Britain. Between 1871 and 1931 (and since 1961) Britain was a **net emigrator**. However the 1931 to 1961 period saw an inflow of immigrants, mainly composed of European refugees and new Commonwealth (largely black) citizens. These immigrants came to Britain for various motives: escape from religious and political persecution *e.g.* Jews from Germany, Asians from Uganda; to take advantage of economic opportunities *e.g.* Pakistanis, West Indians; the attraction of a higher standard of living *e.g.* Indians, Cypriots.

The net outflow since 1961 has been termed a **'brain drain'**, because the better educated and more skilled left. Their reasons were similar to those of the immigrants except that the persecution was claimed to be high rates of income tax which stifled business initiative and penalized people on high salaries. The lowering of income tax, particularly on higher incomes, by the Conservative government since 1979 has not produced any noticeable return of exiles: in fact the 1979 to 1982 outward migration accelerated!

Changes in the size of the population

Birth rate > death rate = **natural increase** in population

Death rate + net emigration > birth rate = **decrease** in population

Optimum size

In theory, there is an ideal population size for each country. This is the level of population at which **income per head is maximized**. This would mean that best use was being made of a nation's **resources**.

If a country's population exceeds the optimum it is said to be **overpopulated** *e.g.* Bangladesh, Mexico. Thus, those nations do not allow immigration and encourage lower birth rates. In contrast, Australia and Canada are underpopulated and they actively seek immigrants so that currently untapped resources, particularly land, can be utilized and output per head can be raised.

It is impossible to estimate the optimum-sized population for a country, because population size varies quickly. It takes time to collect information, and technology improves, making larger populations more sustainable. The optimum size is not just related to space. It needs to be considered in the light of **productive resources** and potential.

In 1798, **Malthus** predicted that the expansion of food supply would be inadequate to meet the growth of population and that **wage rates would fall**, because the supply of land was fixed (and MRP would fall – see Unit 13). But he assumed no technological progress, thus making his gloomy predictions inapplicable to the modern industrialized world. However, they have some relevance to the developing nations, who cannot control the population explosion.

12.3 Structure

1 Age distribution

In looking at age distribution, it is useful to classify the population into three groups:

Those up to **school leaving age**; currently sixteen. They need health, welfare and education services but they do not produce anything. However, their upbringing can be viewed as an investment – a future producer, for society.

Those of **working age**; 16 to 65 men, 16 to 60 women. About one fifth of this group between 16 and 22 are in full-time education and supported by the State. Furthermore, there are many housewives and unemployed people who do not add to the national income. The latter receive benefits. Thus about 45% of the population are producers who pay taxes which can be put towards State services.

Those **above retirement age**; men +65, women +60. Although some pensioners stay in part-time/full-time employment, the bulk of this category need health and welfare facilities. They do not produce much of national income.

The % of population in each category is determined by

(a) changes in birth and death rates

(b) changes in migration

For instance, the fall in death rate has meant a big growth in the retirement age category; from 7% in 1901 to 18% in 1981.

Dependency ratio Ratio of working population to the non-working (dependent) population. At present at least 40% of the population (22 + 18) are dependent on the other 60% (working population), to produce the goods and services needed to sustain them.

Working population All those inhabitants at work or available for work. Its size will be determined by:

(a) Total population size

(b) Ages of school leaving and retirement

(c) % of non-workers within the working age group

(d) Those at work beyond retirement age

(e) Age distribution of population

(f) Sex composition of population

An ageing population—Britain's population is ageing. The numbers leaving the workforce and retiring exceed those entering the workforce. This trend has been quickened by the schemes for early retirement and the expansion of further education.

The **economic effects** of the ageing population are

(a) Changing spending patterns As a population ages, the demand moves from goods associated with the young such as toys, towards products for the old, such as thermal underwear. Faced with a declining birth rate in the 1970s, Mothercare reacted by expanding their 'baby' range to cover children's clothes up to age ten. Conversely, Barratt Homes responded to the increasing number of elderly widows and widowers by developing single accommodation *e.g.* the 'Mayfair' one- bedroomed house. State spending shifts from child care and education towards home helps and old folks homes. Thus, some teacher training colleges in UK were closed between 1978 and 82 because of the declining birth rate.

(b) Increased dependence on working population. As there are more consumers and fewer workers, **taxes** may need to be increased to pay for the necessary services. This could act as a disincentive to production and **slow down** (or halt) **economic growth**. Thus the extra cost of pensions or education falls on a relatively small group who are working and earning, which it could be argued is **unfair**.

(c) Less labour mobility Younger people tend to be more energetic and enterprising. Thus an ageing workforce will tend to be less mobile between jobs and areas. Many workers made redundant from declining industries such as shipbuilding and steel are unlikely to be employed again, particularly those over age 45.

(d) Less adaptive workforce As older people are ingrained in their habits and trades, they are unlikely to seek or get retraining. Thus the nation's productive resources of labour are diminished.

These effects can be overcome if **productivity** and **technology** increase as they enable greater output per head of population. This can bring about a general increase in national income and raised living standards for all of the population.

2 Sex distribution

The sex distribution in UK is of less economic significance than the age distribution, as long as male/female proportions are fairly similar. More males are born, but more women survive, particularly beyond age 45. This is explained by three factors:

1 Work The physical exertion and mental pressure of work affects men more than women, as more men go out to work and they retire later. Thus more men die at, and from, work.

2 Emigration More men leave Britain than women.

3 Wars The majority of women in the population now has been caused by male deaths 1914 to 18, 1939 to 45. This factor is becoming less important and the age (50) at which women outnumber men is getting higher.

In 1980, the number of females (28.7 m) exceeded the number of males (27.3 m), although by 2001 it is predicted that the gap will be slightly narrower.

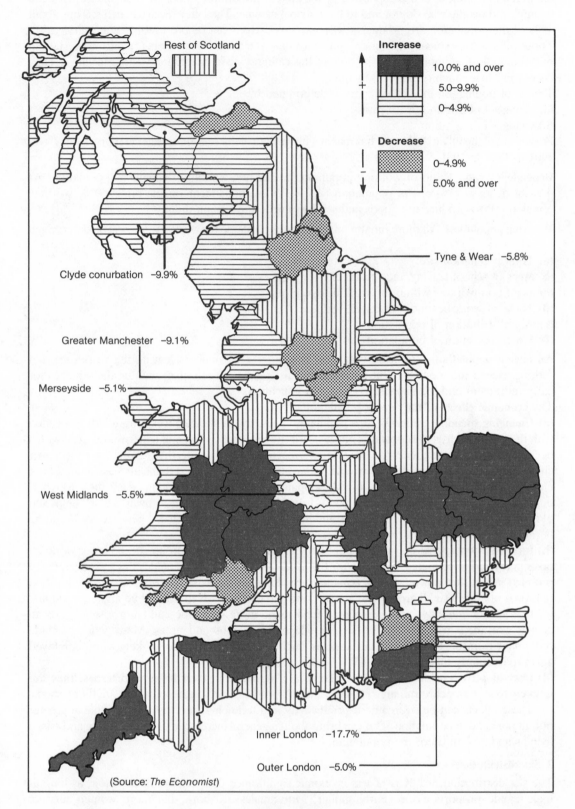

Increase

■ 10.0% and over

▥ 5.0–9.9%

▤ 0–4.9%

Decrease

▦ 0–4.9%

□ 5.0% and over

Rest of Scotland

Clyde conurbation −9.9%

Greater Manchester −9.1%

Merseyside −5.1%

West Midlands −5.5%

Tyne & Wear −5.8%

Inner London −17.7%

Outer London −5.0%

(Source: *The Economist*)

Fig. 12.2 Geographical mobility 1971–81

3 Geographical distribution

The average density of 230 people per sq km in Britain is similar to W. Germany and India. It is one of the denser parts of the world.

The history of Britain shows that before the **Industrial Revolution**, the population was located mainly in **rural** areas. The concentrations were on good **farming land** in the south east beneath an imaginary line from the Wash to the Severn. The population moved into the northern parts of Britain rapidly during the Industrial Revolution, with the development of coal, steel, cotton and shipbuilding. In addition, Scottish and Irish immigrants also went there. This movement **northward** coincided with **urbanization**. Thus by 1901, three quarters of the population lived in towns.

With the decline of these traditional industries, the population distribution again changed, but it remained urban. Thus, between the wars and after 1945, the new **light engineering industries** of the **Midlands and South** attracted labour away from the industrial North.

The heavy concentration of people in urban areas continued until the mid-1960s, with 50% of the population living in towns of over 50 000 inhabitants. However, the 1981 Census (and Figure 12.2) show that the **big city areas lost population** to the more rural areas. For instance, Inner London's population fell by 17%, Birmingham's by 8% and Manchester's by 17%. Places where population increased included new towns, such as Milton Keynes, and remote areas such as the Shetlands. **Overall from 1961–1981**, the population has increased in England, Wales and N. Ireland and declined in Scotland. The main **regions of increase** have been West Midlands, East Anglia, Outer London, the South East and the South West. The areas from which people have migrated were North, North West, Merseyside and Greater London.

4 Occupational distribution

The job distribution of the workforce depends on a country's stage of **development**. Underdeveloped countries typically have 80% of their workforce employed in the agricultural sector, whilst developed nations have less than 10% in this area.

Before the Industrial Revolution, Britain's workforce was largely agrarian. The development of industry necessitated **mobility** into engineering, mining trades etc. In the twentieth century as these occupations have declined, so workers have moved into assembly work and the service sector. Increasing prosperity creates more jobs in the tertiary sector of the economy and fewer in the primary sector. (see Unit 5.2 and Figure 5.1).

Sector	Millions employed	
	1950	*1982 June*
Agriculture, forestry, fishing	0.8	0.3
Mining, quarrying	0.9	0.2
Chemicals	0.5	0.4
Food, drink, tobacco	0.8	0.6
Construction	1.4	1.0
Transport/communications	1.8	1.4
Distributive	**2.1**	**2.7**
Total employed	21.1	20.6

Fig. 12.3 Occupational changes 1950–1982

Figure 12.3 shows the faster decline of employment in the **primary** sector (agriculture, fishing, forestry, mining, quarrying) than in the selected secondary industries (*e.g.* chemicals, construction). The decline of employment varies between types of secondary industry, with some, such as electrical goods doing better than other older ones like textiles. The growth in the distribution trades shows expansion of the **tertiary** sector. The public sector is an increasingly large employer in society, because of these trends and the expansion of the welfare state. An ageing population necessitates more State provision of benefits and services and thus employment in the tertiary sector will continue to increase in Britain.

12.4 Mobility of labour

Mobility is the **movement between jobs**. In an efficient economy it is easily achieved. In **Perfect Competition** (see Unit 7) it is assumed that labour is perfectly mobile *i.e.* an unemployed miner can become a brain surgeon if a vacancy arises. This is clearly unrealistic. However, labour needs to be as mobile as possible, so that **fullest use** is made of it, like any other resource.

Types of mobility

The changing pattern of demand creates growing and declining firms and industries. Thus mobility may be

1 **Occupational** – different **job** but same area, same organization.
2 **Geographical** – different **area** but same job, same organization.
3 **Industrial** – different **organization** but same job, same area.

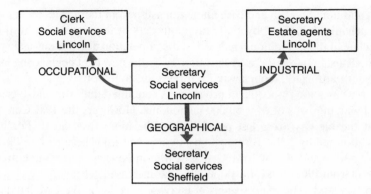

Fig. 12.4 Types of labour mobility

1 Occupational mobility

Obstacles – remembered by **'CARPET'**

(a) Cost The cost of retraining may be a deterrent, so too might be relatively low wages when first starting a new job.

(b) Ability Many white collar workers 'dream' of being professional sportsmen **but** they do not have the basic skills.

(c) Retraining If this is lengthy and involves periods of time away from home, it may deter people from changing jobs.

(d) Personal reasons Personal preference for a particular job and dislike of the alternatives available may discourage movement. A highly specialist worker, such as a glass blower, may be proud of his skill and unable and unwilling to find other employment because of his narrow specialization.

(e) Employment prospects After age 45, many workers are on the 'scrap heap' because employers will not employ them. They are poor prospects for an employer as they only have a short working life (and probably out-dated skills).

(f) Trade Union resistance Trade unions are reluctant to admit retrained workers to certain jobs which involved lengthy apprenticeships. Furthermore, they may have a closed shop agreement whereby union membership is a prerequisite for employment. Similarly, professional bodies *e.g.* solicitors, require certain qualifications before admission.

The obstacles of training, money and trade union resistance can be partly overcome by **government policies**. It has set up skill centres for retraining and paid wages well above the unemployment benefit rates. Since 1980, legislation has been passed to curb the closed shop and weaken trade union resistance. However, the overall effect of these policies has been **minimal**.

2 Geographical mobility

Obstacles – **'FIBPEA'**

1 Family Moving areas poses family problems – changing children's schools, leaving aged relatives, missing close friends. Such factors may deter a worker from moving to another area.

2 Ignorance Information of opportunities may not be available to a prospective migrant.

3 Benefits For lower paid workers with large families there is little incentive to move to a job because the State benefits may be nearly as much as his wage. Furthermore, redundancy pay may cushion the blow of unemployment, particularly in the short run.

4 Prejudice Some people dislike certain parts of the country because of its image *e.g.* 'dirty' North, 'snobby' South. Similarly, London is disliked because of the 'speed'of life and S. Yorkshire because of the 'strange' accents!

5 Expense It may be costly to move, particularly if the worker is buying/selling his own house. The cost of housing varies widely around Britain. Thus a worker moving from Humberside to the South might pay £20 000 more for a similar four bedroomed detached house.

6 Availability of accommodation Workers living in rented property may find it difficult to obtain council housing in the areas where the jobs are located, particularly if there are long waiting lists.

The obstacle of ignorance can be overcome by the better and wider publication of information through **job centres**. However, more people obtain jobs through agencies, such as Alfred Marks Bureau, than through job centres. Expenses may be partly met by **employers**, often government subsidized, but they present a big problem. Recent government policy to **reduce benefits in real terms** means that the differential between work and unemployment is slightly widening, and this might induce more mobility. The regional policies used to encourage geographical mobility are outlined in Unit 6.4. Their lack of success seems to be admitted by the emphasis placed on **increasing capital mobility**.

3 Industrial mobility

This is the easiest type of movement for a worker as it often involves no change of homes and no occupational adjustments. Movement from the public sector into the private sector may involve a change of attitude towards more **profits awareness** though.

An **expanding economy** facilitates industrial mobility. Since 1978, British unemployment has been rising, leaving no scope for industrial mobility. (See Unit 16). The available vacancies have been mainly for skilled tradesmen and thus required mainly occupational (and some geographical) mobility. Sometimes, all three kinds of mobility needed to be combined in a single move.

12.5 World population

The total world population (1983) was 4.5 billion and growing. However, the rate of growth varies. In the **industrialized** nations, the natural rate of increase is **less than 1%** per year. Britain's population of 56 million is almost stationary. In the **developing nations**, the rate of growth of population is 2½%.

In the developing world, the birth rate is 40 compared to a death rate of 10, whereas in the industrialized nations the respective rates are 17 and 10. Such differences are often explained by economic and social factors, such as income distribution and religion.

Within the developing nations, the **middle income nations** (£200 to £500 per head per annum) which are better off have experienced falling birth and death rates. However, the death rate is falling faster so population is bulging. The high rate of population growth per head tends to lower income per head which creates a **poverty trap**. It has been calculated that 50% of population in developing countries live in absolute poverty *i.e.* they cannot afford the bare necessities of life.

The other consequence of fast population growth is the **lack of world resources** to feed and employ the population. In the last twenty-five years, supply has kept pace with food demand. However, the expanding areas of food production are not the regions of growing populations *i.e.* N. Africa needs food whilst Latin America has a surplus. Many developing nations have failed to raise their **productivity** and cannot sell enough to pay for food imports. They need **aid**. However, in 1983 the amount of aid sent by the industrialized nations to the others (except the centrally planned!) fell.

Views of world population problem

Industrialized nations' view Developing nations should do more to reduce birth rate, through birth control principally; otherwise they will remain in the proverty trap.
Developing nations' view Aid is needed to raise their level of development so that family planning programmes will work.

12.6 Links with other topics

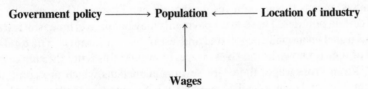

96

13 Trade unions

13.1	Introduction	*
13.2	Methods of payment	*
13.3	Demand for labour	***
13.4	Supply of labour	***
13.5	Wage differentials	***
13.6	Incomes policies	**
13.7	Trade unions (aims, functions, types)	***
13.8	Trade unions (organization, methods)	***
13.9	Government and industrial relations	**
13.10	TUC and CBI	**
13.11	Linked topics	***

13.1 Introduction

Wages and salaries

Wages are the payments made by an employer to the factor, labour, for its use. Wages are the **price of labour**. It is a general term which covers many different types of payment.

Usually 'wages' refers to payments made on an hourly/**weekly** basis which **vary** according to the work done. Extra work (overtime) is usually rewarded at a higher rate, because the worker sacrifices some leisure time in order to work *e.g.* 'Time and a half' may be given (£3 per hour rather than £2 per hour) to a shop assistant for working on her day off. In the past, wages were paid to **manual** workers in **cash**.

Salaries, on the other hand, are usually paid **monthly** with the **same amount** being given each month. Any overtime performed was often considered to be 'part of the job' because salaries were paid to white collar (**clerical**) workers. In the past they were paid by cheque, unlike wage earners. However, increasing numbers of workers are being paid monthly and by credit transfer. So this difference between wages and salaries does not apply.

Earnings

The term **'earnings'** means the amount received from employment. This may be composed of a basic wage and certain bonuses. These extra payments may be for overtime, shift-working, etc. The **basic wage rate** is usually nationally negotiated and less than total earnings. The total amount earned during a period of time is known as the **Gross wage**. However, this is not the sum of money received by the worker. From gross wage, there are several **deductions** which are compulsory – national insurance, income tax and pension. The amount which is received after these, and any other deductions, such as savings and trade union subscriptions which are voluntary, is known as the **Net wage**. These are illustrated in Figure 13.1.

Monthly Pay		£875 ← Gross wage	
Deductions:			
National Insurance	63.00		
Income Tax	180.50		Compulsory
Superannuation	52.50		deductions
	296.00		
Other deductions:			← Voluntary deduction
Trade union subs.	4.00		
Total deductions		300.00	
Net pay		£575.00 ← Net wages	

Fig. 13.1 Wages and deductions

13.2 Methods of payment

1 Time rate (sometimes called 'Day' rate)

This is the most common method of payment *e.g.* most salaries and some wages. Workers are paid on the basis of **how many hours** they work *e.g.* 40 hours at £2.50 per hour = £100 per week gross. The amount paid per hour may depend on the person's age, experience and responsibilities. (see Unit 13.5). Any overtime is usually paid at a higher rate.

Time rate is paid where output is not easy to measure, *e.g.* teaching, and where the payment for speed may lead to lower standards *e.g.* doctor. It usually enables quality output to be produced by the worker. However, it suffers from **three disadvantages**:

(a) It is not easy to distinguish (and thus reward) **efficient** and inefficient workers.

(b) It gives no **incentive** to work hard and encourages skivers.

(c) **Supervision** of workforce is needed and this adds cost to the employer.

2 Piece rate

Workers are paid for **how much they produce**. Their output is counted or measured for the jobs or processes which they perform *e.g.* an assembly line operative gets £4.20 per dashboard fitted to a motor car. He fits 50 in one week and so receives £210.

Piecework overcomes the three disadvantages of time rate and often enables a fuller use of capital but it too has disadvantages:

(a) **Shoddy** workmanship may result from the accent on speed.

(b) More needs to be spent on **inspection**.

(c) **Strain** on workers of working at speed. Also **boredom**.

(d) **Wages vary** with jobs performed and this creates uncertainty for the workers.

(e) **Disputes** may arise over the rate for the job and this may cause an industrial relations conflict.

3 Fees

Professional groups, such as solicitors, charge fees for specific work done over a period of time *e.g.* conveying a house.

4 Commission

Employees are paid a certain percentage of the value of their output. This is most commonly found amongst sales personnel who have a low basic wage, as an incentive to sell more. Insurance brokers receive, from the insurance company, a percentage of the premium paid on policies which they have arranged for the company.

5 Profit sharing

Some firms give their employees a share of the firm's profits. They may be in the form of free (or cheap) shares or an annual bonus. The idea is to strengthen the loyalty of the workers to the company, increase their efficiency and reduce potential industrial relations conflict.

13.3 Demand for labour

All workers incur an Opportunity Cost, *i.e.* what they could be doing if they were not at work. In order to compensate them for this sacrifice they receive wages. As with any other commodity in theory, the price of labour (wages) is determined by the interaction of Supply and Demand for Labour.

The demand for labour is influenced by:

1 The productivity of labour

No employer wants to purchase labour merely to have a factory full of workers. Labour will be demanded only if it can increase the firm's profits by increasing production.

Number of workers	Total output	Marginal physical product
0	0	—
1	10	10
2	22	12
3	32	10
4	40	8
5	45	5
6	46	1
7	45	−1

Fig. 13.2 Diminishing marginal productivity

Marginal Physical Productivity is defined as the 'addition to total output resulting from the employment of one extra unit of labour'.

A farmer employs successive workers to harvest his crops. Figure 13.2 shows the effect on total output of increasing the level of employment. As employment rises so too does total output. Initially the farmer will benefit from increased specialization and more extensive use of fixed capital *e.g.* combine harvesters. However, as further workers are employed each one adds less and less to total output until the seventh worker actually reduces total output. This may be because the employees now find themselves getting in each other's way.

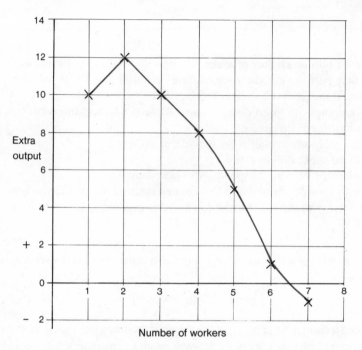

Fig. 13.3 Diminishing marginal productivity

The Law of Diminishing Marginal Productivity. This principle is clearly illustrated in Figures 13.2 and 13.3. As successive units of a variable factor production (labour) are added to fixed factors, marginal productivity will start to decline and may eventually become negative.

This principle plays an important part in determining the demand for labour. For example, in times of slavery employers will increase the labour force as long as there is some addition to total output, no matter how small – *i.e.* as long as MPP>0. This situation is not necessarily unrealistic for in many Third World countries agricultural employment could be significantly reduced with no loss in output *i.e.* MPP=0.

However, in most situations labour is scarce and thus commands a price. A rational profit-maximizing employer will continue to employ additional workers as long as what they add to **Total Revenue** exceeds that which they add to **Total Cost**. However, in practice not all employers are rational and/or profit-maximizers.

2 The demand for the final product (which the labour helps to produce).

It is clear that there cannot be any sense in employing labour, no matter how productive, if the extra output (MPP) cannot be sold. Thus we can see that the Demand for Labour ultimately depends upon the Demand for the Final Product hence the Demand for Labour is a **Derived Demand**. For instance, between 1950 and 1983 the demand for steel fell from 18m to 15m tonnes per annum. In the same period the workforce was reduced from 300 000 to 78 000.

In Figure 13.2 we will assume that a bushel of wheat can be sold for £10 and that wages for farmworkers are £75 per week.

The fourth worker adds £80 (8 units × £10 *i.e.* MPP × Price) to **Total Revenue**. Thus it is profitable to employ this worker because the addition to total **revenue** (£80) is greater than the extra **cost** of employing him (£75 wages). However, the fifth worker only adds £50 (MPP × Price) to Total Revenue whilst adding £75 to the wages bill, thus it is not profitable to employ him/her.

Marginal Revenue Product is defined as the addition to Total Revenue resulting from the employment of 1 extra unit of labour.

The MRP is calculated by MPP × Price. In the example above the MRP of the fourth worker is £80. From Figure 13.2 we can see that the MRP of the seventh worker is £−10.

Thus we can see that MRP tells us whether or not it is profitable to employ successive workers. Therefore, we may regard the MRP as the Demand for Labour.

The MRP varies with market conditions. So far we have assumed that a firm's output can always be sold at a fixed price *i.e.* the firm is in a perfectly competitive market (Unit 7).

However, in most markets demand theory suggests that in order to increase sales price must be reduced. In our example, for the farmer to sell the output of the last, or marginal, worker, the price of **all** the bushels must be reduced. In that case MRP will be equal to MPP $\times$ MR (rather than price). Thus MRP will decline steeply as both the extra output (MPP) and price obtained for it (MR) are falling.

Factors affecting demand for labour (SPED)

(a) Substitution of Factors of Production If **capital** can be easily substituted for labour then, in the long run, demand for labour will fall. For example, robots in the car industry take the jobs of people and thus MRP curve shifts to the left. In Figure 13.4. MRP_2 shows the fall in demand for labour.

(b) Productivity If labour becomes more productive *i.e.* MPP rises. This will have the effect of increasing the demand for labour assuming other things remain unchanged. MRP_3 in Figure 13.4. illustrates this.

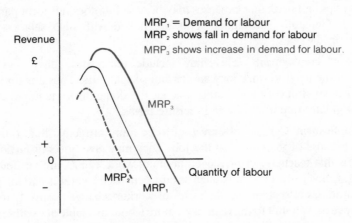

MRP_1 = Demand for labour
MRP_2 shows fall in demand for labour
MRP_3 shows increase in demand for labour.

Fig. 13.4 Changes in Marginal Revenue Product (MRP)

(c) Elasticity of Demand for the Final Product This affects the shape of the Demand curve for labour (MRP). The more elastic is the demand for the final product, the **more elastic** will be the demand for labour. The elastic demand for toys, for example, or ice cream, has meant that the demand for workers in such industries fluctuates greatly unless other products are made to level out the demand for labour.

(d) Demand for the Final Product If there is an increase in demand for the final product there will be a similar shift in the demand curve for labour. A reduction in demand for the product will produce the opposite effect. This factor goes a long way towards explaining the considerable increases in unemployment in such declining industries as coal and shipbuilding.

13.4 Supply of labour

Labour is not a homogeneous factor, indeed it is characterized by **diversity**. *e.g.* a roadsweeper and a brain surgeon are both 'labour' to the economist although they clearly need different skills. As the wages of a particular occupation rise then more people will be willing to work in that industry. Thus the supply curve of labour **slopes upwards** from left to right as in Figure 13.5.

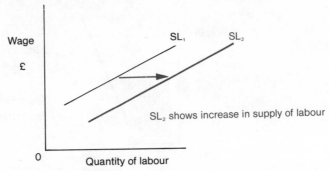

SL_2 shows increase in supply of labour

Fig. 13.5 Increase in supply of labour

General factors affecting the supply of labour

1 Total population This generally determines the potential labour force for an economy. An expanding population, sooner or later, creates an increase in the number of workers available for employment. The factors determining population growth are explained in Unit 12.

2 Labour law School leaving age and retirement age will determine the actual number available for employment. The trends are towards a higher school leaving age and a lower retirement age. This makes more non-workers dependent on the workers in the society.

3 Immigration law An increase in the number of immigrants raises the potential labour supply – see Unit 12.

Specific factors affecting supply of labour ('PICTSE')

1 Pay The wage rate offered will influence the quantity of labour supplied. *e.g.* low pay puts people off whereas high pay encourages. Thus many wish to be business executives but few want to be doormen.

2 Income in kind Many jobs have perks and fringe benefits which are an indirect form of payment. For instance, the use of company cars, expense accounts, luncheon vouchers and cheap mortgages all save the employee from expenditure which others might have to undertake. In certain jobs the income such as tips and travelling expenses may be cash but does not form part of the gross wage which is taxed. Generally substantial perks are linked with high salaries rather than being compensation for low ones.

3 Conditions of employment This may include dangerous, dirty and unpleasant work surroundings, or the need to work long and/or anti-social hours. Thus a night shift worker will be paid more than a day shift colleague in the same factory doing the same job to compensate him/her for incurring a greater opportunity cost in leisure terms.

4 Type of employment Certain jobs are said to be more attractive than others offering similar remuneration because of the nature of the job. They may give 'job satisfaction'.

Society feels that teachers get privileged hours of work, nurses are virtuous and lawyers gain social standing. Conversely, other jobs such as dustmen, social workers and lorry drivers are of low status. If the attitudes in society and the tastes of workers change positively towards certain jobs then the supply curve will shift to the right, with more labour available at existing wage levels. Figure 13.5 shows movement from SL_1 to SL_2.

5 Security Employment legislation has made most jobs more secure than in the past. For instance, 'on the spot' dismissal rarely occurs because warnings and notice need to be given to employees.

However, some specialized labour still faces a short or uncertain working life. For instance, actors, footballers, models, pop stars, etc., **can** earn very high incomes. However, part of this is compensation for the fact that they may only have a short working life *e.g.* 3 to 4 years or long periods of unemployment. *e.g.* an actor or actress may earn £200 to £300 for one or two lines and one day's work and then be unemployed for the next four months.

6 Entry requirements The supply of labour is **limited** for many jobs by factors such as:
(a) **Minimum qualifications** and training *e.g.* degree to become a school teacher.

Unskilled work is likely to be characterized by an elastic supply curve. SL_1 in Figure 13.6. Road-sweeping requires no special skill. Thus only a small rise in wages would be needed to encourage a relatively large number of workers to become road sweepers. Alternatively a brain surgeon requires years of training and few people have the dedication and ability to make the grade. In this case even a large rise in salaries will be unlikely to raise the supply of brain surgeons more than a little. Thus the supply curve is relatively inelastic *i.e.* SL_2 in Figure 13.6.

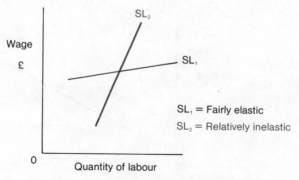

Fig. 13.6 Elasticity of supply of labour

(b) Trade union membership *e.g.* in some jobs you cannot be employed unless you have a 'union card', or agree to join a trade union. Such closed shops, *e.g.* journalism, enable the existing labour to restrict supply and strengthen trade union bargaining position.

Wage determination

1 In theory wages are determined by the interaction of supply and demand for labour as in Figure 13.7.

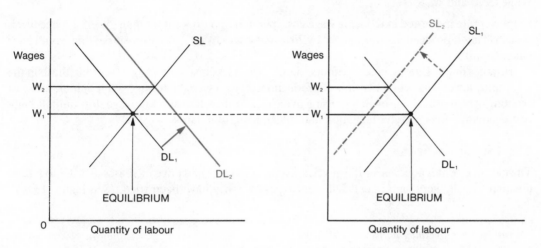

Firm A – Increase in demand for labour   Firm B – Fall in supply of labour

Fig. 13.7 Wages changes caused by shifts in demand and supply

Wages can **increase** from either:
(a) an increase in demand, or
(b) a fall in supply.
These are illustrated in Figure 13.7.
Alternatively in theory wages can fall through either:
(a) a fall in demand, or
(b) an increase in supply.

The factors causing these demand and supply changes are termed **'compensatory wage differentials'**. Higher wage rates offered to attract labour (expand supply) eliminate shortages *e.g.* if North Sea divers were not paid more than swimming pool attendants, there would be a serious shortage of people willing to work on North Sea rigs.

2 In practice wages have not fallen (in money terms) because of institutional factors, principally trade unions. They create **non-compensatory differentials** by interfering in the free workings of demand and supply. Similarly, minimum wage laws artificially raise wage levels. Three million lower-paid workers are in industries governed by twenty-seven **wage councils** which set minimum rates of pay. However, some employers ignore the councils and government inspectors who check on pay regulations.

13.5 Wage differentials

Most of the reasons why some jobs are paid more than others can be explained using Supply and Demand factors. For example the differentials between manual and non-manual largely reflect the relative education/training intensities of the two groups.

The differentials between the wage rates paid to different people doing different jobs may arise **between**:

1 Industries. Capital intensive industries such as oil tend to pay higher wages to manual workers than labour intensive ones, because wages are a very small percentage of total cost. Similarly the workers in **growth** industries find it easier to get wage increases than those in declining industries, *e.g.* platers in shipbuilding fell from 4th to 16th in manual workers' pay league, between 1976 and 81. **Public sector** manual workers are better paid than their private sector equivalents. Such differences between similar jobs which are created by employers are termed **relativities**.

2 Job requirements Occupations requiring qualifications, training, skill, responsibility, and risk are paid more than jobs which do not need these qualities. For instance, gross earnings for coalface workers in 1982 were £165.30 per week compared with £137.30 for chemical workers.

3 Individual characteristics Where several people do exactly the same job, their gross pay may vary because of their age, sex or experience. For instance, a new 17-year-old shop assistant will probably earn less than an experienced forty-year-old.

4 Trade union power Strong and effective trade unions like NUM may be able to maintain, and even extend, their differentials compared with weaker groups such as toolmakers. Between 1976 and 1981 the pay differential between these two widened from £13 to £38.

Wage levels and wage costs

Employers are interested in reducing wage costs per unit of output rather than lowering wage levels as such. Thus if productivity were to rise by 20% and wages by 10% wages costs per unit would have fallen (by 10%).

Britain's major European competitors, despite wage levels some 50% greater than those in the UK, enjoy lower wage costs per unit of production. They have a high wage, high output, low-cost economy which provides growth and rising living standards, whereas a low wage, low output, high-cost economy offers merely stagnation and falling living standards.

13.6 Incomes policies

The idea of incomes policy is for the government to limit wage and price increases in order to **reduce inflation** (usually very high rates). Different types of policy have been tried. (See Figure 13.8.)

Year	Governing party	Policy	Comment
1966	Labour	Pay freeze	Legal
1972–73	Conservative	Stage 1 – Pay freeze	
1973	Conservative	Stage 2 – £1 + 4%	
1974	Conservative	Stage 3 – 7% or £2.25 max.	
1974–75	Labour	Social contract	Voluntary
1975–77	Labour	Norms Stage 1 £6 max.	Legal
		Stage 2 5%	
		£2.50 min. to £4 max.	
1977–78	Labour	10% Guideline	Voluntary
1978–79	Labour	5% Guideline	

Fig. 13.8 Incomes policies

It is difficult to judge whether income policies work. It is not just a matter of comparing periods of incomes policy (*e.g.* November 1972 to March 1973 Heath Stage 1) with periods of no policy (July 1978 to May 1979). The effects of a policy need to be judged against what might have happened in the **same period** of time, if incomes policy had **not** been introduced. In a complex subject like Economics this is extremely difficult to test.

It is generally **agreed** that:

1 Wage and price controls can work for a period of time, if firmly applied.

2 In subsequent periods, wages soon catch up again and inflation rebounds *e.g.* from 1978 to 79, 25% inflation.

3 Non-wage factors push up prices *e.g.* imported raw materials (oil).

4 Incomes controls squeeze company profits.

Criticisms of incomes policy

1 Interference with market forces and it distorts the allocation of labour and capital leading to inefficiency – **but** it controls inflation for a short period.

2 Causing government conflict with trade unions. This may cause industrial unrest – **but** fewer strikes during periods of incomes policy.

3 Squeezing differentials leads to the resentment of skilled workers and management – **but** new perks, job reclassifications have been developed to maintain the wage differences.

13.7 Trade unions (aims, functions, types)

They are organizations of **employees** to represent their interests. One employee alone has no power but employees acting collectively are able to negotiate with employers on a more equal basis. They are formed, financed and run by the members. The average weekly subscription is 50p (1983).

At the end of 1982 there were an estimated **11.3 million** trade union **members** in the UK. This represented 40% of the working people and 52% of the employed labour force. The **number** of trade unions in Britain has fallen from 630 in 1965 to 425 in 1982. There are still 69 unions with less than 100 members *e.g.* Pattern Weavers Society with just 70 members. The biggest unions are identified in Figure 13.9. Each, apart form NALGO, has lost members since 1979 with the increase in unemployment being the main cause.

Trade union	Membership in thousands	
	1979	*1983*
TGWU (Transport)	2070	1633
AEUW (Engineers)	1200	1001
GMBWU (Municipal workers)	965	940
NALGO (Local govt.)	729	784
NUPE (Public employees)	712	702
USDAW (Shopworkers)	462	417
ASTMS (Managerial staff)	471	410

Fig. 13.9 Membership of largest trade unions

1 Aims

Trade unions are concerned specifically with improving their members' **terms and conditions of work** and generally with improving the quality of life of working people. They also have wider **political** and economical **objectives**, such as seeking a redistribution of income and wealth and increased state planning in economic affairs. The main TU apart from the NUT, are allied to the **Labour Party** and their members make a contribution to the Labour Party. This **political levy** is paid by more than 70% of trade unionists. Some trade unions such as NUM and TGWU sponsor Labour Party MPs also, whilst the TU as a whole have a 40% share in choosing the Labour Party Leader.

2 Functions 'NIPS'

(a) Negotiation Trade unions bargain on behalf of their members and others (non-union members, ex-members, and unemployed members) for improvements in **pay and conditions**. Empirical evidence suggests that hourly pay in an industry where the workforce is completely covered by a collective agreement is between 8% and 20% higher than the average wage in a non-unionized industry. If a TU is able to **restrict labour supply** successfully it can force up wages. See Figure 13.6. The extent of their success largely depends upon an inelastic demand for the final product. For instance, the NUM benefits from the inelastic demand for coal, particularly from power stations.

Shorter hours, longer holidays, cleaner working conditions, redundancy pay and job security are all features of TU negotiations. They are part of the general TU responsibility to improve **job satisfaction** and the physical environment of the workplace.

(b) Information The trade unions provide important information and advice for management, the government and the nation. Their members views on new developments within a firm influence management decisions. Similarly, they are closely involved with government economic planning through the National Economic Development Council (NEDC). They also attempt to educate the general public to the wisdom of their policies of full employment, State planning, increased pensions, wealth redistribution, and free collective bargaining.

(c) Persuasion The unions are heavily into **Politics**. In the past they have persuaded their members to accept wage restraint during periods of voluntary incomes policy. This has involved close liaison with the government. Furthermore, because of the TU link with the Labour Party, they seek to convert people to their political views (outlined above) particularly at election time. The 1983 election, in which only 40% of trade unionists voted Labour, indicates their diminishing success in this area.

(d) Support The early trade unions operated as **friendly societies**, providing benefits such as sickness and unemployment payments. However, since the Welfare State has taken over such provision, their social function of protecting workers from hardship has become less important. Nevertheless, many unions still have their own insurance schemes, pensions funds and retirement homes.

3 Types

(a) Craft unions The **earliest** trade unions, which grew up in the nineteenth century, were of this type. They contained **skilled** tradesmen who had usually served an **apprenticeship** and tried to maintain certain working **standards**. Initially they were some of the few workers who could afford to pay subscriptions.

They have **declined** in importance, because of their limited size and entry requirements. The **Electricians** (EEPTU) with 380 000 members is the largest craft union. As its members are spread across many industries it is not very powerful.

The craft unions are very conscious of their skills and qualifications. Thus they seek to maintain their **differentials** over unskilled and semi-skilled workers. Furthermore, they are often involved in **demarcation disputes**, as they try to maintain their sole right to perform certain jobs, which other less skilled workers seek to do. With technological change, such 'who does what' conflicts have become more common in British industry.

(b) Industrial Most **types** of labour in one industry belong to **one union,** *e.g.* NUM contains both labourers at the coalface and skilled workmen. In the USA most unions are industrial. It enables **easier** and **tougher** negotiation, because there is only one spokesman for the workers and industrial action (*e.g.* strikes) can be more effective, assuming the union is united. However, the extent of an industry is sometimes difficult to define (*e.g.* engineering) and sometimes **conflicts** within a large union may occur because of the differing interests of various types of worker *e.g.* guards v. ticket collectors in NUR.

(c) General In the late nineteenth century these unions developed to cater for **semi-** and **unskilled** labour, whom the craft unions would not admit *e.g.* dockers. Traditional crafts declined with industrialization and mechanization and so general unions were formed to represent workers of **varying interests and skills**. TGWU, formed in 1918, is the largest union in Britain but it is difficult to control and often has **internal conflicts** between its members, *e.g.* seamen and dockers over cargo handling.

(d) White-collar These unions are the most **recent** and fastest **growing**. They contain **non-manual workers,** *e.g.* NUT. They are dubbed 'white-collar' because their members typically wear white shirts, rather than overalls, and work in offices rather than factories. Their expansion has been prompted by **envy** at the wage increase successes of manual trade unions and the **decline** in pro-management attitude. The increased number of jobs in the tertiary sector (see Unit 5.2) and the employment of workers with TU traditions in these jobs has given impetus to unionization. Thus, white-collar unions account for 40% of all trade unionists, with ASTMS among the largest unions. These unions have become increasingly **militant** *e.g.* the civil service strike in 1981.

Unions can also be classified into **open** (*e.g.* TGWU) and **closed** (*e.g.* Equity). Open unions do not seek to restrict membership entry to any particular occupation whereas closed unions do.

13.8 Trade unions (organization and methods)

1 Organization

The following outline is a typical pattern, as union structures vary widely.

Each TU member belongs a **local branch**. These are based on large **factories** or several smaller firms in a geographical area. The members elect the local officials and discuss wages, membership and issues at their meetings. However, only 7% of members actually attend branch meetings. In multi-employer branches average attendance is only 4%.

The local branch send representatives to higher organizations, to sit on **district, regional or area committees**. These committees control the running of the branches in their area and occasionally negotiate local agreements with firms. The larger unions have **full time paid officers**, such as district organizers, who deal with immediate problems and negotiate settlements.

The branches also elect delegates to represent them at the annual conference. The **conference** decides union policy. It also elects the **National Executive** which dominates union affairs throughout the year. For instance, it negotiates national minimum wages with the employer's federation. Usually, it alone has the authority to call the union out on strike. The **General Secretary** often acts as leader of the National Executive. He is elected by a ballot of members and responsible for daily affairs of the union.

Shop stewards

They are **elected** (in practice half are elected unopposed) by the men with whom they work on the 'shop' floor (on average forty people). Shop stewards speak and **negotiate** on behalf of the men. It is their responsibility to bring worker **grievances** to the notice of management. They often operate separately from the official union structure. The main duties of shop stewards are distributing union information and recruiting new members. They used to collect subscriptions but now employers collect from over three quarters of workers and charge the union up to 5% of the amount for the service.

In large factories, the shop stewards may be given an **office**, a telephone and time off work to carry out their duties. They usually form themselves into a **shop stewards committee**, composed of shop stewards from the different unions operating in the factory. The elected leader of this committee is known as the **Convenor**. He acts as the spokesman for the workers in discussions with management.

The **influence of shop stewards has increased** because:

(a) More **wage** agreements are now made at **plant** and **company level** rather than industry-wide. This involves the shop stewards as negotiators more than full time trade union officials.

(b) Management recognize and accept shop stewards much more than in the past, because 95% of their work is useful and non-controversial. For instance, in some large firms, a shop steward may have secretarial help provided by the employer.

(c) Full time shop stewards outnumber union officials. There were 3700 full time and over 300 000 part-time shop stewards in 1983.

2 Methods

(a) Bargaining

Trade union activity centres around bargaining with employers, to improve the wages and conditions of the employees. Negotiations take place at national and local levels. The procedure undertaken is usually a union claim followed by a lower management offer leading to negotiation. Occasionally industrial action is taken and only rarely is the Advisory, Conciliation and Arbitration Service (ACAS) involved. (See later).

(i) **National negotiations** involve groups of **unions** in an industry and the corresponding **employer's federation**. They often have voluntary agreed procedures for solving disputes. They discuss and decide **wage rates**, overtime rates, the length of the working week, training initiatives and so on. These then apply throughout the **whole industry**. In some industries, minimum wage rates are determined by wages councils *e.g.* catering, where the unions are weak.

(ii) **Local negotiations** are less formal and are carried out by **shop stewards** and individual employers. These negotiations may be in addition to the national agreements made, or instead of them. If they are in addition, the shop stewards may succeed in getting wage rates above the nationally agreed rate. Usually the local workplace agreements cover factors such as bonus payments, closed shop, working conditions, manning of machinery and holiday periods.

'Free collective bargaining' is a slogan which trade unionists use. They want the right to **negotiate without the interference of the government** and without the legal penalties being placed on them for industrial action. Thus the trade union movement is opposed to statutory incomes policy and most employment legislation which attempts to control them.

ACAS occasionally intervenes in industrial disputes. It was set up in 1975 to provide advice and solve complicated issues, through conducting its own inquiries and recommending a course of action. It does a lot of successful, unpublicised negotiating in which it brings disagreeing unions and management into acceptable solutions.

(b) Industrial action: 'WOBS'

The most common types are:

(i) **Working to rule** The workers stick to the official rules and procedures which in theory determine working practices and safety. Normally these complicated rules may be bypassed or ignored by both employees and employers in the interests of speed and efficiency. The tactic of working to rule is often used by the railway unions in their disputes with BR Board, because it cripples the service by the delays caused.

(ii) **Overtime ban** In jobs where regular overtime is worked by many employees who are low paid, a ban on overtime working may lower production and prove effective *e.g.* bus drivers.

(iii) **Blacking** Trade unions occasionally refuse to handle (or 'black') certain goods. This is often either for political reasons *e.g.* dislike of a foreign government so its products are not handled, or to show sympathy towards another trade union *e.g.* steel workers may refuse to handle coal when NUM are on strike.

(iv) **Strikes** The refusal to work may be **'official'** or **'unofficial'**. Official strikes are backed by the union whereas unofficial ones are not. Official strikes tend to last longer and occur in larger organizations than **unofficial strikes**, which are usually **small-scale, brief, unpredictable** and confined to **one factory**.

Strikes have been termed 'the English disease' which is unfair as our strike record is 'fair to middling' among the major industrialized nations. The working days lost per employee 1968–77 in Britain was .45 compared with .02 in West Germany and 1.45 in Italy. However, this figure of about ½ day lost per employee is much worse than for the period 1961 to 69. In contrast we lose 13 days per employee in absence through sickness. Strikes are not more frequent now and do not involve more employees **but** they tend to last longer.

Likelihood of strikes

1 Major industries are **coal, cars** and **docks**. They account for 40% of days lost but only 6% of all employees work in them.

2 Small firms are less likely to have strikes than large firms.

3 More strikes occur in **manual** industries and few where there is abundant female labour. White collar workers are more likely to ban overtime and work to rule.

4 Main cause is **pay** – 60%; 16% demarcation; 16% redundancies.

Effects of strikes

1 On the firm involved
(a) Loss of production thus average costs raised.
(b) Loss of revenue thus extra cost of borrowing.
(c) Potential loss of market to rivals, particularly foreign.
(d) Diminished reputation with customers.
(e) Worse industrial relations in future.
(f) Extra security/warehousing needed, raising costs, again!

2 On employees (strikers)
(a) Loss of earnings:
but (i) Strike pay, depending on union funds (*e.g.* TGWU = £9 a week)
 (ii) Social Security, depending on family size (*e.g.* married man with two children will receive £28 a week from the State, who 'deems' that he will receive £16 a week strike pay also. (Whether he receives it or not!). This 'deeming rule' is a bone of contention with trade unionists.
(iii) Tax rebates.
(b) Part-time jobs and moonlighting may be undertaken.
(c) Loss of 'working habit' if unemployed for a significant period of time. In the long run, this means lower productivity when the striker returns to work.

3 On other firms

A strike in one firm may well affect others, in the same or associated industries. The car industry, because it is an assembly industry, can influence production and employment through the engineering industry, *e.g.* BL strikes lead to lay-offs in the components industry because half of the parts for BL cars come from outside. There are over 7000 suppliers including:

Dunlop	wheels and tyres
BSC	sheet steel
Lucas	battery
Triplex	windscreen
Ferodo	brake linings
GKN	drive shafts

Since 1982 legislation, a trade union involved in a dispute can lawfully call on its members to:

1 **Picket peacefully** at their own place of work.

2 Take **industrial action** only over disputes **'wholly** or **mainly'** about wages and conditions.

3 Take industrial action only at **other firms** if they are direct customers or suppliers of the firm involved in the dispute.

13.9 Government and industrial relations

The government may be **directly involved** in negotiations and disputes:

1 Where it is the **employer**, *e.g.* civil servants, 1981 strike

2 Where it **provides funds** for the employer *e.g.* nationalized industries depend on government for finance. So the government may exert pressure on employers to hold wage costs down, *e.g.* 1980 steel strike.

3 Where it intervenes as a **last resort** *e.g.* Prime Minister invites the two conflicting groups to Downing Street for beer and sandwiches and tries to persuade them to compromise 'in the national interest'. If this fails, the government may 'strike-break' by sending troops in *e.g.* Glasgow dustmen in 1980.

The government may be **indirectly involved** in industrial relations. Many of its fiscal and monetary **policies** influence employment in some way. More blatantly the government may affect the framework of industrial relations by its **legislation**. This has been increasingly the case **since 1970**.

Brief history of government – trade union relationships

1945 to 1969 consultation and agreement between trade unions and successive Labour and Conservative governments.

1969 to 1974 confrontation – Labour (unsuccessfully in 1969) and Conservatives 1971, attempted to use the law to reform trade unions. The 1971 Industrial Relations Act created a Court which could try trade unionists but the employers where reluctant to use it. The Conservative government conflicts with the miners over incomes policy 1972 and 1974 intensified matters and partly contributed to the Government's loss of office in 1974.

1974 to 1978 co-operation – the elected Labour government made a 'social contract' with the trade union movement. In return for wage restraint and incomes policy co-operation, the Labour government repealed the 1971 Act, introduced 1975 Employment Protection Act and implemented several social reforms.

1975 Employment Protection Act. This set up **ACAS** to provide industrial relations advice, conduct inquiries and decide union recognition claims. It made trade union **recognition** by employers easier to obtain and demanded greater disclosure of information by employers. It gave employees better **terms of employment** such as longer notice of dismissal and greater consultation over redundancy and unfair dismissal.

1978 to 1983 great hostility. In 1978 the trade union movement refused to co-operate with Labour government pay policy and called several damaging strikes which became known as the 'Winter of discontent'. In 1979 the Conservatives were elected to power with a mandate to curb trade union power. They pledged to introduce legislation, which the trade unions refused to discuss.

1980 Employment Act

1 Limited picketing to the place of work. Thus **secondary picketing** by workers other than those involved in the dispute became illegal.

2 Provided State money for **secret ballots** by trade unions over industrial action (*i.e.* strikes).

3 Enabled the Secretary of State to publish **codes of practice**, particularly on the closed shop and picketing.

1982 Employment Act

1 Limited **pickets to six** at each entrance to a place of work.

2 Allowed the introduction of **closed shop** (all workers having to belong to a trade union) if **80%** of the workers are in favour. It provided also for regular reviews of closed shop by secret ballot.

3 Made **trade unions liable for damages** if they undertook action to enforce a closed shop.

4 Gave an **individual** the **right** to seek damages if dismissed for refusal to join a closed shop on grounds of conscience or personal conviction.

1984 Trade Union Act This law makes trade unions hold a **ballot** of members every 10 years to see if they are in favour of the **political levy** to the Labour Party. They also become liable for **damages** if they go on strike without first holding a **national ballot**.

It is clear that the **attitude** of the government to the trade unions depends upon which **political party** is the government. Generally, the **Labour** Party is **pro-trade union** for several reasons. There is a long history of mutual help between the Labour movement and trade unions. The Labour Party is financed (90%) by trade unionists' subscriptions and its leaders are chosen through a system (electoral college) which gives the trade unions a 40% say. Above all, they share similar political views of more State planning, less uneven wealth distribution and high suspicion of capitalism.

The **Conservative** Party is more **anti-trade union**. It dislikes its monopoly power in bargaining and its ability to disrupt the economy. In addition, the Conservatives support freedom of the individual which is diminished through the closed shop and threatened by mass picketing. However, the Conservatives are unlikely to outlaw the **closed shop** because some managements prefer it as it gives greater order to bargaining. Closed shops cover over five million workers and occur principally in the public sector *e.g.* gas, electricity, water.

13.10 TUC and CBI

The Trades Union Congress (TUC) and the Confederation of British Industry (CBI) speak on behalf of the employees and employers respectively. They are often consulted by the government on economic matters.

TUC

It is a permanent organization set up in 1868 and now based at Congress House in London, consisting of trade unions representing over **ten million** trade unionists. There were 102 trade unions **affiliated** to TUC in 1983 and this included the major unions.

The trade unions send delegates to attend the **Annual Congress**. At this conference they formulate **policy** on a wide range of issues such as the economy, social policy, education, health and international affairs. The delegates also **elect** the **General Council**, which runs the TUC between conferences. Since 1983, this body has contained **52** members elected in three sections – large unions (at least 100 000 workers with each of 16 largest unions getting between 1 and 5 members according to its size), small unions (11 members in total from 81 unions) and 6 women members (elected by the whole congress). The voting is by **'block' voting**, which means that all a union's votes are given to the candidate/issue which the trade union delegation supports. For instance, a delegation may split 13 to 12 in favour of 'X' and against 'Y', but all its 25 000 votes go to 'X' (rather than 13 000 to 'X', 12 000 to 'Y').

The TUC may **participate** in economic decision-making. This is particularly likely if a Labour party is in power. It will make proposals to any government and **prepare policies**/recommendations on all legislation that may affect its members. In addition, the TUC is represented on many important bodies, such as National Economic Development Council, and in Parliament through its sponsored MPs and peers. Its spokesman is usually its **General Secretary** who represents the General Council.

The General Council also adjudicates between unions. In 1983 it threatened the print union SOGAT '82 with **suspension** unless it handed back 800 recently recruited Fleet Street workers to the electricians union. It rarely has to expel a member union. However, it often investigates and reprimands, but it cannot control its member unions. For instance, if a trade union refuses to negotiate, when the TUC advises, there is **nothing** the TUC can do, except continue to talk and persuade.

CBI

This body represents **employers** and was created in 1965 from three smaller organizations. The firms belonging to the CBI contain about half of Britain's workers. It includes large and small firms and this occasionally creates disunity.

It has a less obvious political role than the TUC. Before **1974** it was hardly **consulted** at all by the government. However, in 1975 it bargained with the Labour government over its Employment Protection Act and gained concessions on Corporation Tax and planning agreements. It tends to take a less partisan stance than the TUC. For instance between 1980 and 1981 it was very **critical** of the Conservatives' economic policy because of its effect on company profits and interest rates.

13.11 Links with other topics

Demand		**Wages**		**Government**
Supply	⟶	**Trade unions**	⟵	**policy**

14 National income and standard of living

14.1 The circular flow of income

In all economies using money, there are flows of income between people. These people can be represented as groups in a **simple model**. (Figure 14.1). In this model, **producers** pay an income to

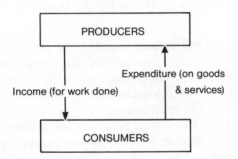

Fig. 14.1 Simple flow of income

workers (who become consumers) for their production. The workers as **consumers** spend their income (expenditure) on the goods which the producers sell. This simple model assumes:

1 No trade with the outside world.
2 No saving, as all income is spent.
3 All the ouput is sold.

The amount of economic activity in a community can be measured by examining the flows of income, expenditure and output in an economy. **In theory national income=national expenditure=national output** because each is measuring the same thing but in different ways. For instance if an economy produces one bag of logs and one loaf of bread then:

National income = **money paid to the factors** that made the logs and bread.
National expenditure = **money spent** on logs and bread.
National output = **money value** of logs and bread **produced**.
The flow of income is said to be **'circular'** because:

1 the starting point is impossible to find in the model, and
2 one person's expenditure becomes another person's income.

A more complicated circular flow model is illustrated in Figure 14.2. This model distinguishes different types of spending and introduces the concepts:

Investment – money spent on capital formation. The main capital items are provided by **producers** and they include factories, offices and shops. The **government** invests in **social capital** such as schools and hospitals, whilst **household** consumers buy houses and other capital assets, *e.g.* video recorders.
Consumption – money spent on goods and services by consumers and by national and local government. In the national income accounts these two groups are treated separately.

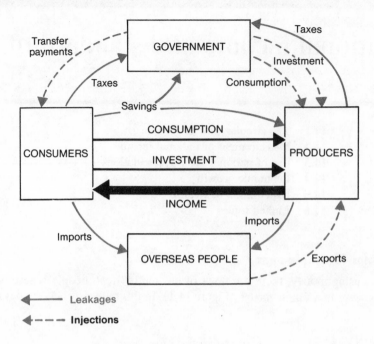

Fig. 14.2 Detailed flow of expenditure

Leakages–the **spending** which is **not returned directly** to the **producers**. Represented by the solid arrows in Figure 14.2, showing taxes, savings and spending on imported goods and services.
Injections–spending by other than producers and consumers. Thus **government expenditure** on investment, consumption and transfer payments and the income from **exports**, add to the circular flow and raise national income. The injections are represented by broken arrows in Figure 14.2.
Overseas sector–payments made to overseas producers and the income received from overseas consumers both affect the flow of income. If export earnings exceed import spending then there is a net inflow of income–an injection into the circular flow.

14.2 Measurement of national income

The national income of a country is the **total value** of the **goods** and **services** produced by a country's **resources** over a given period of time, normally **one year**.

National income is precisely measured by the government in three ways:

1 Expenditure method

This calculation adds together the **spending on consumption and investment** by consumers and the government. It adds on foreign spending on our exports and deducts our spending on imports. This adjustment gives the net **inflow or outflow of income from British trade**. Stocks of unsold goods and partially completed products need to be included because they show expenditure undertaken too.

There are two calculation **problems** which need consideration: **(a) transfer payments**–these are payments such as **pensions** made by the government to people when production has not been given in return. They provide incomes for people who can thus undertake spending. However, as they are a transfer from taxpayer to government to beneficiary, they have to be **deleted** from government spending. **(b) market prices**–the data on spending is collected from the prices paid by consumers. However, market prices are distorted by taxes, such as **VAT**, and subsidies. Thus from gross domestic spending **taxes** need to be **deducted** (as they artificially raise the value of the goods bought) and subsidies added. This then gives the value of production at factor cost.

The expenditure method is useful for detecting changing trends in consumption and investment. It may also show the effects of government policies such as tax raising and reduced public expenditure.

2 Income method

This method adds up to the income received by the **owners of resources**. The share of income from employment is usually about 70% of the total, and includes wages and salaries. Rent includes income from leased property and other assets. The profits of the nationalized industries and other government agencies are kept distinct from those of companies in the private sector.

The imputed consumption of non-trading capital is a small adjustment made for the free use of assets by people for themselves. However, if they let others use them they might charge and thereby earn an income *e.g.* garaging a company car on your own premises. The three main problems with the income method are:

(a) Stock appreciation is an important **adjustment**. With inflation the stocks of goods may increase in value, without anyone touching them. *e.g.* Dunlop increases its tyre prices, thus making unsold tyres more valuable than previously. Thus stock appreciation is deducted from the income because it boosts company profits artificially.

(b) Residual error The main source of information for the income method is the Inland Revenue. However, they only know about what people declare as their income. It has been calculated that £15 billion per annum is earned in the **'black economy'** (see Unit 2.1). Thus, in order for gross domestic product at factor cost to be **equal** by all methods, a balancing figure called residual error is included in the table.

(c) Transfer payments – they are left out of the calculations (as explained in the Expenditure Method).

3 Output method

This method shows the contribution to Gross Domestic Product of the **different sectors of the economy**, as the values added by each industry are summed. Thus comparison with earlier years will reveal the expanding and declining sectors. As shown in Unit 5.2 and Figure 5.2 manufacturing industry in Britain has declined and the service industries have expanded.

There are four main **problems** with this method:

(a) Double counting We take the **value added** by each firm/industry in the calculations rather than the output of each. If we do not, double counting will occur. For instance, if a loaf of sliced bread retails for 40p that is the value of its production to national income; but if we add manufacturers sale price (say 30p) and retailers (say 40p) we get 70p. The value added system of calculation thus gives 30p by manufacturer and 10p by retailer (40p sale price − 30p purchase price = 10p value added) making a total of 40p. This avoids counting output more than once.

(b) Residual error – as explained in income method.

(c) Adjustment for financial services It is impossible to allocate the amount of certain financial services (*e.g.* accountant's fees) at each stage of output in the production process. Thus, this adjustment is made when the total output value of the financial services sector is ascertained.

(d) Valuation of public services As many services, such as defence and education are provided free for the nation it is very difficult to assess accurately the value added and the benefit gained.

4 Income, output and expenditure

The three methods operate differently up to the calculation of **gross domestic product at factor cost**. This shows the total value of goods and services produced **within Britain**. However, beyond that point the calculations are the same, as shown in Figure 14.3.

Expenditure method	billions		Income method
Consumer expenditure	167.1	155.1	Income from employment
Govt. consumption	60.1	19.8	Income from self-employment
Gross domestic fixed capital formation	42.2	33.3	Gross company profits
Increase in stocks	− 1.2	9.1	Gross public corporation surplus
Total domestic expenditure	268.2		⎧ Rent
Exports	+ 73.1	18.8	⎨ Imputed cons of non-
Imports	− 67.1		⎩ trading capital
Gross domestic product at market prices	274.2	0	Residual error
Taxes (net of subsidies)	− 41.7	3.6	Stock appreciation
Gross domestic product at factor cost	232.5	232.5	
Net property income from abroad	+ 1.6		
Gross national product	234.1		
less capital consumption	− 33.0		
National income	201.1		

Fig. 14.3 National income calculation by expenditure and income methods 1982

Gross National Product

This gives the total value produced by all **British owned resources**, both at home and abroad. Thus to GDP at factor cost, we need to **add net property income from abroad**. This total is composed of income earned abroad by British residents less corresponding payments out to foreigners. It is always a positive figure for Britain.

National income

During the year in the course of production, the nation's **capital assets** will be used, thereby wearing them down and lowering their value *e.g.* machines depreciate in value with use. The usage of these assets is known as **capital consumption** and it needs deducting from GNP.

The gross capital formation in Figure 14.3 represents total investment and thus includes capital consumption, which is the amount of capital undertaken to maintain our existing capital stock. Thus the difference between gross capital formation (£42.2b) and capital consumption (£33b) is the net (new) investment during the year.

14.3 The use of national income calculations

The final figure for National Income is really only an **estimate**. Much of the calculating is based on approximations and samples, whilst some activities are under-recorded.

Furthermore, it does not allow for inflation. An increase in national income may occur through higher prices without an increase in production. National income may increase by 10% but if prices rise by 10% then the nation is no better off. Thus, a nation needs to increase its national income in **real terms**.

Real disposable GDP per head rose by 2½% between 1972 and 1982. However, this average masks ups and downs *i.e.* 5% rise from 1978 to 80 but 2% fall from 1981 to 82.

1 Government information

The data collected can enable the government to judge the effectiveness of its previous policies *e.g.* effect of tax changes on consumption. The trends can be used to identify new problems and plan new initiatives.

2 Assessing changes in standard of living within Britain

The standard of living is a relative concept. It shows whether people are **'better off'** when compared, either with other people, or with other periods of time. National income statistics are used as a basis for such comparisons. However, they are subject to many **qualifications**.

Limitations – remembered by 'TRIP TIPS'

(a) Tax An increase in the **burden** of taxation and national insurance over time means that a higher national income per head is needed to maintain the same standard of living. For instance, increased income tax when national income is constant means lower disposable income. Conversely, lower taxes for everyone may make people better off without increases of income.

(b) Regional differences The cost of living may vary within a country. For instance it is much more expensive to live in **London** than elsewhere in Britain particularly because of the cost of housing. Similarly, in 1983 average earnings in the South (man £169) were higher than in the North (£148).

(c) Inflation As mentioned above, adjustment has to be made for **price changes**. For instance, between 1953 and 81 the average weekly wage rose from £8 to £114 per week but a family car increased in price from £750 to £5000. Thus we compare using **index numbers**.

(d) Population An increase in total national income may be achieved because the population rises, through (say) immigration. Thus we need to look at **output per head** unless a false comparison is being made. As Britain's population has now stabilized, this point is becoming less important.

(e) Technical changes The invention of labour-saving devices, improved machinery and better entertainment facilities may enhance the living standards of producers and consumers by making their jobs easier. As we value the output rather than the method of its creation, technical changes may give people an easier, less stressful working life and more enjoyable leisure time. A reduction in the **working week** and an unchanged national income represent an improvement in the standard of living.

However, although mass production techniques may raise the quantity of goods available, the **quality** may fall *e.g.* 'plastic' bread and weak beer!

(f) Income distribution An increase in national income per head does not mean all people are better off. A few may be considerably better off and most might be a little worse off. For example Government tax changes 1979–80, which reduced the high rates of tax on very high earners and increased expenditure (VAT) tax for all, widened the post-tax differentials in Britain.

(g) Personal differences People's needs are different. For instance, pensioners spend a much higher proportion of their income on food and housing compared with well-off households. Thus, the income levels needed to sustain a decent standard of living vary between groups in the community and they change over the years.

(h) State services If the government reduces the free or subsidized services which it provides to the community then the population will be worse off. Such services have been termed the **'social wage'** because the people receive them free without having to pay for them. Thus, changes over the years in State spending and provision will affect living standards.

3 Making international comparisons of living standards

It is useful to make comparisons with other countries because it shows a nation's **economic development**. International **league tables** are devised on the basis of national income per head. In 1982 Britain stood nineteenth with £4300 GNP per head. The table was headed by Kuwait (£11 000) with USA eighth (£6200) and USSR twenty-fourth (£2700).

There are many **problems** of such comparisons. They can be remembered by **'SPICE PAWS'**

(a) Spending habits These differ between nations because of their needs. For example, cold **climate** countries need to spend more on heating than warm nations and thus require a higher national income to maintain the same standard of living.

(b) Prices As rates of inflation differ between countries then adjustments should be made for relative prices. For instance, the **cost of living** in Britain is still less than in Western Europe and America so the national income differential becomes less in **real** terms.

(c) Income distribution The average figures calculated give no idea of the range and distribution of income. For instance, Kuwait has the highest **average** national income but 95% of the population receive less than what would be considered as low wages in Britain. The wealth is concentrated in the hands of a few wealthy sheiks.

(d) Composition of output. A modern society may use many resources for military purposes and these contribute little to the welfare of the people. It could be argued that by changing the pattern of output from **defence** to health and education, the standard of living could be improved without national income changing. Thus a pacifist nation probably can sustain a similar standard of living to a militarist one with a lower level of national income.

(e) Exchange rates National incomes are measured in domestic currencies and then **converted, usually into dollars**. However, because exchange rates are **volatile** and often subject to irrational forces (*e.g.* election jitters), the process of conversion and the timing of the conversion can significantly affect the result. For instance if the dollar moves strongly against the £ but not against other currencies, then the national income of Britain as measured in dollars, appears much worse in comparison.

(f) Political factors Some **intangible** and unmeasurable factors may be important in people's lives *e.g.* **freedom of speech** religion and association. In some nations no political opposition is allowed and the rule of law is not maintained, thereby diminishing the life of the people *e.g.* USSR, S. Africa, etc.

(g) Accuracy The data collected can vary in its quantity and quality. The integrity of the officials and the resources devoted to collection will determine the accuracy of the estimates. Some nations, *e.g.* China, are most reluctant to publish basic economic information. The figures published by others *e.g.* USSR may be doctored for political reasons.

(h) Wealth Although income mainly determines living standards, wealth accumulated in the past can be influential. A nation with a stock of roads, hospitals, schools (**social capital**) and houses, is much better off than a developing nation that needs to develop such assets. The developing nation has to forego consumption (which effectively determines current living standards) in order to invest in capital.

The average net wealth (assets–debts) in Britain in 1982 was £33 000. Each household averaged £38 000 of assets, mainly in the form of financial assets, housing and consumer durables, compared with £5000 of liabilities. Wealth, as well as income, determines the ability to buy **consumer durables**. Britain is well endowed with telephones (507 per 1000 people in 1981), television sets (404 per 1000 people) and computers (most per head in the world).

(i) Social indicators. The quality of life has become an important issue, bearing on the standard of living. Increases in **pollution**, violence, **crime**, heart disease and **pornography** are seen as diminishing the standard of living. Conversely, falls in infant mortality, shorter hospital waiting lists, less emission of lead and fewer patients per doctor all indirectly make us better off. The extent of these factors **varies widely** between nations, again complicating international comparisons. For instance,

114 *National income and standard of living*

Japan's national income has exceeded Britain's but few would argue that its standard of living is better because of its pollution and low level of State provision of services. Figure 14.4 shows certain key indicators which reveal differences between selected economies.

Selected indicators of living standards	USA	West Germany	Britain	USSR	Saudi Arabia	India
Cars per 1000 people (1982)	550	385	286	36	125	1
Telephones per 1000 people (1981)	789	488	507	89	25	4
Higher education % of 20–24 age group (1980)	55	26	20	21	7	9
Divorce – % of marriages ending in divorce (1980)	50	9	36	33	0	1
TV sets per 1000 people (1980)	624	337	404	303	251	36
Doctors per 100 000 people (1980)	192	222	154	357	61	27
Heart diseases – deaths per 100 000 (1980)	435	584	579	500	320	175
Defence expenditure – % of GDP (1980)	4.9	2.7	4.6	13.0	0.1	2.8

Fig. 14.4 Selected economic, social and political indicators of living standards in various countries

4 Calculating economic growth

See 14.4

14.4 Economic growth

1 Measurement

Economic growth is the **% increase in total output of the economy at constant prices**. Such increases mean that real incomes have improved and so probably have living standards. Thus the raising of the standard of living is closely tied to economic growth.

However, the measurement of growth in % terms creates **complications**. Britain's average 2% growth rate of the 1970's does not mean that we are worse off than Spain whose economy grew by 6%. The GNP per head increase in Britain was £200 per year whilst Spain's was just £40. This was because Britain has a **larger base** (starting point) from which the % was calculated. Clearly, a nation with a strong, developed base has less chance of a high **percentage** improvement but more likelihood of a large **absolute** increase.

2 Arguments for – the word 'PENS' may help you to remember:

(a) Poverty – increases in national income can lead to reduction of poverty in society. There is less resistance to the sacrifice of higher taxes paid by high wage earners which may be needed to relieve the poverty.

(b) Efficiency growth – encourages efficiency and best use of resources.

(c) National prestige

(d) Standard of living Growth is necessary to maintain/improve living standards.

3 Arguments against – 'SWAP'

(a) Social costs, such as congestion, noise, crime, pollution, and the loss of beautiful countryside, may increase in the pursuit of economic goals. These costs often have to be paid for by the State.

(b) Waste disposal, particularly nuclear, becomes more difficult and **dangerous**.

(c) Attitudes may become **carefree and complacent** and develop with growth because people have high standards and little incentive for improvement *e.g.* **'throw away' lifestyle**; it is also claimed that much modern employment is depersonalized because of automation. These attitudes, and the increased freedom resulting from higher living standards, may cause more **selfishness** and less trust and co-operation in society.

(d) Private affluence and **public squalor**. If the benefits of economic growth go to a small sector of society then these groups may become very wealthy. Alternatively, the rest of the community will be relatively badly off. The strength of this argument rests on the distribution of income and wealth in a nation and the attitude of the government.

4 Means of growth

Economics need to make use of **idle resources** in order to grow. Once these have been utilized, an economy can only grow through **increased productivity** *i.e.* greater output per person.

This can be achieved by:

(a) Increased quantity of investment It usually means diverting resources from consumption to investment. This may be difficult to manage because it means giving up increases in living standards at the present in order to gain greater increases in the future. It may be a problem of political will.

(b) Higher **quality of investment** More productive and effective capital construction aids growth. Britain's investment in the public sector, particularly in defence rather than communications (which benefit **all** firms in the country), has been criticized because the goods produced are not marketable.

(c) Technological progress Technology can be improved by research and development leading to more efficient machinery and new inventions *e.g.* robots and computers. Each year General Motors in America spends more on research than the whole of India does! The main criticism of Britain in this sphere has been the failure to market inventions, although Sinclair's success with computer technology is a notable exception.

(d) Quality of labour A general improvement in health and better training and education both serve to make labour more productive.

(e) Quantity of labour The size of the working population ultimately limits growth. For this reason many under-populated countries (*e.g.* Australia) and rapidly expanding nations (*e.g.* West Germany – attracting 1½ million migrant workers) encourage immigration (Unit 12).

(f) Incentives Labour output per head can be raised by various inducements *e.g.* bonuses, profit-sharing. These tend to be short-lived rather than fundamental changes in the economy.

5 Britain's growth

Britain's relatively poor post-war growth performance has been analyzed and several causes suggested:

(a) Frequent **changes of government policy** These have disrupted business planning and deterred investment.

(b) Lack of finance British banks have not ventured enough risk capital into British manufacturing. They have preferred to lend to property companies and speculators rather than more productive investors.

(c) Low productivity Caused by inadequate training, a lack of flexibility in working practices, trade union selfishness, and a fragmented workforce all at **shop floor** level. In addition, **middle management** is often underused and not sufficiently rewarded. At **senior management** level, the dominance of the class system, unwise investment and incompetence have been variously quoted as problems which create poor productivity. See Figure 14.5.

| Year | Output per person-hour in manufacturing | | | | |
	UK	USA	Japan	W. Germany	Italy
1973	101	96	102	94	102
1975	100	100	100	100	100
1977	106	108	115	110	108
1979	109	112	132	118	122
1982	117	122	137	121	132

Fig. 14.5 Productivity performance in selected economies

(d) Late entry into EEC meant that Britain did not get toeholds in the European market when its competitors did. It has been calculated that Britain's entry raised the rate of economic growth by 0.3% per annum, via the stimulus to exports. Over the period 1972 to 78 North Sea oil contributed 0.5% to GDP growth.

(e) Low level of investment. The % of income which is invested in Britain is much lower than our industrial competitors. The high interest rates and the high exchange rate, particularly 1979 to 82, have hit recent investment, particularly in manufacturing. UK fixed investment is 15% of GDP (1980 to 83 average) whereas in 1974 it was 20%. The decline has occurred most in steel, chemicals and mechanical engineering. In 1980, 69% of the investment was done by the private sector and 31% by the public sector (of which nationalized industries accounted for 17%).

However, the OECD estimated Britain's growth in 1983 (and predicted growth in 1984) at 2½%, which was still sluggish compared with most of our industrial competitors. It was slightly above the OECD average of 2¼% in 1983 and below the OECD average of 3½% in 1984. Britain's change in real GNP seems to fluctuate less than most other nations, meaning that we **suffer less in slumps** but **gain less in booms**.

14.5 Distribution of wealth

A distinction must be made between income and wealth:

Income is a **flow** of money – usually received on a **regular** basis (Unit 13)

Wealth is a **stock** of assets – these are accumulated over a period of time, either from saving or inheritance. A person's wealth is measured at one point of time. It includes assets which have a **monetary value**.

The general distribution of wealth in Britain is rather more even than in countries such as France and the USA. This is because there are few excessively high top incomes. However, in Britain it is very difficult to 'break into' the top groups because of:

1 **The large council housing system**. In Britain land is the basis of the top people's wealth and 40% of population do not live in their own property. The Conservative Party is encouraging people to buy their own council houses, often at much less than their market price.

2 **The progressive income tax system**. As incomes rise above the poverty line, the Government takes an increasing proportion in taxation. This prevents the build-up of fortunes out of earned income and makes for relative income equality.

Despite these two constraints, the percentage share of total personal wealth held by the most wealthy 1% of the population has declined from 61% in 1923 to 23% in 1980.

Britain does not have a wealth tax, which is an **annual** tax on the value of personal wealth above a certain threshold level. France and Sweden have such taxes. However, Britain has **capital transfer tax**, which acts as a tax on **inheritance**. For instance when a person dies and leaves more than £64 000 worth of assets, the government takes a percentage as a death duty. The scale is progressive as the amount left increases. However, the many exceptions allowed and the current law on trusts and covenants means that the tax take is low and its effectiveness in redistributing wealth is limited. Thus wealth in Britain is largely determined by inheritance as large stocks of assets are handed down through rich families.

Poverty

The opposite of wealth is **poverty**. The definition of poverty is not clear-cut because the **poverty line** changes through the years with movements in earnings, prices and social behaviour. For instance, in 1955 a television set was considered to be a luxury, but in 1983 51% of the population regarded it as a necessity!

Poverty is measured by using the **supplementary benefit level** which averages two-thirds of the national average wage. The benefits paid vary with **family circumstances** but are supposed to be sufficient to allow people to 'keep themselves reasonably fed, and well enough dressed to maintain their self-respect and to attend interviews for jobs with confidence.'

The line below which people are considered to be poor, is usually drawn at **120%** of supplementary benefit level. Thus if a single parent with one child receives £50 per week then the amount needed for them to be out of poverty would be £60 (*i.e.* 120% of £50).

1983 Market and Opinion Research International (MORI) Survey defined poverty in terms of the **necessities needed for a decent life**. The items which most people deemed to be essential were heating for living areas (3.23m families without), indoor lavatory, damp-free home (4.3m without), bath not shared with other families (1.1m without), money for public transport, three meals a day for children (7.0m without).

On this basis, the poor in Britain are concentrated within five vulnerable groups:

1 Single-parent families (900 000)
2 Unemployed (3m)   4½m elderly
3 Elderly   3m adults
4 Disabled and sick   2½m children
5 Low paid

14.6 Links with other topics

Savings and investment ⟶ National income Standard of living ⟵ Wages Trade unions

15 Public finance

15.1 Public expenditure

This term refers to **government spending**, which has become a much larger proportion of national income in recent years. (See Figure 15.1.) Public finance refers to the revenue raised to pay for this expenditure. In 1969 central government revenue exceeded expenditure leaving a budget surplus. However, in every year since, expenditure has exceeded revenue, causing a **budget deficit**. In 1979 the Conservative Government came to power committed to reducing the budget deficit and lowering the government spending as a % of GDP. As yet (1984) it has been unsuccessful. The term **fiscal policy** is used to describe changes in taxation and public expenditure.

	Central government			
Year	Expenditure £ billion	as % of GDP	Taxation £ billion	as % of GDP
1963–64	11	36	9	30
1973–74	32	43	26	36
1982–83	132	47	108	39

Fig. 15.1 Public expenditure, taxation, and GDP percentages

Category	As % of total spending	
	1972–73	1982–83
Social security	20	29
Defence	12	13
Education, science, arts	13	12
Health and personal services	10	12
Industry and employment	8	5
Scotland	6	5
Housing	6	2
Transport	4	4
Agriculture, fishing, forestry	2	2
Other expenditure	19	16

Fig. 15.2 Public expenditure by category

Figure 15.2 shows the main areas of public spending. The major change which has occurred in the last decade is the large increase in the proportion of public money spent on **Social Security**. This has been a direct result of Britain's ageing population, which partly explains the increase in the health and personal services category. A significant fall is in the housing category and this reflects the stable population and the increase in owner-occupation. More money is spent on all of the categories now, than in 1973 to 74, reflecting **inflation**.

Reasons for public expenditure – 'PERM'

1 Public goods They are defined as 'those goods/services which will not and cannot (in reality) be provided by the free market'. Examples are defence, law and order, roads and street lighting. The main reason why the free market does not provide these goods is that it is **impossible to exclude** non-payers from benefiting from the provision of these goods and services. For instance, if you do not purchase an entrance ticket to the cinema then you are prevented from seeing the film being shown. However, if you refuse to purchase the services of the **armed forces** it would be impossible to defend your neighbour, who has paid, without defending you at the same time. For this reason, if public goods are provided at all it must be by the government through taxation.

In the nineteenth century most public expenditure was on public goods, particularly defence, but nowadays it is a small share of the total. However, since 1979 (and the Conservative Government) defence spending has increased its share of the total which had fallen to 11% (in 1978–79).

2 Economic efficiency Governments often feel the need to intervene in the economy either to increase efficiency or to reduce the production of economic 'bads' *e.g.* pollution, whose costs are paid for by society, rather than privately by those responsible.

In order to raise efficiency, a **new motorway** might be constructed which will probably lower the transport costs for firms using it. Other similar policies such as regional grants and youth training schemes also have **social aims**, *i.e.* reducing unemployment. The extent of government intervention aimed at increasing economic efficiency depends on political values. A socialist (Labour) would argue that **nationalization** leads to a better use of resources. In contrast capitalists (Conservative) dispute this view and thus privatize parts of the public sector.

3 Relief of poverty Income is provided for many **disadvantaged** groups in society, so that they are not dependent on charity *e.g.* widows, pensioners, students, unemployed etc. They receive **benefits** from the State. Supplementary benefit is designed to ensure a minimum standard of living for those who do not have full-time jobs. It covers pensioners, single parents working part-time and the disabled, as well as the unemployed. The rate for a married couple is currently (Nov. 1984) £45.55 per week.

Not all of the available benefits are taken up by those who are eligible for them. For instance only 74% of those who qualify for supplementary benefit actually claim it. Many benefits have a lower **take-up rate** than this *e.g.* free school meals 15%. These benefits are termed **'transfer incomes'** because public funds taken from taxpayers are given to the needy.

4 Merit goods They are defined as 'those goods considered to be so important that they are provided by the State at **zero** (or subsidized) **cost**'. The two most important examples in Britain are **education** and **national health**. These services are also provided by the free market (*i.e.* public schools such as Eton, and private nursing homes) but for the majority of the population they are too expensive. In contrast, the government may deter or prevent **demerit goods**, such as addictive drugs, which it considers to be harmful.

15.2 Taxation – aims and principles

1 Aims of taxation – 'MARS'

(a) Management of the economy Taxation and public spending have been used to regulate the economy. In general a higher **budget deficit** seems to reflate the economy because more money enters the circular flow. This stimulates spending and increases the demand for workers, thereby probably **lowering unemployment.** However, some economists (notably the Monetarists) argue that such reflation leads to **inflation**, unless there are substantial increases in productivity. Thus generally lower taxation and more spending reflates, whilst higher taxation and less spending deflates.

(b) Alteration of income distribution Taxes can be used to redistribute income in society. The **Labour Party** as a government tends to seek a reduction in income inequality by **progressive** taxation

Tax	As % of total tax income	
	1972–73	*1982–83*
Income Tax	31.1	27.8
National Insurance	15.3	20.2
Rates	11.1	11.2
Petrol & diesel	7.1	4.7
Corporation Tax	6.7	5.0
Purchase Tax	6.5	—
Value Added Tax	—	12.8
Tobacco	5.4	3.3
Beer, wines, spirits	4.9	3.1
Vehicle licences	2.3	1.7
Death duties	2.2	0.5
Capital Gains Tax	1.3	0.6
Petroleum Revenue Tax	—	4.7
Other	6.1	4.4

Fig. 15.3 Income from different taxes

(see Unit 15.3). Thus it is likely to raise income tax, particularly the rate on large incomes. In contrast, the **Conservatives** since 1979 have reduced the basic and top rates of income tax (from 83% to 60%) and nearly doubled VAT which is **regressive** (see Unit 15.3). This has effectively redistributed income to the higher earners. Such a policy is justified by their desire to increase incentives and encourage investment.

(c) Raise revenue The original aim of taxation was to gain income, usually for the State to fight wars. The contribution of the main taxes towards government revenue is illustrated in Figure 15.3.

In the last decade several important changes have taken place. **VAT** has replaced Purchase Tax and become an important source of income. Also, **Petroleum Revenue Tax** has been introduced (1974) and, together with several other taxes on North Sea oil, it is likely to raise £9 million in 1984 to 85. **National Insurance** (see 15.4) has become more important, whilst the shares of **income tax** and **excise duties** on petrol and diesel, tobacco, and beer, wines and spirits have fallen.

(d) Specific objectives. Governments sometimes use taxes to discourage certain harmful activities. For instance in the eighteenth century **gin** was taxed to deter excessive drinking which had been increasing the death rate. This policy of **discouraging 'vices'** such as smoking and drinking persists today and the taxes on them raise over £6.0 billion. 70% of the price of a packet of cigarettes goes in tax, raising £1 billion a year.

Similarly, government spending can be used to encourage certain effects. From 1967 until 1975 a **regional employment premium** was paid to manufacturers in development areas (see Unit 6.3) for each employee. This **subsidy** encouraged employment in these depressed areas and was a disincentive to firms thinking of locating in other areas.

2 Principles of taxation

Adam Smith's four canons or principles of taxation are still relevant today:

(a) Certainty It is argued that the easier taxes are to understand the less will be the incentive to evade them. The many exemptions from Capital Transfer Tax (see 15.4) have encouraged evasion, which is unfair to those who pay, and a loss of revenue for the government. Some people say Capital Transfer Tax is a 'voluntary tax'. If people know what is **expected** of them (*i.e.* when and how much they pay) then there is less aggravation *e.g.* PAYE (see 15.4).

(b) Convenience Governments should consider the **circumstances** of tax payers and levy taxes when it is more convenient. Thus income tax is deducted through PAYE weekly or monthly at source (*i.e.* when paid) rather than collected yearly. The latter arrangement would require great organization and disciplined saving by the taxpayer. The self-employed often find paying income tax six months after the 'year end' onerous, because a lump sum is required. Nowadays local rates can also be paid monthly because payment is easier that way, for both ratepayers and councils.

(c) Economy The receivers of tax want a system in which **collection is cheap**. If a tax costs a lot to gather then the the the yield from it is reduced. For instance, in 1982 it was calculated that the collection of dog licences cost over four times the amount received.

(d) Equality This principle is difficult to interpret. Most people argue that taxes should be based on the **ability to pay**. Thus, people bear a fairly equal **burden** rather than all paying the same amount. Those on higher incomes pay more tax (and usually a higher proportion of their income) than those on low incomes. This progressive tax idea for income tax is also **practical**. Equal tax demands for all people would hurt the least well off who probably could not pay and incur high administration costs *e.g.* taking non-payers to court.

15.3 Taxation–types

Taxes are classified in two ways:

  1 Who pays the tax–Direct and Indirect
  2 The economic effects–**Progressive, Regressive, Proportional**

1 Direct and indirect taxation

(a) Direct taxes The **burden** of paying the taxes falls **upon** the income of those from whom the tax is collected. For instance, **income tax** is paid by employees, corporation tax is charged on company profits, and rates are levied on property owners. Income tax and corporation tax are collected by the **Inland Revenue**.

(b) Indirect taxes The **burden** of taxation does **not** fall upon those from whom the tax is collected. **VAT** (see 15.4) is an indirect tax, which is collected from manufacturers, wholesalers and retailers (see Unit 20) but as it is included in the final price it is the consumer who really pays when he buys the good/service. The **Customs and Excise Department** supervise taxes on expenditure.

2 Progressive, regressive and proportional taxation

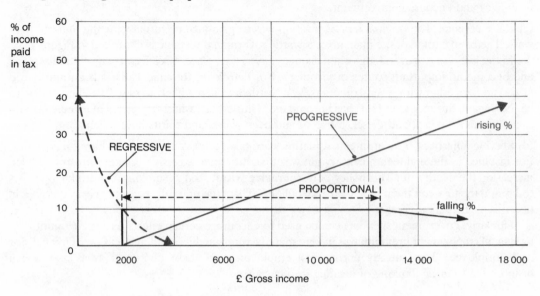

Fig. 15.4 Progressive, regressive and proportional taxes

The **average rate of tax paid** varies between different income levels and different types of tax.

(a) Progressive The **proportion** of income taken in **tax rises as income** increases, above a certain minimum level. **Income tax** in Britain is progressive because taxable income up to £14 600 (1983–84) is taxed at 30p in the £, but taxable income between £14 601 and £17 200 is taxed at 40p in the £. This scale increases upward until all taxable income above £36 000 is taxed at 60p in the £. The full range is shown in Figure 15.5.

Allowances	1983–84 £	1984–85 £
Single and wife's earned income allowance	1785	2005
Married allowance	2795	3115
Additional personal and widows bereavement allowance	1010	1150
Single age allowance	2360	2490
Married age allowance	3755	3955
Age income limit	7600	8100

Income tax rates	Bands of taxable income	
per cent	1983–84 £	1984–85 £
30	0–14 600	0–15 400
40	14 601–17 200	15 401–18 200
45	17 201–21 800	18 201–23 100
50	21 801–28 900	23 101–30 600
55	28 901–36 000	30 601–38 100
60	over 36 000	over 38 100
	1983–84 £	1984–85
Investment income surcharge threshold	7100	Abolished

Fig. 15.5 Income tax and allowances

Using the information for 1983 to 84, a single person 'A' with a gross income of £5785 has taxable income of £4000 (£5785−£1785 allowances) which he pays at 30p in £. His total tax bill is £1200 (£4000 × .30p) which is 20.7% $\left(\frac{1200}{5785}\right)$ of his income. In contrast another single person 'B' with a gross income of £8285 has a taxable income of £6500 (£8285−£1785) which he also pays at 30p in the £. B's total tax bill is £1950 (£6500 × .30p) which is 23.5% $\left(\frac{1950}{8285}\right)$. Thus 'B' pays more tax than 'A' and a higher proportion of his income goes in tax.

(b) Regressive The **proportion** of income taken in tax **falls as income increases** (*i.e.* the average rate of tax falls). **VAT** is regressive because it is charged at uniform rates (see 15.4) irrespective of the purchaser's income.

For instance, if a relatively poor person with an income of £100 per week buys a bouquet of flowers for £11.50 (£10 + £1.50 VAT) then he pays 1.5% $\left(\dfrac{1.50}{100}\right)$ of his income in tax. A much richer person with an income of £500 per week buying a similarly priced bouquet of flowers pays 0.3% $\left(\dfrac{1.50}{500}\right)$ of his income in tax. Thus, the higher a person's income the smaller the percentage of it which will be paid in tax.

(c) Proportional The **same proportion** of income is taken in tax at all income levels. The average rate remains unchanged. **National insurance** payments by employees operate in this way between certain minimum and maximum limits, as shown in Figure 15.4. At present (1984) in Britain employees pay 9% between £34.00 and £250.00 per week. Below £34 there is no tax; whilst above £250.00 no more than £22.50 is taken per week and so the average rate begins to fall, making the tax regressive.

15.4 Taxes on income, expenditure and capital

The main taxes levied in Britain can be classified into three categories:

1 Taxes on income

(a) Income tax Introduced 1799 for incomes over £60 per year, discontinued in 1815, and reintroduced in 1842 at 7d (2.9p) in £. It has since varied between 2d (0.8p) in 1875 and 10/- (50p) during the 2nd World War. Each taxpayer is given certain **tax-free allowances** depending upon their family circumstances. (See Figure 15.5). The difference between their gross income and tax free allowances is their **taxable pay** – the first £14 600 being taxed at the basic rate of 30% (1984). After that the **marginal rate** (the tax charged on the extra income) increases up to a 60% maximum.

Advantages – 'FAYRE'

 (i) **Fairness** As it is levied according to the ability to pay, income tax is **equitable**. Thus very low earners pay no tax and very high earners pay much more than the basic rate.
(ii) **Automatic Stabilizer** As incomes rise generally, so does the total amount paid in income tax. The increased taxation acts as a withdrawal from the circular flow, slowing down the increase in consumption. Conversely, a fall in income during a depression will mean less tax for the government (and lower withdrawals). This **prevents rapid fluctuations** in the economy.
(iii) **Yield** Income tax is a **large revenue** raiser, at least £30 billion annually.
(iv) **Redistribution** of income. As income tax is **progressive**, it takes more from the rich than from the poor. If some of the tax revenue is used to provide free benefits for the poor then income has been redistributed.
(iv) **Efficiency** It is easy to operate through PAYE (Pay As You Earn) and **difficult to evade**. The cost of collection is **cheap** – 1.7% of the yield from PAYE but 6.0% of the yield from self-employed and rent incomes.

Disadvantages – 'DEALS'

 (i) **Disincentive** effects It is often argued that high and progressive income tax rates discourage extra work by employees and deter entrepreneurs. For these reasons, the 1979 Conservative government cut income tax at all levels. There is not much actual evidence that these changes have encouraged greater production and brought the return of famous 'tax exiles'. In general it is very difficult to measure people's responses to tax changes as they react differently in different situations at different times. For instance, someone using overtime earnings to pay for a future foreign holiday may work more as tax rates rise because he gains less from each hour of overtime worked. In contrast, somebody with nothing to save for may react to a tax increase by substituting leisure for work.
(ii) **Evasion** and **Avoidance**. Tax evasion, which is not paying the tax required, is **illegal** and the Inland Revenue employs inspectors to catch offenders. However tax avoidance is **legal** and involves the self-employed and companies employing accountants to reduce tax liability. It is claimed that high direct taxes channel effort into avoidance and evasion.
(iii) **Less Savings** The income tax system in Britain is said to encourage consumption rather than savings. In the long run, a low level of savings (17% of GDP in Britain, compared with 31% in Japan) reduces the flow of funds available for investment and thus limits the potential for economic growth. (see Unit 14.4). In particular, the tax relief given to private pensions, house loans (mortgage relief costs £2.2 billion per year) and life assurance encourage specific savings but these do not go towards productive investment.

(b) National insurance NI contributions are made by both **employers** and **employees**. The current rates are 9% for employees and 10.45% for employers. Earnings below £34 per week are exempt. In practice, national insurance is a tax on earnings and a **tax on jobs**, because every time a firm takes on an employee it has to pay the employee's contribution. It is unpopular with business. However, it is popular with the government as a **revenue raiser** because its contribution to total revenue has doubled in less than twenty years.

(c) Corporation tax This direct tax on **company profits** was introduced in 1965 to replace Profits Tax. The standard rate of **52%** is charged on profits in excess of £500 000. Companies can claim tax relief for many business costs *e.g.* interest paid on loans. Small companies are charged at a lower rate – 38%. In his 1984 Budget, the Chancellor made it clear that by 1987 – 88 the basic rate of Corporation Tax would be reduced to 35%. During the same period also, depreciation allowances on capital equipment would be progressively reduced (for instance from 100% to 75% in 1984 – 85).

2 Taxes on expenditure

(a) Value-added tax – VAT is levied upon the **net** value added at each stage of production for certain goods and services. This is illustrated in Figure 15.6. It was introduced in **1973** as a replacement for

Stage of production	Buying price	Value Added £	15% Tax £	Selling price
Primary producer	—	40	6	46
Manufacturer	46	40	6	92
Retailer	92	20	3	115

Fig. 15.6 VAT at different stages of production

purchase tax and to bring the United Kingdom in line with the EEC prior to our entry. It is essentially a tax on **consumption**, *e.g.* in 1984 the Chancellor introduced VAT on hot takeaway meals such as fish and chips.

There are three levels of VAT. There is the **standard** rate which is 15% on many goods and services, *e.g.* meals out. Some goods and services, *e.g.* food and power are **zero-rated**. This means that VAT is not payable at the retail stage and that any VAT paid at earlier stages of production can be claimed back. Other goods and services, such as education and insurance, do not have VAT charged at the final stage, but VAT paid earlier cannot be reclaimed. This is the **exempt** category.

Advantages – 'FACE'
 (i) **Flexible** VAT can be easily and quickly changed, as happened in 1979.
 (ii) **Automatic** stabilizer As most **consumer durables**, particularly luxuries, are subject to standard rate VAT, increases in consumption expenditure bring about greater tax revenue. This prevents a too rapid surge into a boom (and vice-versa during a slump).
(iii) **Cheap** The administrative costs of VAT are low. In 1976 they were 2% of the yield but now they are only **1.2% of the yield** (mainly because VAT is now at a higher rate). The low collection costs are partly explained by the work done by the VAT payers (*i.e.* business) who virtually act as 'unpaid tax collectors'.
(iv) **Effort** unaffected. VAT is not usually 'seen' by the consumer because it is included in the purchase price. Increases in VAT by making goods more expensive may encourage **extra effort** so that the goods can be afforded.

Disadvantages – 'DIRE'
 (i) **Disliked** by business. Firms bear the **cost** of record keeping and VAT calculation, because the law says they must. In addition VAT inspectors may check their accounts and search their premises. These aspects have made VAT unpopular with small businesses.
 (ii) **Inflationary** The existence of VAT and any increases, such as 1979, are inflationary because **prices rise** in order to maintain profit margins and pay the costs of record keeping. It is possible that trade unions may respond to such price increases by demanding higher wages to maintain living standards.
(iii) **Regressive** Even though many basic necessities *e.g.* food, are zero rated, VAT hits the lowest paid hardest (see 15.3 (2) (b)). Clearly poor people pay less VAT than rich people because they do not buy as many 'vatable' goods or they buy cheaper goods, but they still pay a higher proportion of their income in VAT. Thus VAT seems to be **inequitable**.
(iv) **Evasion** The Black Economy (see Unit 2.1) has thrived since VAT was introduced. VAT payment is evaded by activities such as charging a lower price for **payment by cash** without a receipt (*e.g.* car mechanic servicing motor car) and the **bartering** of services by professional people (*e.g.* accountants and solicitors).

(b) Protective (customs) and excise duties These taxes are collected by the Customs and Excise department and levied **in addition** to VAT on several important goods *e.g.* alcohol, tobacco. Before 1973 (EEC transitional entry) the **excise** duties were taxes placed on **domestic** goods and **customs** duties were taxes levied on **imported** goods. However, since we have 'harmonized' with the EEC the terminology has changed. All duties for **revenue purposes** are now termed **excise** which is payable on both **home produced and imported goods**.

Protective duties refer to customs duties on **non-EEC** goods (rather than just non-British as in the past) and are generally in line with the **Common External Tariff**. This change has arisen because there is a free market within the EEC and so Britain cannot levy customs duties on goods from (say) France. Britain imposes tariffs on cheap textiles from S. Korea and Taiwan, as part of a Multi-Fibre agreement (since 1977).

3 Taxes on capital

(a) Capital Transfer Tax This tax was introduced in 1975 when estate duty was abolished. It has been called a '**Gifts** tax' because it is payable on gifts made during a lifetime and on **transfers of personal wealth** at death. Capital Transfer Tax is intended to reduce the inequality of wealth distribution by taxing its transfer. For instance, it is reckoned that half of Britain's millionaires inherited £500 000 at least!

In 1984, the first £64 000 left was tax free, and after that 30% of each £ was taxed. The rate of tax levied is progressive up to 60% on transfers at death exceeding £2 million. There are many **exemptions** for birthday and wedding gifts (£3000 tax free), business owners and donations to charity. In addition, **lifetime** transfers are levied at half rate. These concessions have encouraged tax **avoidance**, particularly through trust funds, and given CTT the label of a 'voluntary tax'. It contributes a very **small**, declining amount of tax revenue and the collection cost is 3% of the yield.

CTT is a tax on inheritance rather than wealth. Britain does not have a wealth tax, unlike France and Sweden where a tax is paid annually by those owning assets above a certain value.

(b) Capital Gains Tax This tax is charged on **profits** made when certain **paper assets**, such as stocks and shares, are sold. Profits of less than £1000 per annum are exempt whilst allowances are made for inflation. The revenue earned by the government from this tax is thus slight and **diminishing**.

4 Other taxes

(a) Rates – See Unit 19.5

(b) Petroleum Revenue Tax Prior to 1975, production from the UK's offshore gas and oilfields was subject only to **Royalty** payments and Corporation Tax. Since then companies have paid PRT and Advanced PRT which together now take about 75% of an oilfield's net revenue, after certain costs have been deducted. The **complicated system of allowances** permits oil companies to recover most of their capital expenditure within a few years of the oil first flowing. The main advantage of the tax is clearly its **yield** – £10b estimated for 1984 – 85. In contrast, it is argued that very high rates of tax may deter future investment.

15.5 Incidence of taxes

The incidence of a tax occurs in two ways. The **formal incidence** refers to the taxpayer who has to **pay the tax over** to the government. For instance VAT is collected by the retailer and remitted to the government every three months. The **real incidence** refers to the person who has to **bear the burden** of the tax. For instance, whilst a retailer may collect and pay over VAT, he may be able to pass on the tax by raising the price of his goods and not losing any customers. Economists are concerned with this eventual real impact of certain taxation, particularly where it affects demand and supply.

Expenditure taxes, such as VAT, may **distort** the prices and quantity supplied of goods. Such taxes shift a producer's supply curve to the left as shown in Figure 15.7. At each price the producer is now prepared to **supply less** because part of his sales income goes in tax. The supply schedule shows that at £2 price before tax was introduced 15 units were supplied, but since taxation of £1 per unit, only 10 are put on the market. The suppliers total revenue before tax was £30 but now after tax it is only £10 (£20 total revenue less £10 tax). In order to achieve a net revenue of £30, the supplier needs to produce 15 at £3. In that way he pays £15 (15 × £1 tax) to the government and keeps £30 out of the £45 total revenue.

The original equilibrium price was £3 with 20 units supplied. The imposition of tax has caused a fall in the quantity demanded to 17 units and rise in price to £3.30. This result has been caused by the **shape of the demand** curve (*i.e.* its elasticity). The real impact of the tax is shown by the shaded areas in Figure 15.7. The price rise to £3.30 shows that the consumer has to pay an extra 30p because of the tax. On each sale, the supplier has to pay £1 to the government and so really he bears 70p of the tax (£1 to pay but gets extra 30p from customer). It is mainly because the **demand curve** is so **elastic**

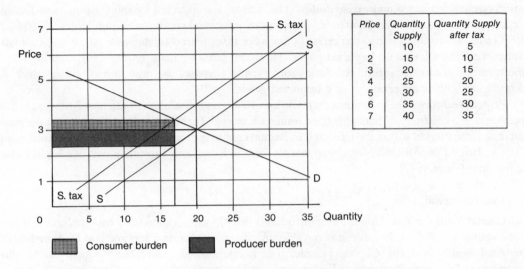

Price	Quantity Supply	Quantity Supply after tax
1	10	5
2	15	10
3	20	15
4	25	20
5	30	25
6	35	30
7	40	35

Fig. 15.7 Tax incidence and effect of a tax on supply

that the bulk of the burden falls on the producer. In Figure 15.8, the demand curve is **perfectly inelastic** (and the supply data is the same as in Figure 15.7) and so the incidence of the tax falls completely on the **consumer**. In practice, taxes on expenditure should be placed on goods (such as tobacco, alcohol?) where demand is inelastic so that the revenue aimed for is obtained.

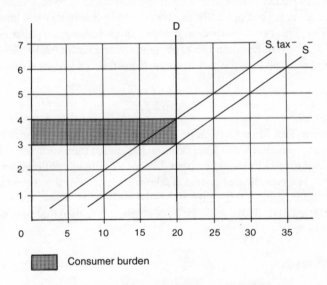

Fig. 15.8 Tax incidence and inelastic demand

15.6 The Budget and PSBR and government policy

The Budget Each year the Chancellor of the Exchequer, on behalf of the government, prepares a budget in which he outlines the **following year's** public expenditure and public revenue **plans**. Occasionally, there is a mini-budget mid-way through the financial year, in the autumn. There is now also an **Autumn Statement** outlining possible options for the following March budget and laying down economic policy objectives.

The budget has become an important economic weapon for the government in the pursuit of certain objectives. (See Unit 19.1). In the past governments sought either to **balance** the budget, or create a **surplus** or produce a **deficit**.

In simple theory, a **balanced budget** has no overall effect on the level of economic activity because the amount withdrawn through revenue is matched by the amount injected by expenditure. In the inter-war years a balanced budget was aimed for as a sign of **good housekeeping**. **Keynes** was one of the first to suggest deficit budgets – the idea being for the amount by which expenditure exceeded revenue, to stimulate demand. Thus, deficit budgets could be used to lower unemployment which had been caused by low demand. However, too large a deficit, by increasing spending possibly faster than output and possibly on imported goods, created two problems – **inflation** and **balance of payments deficits** respectively. Thus, in order to reduce these problems, **surplus budgets** were sought when expenditure was less than revenue and the level of demand fell. In the 1960s the alternation of these types of budgets was known as 'stop-go'. The government was trying to regulate the economy through **fiscal** (taxation–spending) policies. It was trying to manage the level of demand.

Public Sector Borrowing Requirement (PSBR)

PSBR is the **difference** between **the income and expenditure** of the **whole of the public sector** each year. This includes the activities of nationalized industries, public corporations, local authorities and central government departments. A **budget deficit/surplus** just refers to the **central government**.

The increase in public spending in the **1970s** has made PSBR inevitable every year. Thus the economic argument has shifted away from surplus/deficit towards **how large/how small** a PSBR. The main reasons for the **increasing size** of PSBR have been:

1 Effects of **inflation** on spending, particularly on necessary services.

2 **Political spending** commitments *e.g.* Labour to social services, Conservatives to defence, and law and order.

3 **Unwillingness**, for political reasons, of successive governments to **raise taxation** in line with the increases in spending–increased rates of income tax before election time is political suicide!

4 **Ageing population** This has raised the social security share of public expenditure significantly (see Figure 15.2).

5 **Increased unemployment,** particularly since 1979. Each unemployed person costs the State approximately £5000 per year in lost tax revenue and paid benefits.

6 **Debt interest**–each PSBR raises the National Debt (see 15.7) upon which interest needs to be paid. As debt interest is 11% of total public sector expenditure it usually exceeds the PSBR on its own.

The PSBR is a **forecast** for the next financial year. The actual amount borrowed (out turn) is often several billions different from the planned total. Changes in the economy may distort the estimates. For instance, greater unemployment than forecast may increase government expenditure and lower government revenue, thus making PSBR larger.

The significance of PSBR

Year	PSBR £b	% of GDP	National Debt £b	% of GDP
1972–73	2.5	3.9	49.6	77.4
1976–77	8.5	6.8	88.5	70.1
1978–79	9.2	5.4	108.1	63.6
1980–81	13.2	5.7	136.4	58.6
1982–83	9.0	3.3	158.3	54.4

Fig. 15.9 PSBR and the National Debt

Figure 15.9 shows the general upwards trend in the size of PSBR, until 1980–81. **Monetarist** economists argue that the rise of PSBR has caused inflation. In order to finance the public spending, the government has needed to borrow money. In so doing it has increased the supply of money in the economy thus generating inflation (See Unit 9.7).

Another consequence has been **higher interest rates**. In order to borrow, the government needs to offer lucrative interest rates. It is argued by some that investment funds have been attracted by these rates on government stock (gilts, savings certificates, etc) and diverted away from productive industrial lending. This view claims that private sector investment has been **'crowded out'** by the public sector.

The Conservative Party as government takes the view that a high and rising PSBR is a 'bad thing'. It argues that PSBR should fall as a proportion of GDP. On the other hand, the Labour Party is less concerned about the overall size of PSBR. It points out that Britain's PSBR is a very small % of GDP compared with most of our competitors and that it is falling in **real** terms (*i.e.* allowing for inflation). In addition, it disputes the inflation argument, giving the **demand for money** fed by profit-seeking banks and other credit providing institutions as alternative causes of the inflation. The Labour Party dismisses the crowding-out argument and cites the **conservatism of British management** and its unwillingness to invest, as explanations.

15.7 National Debt

The National Debt is the **total** amount **owned** by the **central government** to people both in Britain and abroad. The debt has been accumulated over the years. Whenever there is a PSBR the debt increases. Each year, **interest** is paid to the lenders and, intermittently, **capital** is repaid. However, some debt is undated (*e.g.* 2½% Consols have no redemption date or value). Obviously as the debt increases in size so does the amount paid in interest. However, in **real terms**, the National Debt has become less significant.

Most of the debt is owed to **domestic residents** who hold Treasury bills, medium and long-term government stock and various savings certificates. Less than 10% is owed abroad fortunately, because interest and capital repayments are an outflow from the British economy and a drain on the Balance of Payments.

15.8 Links with other topics

Government policy ⟶ Public finance

16 Unemployment

16.1 Introduction

Unemployment has become a serious economic problem, particularly since 1976 when the percentage of the working population unemployed exceeded 5% and the numbers went over 1 million. As well as labour, capital and land may be unemployed. The unemployment of any factor incurs an **opportunity cost** through the waste of a valuable resource.

The unemployment of the early 1980s has been compared with the 1930s. However, although the total numbers involved are similar, there are several important **differences**:

1 The per cent unemployed in the 1930s was **higher**, because the working population was lower (fewer women workers in particular).
2 The unemployed in the 1930s was much more **regional**. For instance, current blackspots show 30% unemployed in certain towns *e.g.* Hartlepool, compared with 80%, *e.g.* Jarrow in 1930s.
3 **Most occupational groups** were affected in the 1930s with skilled, unskilled and white-collar workers all suffering significantly. This happened because world trade declined in volume by a quarter and GDP fell by a sixth. However, in the 1980s the unemployment has been more concentrated in certain sectors (*e.g.* steel) and occupations (*e.g.* unskilled manual labour).

16.2 Characteristics

1 People

'**YOU**' and '**ME**' is an appropriate mnemonic, as it is important to know who the unemployed are. Five main groups can be identified:

(a) **Young people** A quarter of those aged 16 to 25 are unemployed. This has happened because firms are **unlikely to recruit** young workers during a recession because:
 (i) The **training** costs are high before the young workers become fully productive.
 (ii) The **wage rates** are too high. Trade union power in the 1970s pushed up wages, making young labour less cheap and thus less profitable to employ.

In 1973 the per cent unemployment of males under twenty was the same as the average for all males but in 1983 it was twice the average.

In contrast, firms are **more likely** to make young workers **redundant** because:

(i) Young workers are **less experienced**/less skilled.

(ii) The **'last in, first out'** principle is used by employers when shedding labour, as it rewards loyalty and seems fairer. Young workers are often 'last in'. Thus young workers have experienced several short-lasting jobs.

(iii) It is **cheaper** to lay off the young, as large redundancy payments do not have to be paid. Thus the middle-aged are kept on the payroll.

Figure 16.1 shows the per cent unemployed in each age group.

| | Age group – % unemployed | | | |
	under 25	*25–54*	*55+*	*All ages*
Males	24	11	18	15
Females	23	6	5	9

Fig. 16.1 Unemployment by age group

(b) Older men There are also more older men, aged +55, unemployed than on average, as shown in Figure 16.1. For instance, if cuts in a firm's labour force are necessary then the **declining productivity** of older workers makes them 'natural' targets. Those unemployed after age 50 are unlikely to want (or be considered for) **retraining** and many have taken early retirement anyway.

(c) Unskilled workers These workers have borne the brunt of the unemployment, as shown by the increase in **manual workers** unemployed in Figure 16.2. However, as a percentage of total

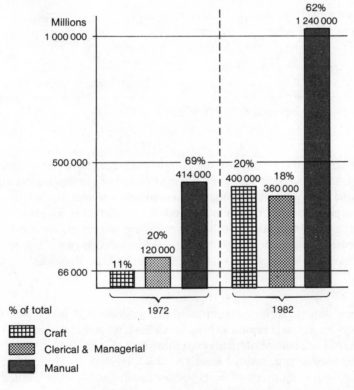

Fig. 16.2 Unemployment by type of worker

unemployed, the manual workers share has fallen and that of craft workers has increased. Unskilled workers are most prone to be replaced by **new technology**. They are also most likely to be employed in (or made redundant from) **labour intensive** industries suffering structural decline. Their relatively **low productivity** makes them likely victims of a recession.

(d) Married people with families There is a direct link between family size and unemployment, if single people who have the highest rate of unemployment (mainly because of their youth) are discounted. Families with four or **more children** are four times **more likely** to have the **male parent unemployed** than families with one child or no children. There are several sociological explanations for this. However, the main economic reason is the **'unemployment trap'** created by low wages and social benefits. Some potential workers with large families are only slightly better off in work than unemployed. Thus, such workers have little financial incentive to find employment.

(e) Ethnic minorities There are proportionally more **non-whites unemployed** than whites in most age groups (see Figure 16.3). For instance, a male West Indian school leaver with five 'O' levels is twice as likely to unemployed as a similar white classmate. Almost no whites with degrees are employed in manual work yet 20% of ethnic minority degree holders work manually. Apart from being unfair, it is a serious waste and misuse of scarce resources.

Great Britain *percentages and thousands*

	Ethnic group				All ethnic groups
	White	West Indian or Guyanese	Indian/ Pakistani/ Bangladeshi	Other	
Unemployment among males *aged* (percentages)					
16–24	19	38	25	34	19
25–44	8	13	13	7	8
45–64	7	17	19	10	8
All aged 16–64	10	21	17	14	10
Total unemployed aged 16–64 (thousands)	1423	31	49	18	1528
Unemployment among females *aged* (percentages)					
16–24	16	28	30	25	17
25–44	8	10	14	10	8
45–59	5	7	10	12	5
All aged 16–59	9	15	18	15	9
Total unemployed aged 16–59 (thousands)	839	18	23	12	894

(Source: *Social Trends* HMSO)

Fig. 16.3 Unemployment by ethnic group (1981)

2 Duration

The length of time unemployed is very important. A short period unemployed is a **financial burden** to the State and a waste of resources. However, a longer period of unemployment incurs a bigger financial sacrifice, **social costs** and a **deterioration of an economic resource**. In 1955 the average spell of unemployment was just under one month, now (1984) it is nine months! The young are less likely to be unemployed for a very long period but those over 55 face longer periods of inactivity. Half of those aged 60+ have been on the unemployment register for over one year. In general, over ⅓ of total have been unemployed for over one year and 60% for at least 26 weeks.

3 Regions

The extent of unemployment varies between regions, as illustrated in Figures 6.2 and 6.3. Generally, the further you go from London and the South East, the worse the problem has become. It is mainly associated with the decline of traditional industries *e.g.* steel, shipbuilding (see Unit 6.3). As a result of high unemployment, **assisted areas** have been created. It is interesting to note that **Scotland** made a small relative improvement in its position because of North Sea oil and its success in attracting high technology electronics firms.

4 Industries

The **manufacturing** sector of the economy has suffered much more unemployment than the service sector. For instance, employment in manufacturing in 1983 had fallen to three-quarters of the 1976 level. This shows the **de-industrialization** referred to in Unit 5. The **steel** industry suffered particularly badly (see Unit 6) losing half of its workforce between 1980 and 1983. Also between 1950 and 1981 employment fell by 50% in shipbuilding, 61% in agriculture, 61% in mining and 64% in textiles.

The **service sector** has maintained its employment levels. This partly explains why the South East had the lowest rates of unemployment in the 1970s.

16.3 Costs

There are costs to the individual and society when unemployment occurs. These can be remembered by the highly appropriate (but contrived) mnemonic – **'DESTITUTES'**

1 DEterioration

Labour, like land, deteriorates if not used. An increasing sense of frustration, apathy and uselessness lead the long-term unemployed to 'a not caring less attitude'. They fail to organize themselves, miss appointments and shun work. This makes them 'unemployable'. Thus their previous experience and training is wasted.

2 STandard of living

When workers lose their jobs, their incomes fall and this lowers living standards. Some may receive redundancy pay which might cushion the fall but most of the unemployed have to **cut back their spending** – thus the demand for goods and services falls. A single person receives £28 (1984) Supplementary Benefit which is one sixth of the average industrial wage. The fall in spending may create further unemployment elsewhere in the economy.

3 Income Tax

As the number of unemployed people rises so the revenue received by the Inland Revenue falls (through less tax and more rebates). This may make the Government's PSBR target (see Unit 15.6) unobtainable because their income falls; and when Supplementary Benefits are paid their spending increases.

4 Unemployment benefit

A whole range of **social benefits** become available to unemployed people *e.g.* free school meals, welfare milk, rate and rent rebates. Their provision increases public expenditure. It is calculated that each unemployed person **costs** the State **£5000** per year through lost tax revenue and benefit payments. These are just the **direct** costs. There are also indirect economic costs, such as extra administration involved, and social costs.

5 Total Economic activity

A major **opportunity cost** of unemployment is the goods and services which could have been produced by the unemployed. Consequently, real GDP in UK actually declined in 1980–81. Thus economic growth is handicapped in both the long and short term by the unemployment of resources.

6 Social costs

There are many dimensions to the cost to society as a whole of unemployment. There is a link between rising unemployment and **crime**. The Toxteth and Brixton riots of 1982 and other **violence** were not unrelated to unemployment. Similarly, increased divorce, **suicide**, heart attacks and stress-related diseases tend to rise with unemployment. For instance, the suicide rate among the male unemployed is twice that of employed men. Although individuals suffer, society bears much of the cost through health, police and law services, which are paid for with taxpayers' money.

16.4 Measurement

Since 1983, the unemployment figure has been based on those **claiming unemployment benefit**. It used to be calculated from those **registered** as unemployed. Furthermore, the figures given are **seasonally adjusted**. This allows for large increases in the summer, when students leave school, and enables an underlying trend to be identified.

Each month the government discloses the '**official** figures' relating to unemployment. Most economists accept that they are not the '**true** figures'.

The actual measurement is an **understatement**, because of:

1 **People not registered** but available for work. It is reckoned that nearly all men but only 67% of women register for employment.

For instance, many **women** do not qualify for unemployment benefit but would take a job if offered one – thus they are 'available, able and willing to work' (usual definition) but unable to find paid employment.

2 People seeking **part-time** employment.

3 **Men aged over 60** – from December 1982 they did not have to claim, thus 250 000 were removed from the figures. However, undoubtedly some are able-bodied and want work of it is available.

4 **Some employees** are kept in employment by their firms (even though not fully employed) to avoid

(a) redundancy payments

(b) loss of skilled men who may be needed when the economy recovers. If these men were lost then new workers would need recruitment and training

(c) litigation from workers against unfair dismissal

 5 Government job creation and **training schemes** *e.g.* Youth Opportunities Scheme (1978-82), Youth Training Scheme (1983 onwards)—see Unit 16.7

Thus, some economists and critics of the Government claim that the true total is about 5 million unemployed. However, others argue that this is an **over-estimate** because it does not allow for:

(a) people changing jobs—each month slightly over 320 000 join the register and slightly less than 280 000 leave it

(b) many of the unemployed are **incapable** of work—because of ill health, age, lack of skill

(c) others are **unwilling to work** (about one-tenth of total)—they may be 'work-shy' or they may find Supplementary Benefit sufficient

(d) some are in the **wrong place** but unwilling to move, *e.g.* a crofter in the Orkneys

Between 1979 and 1982 the population of working age **rose by over half a million** whilst the number of employed and registered unemployed **fell** by over half a million. This indicates that over one million people have disappeared from the labour market. The categories of people so discouraged from employment seem to be women, ethnic groups and young people.

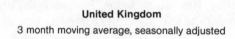

United Kingdom
3 month moving average, seasonally adjusted

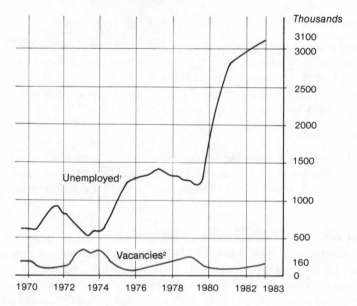

¹Excluding school leavers.

²Vacancies notified to unemployment offices.

(Source: *Employment Gazette*, Department of Employment)

Fig. 16.4 Unemployment and vacancies 1970–1983

Vacancies

Undercounting also affects the statistics of vacancies. The Department of Employment estimates that it records about one third of the job openings that actually exist. Thus, the vacancies figure in Figure 16.4 should perhaps be over 400 000 in 1983. However, even allowing for this, the gap between the numbers unemployed and available jobs has widened markedly since 1979 and shows no sign of narrowing. If there was **perfect mobility** of labour there would be no vacancies.

16.5 Types

The unemployment problem is, in reality, **several** different problems. A useful insight into these problems may be gained by classifying unemployment into several types.

1 Structural

Changes in **demand** and/or **supply** cause this type. For instance, if a particular skill *e.g.* roof thatching, or product *e.g.* matches, suffers a drastic fall in demand then labour becomes unemployed. Competition from other countries *e.g.* **cotton textiles** in Britain facing cheap Third

World products, cars from Japan, may depress the British industry and lead to redundancies. Thus changes in the structure of economic activity, prompted by different consumption patterns, create unemployment. In other industries, demand has expanded but supply is fulfilled by **capital**, such as robots and greater mechanization and so labour is needed much less.

Some parts of the United Kingdom suffer greatly from this type of unemployment *e.g.* North East (coal, iron and steel, shipbuilding, in decline), W. Yorkshire (textiles). As these industries are **localized** in certain areas, structural unemployment is linked with **regional** unemployment, which is essentially geographical.

Structural unemployment is always present in an economy. There appears to be more in British economy now than in the 1960s and early 1970s.

2 Demand deficiency

This modern term has largely superseded **'cyclical'** and 'general' unemployment. It occurs when **total spending** in the economy **falls** and tends to affect most industries, occupations and regions. It is often associated with a decline in **world trade** and growth. With its open economy, Britain is particularly susceptible to this type. It partly explains the large increase in unemployment since 1979 in Britain. Government policies of controlling money supply and limiting public expenditure have contributed to the demand deficiency and could again be partly blamed for the rise in unemployment.

3 Frictional

This type is sometimes known as **'search'** unemployment. It refers to people **changing jobs** and the period of transition from one job to another. As it is temporary, there is little hardship. A lot of frictional unemployment indicates a healthy and dynamic economy. It shows **labour** being **mobile** and moving from declining to expanding sectors. Currently in Britain the low level of vacancies and the mismatch between job specifications and the unemployed's skills (or lack of them) suggest that there is little frictional unemployment.

4 Natural

Monetarist economists argue that there is a 'natural rate of unemployment' which is defined as 'that rate of unemployment at which **inflation is constant**.' This is a very controversial viewpoint which suggests that a government can only reduce unemployment below the natural rate for short periods and then at the cost of accelerating inflation. This view underlines Conservative government thinking on unemployment.

5 Technological

Improvements in science and technology have made it possible to replace workers with **machines** (labour with capital) in specific industries *e.g.* robots building motor cars. The Service sector is perhaps less susceptible to this type of unemployment, particularly where personal contact is important *e.g.* estate agents, solicitors.

On available international comparisons, the UK appears relatively sluggish in its record of **investment** in new technology. This perhaps suggests that there is more of this type of unemployment still to come in the British economy. On the other hand, in the long run technology **creates more jobs** than it destroys, on American evidence. For instance, computers need hardware and software.

6 Seasonal

Certain jobs are only available at certain times *e.g.* Santa Claus at Christmas, strawberry pickers in July and August. This type of unemployment is of **little** economic importance. Many such jobs are taken on by part-timers or occupational pensioners; the holiday season is lengthening, *e.g.* Christmas pantomimes now run from up to four months in some places; and seasonal workers have diversified to other times of the year *e.g.* ice-cream salesmen.

7 Voluntary

This is said to occur when people are unwilling to work to existing **wage rates**.
In Figure 16.5 if W1 is the existing wage rate then N1-N2 people may be said to be voluntarily unemployed as they will only supply their labour at wage rate W2. Some argue that a high level of **Supplementary Benefit** and other free services encourages voluntary unemployment.

In contrast, **involuntary** unemployment occurs when workers are willing to work at existing rates but cannot find employment. Figure 16.4 seems to indicate that the great majority of Britain's unemployment is involuntary, because there are so few vacancies.

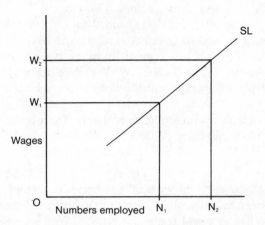

Fig. 16.5 Wage rates and the supply of labour

16.6 Causes

Several causes of unemployment have been implied in the different types explained in 16.5. However, five main underlying causes can be identified. They can be remembered by the word **'WILTS'**.

1 Wage rises

It can be argued that the quantity of labour demanded by firms falls as wage rates increase. (See Figure 16.6). Clearly, if trade unions can achieve **higher wages** then this may be at the expense of some unemployment. In Figure 16.6 if trade unions restrict supply (SLT) then wages will rise and the quantity of labour demanded will fall to N2. This creates unemployment (N2 – N1). The present Conservative government claims that by demanding higher wages workers 'have priced themselves out of a job'.

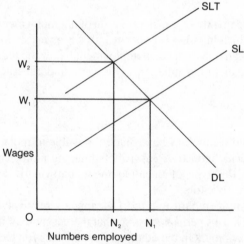

Fig. 16.6 Wages, trade unions and unemployment

However, it is clear that wage levels are a major determinant of the demand for labour. Labour is a **derived demand** based, particularly in the private sector, on the demand for the **final product**. If demand for the final product falls (*i.e.* structural changes, demand deficiency unemployment) then firms will seek less labour, irrespective of the wage rate. Furthermore, in capital-intensive industries, *e.g.* oil, labour is a small **proportion of total cost** and so high wage increases can be more easily absorbed.

A further argument against the view that excessive wage rises cause unemployment is that real wages in West Germany are about 50% higher than in UK but unemployment is considerably lower.

2 Inflation

Throughout the 1970s our rate of inflation has been higher than that of our competitors. This made British **exports relatively** more expensive and **imports relatively** cheaper. Both of which would probably lead (assuming demand not inelastic) to a **fall** in the **market share** of British products and thus fewer jobs for British people. Higher rates of inflation in certain industries can cause structural decline *e.g.* in textiles.

Furthermore in attempting to cure Britain's inflation problem, the Government since 1979 has adopted policies which lead to greater unemployment. For instance less grant given to local authorities has led to a fall in their manpower from nearly 3 million to 2½ million.

3 Lack of demand/output

If the growth of an economy slows down, then demand declines and workers are laid off. Unemployment follows changes in **economic activity** with a lag of 12 to 18 months. Thus GDP rose by 3½% per annum between 1966 and 73 but then slowed down because of the oil crisis. This probably started the rise in unemployment in late 1974 and early 1975 (see Figure 16.4).

Between 1974 and 1982 there was little world growth, made worse by the **1979 oil crisis**. This crisis could explain the take-off of unemployment in Britain in 1980 and its slowing down in early 1984, when the world economy recovered from depression.

This lack of demand in the world, and domestically, leads to redundancies. The redundant workers will **spend less** and thus the demand for other products falls, causing further job losses. Some economists (called Keynesians) maintain that it is the government's responsibility to increase spending (by fiscal and monetary policies) so that unemployment is soaked up. This lack of demand/output is probably the **main** cause of Britain's recent unemployment. An international trade war or policies of **protection** (see Unit 17) make matters worse.

4 Trade unions

The increased power of trade unions in the 1970s (Units 13.7, 13.8, 13.9) may have contributed to unemployment in two ways:
(a) Wage rises, obtained by trade union militancy, may have fuelled inflation in some sectors.
(b) By maintaining established **working practices**, rigid **demarcation** and **closed shops**, and by resisting certain new innovations (*e.g.* printworkers), trade unions have not helped manufacturers to raise their efficiency. This may have contributed to rising costs and prices, leading to lower sales and less employment.

5 Social security

Some economists believe that 'high' levels of unemployment and supplementary **benefits encourage unemployment**. If these benefits were lowered then unemployment would be reduced as workers would not refuse jobs where the wages made them only slightly better off. The present level of benefit seems to these economists to be an **incentive** to stay unemployed until a very lucrative job comes along, hopefully or indefinitely.

In 1982 the Government took away earnings-related benefits and made unemployment benefits taxable in an effort to reduce the **real** value of benefits. However, there are still some people, often with large families and low incomes when in employment, who can get almost as much income from being unemployed. This **unemployment trap** affects about 5% of the unemployed.

(Married man with two children)			
Income when unemployed		*Income at work*	
Unemployment benefit	41.70	Wage	100.00
Child benefit	11.70	Child benefit	11.70
Supplementary benefit	6.10	Rent rebate	7.32
Rent and rates (paid)	20.00	Rate rebate	2.41
Tax rebate	3.69	Tax	−13.94
		National Insurance	−9.00
	£83.19		£98.49

(Source: *Economist Oct. 1983*)

Fig. 16.7 Wages and social benefits

Figure 16.7 shows how a worker's income is replaced by various benefits and tax rebates if he becomes unemployed. In this particular example, his out-of-work income is 84% of his in-work income. This is known as the **replacement rate**. The average rate is 66% in the short run and 50% in the long run (because tax rebates are lost).

Prof. Minford (Liverpool University) claims that such generous unemployment benefits set a floor for wages in the whole economy. Firms find it hard to recruit workers, wage rates do not fall and supply exceeds demand causing unemployment.

16.7 Policies

There are no 'cures' for unemployment but some remedies may be less ineffective than others. The policies proposed depend upon the view taken of the **causes** of unemployment and the **types** that have resulted. The policies can be divided into two approaches: general remedies and specific measures.

1 General remedies for:

(a) Structural unemployment

In the **short run**, this can be minimized by increasing labour mobility, both occupationally and geographically *e.g.* improved **training** facilities (see Unit 2).

Also in the short term the impact of decline can be lessened by government assistance – this may be by subsidy or overt **protection** *e.g.* Multi-Fibre agreement since 1977 protecting British textiles from cheap imports.

The long-term remedy is a vigorous, expanding economy in which new industries develop. They replace the declining sectors. Thus Britain in the 1980s needs to develop **new technology** and **service** industries for the future.

(b) Demand deficiency unemployment

The remedies here rather depend on the **cause** of the unemployment. Clearly if excessive wage increases are the problem then a reduction of **trade union** power may be one answer (see Unit 13.9). **Incomes policy** could be another (Unit 13.6). Both of these may involve deep government intervention through changes in the law (even).

If a lack of output is the cause then several approaches are possible – **increased government spending** through a larger PSBR (see Unit 15.6), expansion in **world trade** through international co-operation (Unit 17.6), **lower interest rates** (see Unit 9.8) and **increases in money supply** (see Unit 9.8) all help.

(c) Frictional unemployment

This type is less serious than the previous two. However, **lower welfare benefits** and **more efficient** job centres could cut 'search' unemployment. A Government survey in 1981 showed that four-fifths of the unemployed finding jobs did so **without** the help of job centres.

(d) Natural unemployment

The answer here is simply reduce the level of **inflation** because it causes the unemployment. (See Unit 9.8). The usual ways advocated by the monetarists are through restricting the growth of money supply and higher interest rates. They seek to lower 'inflationary **expectations**' (*e.g.* large annual pay rises) by their predictions and policies. This policy also involves the limitation of **trade unions'** power, because they make unrealistically high claims and in the 1970s they achieved substantial wage increases.

(e) Technological unemployment

In some economies, technological advance has not created excess unemployment. Job preservation and opposition to innovation are short-term ways to stave off this problem **but** they damage the economy's productive capacity. Ideally, alternative employment needs to be available – this occurs if there is **retraining, mobile labour, government assistance** and **investment** (both public and private).

(f) Seasonal unemployment – very minor and largely acceptable.

(g) Voluntary unemployment

This type of unemployment is publicized as consisting of 'work-shy' skivers living it up on social security! The reality was about 10% of the 1978 total in a Job Centre survey. The proportion is probably much smaller now as unemployment has increased, the real value of **social benefits has fallen** and the replacement rate has fallen. Also, Health & Social Security unemployment review officers have proved very effective in finding **fraudulent claimants** and deterring doubtful claimants.

In the short term the measures above may have improved the incentive to work. However, they also harm those involuntarily unemployed. The advocates of tax and social security harmonization seek administrative changes so that benefits can be better directed to the needy without encouraging the fraudulent.

Again, in the long run, economic growth is the answer (see Unit 14.4).

(h) Regional unemployment (See Unit 6.3)

2 Specific measures

The growth of unemployment is bad both economically and politically. Thus, successive governments have taken specific measures to **reduce the total** number unemployed. Critics call this 'massaging the figures' so that the problem does not seem as bad as it really is – see Unit 16.4 (5).

These programmes began in 1976 and reached a peak of +1 million in early 1981.

The **Youth Opportunities Programme** ended in 1982 and was superseded by the **Youth Training Scheme**. Both were aimed at finding 'employment' for school leavers.

Youth Training Scheme (YTS)

Advantages

(a) Useful **training**, particularly in big organizations. In the YTS each trainee has a 3-month off-the-job training spell in the year. However, much of the training has been criticized as 'traditional'.

(b) It teaches the **'work habit'** and gives experience of working life and dignity to individuals.

(c) It keeps 350 000 teenagers off the streets and **reduces the social costs** associated with juvenile delinquency.

(d) Some of those trained find **employment**. The YOP Scheme claimed a 40% success rate, and YTS 54%.

(e) Better **quality** workforce is developed.

Criticisms

(a) YTS trainees **replace adults**, raising unemployment in other age groups

(b) **Cheap labour.** The employer receives £1950 grant per person. He pays £1250 in wages (£25 per week), has administration costs of perhaps £150 and should use the remaining £550 for training.

(c) **Public cost** – £1 billion per year.

(d) **Artificial, not real jobs**. Few will get permanent employment and will become disillusioned. The YTS may postpone the problem by one year.

(e) **Lower wages** for young people because YTS is cheap employment. However, some might argue that this lowers costs and expectations and helps minimize inflation (thus being a benefit).

The Government has intervened in the labour market in three ways:

(a) Measures to increase **quantity of labour demanded** – the **Youth Employment Subsidy**. This scheme pays employers a grant of £15 per week if they employ young people under the age of 18 and pay them less than £40 per week. It no longer takes 16 year olds (since Jan 1984), and will follow on from YTS at 17 in future. However, these 'jobs' are not new – 90% would have existed anyway. In demand terms, they represent a movement along a demand for labour curve (W2 – W1 in Figure 16.6).

(b) Measures to **reduce the supply of labour** *e.g.* **early retirement** and work sharing.

The **Job Release Scheme** pays males +62/females +59 a tax-free allowance on early retirement provided they are replaced by someone currently registered as unemployed. From the point of view of national output and growth, reductions in supply (and compensating increases in leisure) are less desirable than increases in the demand for labour.

(c) Measures to reduce the **registered unemployed**.

 (i) **Young people** – YTS (see above).

Community Enterprise Scheme – 1981 – 82 This provided 30 000 jobs at a cost of £147 million doing useful work caring for sick and elderly (and counting lamp-posts in Manchester!). Payment of Supplementary Benefit to people in further education on a **part**-time basis has encouraged more to stay on in education rather than enter the job market.

 (ii) **All ages** – **Temporary Short Time Working Compensation Scheme** (TSTWCS). This gave a 9-month subsidy of 75% of their wages to all employees put on short time instead of being made redundant.

Enterprise Allowance Scheme – those unemployed between 18 and 65, who have £1000 to invest in their own business venture, receive £40 per week from the Government for one year.

3 Possible side effects

It is important for the Government to identify the correct cause(s) of increased unemployment because if the wrong remedies are applied the problem may be **aggravated** rather than relieved. However, **economists disagree** over the relative importance of the different causes and types. For instance the Conservative Government (since 1979) has blamed world recession for the increase whereas the Labour Opposition attributes at least half of the fault to the Government's economic policies. These policies were designed to deal with a **different problem, inflation**, but in so doing they have made unemployment worse. This happened because demand was reduced, through restrictions on money supply and public spending, and this resulted in increased unemployment.

In contrast, it can be pointed out that a policy to directly lower unemployment through increased public expenditure may have undesirable side effects too. It could increase inflation and cause

Balance of Payments difficulties by sucking in imports (rather than creating jobs in UK). Similarly, if increased wages have led to unemployment then higher public spending by increasing demand for labour will do nothing to slow down wage rises.

16.8 Links with other topics

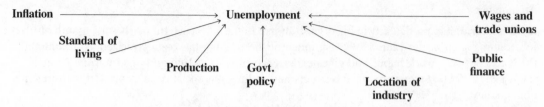

17 International trade

International trade is essentially an extension of **specialization** from **individual** and **regional** to an **international** level. Nations specialize in the production of goods and services and then exchange them for the output of other countries. A country's particular national interest is often best served through international co-operation but there may well be occasions when governments choose to intervene in the trading process in order to protect national interests – as they perceive them.

International trade differs from domestic trade in that **foreign currencies** are used. Thus a British importer of French wine will need to pay the French seller in francs. His bank will deal with the arrangements.

17.1 Advantages of international trade

The case for free international trade may be recalled by the mnemonic **'SMILE'**

1 Specialization

Since resources are unevenly distributed throughout the world it follows that different nations will have differing abilities to produce goods and services. In the same way that the **division of labour** in domestic production has led to considerable increases in living standards, so too can specialization on an international scale.

In theory nations specialize in the production of goods for which they have a **natural advantage**. For instance, Canada uses its land and climate for wheat growing. Some countries acquire advantages. Britain's pop music industry is internationally respected and successful; thus it benefits our balance of payments (invisible account).

Assumptions To demonstrate potential gains from trade we make some simplifying assumptions:
(a) The world consists of two **countries** each producing two products. In Figure 17.1 the countries and products illustrated are those referred to by David Ricardo, the 'father' of much of the economics of international trade.

(b) Production takes place in **two homogeneous units** of production (*e.g.* factories, farms, etc.).
(c) All factors of production are **perfectly mobile**.
(d) There are **no barriers** to trade.
(e) Transport **costs** are **zero**.

Country	Annual output per unit of production	
	Wine (000 barrels)	*Cloth (000 metres)*
England	5	10
Portugal	10	5
World output	15	15

Fig. 17.1 World output before specialization

Absolute advantage In Figure 17.1 it is immediately apparent that England is more efficient at producing cloth while Portugal is more efficient at producing wine. Figure 17.2 shows the result of each country specializing in producing only the product in which it has an **absolute advantage**. World output has increased by 33⅓% (15 to 20 = ⅓).

Country	Annual output per unit of production	
	Wine (000 barrels)	*Cloth (000 metres)*
England	0	20
Portugal	20	0
World output	20	20

Fig. 17.2 Output after specialization

Thus world output of both goods has been increased **without** using any more scarce resources. However, this benefit will not be realized unless international trade takes place, and goods are exchanged. Failure to trade will mean the only people to benefit will be–(1) Alcoholic nudists in Portugal, because Portugal has more wine but no cloth and–(2) Fashion-conscious teetotallers in England where cloth production has doubled but there is no longer any wine production!

Country	Annual output per unit of production	
	Wine (000 barrels)	*Cloth (000 metres)*
England	7	13
Portugal	13	7
	20	20

Fig. 17.3 Output after specialization and exchange

Figure 17.3 shows that by exchanging 7000 metres of cloth for 7000 barrels of wine, both nations end up better off than in Figure 17.1 (before specialization and trade). Thus, from specialization and trade, at this exchange rate, England has gained 2000 barrels of wine and 3000 metres of cloth.

Comparative advantage It is somewhat unrealistic to expect the situation described above to occur very often in the real world. Far more likely is a situation in which one country is more efficient than its trading partner in producing a whole range of goods.

Country	Changes in output	
	Textiles (000 garments)	*Computers (000s)*
England	100 (1/20 C)	5 (20 T)
India	50 (1/25 C)	2 (25 T)

Fig. 17.4 Comparative advantage example (opportunity cost)

In Figure 17.4 England is more efficient in the production of both textiles and computers than India. On the face of it there seems to be no basis for mutually beneficial trade. However, an examination of the **opportunity costs** of production proves otherwise.

The opportunity cost of producing 5 computers in England is the 100 garments which could have been produced instead. Thus the opportunity cost of 1 computer is $\frac{100}{5} = 20$ garments. Figure 17.4 shows all the opportunity costs.

It is clear that the opportunity cost of producing computers is the **reciprocal** $\left(\frac{1}{?}\right)$ of the opportunity cost of producing textiles (*i.e.* $\frac{1}{1/20} = 20$). This will always be true in a 2-good model and is an important check on whether your own workings are correct.

From the example we can see that the opportunity cost of producing computers is **lower** in England than in India, thus to the economist, England has a **comparative advantage** in production of computers. Put simply, England does not have to give up as much (only 20 textiles) to make computers as India does (25 textiles). Similarly India has a comparative advantage (lower opportunity cost) in the production of textiles. England may be said to have a **comparative disadvantage** (higher opportunity cost) in producing textiles (England gives up ½₀ of computers whereas India only gives up ½₅).

Economic theory predicts that international trade will be mutually beneficial if countries **specialize according to their comparative advantage(s)**.

This is a little harder to demonstrate than the gains from specialization according to absolute advantage. It will be necessary to assume there are a large number of 'units of production' in each country. Specialization thus involves England transferring production out of textiles into computers whilst in India the process is reversed. Suppose England switches 3 units of production from textiles into computers, whilst India transfers 7 units from computers into textiles. Figure 17.5 shows the net results of such a change: 1000 more computers and 50 000 more textiles. Again through trade at a suitable exchange rate both nations can gain.

Country	Changes in output	
	Textiles (000 garments)	*Computers (000s)*
England	−300	+15
India	+350	−14
Net change	+50	+1

Fig. 17.5 Comparative advantage and specialization gains

It might be noted that in practice, specialization leads to the benefits of large-scale production (see Unit 5). Such **economies of scale** mean that when all of a nation's resources (Figure 17.2) are concentrated on one product rather than half of them (as in 17.1) output is **more** than doubled. Thus in Figure 17.2 world output of wine and cloth would exceed 20 000 giving each more benefit.

Conclusion If countries specialize according to their comparative advantage then total production from a given set of resources will be increased. Futhermore, the greater the degree of specialization the greater the potential gains from trade. These potential gains explain why so many economists and politicians are supporters of free international trade and opponents of any attempts to restrict this trade.

2 Monopolies

International trade enables foreign competitors to enter domestic markets which would otherwise be controlled by monopolists or oligopolists. All other things being equal (see 17.5) this increase in **competition** will benefit the consumer through lower prices and improved efficiency (see Unit 7). For instance, British firms do not have to buy British steel and can import from elsewhere, notably West Germany.

3 Increased choice

There is an obvious benefit from international trade in that a country may gain access to goods or services it cannot produce itself. However, a more significant aspect of increased choice lies in consumer demand for foreign alternatives to domestically produced goods. For example even though the UK produces, and indeed exports, motor vehicles, British consumers obviously value being able to choose Japanese or European vehicles. However the price of increased consumer choice may well be increased unemployment in domestic industries.

4 Links with other countries

To the extent that international trade increases both understanding and, more importantly, economic interdependence, trade may be said to be a force for international harmony. On the other hand it is, regrettably, true that conflicts of commercial and business interests have led to international crises, *e.g.* the European supplying of Soviet pipeline in 1982 angered the USA. Britain and France have clashed over milk, beef and apples in recent years.

5 Economies of scale

The size of the market represents the most important restriction to the **division of labour**. By opening up new markets, international trade creates new opportunities to exploit economies of scale. Thus more trade between nations is beneficial to countries involved, although they do not always see the immediate gains. The scope for specialization and economies of scale may be limited by transport costs, national considerations and protectionist measures (17.6 and 17.7).

17.2 Patterns of UK trade

1 Commodity structure

Traditionally the UK has been thought to possess a **Comparative Advantage** in the production of manufactured goods and a **Comparative Disadvantage** in the production of food and raw materials. Economic theory would, therefore, predict that we would export manufactured goods and import food and raw materials (see 17.1(1)).

Exports – Description	1955	1965	1975	1980
Engineering Products	36.5	43.5	45.3	37.5
Machinery	21.1	26.5	30.4	25.3
Road Motor Vehicles	8.9	11.6	9.5	6.7
Other Transport Equipment	5.7	3.3	3.4	3.5
Scientific Instruments	1.2	2.1	2.0	2.0
Semi-Manufactures	29.7	26.8	24.0	22.7
Chemicals	7.8	9.2	10.9	11.2
Textiles	10.1	5.8	3.7	2.9
Metals	11.8	11.8	9.4	8.6
Other Semi-Manufactures and Manufacture	12.6	13.2	12.6	13.4
Non-Manufactures	21.2	16.4	18.1	26.4
Food, Beverages, Tobacco	6.5	6.6	7.3	6.9
Basic Materials	5.6	4.0	2.7	3.1
Fuels	4.6	2.7	4.2	13.6
Other	4.5	3.0	3.9	2.8
Total	100.0	100.0	100.0	100.0

Imports – Description	1955	1965	1975	1980
Food, Beverages, Tobacco	36.2	29.7	17.7	12.4
Fuel	10.4	10.6	17.7	13.8
Industrial Materials and Semi-Manufactures	47.9	43.0	34.1	35.2
Finished Manufactures	5.2	15.3	28.3	35.6
Unclassified	0.3	1.4	2.2	3.0
Total	100.0	100.0	100.0	100.0

Fig. 17.6 UK exports and imports by commodity 1955–1980

In Figure 17.6 we can see that the traditional picture of UK trade remains true as far as **exports** are concerned. There are two notable exceptions:

1) the growth of **North Sea oil** into a major UK export.   2) the decline of **textile** exports.

In Figure 17.6 we can also see in 1955 the notion of Britain as an **importer** of Food etc., and Industrial Materials was largely accurate. However by 1980 the picture was very different. **Finished Manufactured goods** are now the most important single category of imports whilst Finished and Semi-Finished manufactures now account for +70% of total imports. The food category has plummeted dramatically to 12%.

Significance of changing trade patterns

It should be noted that given the **income inelasticity** of demand for **primary products** and fairly stable population, it is not surprising that the percentage of food imports has declined.

The increasing importance of **manufactured goods** may be seen as inevitable as world and UK incomes rise. Both France and West Germany are more dependent on imported manufactures than the UK. However certain aspects of the UK's recent trading performance do give rise for concern.

Britain is now a **net importer** of manufactured goods.

1982 was the last year in which there was a surplus on balance. Of all the individual industries listed, only metal goods seems to be going against the general pattern of increased imports.

It may be possible to explain this trend by suggesting that our **Comparative Advantage** now lies in **oil** rather than manufactures. However, it is clear that once the oil has run out the **import penetration** and consequent **de-industrialization** process (see Unit 5) will have so weakened our manufacturing sector that the UK will suffer serious balance of payments problems (see Unit 18).

2 Area structure of trade

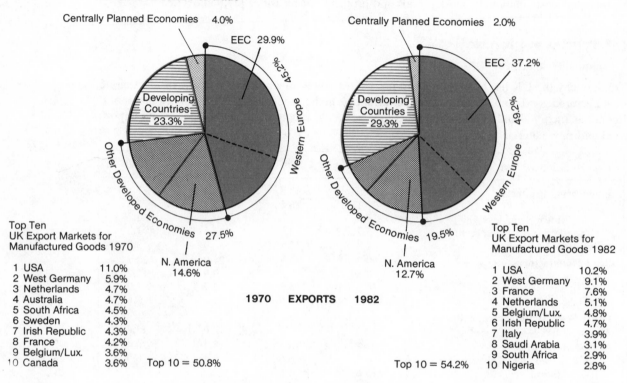

Top Ten
UK Export Markets for
Manufactured Goods 1970

1	USA	11.0%
2	West Germany	5.9%
3	Netherlands	4.7%
4	Australia	4.7%
5	South Africa	4.5%
6	Sweden	4.3%
7	Irish Republic	4.3%
8	France	4.2%
9	Belgium/Lux.	3.6%
10	Canada	3.6%

Top 10 = 50.8%

1970   EXPORTS   1982

Top Ten
UK Export Markets for
Manufactured Goods 1982

1	USA	10.2%
2	West Germany	9.1%
3	France	7.6%
4	Netherlands	5.1%
5	Belgium/Lux.	4.8%
6	Irish Republic	4.7%
7	Italy	3.9%
8	Saudi Arabia	3.1%
9	South Africa	2.9%
10	Nigeria	2.8%

Top 10 = 54.2%

Fig. 17.7 UK Exports (Manuf. goods) by area

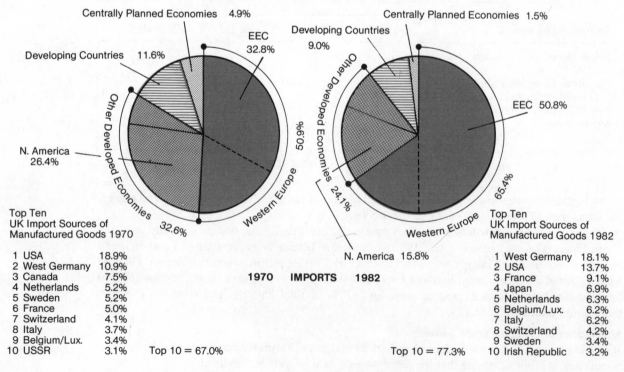

Top Ten
UK Import Sources of
Manufactured Goods 1970

1	USA	18.9%
2	West Germany	10.9%
3	Canada	7.5%
4	Netherlands	5.2%
5	Sweden	5.2%
6	France	5.0%
7	Switzerland	4.1%
8	Italy	3.7%
9	Belgium/Lux.	3.4%
10	USSR	3.1%

Top 10 = 67.0%

1970   IMPORTS   1982

Top Ten
UK Import Sources of
Manufactured Goods 1982

1	West Germany	18.1%
2	USA	13.7%
3	France	9.1%
4	Japan	6.9%
5	Netherlands	6.3%
6	Belgium/Lux.	6.2%
7	Italy	6.2%
8	Switzerland	4.2%
9	Sweden	3.4%
10	Irish Republic	3.2%

Top 10 = 77.3%

(Source: **Overseas Trade Statistics of the United Kingdom**)

Fig. 17.8 UK Imports (Manuf. goods) by area

Imports

Britain's EEC partners have become far more important to the UK in terms of both imports and exports as can be seen from Figures 17.7 and 17.8. Manufactured imports from the Common Market have risen much faster than UK sales to Europe since our entry in 1973. West Germany, France, Italy, Belgium and Luxembourg increased their percentage and moved up the top ten table.

Perhaps the most significant change has been the rise of manufactured imports from Japan from nowhere to fourth. On overall trade a small UK–Japan trade surplus in 1970 was turned into a deficit in excess of £2 billion in 1983.

Exports

Although USA and West Germany remain our two largest single markets the shares of our EEC partners have risen to the detriment of the old Commonwealth. In 1982 Australia and Canada had disappeared from Top 10 and South Africa's share had dropped. Sweden's decline as an export market also reflects Britain's entry into the EEC because Sweden remained outside in EFTA to which Britain used to belong.

It should be clear that, given the nature of **international specialization**, there is an obvious link between changing commodity structures and changing area structures.

17.3 The terms of trade

The terms of trade represents the purchasing power of a country's exports in terms of imports. It shows the **price** changes of **goods** in international trade. It compares the average change in the price of exports with the average change in the price of imports. The calculation is through **index numbers**. The figure for the terms of trade is a percentage based on the movement of two index numbers (one for imports, one for exports).

Year	Terms of trade index
1972	121.2
1975	100.0
1977	100.1
1979	106.3
1982	100.6

Fig. 17.9 Terms of trade

The **Measurement** formula $= \dfrac{\text{index for export prices}}{\text{index for import prices}} \times 100$. Thus in 1972 the value of terms of trade was 121.2. The two indices are **weighted** averages (adjusted for the volume of trade in each product). The export weights reflect the importance of the different categories of goods which Britain exports. As with the retail price index (see Unit 9) a base year is chosen (in Figure 17.9 it is 1975) and variations in the index show changes of price since that date.

The two basic **causes of price increases** are:

1 Production costs rising. The seller in order to maintain his profits may have to raise his market price. In Britain's case higher domestic costs of production lead to more expensive exports.

2 Exchange rate rises–since fixed exchange rates were abandoned (see Unit 18.4), freely fluctuating rates have greatly affected prices in world trade. For instance, if the £ rises in value, then British exports go up in price *e.g.* at £1 = $1.50, a £4000 British car sells in USA for $6000; but if the exchange rate rises to £1 = $1.60 then a £4000 British car now sells at $6400–a price increase of $400. Changes in demand and supply patterns influence exchange rates. For instance, North Sea oil artificially raised the value of sterling, which in turn raised export prices and cheapened imports–this improved the terms of trade for Britain.

If the terms of trade index **exceeds 100**, then it shows that export prices are increasing faster than import prices. For instance, between 1977 and 1979 the terms of trade increased from 100.1 to 106.3. The terms of trade are then said to be **favourable** to us. Each £ earned from a given quantity of exports can pay for a greater volume of imports. Conversely, a fall in the terms of trade between 1979 and 1982 means that more British goods will need to be exported to pay for a certain quantity of imports.

This supposedly favourable movement in the terms of trade indicates a **worsening** of Britain's **competitive position**, as it shows dearer exports and cheaper imports. Thus, where our exports compete with foreign goods in a third market then we will lose trade.

Terms of trade and the balance of payments

The terms of trade just looks at the price effect. It does **not show** the volume effects. These depend on:

1 the relative demand elasticities. For instance, if British **export** prices rise then assuming demand is **elastic** the quantity demanded will fall. This fall in volume and total revenue will lead to a **current account trade deficit**, other things being equal. At the same time if the price of **imports** into Britain

Movement in terms of trade	Cause	Elasticity of demand	Effect on balance of payments
Adverse	↓ Export prices	Inelastic	–
	↓ Export prices	Elastic	+
	↑ Import prices	Elastic	+
	↑ Import prices	Inelastic	–
Favourable	↑ Export prices	Inelastic	+
	↑ Export prices	Elastic	–
	↓ Import prices	Elastic	–
	↓ Import prices	Inelastic	+

Fig. 17.10 Terms of trade and balance of payments

falls, assuming demand for them is **inelastic**, the quantity demanded will remain unchanged but total revenue will fall. This will tend to **benefit** the **current account**. Figure 17.10 summarises all the demand possibilities and their effects on Balance of Payments;

2 the supply elasticities. The terms of trade looks at price changes, which means movements **along** a demand curve for exports and imports. It does not examine the impact of factors other than price which produce a shift in demand. For instance, if **supply is elastic** then traders can take advantage of changes in demand to expand their **share of world trade**. This may occur irrespective of price changes and produce extra current account earnings – see Figure 17.11.

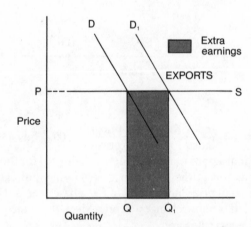

Fig. 17.11 Terms of trade and export earnings

17.4 Government control

In view of the advantages of international trade it may seem surprising that governments seek to regulate international trade. Countries often place national interests before international interests and so protect their trade.

1 Reasons

The reasons for such intervention can be remembered by the mnemonic **'BRIDES'**

(a) Balance of payments

If a country is faced with a persistent balance of payments **deficit** (see Unit 18.3) it may attempt to reduce its import bill by imposing import controls (see 17.6). The danger is that trading partners affected by the import controls may retaliate and thus British export demand will fall, making the protecting nation no better off.

(b) Revenue raising

Just as domestically-produced goods attract **indirect taxation** so too will imported goods such as wines, spirits and tobacco. Revenue raising is not a major objective of import controls. If it was then duties are likely to be levied on goods with an **inelastic demand**. The disadvantage of such tariffs is that domestic consumers pay higher prices and the cost of living is raised.

(c) Infant industries

It is argued that new industries need protection. This argument is particularly applicable to Third World countries where newly-formed manufacturing industries may not be able to grow fast enough to fully realize **economies of scale**. Also, they may face competition from the already industrialized nations. Import controls, therefore, allow the 'infant industries' a breathing space during which they can expand and exploit scale economies and thus compete on an equal basis. The main **problems** with this line of argument are:

  (i) Protection from competition may merely encourage inefficiency.
 (ii) When does the infant come of **age**? It is hard to imagine domestic industry ever being totally willing to give up the benefits of protection.

For instance, Britain has protected its film industry from American competition since the 1930s, by restricting the percentage of American films which could be shown in British cinemas.

(d) Dumping and unfair competition

Much of the protectionist argument centres on the claim that other countries indulge in 'unfair competition', particularly **dumping**. This tactic involves **selling exports** at **artificially low prices**. This may be done to benefit from economies of scale in production or to gain a toehold in the market *e.g.* Japanese electrical goods.

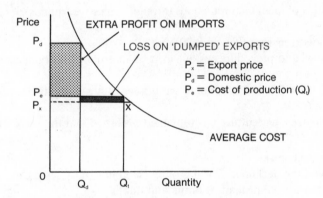

Fig. 17.12 Dumping abroad (and profits at home)

Figure 17.12 illustrates how dumping works. The size of the domestic market provides a restraint on the ability to exploit economies of scale. The average cost for home sales of Q_d is shown by P_d. If Q_t is produced then average cost falls to P_e. The extra production $Q_d - Q_t$ can be exported. If it is sold at below cost price (dumped) then a loss is made (red area). However, if domestic production Q_d is sold at P_d extra profit is made (shaded area). By selling quantity $Q_d - Q_t$ abroad at price P_x **below factor cost** P_e output has risen to Q_x and average cost has fallen to P_e. Despite the losses on the dumped exports the exercise is successful because of the high profits on the home market.

Many protectionists would prefer free trade but are concerned by what they see as the unfair practices of some of our trading partners. Objectively it is very difficult to decide what constitutes 'fair trading' and what does not. In the 1984 lamb dispute with France, a central factor in the French farmers' case was that Britain, in subsidizing her farmers, was guilty of unfair competition. The Americans have said the same about British steel. One is tempted to conclude that 'fair trade', like beauty, 'is in the eye of the beholder!'

(e) Employment

Since 1973, in Britain, a major argument for protection has been either to maintain home employment or to minimize the increase in unemployment. In demonstrating the advantages of international specialization (17.2) we assumed both homogeneous units of production and perfect factor mobility. We thus envisaged that textile mills and textile workers would instantaneously become computer plants and operatives as the UK specialized according to its comparative advantage.

However, in the real world, such assumptions are unrealistic because of factor immobility. In the West Riding of Yorkshire, only a tiny fraction of workers made redundant by the decline of the textile industry have even the remotest chance of finding work in the new computer firms such as

Systime. Thus the price paid for cheap foreign textiles has been **extensive localized unemployment**. In contrast to our hypothetical examples (Figures 17.1 to 17.4) the gains from trade may well be outweighed by other **costs**, which may be indirect. Thus to limit the public cost of unemployment (and ease pressure on PSBR) and reduce social costs, protection may be encouraged.

The Multi-Fibre agreement limiting cheap textiles into Western Europe was adopted in 1975 to ease the unemployment problems threatening declining textile industries.

A number of politicians and economists, notably the New Cambridge group, have advocated **selective import controls** to maintain and increase employment levels. Protectionists further argue that if import controls successfully reduce unemployment then national income will increase, thus enabling Britain, as a nation, to afford to purchase **more imports**. Thus the effect of import controls may **not** be to reduce the volume of imports but to increase national income, in the **long run**.

(f) Strategic reasons

In times of international conflict certain products may be considered 'essential' making home production desirable even when other countries are more efficient. Since World War II the UK has 'artificially' encouraged the development of home-produced foodstuffs by heavy subsidization of agriculture. Similarly for **security** reasons the export of high technology products to Comecon is restricted. Also the export of natural gas from Britain is prohibited. An obvious difficulty with this line of argument is that what is considered to be 'essential' may well be largely a matter of opinion.

2 Post-war trends

1945–72 Trade became freer
The main reasons for this liberalization were:
 1 Removal of quantitative restrictions.
 2 Reduction of tariffs of manufactured goods through successive 'rounds' of cuts *e.g.* 1973 Tokyo round.
 3 Convertibility of currencies achieved in 1950s.
 4 Rules, conventions and procedures established by international organizations such as GATT and IMF.
 5 Enlargement of the EEC and agreement with other States bringing about more free trade in Europe.

Despite these changes, **agriculture** has remained **protected** and the trade in **services** is still not very liberated.

Since 1973 'New Protectionism'
Since the oil crisis and the decline in world growth (see Unit 14.4) newer, more **subtle**, restrictive devices have been introduced instead of tariffs and quotas.

Trade is now **'managed'** by many governments in certain ways. For instance selective temporary tariffs, voluntary export restraint agreements and export subsidies mean that half of world trade is not free, compared with 40% in 1974.

17.5 Methods of Protection

1 Types of import control
One of the main forms of import control also serves as a mnemonic for the others–**'QUOTAS'**.

(a) QUOtas
There are restrictions on the amount of imports. They may refer to either the total quantity or total value of a commodity which may be imported during a given period of time. They may also refer to the quantity or value which may be imported from a particular country or group of countries.

GATT (see 17.6) has tried to stop quotas. However, it has allowed **exceptions** for nations with balance of payments difficulties and industries suffering injury. It has also been undermined by the signing of **voluntary export restraint** agreements (VERA).

In recent years the Japanese car industry has voluntarily negotiated with Britain a limit of 12% of all domestic UK car sales. Britain also limits T-shirts, radios, cutlery and watches from other less-developed nations.

(b) Tariffs
These are taxes placed on imports. They may be **ad valorem** (*i.e.* a given percentage of import price) or **'specific'** (*i.e.* a set amount per unit *e.g.* per bottle of wine). Tariffs levied on goods with an **elastic** demand will be more effective in reducing the volume of imports, whilst those levied on goods with an **inelastic** demand will raise revenue rather than reduce imports.

(c) Administration
A 'hidden' form of import control is the use of deliberately obstructive bureaucratic **procedures**. For years European exporters have complained about Japanese use of red tape (form filling) to slow

imports into Japan. In 1983 France retaliated by insisting that all Japanese videos imported into France had to be processed through the customs office in Poitiers. This tiny office has a staff of only eight officials, thus the processing is a slow business!

This subtle form of protection has become more commonplace since 1973.

(d) Specifications
The less visible the protection the less likely it is to invite retaliation. For this reason, recent years have also seen a proliferation of **technical and safety regulations** imposed by many countries. For example, Rowntree-Mackintosh are required to produce several different shades of Smarties in order to satisfy food colour regulations in many countries. Similarly the American fuel emission regulations have acted as an indirect barrier to BL's Rover and Jaguar exports.

2 Disadvantages of import controls – 'WIRE'

(a) Welfare loss
17.1 showed that unrestricted international trade leads to an increase in production and thus in total economic welfare. Thus the greater the barriers to trade the greater this loss of welfare.

However, individual nations are concerned with how the welfare gains are **distributed**. If a nation feels that it is not sharing in these gains but losing out then it may protect itself.

(b) Inefficiency
Protection from international competition may encourage inefficiency in a number of ways. Within specific firms and industries it may prevent or delay the introduction of modern technology and encourage overmanning etc. On a general economic level it may encourage an inefficient allocation of resources by delaying the movement of resources out of declining and into expanding industries.

(c) REtaliation
The imposition of import controls may provoke trading partners to take similar action. For instance British efforts to keep French UHT milk out were followed by French moves to stop British meat imports.

3 Encouraging exports

Since 1973 exports from Britain have been artificially stimulated by:

(a) Subsidies Exporters can claim VAT refunds. This makes their goods artificially cheaper than otherwise and probably more competitive in world markets.
(b) Export credits British Government bodies and banks give cheap loans to British exporters to tide them over, until the goods are paid for by the foreign buyers. Also, the Export Credits Guarantee Department gives cut price insurance against non-payment by foreigners. This enables exporters to be paid (by ECGD) even if the buyer defaults.
(c) General advice/information Official support is often given for export deals. This is done by Ministerial influence, British Embassy contacts and trade fairs.

17.6 International economic organizations

1 GATT

The General Agreement on Tariffs and Trade was founded by 23 nations in 1947. It is now composed of over 80 (non-communist) countries and based in Geneva. It lays down rules for international trading.
The broad **aims** are twofold:
(a) To reduce tariffs. There have been a series of **'rounds'** in which tariffs were cut. By 1967 the average tax on manufactured goods had been reduced to 7%. This was further lowered by the Tokyo round launched in 1973 and concluded in 1979.
(b) To eliminate quotas. This was most successful up to 1973 but 'VERAs' (see 17.5) have recently undermined this aim. GATT rules allow **exemptions** on a **temporary** basis if:
 (i) A nation has balance of payments difficulties.
 (ii) Home producers suffer injury.
The weaknesses of these allowed exceptions are that they are difficult to disprove and tend to become more than temporary, *e.g.* Multi-Fibre agreement since 1974!
The **importance** of GATT is **declining** for several reasons:
(a) Regional trade groupings such as the EEC are growing. They have their own regulations which may contradict GATT *e.g.* EEC has a common external tariff (see 17.6(3)). 50% of world trade takes place within W. Europe.
(b) Exemptions to GATT are increasing. This undermines the principle of equal treatment which GATT has tried to develop. The 'New Protectionism' since 1973 has been counter to GATT's aims.

(c) Under-developed nations are critical of GATT (see UNCTAD). In 1971 the Generalized System of Preference (GSP) was introduced to help poor nations. The rich countries gave tariff concessions to the less developed without expecting them to reciprocate (*i.e.* make tariff cuts in return). However, the benefits of this were lost with the oil crisis 1973 which made the under-developed world bigger debtors than before. They feel that GATT has not adequately catered for them. In particular, the new protective measures since 1973 during the World Depression hit the poor nations more than the rich.

(d) Trade in services has been largely ignored.

(e) Agricultural trade is still restricted.

2 UNCTAD

In 1964, seventy-seven poor nations set up a United Nations Conference on Trade and Development (UNCTAD). It holds conferences every **four years** to pressurise the developed countries to help the poor. UNCTAD wants:

(a) free **access** to world markets. GSP (above) went some small way towards improving their access. The Lomé conventions agreed with EEC in 1975 and 1979 gave sixty less developed nations free access to EEC;

(b) commodity agreements to **stabilize prices** (mainly primary products). For instance, +80% of Zambia's export earnings are from copper. Thus if the price of copper falls dramatically, the economy of Zambia is badly affected.

(c) One per cent of GNP of developed nations to be given in **aid**. They have achieved little success with this as Britain gave 176 million (0.53%) in 1964 but 766 million (0.34%) in 1980.

3 Trading blocs

There are two types of group (which GATT allows).

(a) Free trade areas

There are **no internal restrictions** on trade **between** members. However, each member decides its **own external** policy in relation to trade with non-members. Examples are EFTA (European Free Trade Area) of which the UK is a former member and LAFTA (Latin American Free Trade Area).

(b) Customs unions

A customs union is a **free trade area** where members agree to adopt a **Common External Tariff** to be levied on all imports from non-members. The European Economic Community is a customs union (see Unit 17.7).

4 Suppliers' organizations

Producers sometimes co-operate in a **cartel** to exploit a world market. The Organization of Petroleum Exporting Countries (OPEC) is a good example. In 1973 they forced a four-fold oil price increase, by making supply elastic at an agreed (high) price (P_1). Figure 17.13 shows the increase in total revenue (gained black area exceeds lost red area) which was achieved because D was very **inelastic**.

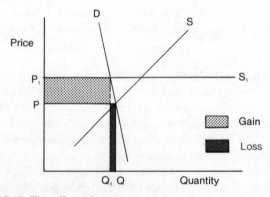

Fig. 17.13 The effect of total revenue on oil price changes

Since 1979 OPEC has **lost** its **power** because of:

(a) Disagreement among the members. Unity is important. If price is agreed then one member selling cheaper creates competition, breaking the monopoly. Britain has done this with North Sea oil since 1981. Similarly, if supply levels are agreed and one member exceeds its 'quota' this makes supply more elastic and destroys the monopoly position again. Iran and Iraq have done this to gain extra revenue for war financing (against each other!).

(b) The **fall in world demand** for oil. This demand is derived from the level of world production. If output does not continue growing substantially, as happened 1973–1981, then oil demand falls. This declining market means less for each oil-producing nation, unless it acts unilaterally to increase its market share. Such action breaks the unity of the cartel, and has weakened OPEC.

The world economy can be divided into four major trading groups:

OECD (Organization for Economic Co-operation and Development) Containing twenty-four leading industrial nations including Britain, they account for 62% of world trade.

OPEC – 15% of world trade.

Developing nations – 13% of world trade.

COMECON – Communist economies which are centrally planned. This group includes Eastern Europe, Cuba and other communist states. They are responsible for 10% of world trade.

17.7 The European Economic Community

In 1957 the **Treaty of Rome** created the EEC. It was composed of Belgium, France, West Germany, Holland, Italy, Luxembourg who had previously combined in the European Coal and Steel Community (ECSC) since 1951.

The UK joined the EEC on 1 January 1973 as did Eire and Denmark. The Labour Government completed its renegotiation of British membership conditions in March 1975 and the issue was subsequently ratified by a referendum in July 1975. However, our participation remains a controversial issue and at the very least it remains a possibility that a future government may bring us out of the market.

Main features of Common Market

1 Free trade within the market There are no customs duties between members. However, there may be more subtle protective measures (see Unit 17.5). This market of just under 300 million people should enable large-scale investment and economies of scale resulting in lower prices for consumers.

2 Common External Tariff (CET) Most imports from outside the market face this tariff. The exceptions include 14 000 tons of New Zealand meat imported under licence into Britain, and agreements (such as Yaounde made with former French colonies) with associate members.

3 Common Agricultural Policy (CAP) This seeks to increase agricultural earnings and to eliminate fluctuations in prices and supplies. Farm products are guaranteed an **intervention price**. If the market price falls below this the Community guarantees to buy excess supplies at the intervention price. Imported foodstuffs are taxed so that they are above the intervention price.

CAP subsidises farmers and by doing so it has created excess production *e.g.* butter mountain, wine lake. CAP accounts for two-thirds of the EEC budget.

Its effect on Britain has been:

(a) To raise food prices (faster than otherwise but only slightly).

(b) Many small efficient British farmers have become extremely well off. They have ploughed up hedgerows to get more land for agricultural production. Their output and incomes have increased.

(c) The Budget expenditure on CAP means less for other EEC programmes from which Britain might benefit *e.g.* regional and social funds.

(d) Disproportionately large budget contributions *e.g.* £700 million per annum on average, with low amounts in the early years and larger amounts (+£1 billion) since.

Generally, it would seem that there has been a redistribution of income from British taxpayers and consumers to farming sector. However, consumers have probably benefited indirectly from the increase in economic growth (0.15% a year) as a result of joining the EEC.

4 Free movement between nations, of capital and labour. For instance, entry visas and work permits are no longer required but passports remain. In 1979 Britain ended exchange control which has made capital movement much easier.

EEC finance

The EEC is financed by 'its own resources' *i.e.* 90% of all import duties and agricultural levies from non-EEC sources (the remaining 10% covers administrative costs) are put into the EEC. It also receives a proportion of VAT receipts.

The UK contributes about 20% of EEC revenue **but** our GNP is only 16% of EEC total. Thus in recent years, British governments have attempted to negotiate temporary reductions in our contributions. For instance, in 1981 Britain received +£800 million refund. However, a permanent solution requires the reform of CAP.

British trade with EEC

The volume and value of UK exports to, and imports from, the EEC have increased since British entry. From 1973 to 1980 deficits were made on total EEC trade. However, since 1980 a surplus has been achieved.

In January 1983 Lloyds Bank Economic Bulletin did a thorough analysis of the gains of EEC membership. It concluded:

Year	% of total UK exports to EEC	% of total UK imports from EEC
1970	29.7	28.4
1975	32.2	38.5
1980	43.1	42.7
1982	41.8	44.7

Fig. 17.14 UK–EEC trade

It is difficult to believe that the UK economy has benefited from EEC membership, because its performance has been so poor over the last decade. The evidence is, however, that the UK economy would have done and would do **even worse outside** than inside the EEC.

17.8 Links with other topics

Balance of payments —————→ **Trade** ←————— **Government policy**

18 Balance of Payments

18.1	**Balance of Payments account**	***
18.2	**Balance of Payments problems**	***
18.3	**Balance of Payments policies**	***
18.4	**Exchange rates**	**
18.5	**International Monetary Fund (IMF)**	*
18.6	**Linked topics**	**

18.1 Balance of Payments accounts

In the same way that companies calculate their profits and losses, so nations calculate their trading positions. However, for **nations** the calculations are larger and more complicated. For instance, imports into Britain need to be paid for in **foreign currencies** whose value now fluctuates daily. Thus, exchange rates have a big influence over the balance of payments.

The Balance of Payments is a national account, showing the **financial transactions** of **one nation** with the **rest of the world** over a **period of time**. Although monthly figures are calculated, quarterly and yearly totals are more useful indicators of trends, because the official figures (particularly invisibles) are often revised. This is caused by the use of estimates and the different dates for collecting information. The statistics are collected by the government. The format of the accounts has been changed over time, but the basic intention remains the same.

If total payments exceed total income, there is a net outflow of funds and vice versa. All nations seek a **net inflow**, but obviously they cannot all achieve it, because everybody's surplus is equivalent to someone else's deficit. Thus, 1973–77 surpluses in the oil rich countries were matched by deficits in the industrialized world (except Japan and West Germany) and the developing world.

The Balance of Payments is divided into three sections:
1 Current Account
2 Capital Account
3 Official Financing

The addition of the **totals on current and capital account equal** the **total for official financing**. Thus, if in Figure 18.1 –

A+B+C+D=£3000m, this amount would be added to the reserves or repaid to borrowers and the official Financing figure would be £−3000m (in this part of the accounts the minus represents a gain!)

1 **Current Account**

Visibles	Export +	+
	Imports −	−
	Balance of Trade	A
Invisibles	Credit +	+
	Debit −	−
	Net Invisibles	B
Current Account Balance		A + B

2 **Capital Account**

Short term capital flows (inflow +, outflow −)	net
Long term capital flows (inflow +, outflow −)	net
Total investment and other capital inflows	C
Balancing item (+ or −)	D
Balance for official financing	A + B + C + D

3 **Official Financing**

Foreign currency borrowings (+) or landing (−)	net
Changes in reserves (addition −, drawings +)	net
Transactions with IMF and other central banks	net
Total Official Financing	− (A + B + C + D)

Fig. 18.1 Balance of Payments Accounts

1 Current Account

This part of the balance of payments is regarded as the most **important**, as it shows a nation's trading strength. If payments are greater than receipts, there is a **deficit** which is undesirable.

This account is subdivided, as shown in Figure 18.1 into,

A **Visible** Trade – trade in **goods**

B **Invisible** Trade – trade in **services**

A Visible trade

The money earned from British **exports of goods** (*e.g.* tractor sold to Zambia) is **credited** (added) to this account, whilst payments for **imported goods** (*e.g.* Japanese car sold in Britain) are **debited**. The difference between the totals is known as the **balance of trade**.

In most years, Britain has suffered a visible trade deficit which reached a peak in 1974 of £5.2 billion. However, by 1980 it had moved into surplus and in 1981, it showed +£2.9 billion (1982 – £2.2m). This change round was caused by:

 (i) the **world depression**. This produced lower primary products prices which lowered import spending. Usually during periods of depression, British trade suffers less than most, making our relative trading position slightly stronger.

 (ii) **Destocking** by British firms who kept fewer stocks of goods (*e.g.* imported raw materials) in order to save money, during Britain's **recession**.

(iii) **The oil position**. Britain, with its own supplies, needed to import less oil and could export more, thus improving her visible trade in oil.

The trade in oil has become so important that the accounts are often analysed in terms of oil and '**non-oil trade**'. The latter category is now in deficit because of increased imports and stable exports. This trend is likely to return the total visibles to a deficit in the mid 1980s, particularly as Britain's **imports of manufactured goods** now exceed her exports of manufactures (for the first time ever).

B Invisible trade

The income earned from the sale of British services abroad is known as an invisible export *e.g.* an insurance premium paid by a Greek shipowner to a Lloyds broker. When British residents spend money on foreign services *e.g.* a week's accommodation in Benidorm, they are creating invisible imports, because payment is going out of Britain.

The main invisibles are:

 (i) **Government expenditure** on embassies, contributions to EEC and other international bodies, military bases/forces abroad, and overseas aid. These all create a substantial **deficit**.

 (ii) **Interest, profits and dividends** These earnings from loans, companies and shares, respectively, earn substantial **surpluses** for the British economy.

(iii) **Other financial services** The earnings of solicitors, brokers, merchants and pension funds investments also contribute benefits to the invisible account.

(iv) **Transport**. Britain's former dominance as a passenger carrier by sea, particularly, and air has disappeared and payments are now roughly **equalled** with earnings in most years.

(v) **Tourism** This covers the expenditure of travellers abroad. From Britain's point of view, the debits and credits roughly **balance**.

(vi) **Private transfers** – individuals transfer money to other countries. Most industrialized nations contain migrants who remit funds to relatives in their family of origin. Such monies are a small but slowly increasing deficit in the invisible account.

A large **invisible surplus** has always been a feature of the British current account in modern times (see Figure 18.2). The figure is subject to **great fluctuation** and frequent revision. However, the general trend has been upward, with a peak reached at **+£3.0 billion** in 1981. The decline to £1.76b in 1982 reflected the low levels of world economic activity which created significantly fewer interest, profits and dividends earnings and the temporary increase in value of £ sterling. A decrease in £'s value is good for the invisibles *e.g.* at £1 = \$2.4, a \$2400 insurance premium earns £1000, but if £ depreciates to \$2.0, the same \$2400 is worth £1200 $\left(\frac{£ \times 2400}{2.0}\right)$

Thus, assuming the demand for British services is inelastic, a **depreciating pound** raises extra income.

Britain's successful trade in services (invisible) has been explained by:

(i) The expertise accumulated over the years.

(ii) London housing the world's largest insurance market and key markets in agricultural products and metals which often do not touch British soil.

(iii) The British reputation for probity (honesty) and variety.

This invisible trade success may be more limited in the future as there is likely to be extra competition particularly in banking and insurance.

A + B Current Account Balance

The balance of trade (visible) and net invisibles are added, as in Figures 18.1 and 18.2, to give the current account balance. The net figure may be +/−. A **deficit** (−) on the current account is a warning that the **nation is spending more than it is earning**, in the short run *e.g.* 1973, 1979. This usually leads to changes in government policy if the deficit is persistent (see 18.2).

2 Capital Account

C Investment

This account includes investment and other capital movements. **Outflows create deficits** (−) and inflows give surpluses (+) in the account. For instance, if Marks & Spencer purchase a new shop in France, this is an outflow of capital. Conversely, if Nissan (Japan) build a car plant on Wearside, then there is a **capital inflow**.

Expenditure on portfolio (paper) assets is also included in this section of the accounts. Thus, if a British citizen buys shares in MacDonalds (hamburgers in USA) this counts as a capital outflow.

The investment can also be distinguished between private and public sector. **Private** sector investment tends to be in **buildings** and **paper assets** held for a long period of time. Public investment, on the other hand, consists of low interest **loans** to underdeveloped nations (*i.e.* aid) where the aim is not always profitability.

Capital flows may be **short term** or long term. The short term ones tend to be **unpredictable** and **volatile**. They feature the shifting of very liquid assets (*i.e.* 'hot' money) between nations to gain the advantage of favourable interest rate differentials. They may also occur for non-economic reasons. For instance, the long standing Arab-Israeli conflict has led to Arab oil money being taken from nations with pro-Israeli sympathies *i.e.* a **political** reason for a capital movement.

During the post war period up to 1970, investment on balance tended to be outward. However, during the 1970s, as shown in Figure 18.2, net investment has been **inward**. This trend has been caused by:

(a) **British entry into the EEC** which has encouraged American and Japanese investment. Their

£m		1971	1973	1975	1977	1979	1981
Visible	(A)	+299	−2375	−3195	−1612	−3312	+4066
Invisible	(B)	+743	+1089	+1560	+1577	+875	+2785
Current Balance		+1042	−1286	−1635	−35	−2437	+6851
Investment etc	(C)	+1821	+919	+360	+4802	+3525	−7538
Balancing item	(D)	+365	+577	−190	+2596	+623	—
Balance for Official Financing		+3228	+210	−1465	+7363	+1711	−687

Fig. 18.2 Balance of Payments selected years 1971–81

firms could then sell in Europe without having to pay tariffs, which would be imposed if they had exported from home.

(b) North Sea oil By making the £ a strong, 'petrocurrency', this encouraged investors to regard investment in Britain as relatively safe, compared with industrialized non-oil producers, such as France.

(c) High interest rates attract hot money, whilst generous regional aid induces real capital investment.

The ending of exchange controls in 1979 does not appear to have slowed down the net inward increase in investment, but it is encouraging excessive capital outflows.

In the **short run**, net inward investment **benefits** the balance of payments accounts because official financing is not needed – reserves can be accumulated and borrowing repaid. However, in the long run, it may be detrimental. The profits, interest and dividends from the investment are remitted abroad and become invisible imports, thus weakening the current account.

D Balancing item

A balancing figure is **added to** or **subtracted from** the combined balances of the current and capital accounts. The balance of payments accounts **always balance** because the current and capital account totals together equal the official financing undertaken. As the latter figure is more accurate than the **varied data** in the other two accounts, the balancing item is calculated from it and is used to make the two totals the same. It is a **net** figure. For example, in 1979, the current account and capital investment came to £+1088 (3525–2437 see Figure 18.2) and the official financing was £+1711. These figures showed an under-recording of £623m. Thus, a balancing item of +£623m was added to the capital account to achieve a balance.

3 Official financing

The Balance for official Financing (which used to be termed total currency flow), shows the **balance of monetary movements** into and out of the country. A positive figure reveals a net inflow of funds into a country *e.g.* 1979 £+1711m. Alternatively, a net outflow is represented by a negative figure *i.e.* 1975 £−1465.

When there is a negative figure, the amount has to be paid for either by:

(a) borrowing from other central banks and international organizations or;

(b) using up **reserves** which have been saved over the years or;

(c) borrowing **and** withdrawing reserves.

When the balance for official financing is positive, then loans can be repaid and reserves replenished. Governments do sometimes borrow even when the balance for official financing is positive; this is in order to build up reserves for the future.

The fact that the amount of official financing **equals** the balance for official financing ensures that the balance of payments always balances.

18.2 Balance of Payments problems

A country has a balance of payments problem when a section of its accounts are in regular deficit or surplus. Deficit problems are more serious than surplus ones, as surpluses usually result from successful international trading, whilst deficits indicate failure. Persistent imbalances indicate that the balance of payments is in **fundamental disequilibrium**. This usually requires the **government** to undertake rectifying policies.

The **seriousness** of a deficit depends upon its size and the section of the accounts in which it occurs. A **Balance of Trade** deficit has plagued Britain for decades but whilst Net Invisibles covered it, the problem was not too great. However, if the **Current Account** balance became negative, because net invisibles did not supersede the deficit trade in goods, then the alarm bells started ringing. This was because such a deficit, if large, showed trading weakness and tended to depress the exchange rate. A negative Balance for official Financing could also be worrying. This would need paying for out of reserves or by borrowing, again weakening the exchange rate position. If it were caused by investment outflows, there might be concern that resources were being utilized abroad rather than at home, thereby limiting economic growth potential. However, in the longer term, the returns on these investments would benefit the current account invisible earnings.

1970–1980 Up to 1980, **Britain** faced intermittent balance of payments crises, caused by current account **deficits** – see Figure 18.2. In 1967, sterling was **devalued** by 14.3% and this contributed to a steady improvement in the current account. However, after 1971, because of the accelerating inflation and the expansion of credit in the economy, imports zoomed. In 1972, the Government **floated** sterling in order to get a lower exchange rate (which would hopefully reduce imports by making them more expensive and encourage exports by making them relatively cheaper). This did not work for many reasons – 1973 rising oil prices, faster growth from our competitors, lower inflation of our trading rivals. However, the world depression created by the **oil crisis 1973–4** dampened the demand for imports, as did reduced public expenditure (undertaken under IMF instructions), whilst a further sterling depreciation stimulated exports, resulting in a moderate surplus in 1978.

1980 onwards. Since 1980, Britain has gained a balance of payments **surplus** on current account. This has been caused almost solely by North Sea oil. On stream oil has reduced oil imports and increased oil exports. Although goods and services were imported for the oil exploration and construction work and invisible debits occurred through remitted foreign company profits, the overall impact has been beneficial. In addition expenditure on imports has decreased because of the recession and this has helped.

The disadvantages associated with a surplus are:

 1 It **masks underlying weaknesses** in the economy. In Britain's case, the oil revenues may only be significant until 1990 and the non-oil visible trade is declining markedly (see 18.1 above).

 2 It leads to an **unwanted rise in money supply**. This may prevent internal monetary policy from working and stimulate inflation.

 3 It may be used to **finance current consumption** rather than future investment. The government may use taxes from oil sales to increase existing living standards at the expense of investment in new industries and technology. *e.g.* 1983 British Rail electrification has been put off again because the Government fears that it will raise public expenditure, but Social Security is paid to 3m unemployed.

A surplus on the combined capital and current accounts may also be disadvantageous for the same reasons. In addition,

 4 **Excessive inward investment** (Capital Account) may take up opportunities which domestic firms should have been developing; and lead to a long-term drain on the invisibles through interest, profits and dividends sent abroad in the future.

 5 It may cause an **Exchange Rate appreciation**, but this decreases the competitiveness of visible exports in world markets and increases the attraction of imports. If this leads to domestic unemployment, then the oil revenues may be 'lost' financing unemployment benefit.

However, governments find it much easier to live with surpluses than deficits. They give the appearance of successful economic policies, prestige and political strength.

18.3 Balance of Payments policies

Governments are expected to remedy persistent balance of payments **deficits**, particularly those on current account. The policies adopted depend on the causes. From British experience, the most **common causes** appear to be:

 1 an overvalued exchange rate making our goods uncompetitive;

 2 domestic spending exceeding domestic output, leading to inflation, which made imports relatively cheap and exports relatively dear;

 3 an excessive supply of money in the economy causing inflation;

 4 structural weaknesses in the economy.

Policies – 'DEDECTS'

1 DEvaluation or Depreciation

These mean a reduction in the foreign exchange value of a nation's currency. Thus, in 1949 the £ value was lowered from $4.03 to $2.80 when there was a system of **fixed exchange rates** – this was a **devaluation**.

However, since 1972 (see Unit 18.4) exchange rates have floated. If an exchange rate **floats** downwards, the fall in value is known as a **depreciation** *e.g.* during winter 1983–84, £1 fell from $1.80 to $1.20.

The **role** of the **government** varies between devaluation and depreciation. In the case of devaluation, the government applied to the IMF (Unit 18.6) for permission to lower its fixed exchange rate as a **last resort**, after trying other policies to reduce the deficit. When exchange rates are floating, demand and supply factors cause the rate to fall. However, a government can affect them by its policies, thus having an **indirect influence**. For instance, a government may act to raise interest rates, which should attract demand for £ and thereby slow-down/stop a depreciating £.

The effects of devaluation and depreciation are the same – **cheaper exports** and **dearer imports**. The following example illustrates how this results: at the exchange rate of £1 = $2, a British export priced £5 sells for $10 in USA, and an American import costing $20 sells for £10 in Britain. If the exchange rate falls to £1 = $1, then the British export now sells for $5 (*i.e.* $5 cheaper) and the American import is priced at £20 in Britain (*i.e.* £10 dearer). Thus devaluation/depreciation restores competitiveness to a nation's goods. However, the Balance of Payments only benefits if proportionately more exports are sold and many fewer imports are bought. The likelihood of this occurring depends on the **elasticity of demand** of the goods being traded. Devaluation/depreciation is only effective if the demand for **exports** is relatively **elastic** and the demand for **imports** is relatively **elastic**. This is because in these cases, the total revenue from exports will increase and the total spending on imports will fall, giving a net gain. There is little evidence that the elasticity of demand for imports and exports are sufficiently elastic to have a big impact, in Britain's case.

The effectiveness of depreciation/devaluation is further **limited** by other factors:

(a) The ability of domestic suppliers to meet the extra demand created by cheaper exports and home consumers switching away from imports to British goods. If home **supply** is **inelastic**, then the advantage of depreciation may be lost.

(b) Inflation – if the costs of production in Britain are rising faster than elsewhere, the price advantage from devaluation may be lost.

(c) Price is just one factor. The **conditions** of **demand** (Unit 4.2) might change, or be more important in some markets *e.g.* in engineering the design, safety and efficiency of a product may be more important than its price.

(d) Other nations may **retaliate** by lowering their exchange rates, thus nullifying the impact. In practice, this has rarely happened.

2 DEflation

This is a general policy designed to reduce the **level of spending** in the economy. In doing so, it will curb the **demand for imports** in particular, as Britain tends to suck in imports during boom periods. It can be operated through fiscal and monetary policies. The government can cut its own **public spending, raise taxation** and increase National Insurance contributions so that less money is available for spending on imports. Alternatively, a monetary policy of **credit control** can be introduced to curb spending. It is further argued that the fall in purchasing power will affect domestic producers who may switch resources towards seeking export markets, thereby further benefiting the balance of payments. An additional effect of the government's deflationary policies 1979 – 1982 was to **weaken trade union bargaining power** by introducing the fear of unemployment. This may have produced lower wage increases and restrained costs.

Deflation has been tried many times in the British economy. It tends to be a short term policy. As balance of payments crises have recurred, it would indicate that deflation is not a long term solution, and not effective. The **costs** of deflation make it unpopular because spending cuts lead to **unemployment** and **falls in output**. In turn these changes make it self defeating because taxation revenue falls and public spending, through Supplementary and other Benefits, increases, which is what the government did not want. Also, it clearly conflicts with policies designed to stimulate growth by depressing business optimism and lowering investment, both public and private.

3 Control of money supply

The monetarist economists believe that uncompetitiveness in international trade can result from domestic inflation caused by an excessive growth in the supply of money in the economy (see Unit 9.7). If Britain's inflation rate outstrips her trading rivals, then we suck in imports and lose export markets, thereby probably creating a deficit.

Thus, the supply of money could be controlled by **raising interest rates**, to deter borrowing, and **restricting credit**, using the usual monetary weapons (see Unit 10.8). Both policies would reduce spending on imports and strengthen employers' resistance to wage demands thereby lowering domestic costs of production and making British goods more competitive. In addition, higher interest rates attract **capital inflows** and temporarily strengthen the capital account. However, they may raise the exchange rate and make our goods less competitive too! This policy has similar consequences to deflation – namely lower output and increased unemployment.

4 Trade controls/incentives

This policy is less general and more **specific**. It involves direct measures aimed in certain areas:

(a) Tariffs (see Unit 17) These can be used to raise the price of imports and, if demand is elastic, choke off the demand for imports. As a member of GATT, Britain can make little use of this option. However, in 1977, we imposed a duty on certain Japanese steels.

(b) Quotas (see Unit 17) These can be introduced to limit the quantity of imports, thereby strengthening the balance of trade. The British government has tried voluntary quota restraint with Japanese cars, with little success. However, GATT does allow the imposition of quotas on a temporary basis for a nation with balance of payments difficulties. Britain currently (1984) has restrictions on cheap clothing from South East Asia.

(c) Exchange control Capital account deficits created by **investment outflows** can be countered by exchange controls. In 1947, the government introduced controls over overseas transactions, restricting the amount of currency available for investment abroad. This meant that British citizens buying shares and British companies building factories overseas needed government permission to obtain the necessary foreign currency. In 1979, the Government relaxed this policy and finally abandoned it so that British resources could be more freely invested overseas. On average £2 billion has flowed out each year since. However, the buffer of North Sea oil revenue and high interest rates have largely cushioned the impact.

The Labour Party is pledged to re-establishing exchange controls. They also form part of the **alternative economic strategy** based on trade controls and expansionary public spending which has been proposed (by the 'new' Cambridge School of Economists) to generate domestic economic growth.

(d) Administrative controls There are many non-tariff barriers to trade which are not easily dealt with under GATT rules. Frequent changes in a country's **laws** and administrative **procedures** on **health standards, invoicing** procedures, **safety specifications** and product designs can be used by unscrupulous governments to keep out competitive imports. **France** and **Japan** are renowned for such tactics. Some people argue that Britain should adopt similar 'unfair' trading practices, in order to improve its visible trade.

(e) Subsidies Governments may subsidize exports to make them more competitive. This is not allowed by GATT rules, but the subsidies may be disguised as payments for services. Thus **West Germany** subsidizes its **steel** industry in particular and industry fuel bills in general. **British exports are exempted from VAT** which is a subsidy as it reduces the costs of production. Export credits (lending funds to buyers of British goods) are subsidized by most governments. In a normal year this subsidy costs British government £500m. Apart from direct help, the Government, through the Department of Trade promotes **trade fairs, exhibitions** and publicity to aid British exporters. There is a good case for raising this currently low budget activity, so that more indirect financial and advisory help can be given.

5 Structural changes

Certain parts of the British economy are weak. It is argued that it is in these **sectors** where changes ought to be made. The declining manufacturing industries, such as textiles, shipbuilding, coal and steel, should not be supported with funds which could otherwise be spent on **investment in new industries** *e.g.* information technology. The government could give a lead in this direction by its spending policies and attitude.

General **underlying problems** such as low investment, low productivity and high wage costs/unit could also be tackled. The 1979 Conservative Government was elected to make radical changes in Britain's economy in order to overcome these problems. So far, it has used monetary policy and trade union legal reforms to invigorate the **supply side** of the economy. Labour productivity has clearly improved but this has been more through unemployment and less from higher output. However, direct government action in several areas of the economy is unlikely because the Conservative Party believes in less, not more, government participation in economic decision-making.

18.4 Exchange rates

An **Exchange Rate** is 'the **external value** of a currency **expressed in another currency**' (or as a weighted average of the currencies of its **main** trading partners), *e.g.* £1 = $1.56 (or £1 = 86.2 trade weighted index).

In international trade, foreign currencies are needed for the payment of imports. Thus, the exchange of currencies is vital for **trade**. For instance, a British garage owner importing cars from Japan will require his bank to obtain yen and pay the seller with them, Thus, the rate of exchange between £ and yen must be established. This rate may be determined by the conditions of demand and supply on a daily basis. This is known as a **freely fluctuating** or floating exchange rate. Alternatively, the rate may be fixed by the country's central bank – a **fixed exchange rate**.

1 Floating exchange rates

The **theory assumes** that a currency is demanded for just **trade** (rather than speculation) *i.e.* to purchase imports. Also that demand and supply elasticities are perfectly **elastic**.

The D and S curves for a currency show the amounts that traders wish to buy and sell at various prices (exchange rates). The **lower the exchange rate**, the **greater the demand** for pounds and the lower the supply of pounds. The demand for pounds is a **derived demand** reflecting the demand for

British exports. Similarly, the supply of pounds is produced by the demand for British imports. Thus, if the exchange rate falls from 1.50 to 1.25, the supply of £ will fall (Qs) because imports become more expensive and so their quality demanded falls (fewer £ supplied). Conversely, the quantity of £ demanded will rise (Qd) because exports become relatively cheaper.

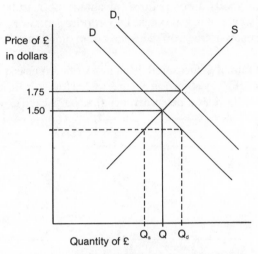

Fig. 18.3 Floating exchange rate changes

A change in the conditions of demand, such as a new government or North Sea oil raising confidence in the nation's trading performance, will raise the exchange rate. In Figure 18.3, the increase in demand to D_1 causes the exchange rate to rise to $1.75.

Advantages of floating rates

(a) Artificially high exchange rates are not possible and the rate is subject to demand and supply. For instance, in 1978, Japan had a 17 billion dollar current account surplus similar to USA's deficit. In 1979, Japan had a current account deficit because the yen appreciated against the $. This appreciation made Japanese exports more expensive and less competitive, leading to their contraction and the reduction of the surplus.
(b) Market prices reflect changes in demand and supply and thus lead to **efficient use** of world **resources**.
(c) The exchange rate ceases to be a policy objective. In order to maintain a favourable exchange rate, governments may adopt domestic policies such as deflation to prevent balance of payments deficits. Thus internal **fiscal** and **monetary policies** are **freed** from external trade limitations if rates float.
(d) As any balance of payments deficit will be corrected by automatic exchange rate adjustments, there is no need to tie up **resources** in **reserves**. Instead, they could be used internally for (say) investment.

Disadvantages

(a) Currency speculation This has two effects:
 (i) Hot money flows into a country forcing artificially high exchange for a short period. It then leaves for elsewhere causing violent fluctuations in the external value of the currency. This weakens the stability of the system.
 (ii) Speculators may rush to sell a weak currency and force its price down, before buying back at a lower price and making a **capital gain**.
(b) Inflation has been encouraged because floating rates transmit inflation and weaken the government's resolve to control domestic expenditure.
(c) Increased business **uncertainty** reduces trade because traders cannot be sure of the exchange rate which they will receive when goods are sold, because the rates are ever changing.

Since the floating of the major currencies, 1972, these disadvantages have not been borne out. Traders can guard against the risk of exchange fluctuations to some extent by buying currency in the **forward market** at a certain rate. Similarly, governments can minimize these fluctuations by **intervention**. They use reserves to buy their currency in order to maintain and/or raise demand artificially, thus keeping the exchange rate up. If the currency is too strong, they sell it and buy foreign currencies, thereby replenishing reserves.

Consequences of floating

(a) However, markets have tended to 'overcorrect' exchange rates. In 1981, the £ appreciated from $1.80 to $2.45 in six months. This fast rise was bad for trade and investment.

(b) Another criticism has been the emergence of **'dirty floating'**. This is where a government has an exchange rate target, and intervenes in the foreign exchange market by buying or selling in order to maintain this target. This is considered 'dirty' if the desired exchange rate target is artificially low, thereby giving its national goods a competitive advantage. An artificially low rate may thus stimulate employment. However, it will also raise import prices and worsen inflation. Thus, in dirty floating, the government makes a 'trade-off' between a rate of inflation and the number of people unemployed.

(c) The effective exchange rate of £, measured by an index of currencies weighted to reflect British trade, fell down to 81.5 in 1978, as shown in Figure 18.4. However, it increased to 82.0 in 1984 reflecting the importance of the £ as a **petrocurrency** (*i.e.* oil backed).

Year	Value
1972	123.3
1975	100.0
1978	81.5
1981	94.9
1984 (March)	82.0
1984 (October)	75.0

Fig. 18.4 Effective exchange rate in £ in selected years 1972–84

(d) In March 1979, the **European Monetary System** (EMS) was created. Britain did not join. All the major European nations link their currencies to each other and to a central rate, expressed in terms of a European currency unit (ecu). The EMS operates like managed flexibility within certain bands.

2 Fixed exchange rates

(a) The Gold Standard

In the nineteenth and early twentieth centuries, exchange rates were fixed in terms of gold. Balance of payments deficits were paid for in **gold**. Thus, a deficit country's stock of money would decline. This contraction of money and credit would cause **deflation** and in theory, lower prices, thereby improving competitiveness and removing the deficit. Vice versa in surplus nations. This system was known as the Gold Standard, but its ideal (above) operation did not occur **in practice** as (i) instead of prices falling in the deflation, output and unemployment declined, and (ii) reserve currencies such as £ and $ were developed. The shortage of gold meant that in order to finance expanding world trade, nations were prepared to accept other safe currencies. It fell down after 1931, when Britain came off the Gold Standard *i.e.* it refused to convert.

(b) Managed exchange rates

The 1944 Bretton Woods Conference created a system of managed exchange rates which began to operate from 1947. The International Monetary Fund was set up to supervise it. USA and UK were behind the scheme which planned to be more **flexible** than the Gold Standard and more **stable** than freely fluctuating exchange rates. By removing violent fluctuations, it encouraged trade and

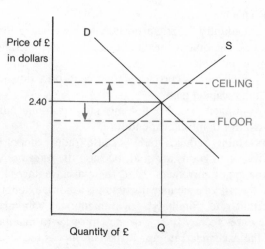

Fig. 18.5 Managed exchange rate changes

removed uncertainty. However, it made exchange rates less reflective of economic conditions and less easy to adjust. In the new system, exchange rates were fixed, but allowed to fluctuate daily within 1% above and below the agreed rate or 'peg'. This is illustrated in Figure 18.5.

This system operated until 1972. It ended because the dollar was less desired as a reserve currency (Central Bank reserves were held in gold and certain currencies, principally dollars and pounds) when America was running persistent balance of payments deficits. They indicated that the dollar needed devaluing, but other countries did not want that as it would reduce the value of their reserves (held in dollars). However, when America devalued, other countries floated.

18.5 International Monetary Fund

The IMF was created in **1944** at the Bretton Woods Conference, which met to establish a stable system of international exchange. The World Bank was also set up at the same time.

The IMF has **138** member countries. The centrally-planned nations, such as the USSR, are not members. Each member pays subscriptions, called **quotas,** determined by the size of their economies. They pay three-quarters in their **national currency** and one quarter in **reserves**, such as gold, dollars and SDRs (Special Drawing Rights – see later). It is run by a board of twenty-one executive directors. Six directors are appointed by the big economies *e.g.* the USA, West Germany and fifteen elected by the other members.

Functions – 'SAL'

1 Supervision and surveillance of exchange rates. Initially, the IMF supervised the fixed rates adopted and gave approval to devaluations. However, after the ending of managed flexibility in 1971, this role became less important. The IMF now **recommends** exchange rates for economies, when lending to countries with exchange rate problems. It also recommends domestic economic policies to be adopted, usually lower public spending and domestic credit limitation. It usually objects to nations attempting to get an artificially low exchange rate in order to gain a competitive advantage at the expense of the rest of the world.

2 Advice IMF **consults** and helps its members. It seeks stability in exchange rates. However, its **influence** over countries, such as Japan and West Germany, with persistent trade surpluses, is limited.

3 Lending The IMF aimed to promote world trade by increasing international **liquidity**:
(a) When nations went into **temporary** balance of payments **deficit** they could borrow from the IMF for short periods, during which they tried to rectify the problem. Each member could borrow so much **automatically** and obtain extra credit at the discretion of the Fund. The stand-by credit to Britain in 1976 was given subject to certain conditions. The money comes from the quotas which each country subcribes when it joins. The IMF has also created **special oil facilities** for borrowing by countries specifically hit by the oil price rises of 1973 and 1978.
(b) The reserve role of the dollar has limited the growth of international liquidity and so the IMF has sought an alternative. It developed **Special Drawing Rights** (SDR), which is a kind of paper money. Its value is based on a basket of 16 major trading currencies and holders of SDRs receive interest. The IMF's supply of SDRs is 10% of total world reserves (see Figure 18.6). However, many countries lack **faith** in SDRs (and, as with all money, acceptability is important).

Type of currency	Total value
Gold	34
Foreign Exchange	292
IMF (SDR)	21
SDR	16
	363

Fig. 18.6 Total world reserves 1981

These functions are carried out in order to meet certain general objectives:
(a) to promote international monetary co-operation.
(b) to encourage/establish stability in exchange rates and balance of payments.
(c) to seek full convertibility between currencies and an ending of exchange controls.
(d) to lend its resources to maintain international trade/liquidity and so discourage trade restrictions as a means of resolving balance of payments' crises.

The World Bank

The World Bank, or International Bank for Reconstruction and Development, was created in 1944 at Bretton Woods. Its main purpose is to provide aid to developing countries for capital projects *e.g.* dams, airports etc. It is composed of most major nations, except the eleven centrally planned, and raises revenue from its members and by issuing bonds. In 1982 it spent £3000m.

18.6 Links with other topics

Trade ⟶ Exchange rates ⟵ Government policy

19 Government policy

19.1 Objectives

In a mixed economy such as Britain's, the government has a very important role to play. As explained earlier, (see Unit 3.1) the two major parties disagree over the best **size of the public sector**. (Labour favours a larger public sector, Conservatives a smaller one.) The Government's annual expenditure (1984 to 85–£128 billion) is at least 46% of GDP and therefore very substantial and influential. Even the Conservative Party, which believes in less interference in the economy, realizes that the government has a major role to play. All political parties have a general desire to **raise the standard of living** of society. This could be done if certain **aims** are achieved:

1 A low level of unemployment
2 A low inflation rate
3 A surplus on the Balance of Payments
4 An improvement in economic growth
5 A realistically-valued exchange rate.

Since 1945 successive British governments have sought to achieve these rather **vague** aims. Prior to 1971 the fifth aim was unnecessary as we had a fixed exchange rate (see Unit 18.4).

These aims are extremely **difficult** to achieve individually, and almost impossible to attain simultaneously. Thus, a government usually lays down a **priority**, for example between 1967 and 70 Labour's objective was to remove the balance of payments deficit; and betweeen 1979 and 83 Conservatives have aimed to reduce the inflation rate. In recent years, the priorities have **varied between political parties**. For instance in 1983 the Conservatives saw inflation as the main priority but Labour stressed the reduction of unemployment. Figure 19.1 gives a summary of the main party's election proposals for the economy. It shows Labour's specific commitment to a redistribution of income and wealth. However, it is not included as a general aim, because the Conservatives do not agree with it.

CONSERVATIVES	Main priority remains to reduce inflation Control of public spending, borrowing and money supply
LABOUR	'Massive' rises in public spending Annual national economic assessment agreed by TUC and Government on how to distribute national income
ALLIANCE	Increased Government borrowing to reduce unemployment

Fig. 19.1 1983 Election proposals for the economy

In practice each aim usually involves a **specific target**. For instance, in 1979 the Conservative Government promised to 'reduce inflation to single figures', a lower rate than that which occurred in the previous five years. In order to achieve this it devised a medium-term financial **strategy** which incorporated several economic indicators *e.g.* growth of money supply M3.

However, the targets may change. In 1977 the unemployment of one million people was thought to be a 'shameful failure'. If this target were achieved in 1985 it would be heralded as a 'fabulous triumph'. Thus, changing **economic circumstances** lead to revised targets. A total of three million unemployed in 1984 has made one million seem a desirable figure and unemployment at that level would now be seen as a 'success'.

19.2 Limitations

The effectiveness of a government's action is curtailed in many ways. These limits can be remembered by **'COPPIT'**. .

1 Conflict between aims A policy which leads to the achievement of one aim may prevent the obtaining of another. For instance, a low level of unemployment could be achieved by massive public expenditure financed by borrowing and credit creation (fiscal and monetary policies). However, the rapid increase in the money supply would probably lead to higher inflation and so the inflation goal would not be obtained. There are potential conflicts between many of the objectives.

2 Open economy As a nation dependent on trade and committed to more free trade, the British economy is **vulnerable** to world problems. For instance, a world economic recession will intensify British problems because the export markets will decline, thereby weakening the balance of payments and probably the exchange rate value, as well as raising unemployment. The growth in unemployment in Britain between 1979 and 1983 was attributed to two factors – government policy and world depression. It could be argued that the openness may 'blow a government's policy off course' by introducing an unconsidered factor which distorts its calculations and policies, thus preventing the fulfilment of an economic aim.

It has also been argued that balance of payments problems, made worse by fair and free trading, have led to undesirable domestic policies, such as deflation, which have prevented the achievement of improved economic growth. Some have proposed a 'Siege Economy' in which Britain would withdraw from the EEC and erect trade barriers, behind which public spending would be increased substantially to generate economic growth. This forms part of the **alternative economic strategy** championed by some economists and left wing Labour politicians.

3 Previous Policies

A government often does not have much room for manoeuvre because of the policies which it has inherited and the substantial commitments that all governments have. In the short term, a government has to carry out the spending plans for the current financial year. After that it is less tied, although much **financial spending is long term** (*e.g.* motorway construction) and needs to be continued. Also, much of public spending is in the form of transfer payments (*e.g.* pensions) and these cannot be cut or stopped. For instance in 1983, the Conservative Government slowed down the increase in spending on social welfare programmes but only in the face of much opposition and criticism. Only about 20% of public expenditure each year is subject to government discretion.

Even in the field of legislation, a new government is rather limited. Much legislation is introduced irrespective of which party is elected and the power of the **civil service** may minimize a government's impact. For instance the 1980 and 1982 Employment Acts were less radical than many Conservatives wanted and had promised. Similarly, between 1980 and '84 several privatization proposals were scaled down.

4 Information

The government lacks perfect knowledge of the economy. It collects many **statistics**, related to its targets and general aims, but their accuracy leaves a lot to be desired. For instance, the **Balance of Payments figures**, which are published monthly are based on estimates, later often revised substantially. The export earnings from insurance premiums accrued at Lloyds are particularly difficult to calculate, as the accounting is done over a three-year period (to balance good and bad years). **Similarly**, the **'black economy'** indicates the problem with domestic statistics.

The information received is **out of date**, because of the time needed for collection. Things may change between the date of collection and the time when the figures are analyzed. Governments therefore tend to base decisions on **trends** rather than figures in isolation.

Economic decisions also require information about the **future**. This type of information is very susceptible to error because it is based on **assumptions** and **predictions**. For instance there are various models of British economy and each will give different **forecasts** from the same input data.

Generally, there is plenty of reasonably accurate information available but government post-war policies indicate that either (i) the inter-relationships between the figures are not very well understood, or (ii) the wrong conclusions are drawn and thus the wrong policies are applied.

5 Time

From the point when a policy decision is made, time elapses before the policy is implemented and carried out. During this period of time **circumstances** may have changed which may make the policy unnecessary. Some policies do not have immediate effect. For instance, changes in income tax usually take three months to implement and six months before they have any **impact**. So timing is clearly very important.

The 1979 Conservative Government came to power aiming to bring about a 'fundamental change' in attitudes to work. They claimed that this would require two terms in office (*i.e* up to ten years). This made their economic policy **long-term** and dependent on political factors such as winning another election inside five years–which they did in 1983. Thus, the Conservative Government will have the time it needs. However, often this is not the case, for example in 1970, 1974 and 1979 when governments fell from power without lasting the full five years.

19.3 Methods

The government plays several roles in society. Each entails a type of action which can be influential. They can be remembered by the word 'LEST':

1 Legislation The State passes laws which affect the economy *e.g.* Equal Pay 1975 raised the costs of production because women had to be paid the same as men when doing comparable jobs. Most government policies have some legal aspect to them, including the need for Parliamentary approval.

2 Employment The Government is a major employer–30% of the labour force are employed in the public sector. It often sets an example to other employers in the economy for instance in incomes policy and wage restraint.

3 Spending Public expenditure and government planning are vitally important in a mixed economy. Cuts in public expenditure in real terms affect the private sector and can be used to achieve certain economic objectives; for example to reduce consumption, to prevent tax increases, or to reduce the supply of money.

4 Trouble shooting The State often acts as a mediator between groups in society. For instance, in industrial relations it provides services (such as ACAS) to resolve disputes between trade unions and employers. Since 1979 the Conservative Government has been less interventionist. Generally, the government tries to right the wrongs of the economy through its various policies, *e.g.* regional policy to assist depressed areas.

Types of policy

1 Fiscal–the use of public spending and taxation. (see Unit 15.) Very general policy.

2 Monetary–the use of interest rates and credit creation (see Unit 10.8.) Very general policy.

3 Industrial–the use of specific policies affecting different aspects of British industry, for example:
(a) Manpower–trade union law (see Units 13.8 and 13.9), incomes policy (see Unit 13.6).
(b) Competition–monopolies legislation (see Unit 7.4), privatization (see Units 3.1, 3.2 and 2.4), small firms (see Unit 5.8).
(c) Regional policy (see Units 6.3 and 6.4).

4 International–the use of specific policies affecting British trading relations with the rest of the world:
(a) Balance of Payments   (see Unit 18.3)
(b) Exchange rates   (see Unit 18.4)
(c) Trading   (see Units 17.4 and 17.5)
(d) Membership of international bodies (*e.g.* IMF) and trading organizations *e.g.* EEC (see Unit 17.6).

5 Social Many social policies have economic implications, and vice versa. For instance, the relief of poverty could be tackled by massive public spending and negative income tax. Each of these policies would have far reaching effects on inflation and incentives.

The main social areas with economic links are:
(a) Housing Owner occupation is encouraged by the government through its provision of tax relief on mortgages. It gives incentives to home improvement through grants; and provides central government revenue to local authorities for the building and maintenance of council houses. In 1979 the Conservative Government began the controversial policy of council house sales at reduced values.

(b) Health The State provides the National Health Service, which consumes 10% of public expenditure. The role of the NHS is influenced by population needs. Thus Britain's ageing population (see Unit 12.3) will require more health care and increased public expenditure in that field.

(c) Pensions As these are provided out of public funds, although based on workers' earnings-related contributions, their rising cost imposes an economic burden (as with health care).

(d) Poverty Many politicians and economists believe that poverty can only be alleviated by increasing the size of national output, so that all people can benefit from an improvement in living standards. The uneven distribution of income is seen by others as a problem which makes poverty relief difficult.

Overall, there is a general belief that certain social problems can be minimized by increased public spending. Such spending is easier to fund if **economic growth** is achieved (see Unit 14.4).

19.4 Problems and policies

In addressing an economic problem, it is unusual to find only one policy in use. More often than not **several policies** are involved, in achieving the objective, or **several** objectives. These policies may have **side-effects** which make other aims impossible to achieve.

The wisdom of using certain policies may be questioned. **Different schools of thought** may vary in their support and underlying variations may be political as well as economic. For instance, the Monetarist economists, who support Capitalism, believe that strict control over the money supply will lead to a reduction in the rate of inflation. They are prepared to accept cuts in services and greater unemployment in order to achieve their inflation goal. Conversely, Keynesian economists, who believe in greater State involvement in society, consider money supply policies deflationary and misplaced, because they see an unemployment goal as more important.

Figure 19.2 provides a simple summary of some policies which have been proposed to achieve certain aims. More detailed explanations appear in the relevant units. The table is not all-embracing, and on careful study some policies may be seen as contradictory.

| | **General policies** | | |
Aim	*Fiscal*	*Monetary*	*Other*
Bring down the level of unemployment	Increase public spending Lower taxes	Create more credit Lower interest rates	Investment grants Industrial training Tariff barriers
Lower rate of inflation	Higher taxes Less public spending	Reduce credit	Incomes policy Lift trade controls Encourage competition
Balance of Payments improvement	Higher taxes Less public spending } deflation	Limit credit Raise interest rates	Tariff barriers Exchange control
Greater economic growth	Lower Income Tax Reduced Corp. Tax	Easy and cheap credit	Privatization Help small firms Encourage competition
Higher valued exchange rate	Cut public spending	Raise interest rates	

Fig. 19.2 Summary of economic aims and some possible policies

19.5 Local government

In the British political system, local government is largely controlled by central government. Since the 1972 reform, local government has been divided into several types of authority. There are six **Metropolitan counties**, responsible for overall planning, transport, police and fire services, and forty-seven **non-metropolitan** counties with the same functions and, in addition, responsibility for education and personal social services (in England–*except* London, and Wales). The Metropolitan counties are subdivided into **districts** which are responsible for education and personal social services, housing, local planning, environmental health and leisure services. Similarly, the non-metropolitan counties include districts with similar powers (except education and personal social services). **Scotland** is divided into nine regions, with similar functions to the non-metropolitan areas. These are subdivided into districts with power over housing and local planning only.

London has a system of its own (since 1963) composed of the Greater London Council (GLC) which is responsible for transport, overall planning and some housing, the Inner London Education Authority (ILEA), and thirty-two boroughs which provide all of the other local services. In 1985 the Conservative Government plan to abolish the GLC and to restore some of its functions to the county boroughs and transfer others to special agencies.

The term 'Local Government' is used to cover all the elements of this diverse structure and all the different types of local authority. In total, local government accounts for 20% of public expenditure and employs just under **2½ million people**. Out of the total spending, roughly **80%** is **current expenditure**,–*i.e.* annual expenditure on consumption, such as teachers' salaries, dustmen's wages and maintenance of old folks' homes. The most expensive provisions are education and personal social services which account for two-thirds of **current** spending. Some services such as transport are subsidized, for example in South Yorkshire. The other 20% of the total, which is a declining proportion since recent central government policy changes, is **capital expenditure**. This is investment, mainly in housing (council houses) and social assets such as schools.

Each year, local authorities **budget** (plan) their spending in the light of what they need to provide in their area. They usually intend to spend more than the central government wishes them to spend. However, their **actual spending** in total is about 3% less than they planned. Central government has become increasingly concerned over the growth of local government expenditure. However, the growth in real terms after allowing for inflation has been very slight (1% per year on average).

Local revenue

	1963–64	*1973–74*	*1983–84*
Rates	39	30	26
Govt. grants	40	49	53
Other income	21	21	21

Fig. 19.3 Local government sources of income

1 Government grants

The Rate Support Grant given by the government is now the largest source of local authority finance. It was 61% of the total spending from 1978 to '79, but it has declined somewhat to 52% (1984–'85). The system of grant allocation has been reviewed and changed since 1981. As local authorities carry out many policies and laws on behalf of central government, central government makes a substantial contribution towards them and requires certain minimum standards and nationwide uniformity. In addition, the government may give financial assistance in emergencies *e.g.* in cases of flood damage. Since 1981 it has also told local authorities what they should be providing and how much it should cost, based on a standard formula. This is known as **grant related expenditure**. Each authority now gets a **'block grant'** for this expenditure.

Before 1981 the rate support grant was based on the past spending patterns of authorities. Each authority was paid a grant on the basis of their **needs** (the services they had provided) and their **resources** (income from rates). Under the new system, local authorities which overspend government limits will have their **grants cut**. Any attempt by local authorities to raise rates in order to finance extra expenditure beyond these limits, as happened in 1983 to '84 may soon be stopped by law (1984 Local Government Bill). This is known as 'rate-capping'!

Central government can control local authority spending by:

(a) Financing a smaller % of its local expenditure *i.e.* **less block grant**.

(b) Allowing less for inflation than necessary *i.e.* setting a **cash limit** of 5% when inflation is 8% so that economies have to be made.

(c) **Penalizing** them for over spending *e.g.* In 1983–84, £292m of Rate Support Grant was withheld from big overspending councils.

(d) The government can also **change** the **formula** by which the grant is distributed to local authorities. For instance, the present subsidy to domestic ratepayers in Wales is greater than it is in England.

2 Rates

Rates are a local tax on property. All property in an area is given a **rateable value**. This is the estimated annual rent (less the cost of upkeep) that the property is worth in its present condition and location. It is assessed by the Inland Revenue department. An authority will know the total rateable value of its area, say £10m. It estimates each year how much income it needs from rates, say £8m. It can then fix the rate in the pound necessary to raise the required amount of revenue. This is called **the rate poundage** and in this example it is 80p in the £. Thus a house-owner whose property has a rateable value of £300 pays £240 per year $\left(300 \times \frac{80}{100}\right)$ in rates.

Rateable values are reviewed every five years, whilst the rates may be changed (and usually increase) annually. The rateable value of an individual property will increase when **improvements**, such as central heating, are made. Rates are charged at a higher rate on business premises but church and agricultural land is exempt. Commerce and industry contribute over 55% of the rate income.

Rates are a declining proportion of local government income (see Figure 19.3).

Advantages of rates

(a) **Easy to collect** – a twice yearly bill is sent and payment can be made in instalments (unlike VAT).

(b) **Cheap to administer** – an annual calculation of rates per property (rather than monthly as with PAYE). Administration is 2½% cost of yield.

(c) **Difficult to evade** – ownership or use of a property is easy to establish and check upon.

(d) **Large, reliable** sources of income – this is also fairly stable.

Disadvantages of rates

(a) **Unfair** Not related to income or spending and not everyone pays. Roughly one third of households are not ratepayers directly. Businesses pay whether they are profitable or loss-making.

(b) **Regressive** – the system tends to hit the less well-off more than it does the better-off (*e.g.* a large house may mean a large family rather than a large income), although **rate rebate** schemes do operate.

(c) **Penalizes improvements**, as improvements lead to higher rates being paid.

(d) **Highest in poorer areas** The inner city areas have few valuable properties and need to provide more services. So rate poundages are higher, often as high as £2.50 in the £.

(e) **Unequal** The same type of property may incur vastly different rates in different areas. *e.g.* rates in Cardiff are nearly half as much as those in the West Midlands (for the same type of property) and less than half of those in London.

The Conservative Government in 1984, plans a system of 'rate-capping'. This is intended to limit rate increases by local authorities. It clearly makes rates less easy to increase and thus reduces the local authority's ability to raise its revenue.

3 Other income

Local government also obtains income from the amenities and services which it provides. It receives **rents** from council house tenants, **fees** from leisure centres, and **payments** such as bus fares and from the use of other **facilities**. Many of these services are run at a loss and thus subsidized from the rates and from government grants.

4 Loans

Capital expenditure is usually financed by borrowing. The money is raised publicly from the Public Works Loan Board and privately by the issue of bonds. Large capital projects such as housing estates usually require the central government's financial approval.

Alternatives to rates

1 Local sales tax Unless the tax on sales was levied at a fairly high level it would not raise sufficient income to replace rates. It would not be very stable and would involve much administration. However, such taxes are used in the USA and they are generally fairer than rates.

2 Local income tax This would only be a partial source of revenue, rather than a direct replacement for rates. It would seem to be fair and suitable, but subject to fluctuations, regional differences and central government interference.

3 Assigned revenues In this system, all the revenue would be raised by central government and certain amounts would be given (assigned) to local authorities. It would seem to be fair, suitable and practical, but it would end local government independence. So for political reasons it is unlikely to be adopted.

4 Reformed rates It is likely that rates will survive, but in a modified form. The valuation of property on a **capital**, rather than **rental** basis, could be introduced. Consideration of **multi-member** households paying higher rates than single occupants might be attempted; and the **rebate** scheme could be changed.

20 Consumption and distribution

20.1 Introduction

The aim of this unit is to cover several topics which are not 'mainstream' Economics but which appear in some syllabuses, particularly of the 'Social Economics' type.

Topics such as retailing are among those which **overlap** Economics and Commerce. The treatment will be to identify the main aspects of a topic, apply economic concepts where appropriate and show the links with other units. If more detailed knowledge is required (*e.g.* Unit 20.4 Retailing) then a specialist O-Level **Commerce** book should be consulted.

The distribution of primary products **differs** from manufactured goods in two respects. Firstly, many raw materials are extracted and grown in different parts of **the world** a long way from the manufacturers. For instance, tea grown in India is made into a saleable commodity in Europe. Therefore specialized **commodity markets** (see Unit 7.1(6)) have been established so that firms can buy the materials months before they need them (to allow time for transport).

A second difference relates to **government interference**. For certain primary products in Britain, the government is involved in the distribution. This is very different from public corporations (see Unit 3.2) where the government is concerned with the manufacture **and** distribution. The government performs a wholesaling function though the **Milk Marketing Board**. The intention is to control the output and sale of this vital product, as well as to help the farming community. The government, through the board, **fixes prices**, grades and tests goods, packs and transports the milk and decides on the terms of sale. Thus, all farmers receive the same price for the same quality milk irrespective of transport costs (MMB collect the milk churns).

The MMB's factories store and use any surplus milk not sold retail. They advertise milk to encourage sales *e.g.* 'Drinka Pinta Milka Day' and 'Milk Has Gotta Lotta Bottle'. They also conduct research into cattle breeding and milk production, so that better quality milk can be produced.

20.2 Distribution

The main effect of division of labour is that the goods produced by specialist workers need to be transferred to consumers. There are several **different routes** which goods can take. These are illustrated in Figure 20.1 with the red route being the **traditional pattern**. In this pattern (1) the manufacturer sells in large quantities to wholesalers who redistribute them in smaller quantities to a

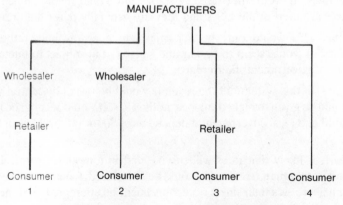

Fig. 20.1 Different patterns of distribution

larger number of retailers. The retailers then sell in ones and twos to the consumer. Most **fruit** and **vegetables** are distributed in this manner.

In distribution pattern (2) the **retailer** is omitted. His functions are undertaken by the wholesaler. Increasingly, **consumer durables**, *e.g.* furniture, dresses, etc., can be bought in this way, usually through the medium of a newspaper/magazine advertisement. Many wholesalers around big cities sell directly from their warehouse premises. The reasons for this development are:

1 Lower overheads–expensive High Street sites not needed.

2 Lower prices–the retailer's profit margin disappears, so cutting out a profit mark-up, often as high as 50% of cost price. Lower prices attract customers.

3 Reduced transport costs. However, this saving may be balanced by the extra expense on advertising.

The **wholesaler** is omitted in the third pattern (3), on Figure 20.1. His function is usually performed by the retailer who has large premises, particularly for storage. Supermarkets, *e.g.* Tesco, and Discount stores, *e.g.* Trident, which utilize the **advantages** of **large scale production**, buy in bulk direct from the manufacturers and usually sell in single units to the consumer *e.g.* bread and electrical goods respectively. Some manufacturers prefer to sell directly to a retailer so that their product can be pushed, more than a wholesaler would. Other manufacturers have established their own retail outlets *e.g.* British Leyland's Unipart Shops.

In pattern (4) both the **wholesaler** and **retailer** are **eliminated**. The manufacturer will carry out the functions of both, except in the case of mail order, where the agent acts like a retailer, by collecting money and organizing the distribution of information and goods. Avon cosmetics are sold in this way. Again the manufacturer has control over sales promotion and can benefit from **economies of scale** (see Unit 5.6).

Each of the functions in the process of distribution needs to be rewarded. It receives **profit** for adding value and providing products in the form at the time required. The profit gained is usually termed the **profit margin**, or **mark-up**. Figure 20.2 shows the different stages in the distribution process and hypothetical profit margins at each stage.

	Activity	Cost (p)	Profit per unit (p)	Profit % mark up
Manufacturer	creates good	40	—	—
	sells to wholesaler	50	10	$\frac{10}{40}=25\%$
Wholesaler	performs functions	60	—	—
	sells to retailer	80	20	$\frac{20}{60}=33.3\%$
Retailer	performs functions	85	—	—
	sells to consumer	102	17	$\frac{17}{85}=20\%$

Fig. 20.2 Different stages in distribution process

20.3 Wholesaling

The wholesaler provides many functions. Some mainly benefit the manufacturer whilst others help the retailer.

1 Services provided for manufacturer – 'CARS'

(a) Convenience It saves him **time/money** by buying in bulk – if there were no wholesalers then each manufacturer would have to deal with each retailer. This would mean more orders, invoices, statements and representatives. The wholesaler also saves manufacturers the trouble and expense of more staff, packing costs and so on. *e.g.* 1 manufacturer to 400 retailers = 400 orders.

But 1 manufacturer to 10 wholesalers (to 40 retailers each) = 10 orders.

(b) Advertising The wholesaler markets the manufacturer's goods and advertises them, usually informally. Also he gives feedback to the manufacturer on sales of his goods and he pushes new products.

(c) Risk bearing The wholesaler provides a ready market for the manufacturer's output. He bears the manufacturer's risk of not being able to sell his goods and gives him prompt payment (which enables the manufacturer to finance the next batch of goods).

(d) Storage Wholesalers provide **warehousing facilities**. Manufacturers need to sell goods quickly. The wholesaler enables them to do this because he buys their output in bulk and stores it until required by the retailer.

2 Services provided for retailer

(a) Warehousing Without wholesalers, retailers would have to buy in much larger quantities, and store them on their own premises. The wholesaler is a reservoir, or source of supply, for retailers. He has a wide selection of goods from many different manufacturers and saves the retailer's time and effort of having to visit and receive many manufacturers.

(b) Breaking bulk Wholesalers break large quantities down into smaller quantities which are more manageable. Some packaging is often undertaken *e.g.* potatoes. In addition, the grading of goods is occasionally done.

(c) Price stability The wholesaler buys stock and releases it gradually over the year. This may eliminate wide price fluctuations. If no one held stocks and all flooded on to the market at once, there would be falling prices *i.e.* excess supply (see Unit 4.3). Later, there would be a shortage and prices would sharply rise.

(d) Credit Few retailers pay cash immediately. Most pay monthly or on a sale or return basis. Thus the wholesaler takes the risk that the retailer may default and gives him short term credit.

(e) Delivery – if wholesalers deliver goods they save the retailer the expense of having under-utilized lorries.

(f) Information – wholesalers tell retailers about new products/bargains.

Types of wholesaler

Wholesalers can be classified according to either:
 1 the range of goods which they handle (a) and (b), or
 2 their trading practices (c) and (d).
    There are:

(a) General wholesalers – they serve a local or regional market, normally stocking a very wide range of goods. They have much capital tied up in stock and operate on a fairly large scale.

(b) Specialist wholesalers – they concentrate on a much narrower range of goods, usually a particular trade. For instance, a builder's merchant who supplies local builders and hardware shops.

(c) Conventional wholesalers – traditional wholesalers deliver goods to retailers who pay for them on a monthly credit basis.

(d) Cash and Carry wholesalers – in the early 1960s some wholesalers began to offer lower prices to retailers if they paid cash and collected their goods. This saved the wholesaler the costs of delivery, salesmen, bad debt provision and credit control. It enabled the retailer to collect goods when necessary and pay lower prices (although he had to bear the delivery costs, he lost free credit and he needed to plan ahead). Many small scale independent retailers utilized 'cash and carry' because they can better compete with supermarkets. The catering trade is particularly well suited to this type of operation.

20.4 Retailing

As the retailer is the last link in the normal chain of distribution, he provides essential functions for the manufacturers/wholesalers on the one hand and for consumers on the other.

Services for manufacturers/wholesalers

 1 Breaking bulk – wholesalers deal in large quantities which they sell to retailers. The retailers break this bulk and usually sell the products in single units.

 2 Quality control – in handling the goods, retailers, particularly of electrical goods, check that they are 'fit' for selling. Usually unworkable equipment and damaged goods are withdrawn or sold off cheaply. Such action may preserve a manufacturer's reputation for quality.

 3 Information – retailers, through their comments and orders, feed back to the wholesalers how goods are selling. This may determine future production and planning.

 4 Selling goods in the quantity, at the place and at the time required.

Services for consumers

 1 Variety of goods Retailers usually sell several brands of each good. By doing this, they give consumers a choice.

 2 Local supplies Retailers are usually located near their customers (except hypermarkets). They provide easy access for customers. Without retailers, consumers would waste time and money travelling to wholesalers' and manufacturers' premises.

3 Credit – most retailers give credit to encourage sales. For small amounts it may be an arrangement to pay the local shopkeeper at the end of the week. On large items *e.g.* motor car, it will be a formal contract. However, supermarkets operate on a 'cash and carry' basis.

4 Delivery – very large organizations, such as department stores who can afford the overheads of a transport fleet, deliver large items such as furniture etc., to their customers. At the other end of the scale, local corner shops may deliver goods for certain (usually aged) familiar customers, as part of their service. However, with the development of transport, particularly the family car, fewer retailers provide a delivery service nowadays.

5 Advice – most retailers help customers by giving them the benefit of their detailed knowledge and experience of products *e.g.* DIY shop – advice over types of paint.

6 After Sales Service – retailers often deal with complaints on behalf of the wholesalers/ manufacturers. By law they must replace or repair faulty goods or give refunds. In performing these functions they clearly help the consumer, too.

1 Department stores *e.g.* House of Fraser
2 Specialist multiples *e.g.* BHS, Halfords
3 Mail order *e.g.* Littlewoods
4 Discount stores *e.g.* Comet
5 Independants *e.g.* Roberts Stores
6 Voluntary groups *e.g.* Spar
7 Variety chain *e.g.* Woolworths
8 Co-op retailer *e.g.* local Co-op
9 Supermarket *e.g.* Tesco
10 Superstore *e.g.* Asda
11 Hypermarket *e.g.* Carrefour

Fig. 20.3 Types of retailer

Trends in retailing

1 Large-scale outlets Many retailers are getting larger, in size and turnover, to benefit from **economies of scale**. For instance, supermarkets (+2000 sq ft) have been superseded by **superstores** (+25 000 sq ft) who can make even better use of specialist staff and gain big discounts from suppliers (because of the volume they buy and sell). As yet, hypermarkets (+50 000 sq ft) have not been developed as extensively in Britain as in Europe. The consequences of such changes in the size of retailers have been fewer independent retailers and fewer small shops. (see Figure 20.3).

Consumers have benefited through lower prices and easier shopping *i.e.* all at one go, called **'one-stop shopping'**.

2 Competition has intensified. There are plenty of retailers competing in the main markets. Some features of **Perfect Competition** (see Unit 7.2), such as many sellers and identical products, are relevant to the type of market structure in retailing. No one firm dominates food retailing, with Sainsbury's at 13% having the largest market share.

In other respects such as **branding** and **advertising** (see Unit 20.5), retailing shows characteristics of **Imperfect Competition** (see Unit 7.5).

Most products are now better marketed because of the competition and also because of the development of **self-service**. When consumers are choosing their own goods, without the advice of an assistant in many cases, attractive packaging can be crucial. Many families buy prepacked **convenience food**, such as frozen peas, meat, chips etc., because man and wife may be both at work and the meals need quick preparation. Thus the growth of private transport, labour-saving devices, refrigerators and working women have revolutionized retailing.

In order to increase sales and make a better return on assets, many retailers have moved out of their traditional markets. For instance, **multiples**, such as Marks & Spencer, have moved **upmarket** and begun competing with department stores in luxury goods. In contrast, many **department stores** which previously catered mainly for middle and upper class customers, are moving **down market**. They are selling less expensive products and trying to appeal to better off working class consumers. The gradual breakdown of social class in Britain and the general improvements in living standards have made such a policy necessary and possible.

Department stores such as Debenhams and House of Fraser have attempted to make better use of their **floor space**. As shoppers are less willing to be lured into lifts, many upper floors are being converted into offices (to earn rent). In addition, space has been let to specialist sellers such as booksellers, opticians, tailors and (even) the Electricity Board. In 1982 these concession holders accounted for over 20% of the sales in Debenham's 70 stores.

3 Diversification In making better use of their resources large retailers have tended to diversify into different product areas. Many **specialist** chain stores have become **variety chain stores**. For instance, W. H. Smith started as booksellers but in recent years they have moved into electrical games, computers and records. In 1982 to '83 a quarter of W. H. Smith's profits came from wholesaling and this side of their business was expanding much faster than the retailing side.

Food retailers, such as Asda, have diversified. As the income elasticity of demand for food is low/inelastic, then in order to increase turnover Asda needs to shift into other income-elastic markets such as consumer durables, wine, etc.

These trends have led to the **demise of the small shop**. Some such shopkeepers have responded by joining voluntary groups/chains such as Spar. This has enabled them to benefit from bulk buying and advertising, but in doing so they forfeit independence.

20.5 Advertising

Advertising makes distribution easier, because it informs consumers about the products and services. In 1982, £3200 million worth of advertising was undertaken (see Figure 20.4). Over 90% of the advertising expenditure is through newspapers and television. The buying and selling of advertising space in these media is very **competitive**. To be successful, advertising needs to be at the **right time**, in the **right place** and at the **right price**.

Media	% of total 1962		% of total 1982	
Newspapers				
National	22		16.5	
Regional	24	70	23.6	63.5
Periodicals	24		23.4	
Television	24		29.7	
Posters & transport	4		4.0	
Radio	0		2.2	
Cinema	2		0.6	
	100%		100%	

Fig. 20.4 Advertising media (1962 and 1982)

Aims of advertising

1 Higher sales – as higher sales usually mean greater profits then most businesses seek this. As sales rise, overheads become lower per unit of output and **average cost falls**. For instance, if fixed costs are £20 000 and variable costs £5 per unit sold, sales of 4000 units cost £10 each $\left(£20\ 000 + £5 \times 4000 = \frac{£40\ 000}{4000}\right)$.

However, if sales increase to 6000 units, the cost of each item falls to £8.33 $\left(£20\ 000 + £6 \times 5000 = \frac{£50\ 000}{6000}\right)$. If advertising is successful it reduces average cost of production.

Increased company turnover can also be obtained through promoting **new products** and generating a popular **company image**. An increasing amount of advertising is company-wide rather than just concentrated on one product. Most advertising is **persuasive**. It aims to persuade people to buy one good or service rather than another. Firms **compete** for a share of a market for their particular **brand**.

Some advertising to increase sales is undertaken on behalf of the **whole industry**. This is known as **generic** or **collective** advertising. In these advertisements the general product, such as milk, is advertised, rather than a particular dairy *e.g.* Express, Co-op, Clover.

2 Information Most advertisements provide some information, even if it is only a brand name. However, some advertisements are intended to inform rather than persuade. For instance, **government departments** issue advertising on health, road safety and crime prevention with the general aim of advising people. In 1982 the Government spent over £70 million; and the nationalized industries, often in competition with one another, (*e.g.* gas v electric), spent a similar amount.

Other mainly **informative** advertising can be found in technical and trade journals. There are over 1000 directories, in addition to the Yellow Pages, which accept business advertisements.

Informative advertising usually states the **facts** e.g. date/time/place of an event rather than making claims for goods or services.

Cost of advertising

The rates charged for advertising depend on the medium used. Television is more expensive than newspapers because it tends to attract a larger audience and has more visual impact.

The rates charged for TV adverts vary with the TV station (thirteen different ones), the time of day, the likely viewers and the length of the advertisement. A 30-second advert on Anglia TV may cost around £1000 whereas a similar advert on Thames TV during a James Bond film will cost about £30 000. Occasionally, companies make special deals with the television network. For instance, the Shadows Silver Album advert only cost £60 for one minute. This was because ITV was given 30% of the record sales.

Similarly, there are several factors which determine **newspaper** rates – the size of the advertisement, the position in the publication, the day of the week and if it is coloured. For instance, a one-page spread in a local newspaper may cost about £1000 whereas a colour page in the *Sunday Times* magazine costs about £14 000.

Public companies in Britain spend millions of pounds annually on advertising. **Proctor & Gamble** who make cleaning materials such as Bold, Ariel and Fairy Liquid spend about **£50m/year** on advertising. This works out at roughly 20% of the cost of the product. They are clearly trying to promote brand loyalty and gain an increase in demand. Thus they are trying to make the demand curves for their products more **inelastic**.

Advantages of advertising 'SPECKS'

1 **The Standard of living** is increased because advertising introduces new products to consumers.

2 **Prices** are kept **lower** – the competition of advertising forces firms to make prices lower than they would otherwise be.

3 **Employment** is created – the advertising industry provides jobs for many people.

4 **Costs** are lowered because advertising enables larger scale production (see Aims).

5 **Knowledge** of goods/services is increased by the existence of advertising. It may give people a better choice of goods.

6 **Subsidized** newspapers, television and periodicals result, because advertising revenue keeps their prices down. For instance, 50% of the *Radio Times'* revenue is from adverts. The *Woman's Own* magazine takes £15m in advertising revenue annually. **Free** newspapers now exist because they are financed by the advertisers.

Disadvantages of advertising 'CREW'

1 **Creation** of unnecessary **needs** can be done by persuasive advertising *e.g.* people lived healthily without double glazing before its introduction. Improvements in the standard of living mean that more 'luxuries' can be advertised and sold as 'necessities'.

2 **Raised prices** may be the result of advertising. The extra costs caused by advertising may not be covered by the increased sales.

3 **Exploitation** may occur. Certain products may be advertised in such a way as to suggest to people that if they do not buy the product then they are not treating their family properly. Similarly the advertising in a glamorous way of potentially harmful practices such as drinking and smoking may be encouraging reckless attitudes and behaviour.

4 **Wasteful use of resources** may take place. If a firm/firms in a stable industry advertise just to maintain their market shares (*e.g.* bread) then they are perhaps not making the best use of their resources. In the long run sales are not likely to rise and they might do better by using the money elsewhere, in research, or by lowering prices. For instance, in 1981 the Army spent £3½m on recruiting soldiers, using the slogan 'Join the Professionals NOW!'.

Advertising agencies

Most individuals organize their own advertising without specialized help. Most large firms who want a **national campaign** lack the necessary skills that are needed to devise, make and place advertisements. So they consult advertising agents such as Saatchi and Saatchi, who are perhaps the best-known name. One of the biggest and widest ranging agents is McCann-Erickson, whose accounts cover beer (Carling Black Label), groceries (Tetley, Shredded Wheat), clothing (Levi jeans), milk (Milk Marketing Board) and cigarettes (Rothmans).

The **functions** of advertising agents are to:
1 find out about the product and its market
2 plan the campaign
3 produce the advertisements
4 place the advertisements in the media
5 advise the producer about the image and brand perceptions of the good/service.

Advertising Standards Authority

This body was created in **1962** to oversee the advertising industry. It is composed of people from within advertising and outsiders. Its job is to protect the consumer from misleading and harmful advertising. In order to do this, it devised a **code of practice**, telling advertisers how to operate. These rules have often been revised. For instance, beer advertisements should no longer glamorize the habit of buying large rounds in a pub or suggest that a drinking man is more attractive to women! Anyone shown drinking must appear to be over 21.

The ASA investigates **complaints** against adverts which people found misleading. In addition, ASA publishes helpful leaflets for the producers of goods, so that they do not infringe the code of advertising practice. The ASA also advertises itself through its 'legal, decent, honest, truthful' adverts.

20.6 Marketing

Advertising and selling in large organizations is handled by a marketing department. They seek to co-ordinate work in several departments so that the good or service has public appeal. Their work covers four areas:

1 **Market research** Firms need detailed information about their product and its rivals in the market. Thus, they collect such information through questionnaires, reports on the use of sample products, experiments in small areas with new goods and tests in shops. The information accumulated is used to plan the following activities.

2 **Branding** A 'brand' is the **maker's** name for their product *e.g.* **Heinz** beans, **Crosse & Blackwell** beans, **H.P.** beans. Often manufacturers in their advertising emphasize the brand name rather than a specific product because they make many different products *e.g.* Heinz soup, Heinz tomato ketchup, etc. They are encouraging the shopper to select goods by **brand name** rather than by the quality of the product. They seek **consumer loyalty**. This differentiation between products shows imperfect competition (Unit 7) and attempts to make demand for the manufacturers' products more inelastic. 'Branding' tends to cause intense competition generated through advertising.

Occasionally, branding is done by **retailers** *e.g.* Marks & Spencer sell their **'own label'** food products. They do not produce the goods but they place large orders with manufacturers on condition that they are labelled with their name. By omitting the wholesaler and getting bulk discount they are able to sell at **below market prices** and increase turnover. The manufacturer also benefits as he has an assured order.

3 **Packaging** – the way in which goods are presented to the consumer has become increasingly important and costly. The advent of **self-service** requiring customers to select their products stimulated manufacturers into attractive and eye-catching packaging, in order to raise sales. Thus packaged food, such as fish fingers, cornflakes etc., is often sold because of the way it is made to **appeal** rather than on the nutritional value of the contents. With certain products, such as perfume, the packaging costs may be half of the total cost. However, generally the extra cost of packaging is less than the cost of selling (employee's wages, etc.) so the consumer does not suffer because of it.

4 **Sales promotion** – the branded, packaged product needs to be convincingly, and persuasively promoted. Most manufacturers allocate a **'budget'** (proportion of the firm's yearly expenditure) for such publicity. The marketing department has to decide how to spend the money which it is allowed. The normal regular means of sales promotion for many consumer goods is by using a **salesman** to tour existing and potential buyers (usually retailers/wholesalers). He may provide information, display material and give free samples which can be used to attract the consumer. In return, he will receive firsthand information on best selling lines and stocks and he can feed this back to the manufacturer. Thus, he is a vital link in the chain of distribution.

20.7 Consumer protection

The expansion in the **role** of the **government** in a mixed economy has meant that today consumers are much better protected than in the nineteenth century. **Unscrupulous traders** are now less likely to 'get away with' cheating their customers. Many laws have been introduced to protect consumers from practices such as:

1 Incorrect weights and quantities being sold
2 Failure to replace faulty products
3 High fixed prices exploiting weak consumers
4 Misleading claims about goods
5 Dangerous substances contained in products

With the growth of interdependence in society, in place of self-sufficiency, people became more dependent on others and the need for government supervision of trading relationships emerged.

1 Consumer legislation – a brief summary

1893 (updated 1979) Sale of Goods Act. Under this act:

(a) Goods must be of **merchantable** quality *i.e.* fit for normal use.

(b) Goods must be **as described**, whether this is written or verbal.

(c) Goods must suit the **purpose** for which they were sold.

In the event of these conditions not being fulfilled then the consumer has three rights – the 3 'R's – **refund, replacement** or **repair**. However, this Act does not totally apply to private sales (as in classified adverts) or to the sale of second-hand goods (although they should be in a 'reasonable' condition for the price charged).

1955 Food & Drugs Act

(a) It is illegal for sellers to offer for sale food which is **unfit** for human consumption.

(b) The premises must also be **hygienic** *e.g.* no smoking when food is handled.

(c) Products must be **correctly labelled**, with the contents correctly described.

The local **public health** department enforce this act.

1963 Weights & Measures Act

(a) It is illegal for goods to be less than the **weight stated** on the package or materials.

(b) Certain common foods, such as tea and butter, may only be packed in **standard sizes/weights**.

(c) Weighing machinery should be working accurately – this is checked by **Trading Standards Officers**.

1968 Trade Descriptions Act

(a) It is a criminal offence for a trader to describe goods or services **falsely**, either in words or pictures.

(b) It limits the ability of traders to offer **spurious 'bargains'**, price reductions, and claims, *e.g.* watches that let in water cannot be sold as 'waterproof'.

The Trading Standards Officers also enforce this Act.

1971 Unsolicited Goods and Services Act

It is illegal for traders to **demand payment** for goods supplied which have not been ordered. The householder has the right to keep the goods if they are not collected within **six months**. If the householder **writes** to the sender asking for the goods to be collected, he/she can keep them, if they are not collected in **one month**.

1974 Consumer Credit Act

This Act refers to goods bought on credit and costing less than **£5000**. It gives the consumer four basic rights – remembered by **'WRIT'**:

(a) **Withdrawal** If a buyer goes to business premises and signs a credit agreement then he/she is totally bound by the contract made. However, goods bought **at home** are subject to a **5-day 'cooling-off'** period during which the buyer can change his/her mind. This was introduced to stop unscrupulous door-to-door salesmen.

(b) **Retain possession** Once **one-third** of the price has been paid by the buyer on credit, the **seller** cannot repossess the goods without going to **court**. The court may allow the seller to retake the goods or it may allow the buyer to repay on slightly different credit terms.

(c) **Information** The customer should receive **written details** of cash price, HP price, goods description, frequency/amount/number of repayments and their rights and duties under the Act. In addition, a buyer on credit has the right to see a copy of any file which a **credit reference agency** has about him/her for 25p fee.

(d) **Termination** The borrower can end the agreement once he has paid **half** of the repayments **but** the lender gets the goods back. The hirer may have to pay for any damage done to the goods. In some agreements, the lender has the right to terminate the loan by giving at least seven days notice.

1976 Credit Trading Act

This Act enhanced the rights of buyers in three more ways:

(a) All businesses lending money or giving credit had to be licensed. Licences are issued (and refused) by the Office of Fair Trading (see below).

(b) Buyers can **repay** the loan at any time and get a **rebate**.

(c) Lenders must show on the agreement the true cost of the credit, namely the **Annual Percentage Rate** (APR) of the total charge for credit. 'Total Charge' means interest **and** any administrative charges. For instance, £100 borrowed for one year at 10% interest (flat rate) has an APR of 22.2%, as shown in Figure 20.5. This arises because the APR is based on the average amount owed rather than the total amount owed. The amount owed decreases each month and this makes the actual interest rate higher.

		£100 borrowing at 10% flat rate interest		
Repayment month	*Amount repaid £*	*Capital repaid £*	*Interest repaid £*	*Total amount of capital owed £*
1st (First)	11	10	1	90 (100 − 10)
2nd	11	10	1	80 (90 − 10)
↓				↓
6th	11	10	1	40 (50 − 10)
↓				↓
10th (Last)	11	10	1	0 (10 − 10)

Total $\frac{450}{10} = 45 = $ Average amount owed

$$\text{True rate of interest} = \frac{\text{interest paid} \times 100}{\text{average amount owed}} = \frac{10 \times 100}{45} = \textbf{22.2\%}$$

Fig. 20.5 True rate of interest compared with flat rate of interest

2 Organizations helping the consumer

	Type of body		
Function	*Government*	*The industry*	*Voluntary*
General supervision	OFT	Trade Associations	—
Proper manufacture & performance of goods	BSI DC		Consumers Association
Selling/services & complaints	Trading Stds CAB	Trade Associations Consultative Councils	Consumers Association

Fig. 20.6 Consumer protection organizations

Office of Fair Trading – created in 1974. This is a **central government** body which looks generally at trading practices. It can get the law changed to meet new problems which arise *e.g.* 1976 Credit Trading Act. Its main activities are to **'WIPE'** out unfair trading by:

(a) Warning/prosecuting traders who persistently commit offences

(b) Issuing/withholding licences to credit traders

(c) Publishing useful information advising people of their rights and where they might get help

(d) Encouraging trade organizations to set up **codes of practice**

Trading Standards/Consumer Protection Departments Local **councils** set up such departments to investigate consumer complaints about goods/trading practices in their area. The local **Environmental Health Department** performs a similar function related to dirty premises where food/drink are prepared.

British Standards Institute This body lays down desirable standards of manufacture and performance for a large range of goods. Approved products are awarded the **kitemark** and a safety mark where applicable.

Design Council British goods, which are well designed, of high quality, are very safe and most efficient, qualify for the Design Centre label.

Both of these organizations are partly backed by government funds. Both aim to protect the consumer by ensuring high standards in the **manufacturing** of goods.

Citizens Advice Bureaux There are over 700 CAB in Britain, which offer **free** and **confidential advice** to the public. They are partly funded by the government. They deal with family, legal and private matters as well as trading problems.

Trade Associations Most trades and professions have such organizations, *e.g.* Association of British Travel Agents, British Insurance Association. Their members usually abide by **voluntary codes of practice** in their dealings with consumers. These codes outline the **correct complaints procedure** and how firms should deal with customers generally. The firms in the industry pay for the trade association to function, which may mean investigation of compaints, **arbitration** between buyer and seller and (possibly) **compensation** payments.

Consumers Association This is a **private** organization set up in **1963** to protect and inform the public about goods and services. In return for an annual fee, members receive *'Which'* magazine. This explains the good and bad points of products, carries out its own tests, and recommends 'best buys'. Such reports are respected by manufacturers/retailers and have thus been influential.

Consultative Councils The government has insisted that each **nationalized industry** should set up a consumer council to keep a check on its operations. The councils receive **complaints** and offer advice, but are generally accepted as not being very effective watchdogs, *e.g.* Post Office Users National Council.

20.8 Credit

When people buy goods and services they can **pay** either immediately in **cash** or by **credit**. In the latter case, payment may be delayed for days (*e.g.* with a cheque until it is cleared – see Unit 10.3), for weeks (*e.g.* with a cheque card – see Unit 8.5) or for months/years (with a loan – see Unit 10.3 for bank loans).

Retailers in buying goods from manufacturers often receive **trade credit**. The goods are paid for within a month of obtaining them. A retailer paying sooner may receive a discount for prompt payment.

Consumers have many possible **ways** of obtaining credit. They vary with the individual's needs, circumstances and credit-worthiness. They are briefly explained below (more detail will be found in most Commerce textbooks).

1 Means of credit

Cheques They give credit until the cheque is cleared, usually three days at the most **but** they are interest free! (see Unit 10.3).

Credit cards They provide short-term credit but may be expensive and a temptation to overspend (Unit 8.5).

Retail budget accounts Large shops may operate their own credit system, requiring regular fixed repayments but giving high spending limits.

Monthly accounts Traders often allow acceptable and trusted customers to have goods/services which they can settle for at the end of each month *e.g.* garage petrol.

Trading checks and vouchers Companies such as Provident have agents who allow people tokens which can be used in certain shops. The consumer pays for the token with interest over time. This system is usually very expensive to the borrower, although he/she may be allowed a limit up to twenty times the regular sum agreed.

Bank loans/overdrafts Interest low, and a fairly long repayment period, but not available to nearly half the population, without bank accounts (see Unit 10.3).

Personal loans These may be given by money lenders, pawnbrokers and finance companies. In each case the interest charged is **high**.

Mail order catalogue A popular way of shopping with repayment allowed between 20–40 weeks. There is no credit charge but the same goods could be cheaper in the shops and choice is limited.

Insurance policy loan Insurance Companies are prepared to give loans of up to 90% of the current 'cash-in' value of certain policies. Repayment is made when the policy matures and interest is charged on the loan.

Mortgages Very long term credit for buying property, but a bargain (see Unit 11.3) because the asset bought with the mortgage appreciates.

2 Types of credit

(a) Hire purchase agreements The shop/dealer may put up the money for the goods or an agreement may be arranged with a finance company. Normally a **deposit** is paid and instalments of equal amounts are paid monthly over a period of time. However, the buyer is only the **hirer** until **all** the repayments have been made. The buyer has the advantage of immediate use of the good, and prompt after-sales service, but he may pay fairly high interest charges.

(b) Credit sales agreements (sometimes called **Extended**) When the goods are purchased the **buyer immediately** becomes the **owner**. The advantages/disadvantages of credit sale are similar to hire purchase **but** the repayment period is usually shorter and ownership may be an important factor to the buyer.

Advantages of buying on credit

1 Immediate use of goods, rather than waiting and paying cash.
2 Repayment can be spread out over a longer period of time.
3 More expensive goods can be afforded, because often only a deposit (or small regular repayment) is needed. This improves the standard of living.

Disadvantages of buying on credit

1 Interest to be paid, at varying rates. Consumers lack perfect knowledge of all available credit.
2 Temptation to overspending.
3 Commitment to regular repayments may be a problem if income falls (*e.g.* unemployment).

Advantages of selling on credit

1 More sales than otherwise. People who could not afford the full price may be able to buy on credit. Increased turnover may lead to economies of scale in manufacturing.
2 Customers find credit to be habit-forming and often continue to shop at the credit-givers shop even when the original purchase has been paid off. Thus it may produce consumer loyalty.

Disadvantages of selling on credit

1 More administrative cost for the retailer – records, reminders and debt collection.
2 Capital tied up in debts which can be expensive.
3 No market for returned cheap, second-hand goods.

Part III Self-test questions and answers

Self-test questions

Unit 1 Economic ideas and concepts

1 Is a 'free' school meal classed as a 'free good' by an economist?
2 Are wild blackberries examples of free goods?
3 Name one example of a 'capital service'.
4 Explain the distinction between 'fixed' and 'working' capital.
5 What is 'social capital'?
6 The place where buyers and sellers make contact is known as ....?
7 The alternatives foregone in order to do/purchase something are known as the .... of the decision.
8 Name the three roles which people play in society.
9 Britain's average income per head is .....
10 Describe an underdeveloped country.
11 Explain how people are interdependent in modern society.
12 Define 'efficiency'.
13 What is the basic economic problem?
14 What are the four decisions about production which all societies have to make?
15 How does inflation affect 'real income'?
16 How does a consumer good differ from a capital good?
17 How are the 'scarcity' and 'choice' linked together?
18 What % of the nation do not live in their own property?
19 Name one economic resource.
20 Name three groups in society likely to be poor.
21 The increased pollution which results from the building of a chemical plant is an example of:
   (a) fixed costs; (b) opportunity cost; (c) social cost; (d) total costs.
22
	Price index	Money income index
Year 1	100	100
Year 2	150	200

From the data, it is shown that real income has:
   (a) doubled; (b) halved; (c) increased by 50%; (d) remained unchanged.
23 Any 'man-made' factor of production which is used to help in the production of consumer goods is known as:
   (a) capital; (b) labour; (c) land; (d) money.
24 'Investment', to an economist, means:
   (a) buying stocks and shares; (b) earning a rate of interest; (c) producing capital goods; (d) saving out of income.
25 The satisfaction derived from the use of a good/service is its:
   (a) demand; (b) elasticity; (c) utility; (d) scarcity.
26 From the following, the best example of a consumer durable is:
   (a) a gallon of petrol; (b) a lorry; (c) an oil tanker; (d) a television set.
27 Choices have to be made because:
(a) resources are limited and wants are finite
(b) resources are limited and wants are infinite
(c) resources are unlimited and wants are finite
(d) resources are unlimited and wants are infinite.
28 The stock of assets held by a person is his/her:
   (a) demand; (b) income; (c) investment; (d) wealth.

29 A production possibility curve assumes that:
(a) costs of production are falling   **(b)** international trade takes place   **(c)** resources are fully utilized   **(d)** there is no scarcity.

30 When people contribute their labour to the provision of a service, they are acting as:
   (a) consumers;   **(b)** citizens;   **(c)** producers;   **(d)** entrepreneurs.

Unit 2 Economic systems

1 Name the three main types of economic system.

2 List the main features of a 'free market' economy.

3 What is the main advantage of cut-throat competition?

4 How is economic freedom maximized in a capitalist economy?

5 What happens to wealth distribution in a capitalist economy?

6 Which nation, in practice, has developed mostly along free market lines?

7 The non-market sector of the British economy accounts for ..% of GDP.

8 What role does the State play in the planned economy?

9 What are the disadvantages of the collectivist economy?

10 Name one privilege which the top quarter of a million people in the USSR receive.

11 What is the minimum monthly wage in the USSR?

12 In which sector of the mixed economy is profit not the motive behind production?

13 The selling off of profitable industries and public assets tends to be a feature of .... Party governments.

14 Name one uneconomic service provided by the government in Britain.

15 Why might the government provide a subsidy to a firm or industry?

16 How does the government participate in a mixed economy?

17 What was the function of the subsistence economy?

18 What were the main disadvantages of the subsistence economy?

19 The satisfaction of consumer wants through unofficial trading is a description of the .... economy.

20 Which is the odd one out – Capitalist, Collectivist, Free Market, *Laissez-faire*?

21 An economic system in which there is no government interference and resources are allocated on the basis of price is:
   (a) Capitalist;   **(b)** Collectivist;   **(c)** Command;   **(d)** Planned.

22 In theory, a collectivist type of economy does not:
   (a) acquire economies of large-scale production
   (b) maximize individual economic freedom
   (c) meet the basic needs of most of population
   (d) obtain full utilization of all its resources.

23 The lack of incentive is usually argued as a disadvantage of a:
      (a) Capitalist economy;   **(b)** Command economy;   **(c)** Mixed economy;   **(d)** Subsistence economy.

24 The 'mixed economy' is composed of a mixture of the characteristics of:
   (a) capitalist and collective economies   **(b)** capitalist and subsistence economies
   (c) collective and command economies   **(d)** planned and subsistence economies.

25 In a mixed economy, the public sector provides all of the following except:
   (a) merit goods;   **(b)** mixed enterprises;   **(c)** public goods and services;   **(d)** transfer payments.

26 The subsistence economy declined because of the development of:
   (a) specialization;   **(b)** skill;   **(c)** trade;   **(d)** sharing.

27 The black economy features all of the following **except**:
   (a) barrow jobs;   **(b)** cash payments to avoid VAT;   **(c)** payments in kind;   **(d)** unemployment pay.

28 If a government adopts a *laissez-faire* approach, it:
   (a) allows markets to operate without restriction,
   (b) increases the size of the public sector,
   (c) intervenes in economic decision-making,
   (d) plans the whole economy carefully.

29 In a collectivist economy, it is possible to postpone consumption in order to develop capital goods for economic growth to occur because:
   (a) economies of scale are possible   **(b)** resources are allocated by price   **(c)** the government plans production   **(d)** wealth is not directly created.

30 Nationalization is a feature of all of the following economies, except:
   (a) Capitalist;   **(b)** Collectivist;   **(c)** Mixed;   **(d)** Planned.

Unit 3 Business units

1 Name one business unit in the private sector of the economy.
2 What is the opposite of 'Nationalization'?
3 Which political party created and expanded the NEB?
4 Suggest four reasons for public corporations. Remember **'WEE'** and **'SUDS'**.
5 From whom may a nationalized industry face competition?
6 Give one example of political interference in running of nationalized industry.
7 Define limited liability.
8 What are 'Articles of Association'?
9 For what do the initials PLC stand?
10 Suggest three **disadvantages** of a PLC.
11 How many people are self employed in Britain?
12 Name three main characteristics of a partnership. At least a DUO is needed!
13 What is a producer co-operative?
14 Which organization in Britain owns 133 factories, is the nation's biggest farmer and undertaker and has its own bank?
15 Define trade credit.
16 List four sources of finance for a private company.
17 For whom does ICFC provide finance?
18 Name one firm which has received a substantial grant from the Government.
19 Explain the difference between nominal and market value of a share.
20 Who issues new shares?
21 A private company does **not** have:
   (a) its Board of Directors elected
   (b) its shares bought and sold on the Stock Exchange
   (c) limited liability   (d) to be registered.
22 The only nationalized industry to be denationalized and renationalized was:
   (a) aircraft;   (b) railways;   (c) steel;   (d) waterways.
23 The characteristics of an ordinary share are:
   (a) maximum risk, fixed dividend, voting rights
   (b) minimum risk, fixed dividend, no voting rights
   (c) maximum risk, variable dividend, voting rights
   (d) minimum risk, variable dividend, no voting rights.
24 A company loan may be known as a/an:
   (a) debenture;   (b) equity;   (c) gilt;   (d) preference share.
25 All of the following are institutional investors except:
   (a) insurance companies;   (b) pension funds;   (c) public corporations;   (d) unit trusts.
26 ICI is an example of a:
   (a) nationalized industry;   (b) partnership;   (c) private company;   (d) public company;
27 The distributed profits of the Co-operative Wholesale Society are:
   (a) divided among retail co-operative societies   (b) given to their consumers
   (c) given to their shareholders   (d) paid to central government.
28 Companies in which the Government have bought shares and made loans are known as:
   (a) co-operatives;   (b) mixed enterprises;   (c) private companies;   (d) partnerships.
29 All public corporations have all the following characteristics **except** that:
   (a) they aim to make a profit   (b) they are created by Act of Parliament
   (c) they are publicly controlled   (d) they are managed by a Board.
30 A Memorandum of Association is a document which outlines:
   (a) a company's internal workings
   (b) information for people outside the company
   (c) the annual dividend to be paid
   (d) the price at which a company's shares will be sold.

Unit 4 Demand and supply

1 Price is determined by the interaction of .... and ....
2 What causes a movement along a demand curve?
3 When demand .... supply price will tend to rise. Draw the diagram.
4 Name the four conditions of demand. **CIST** might help.
5 In the short-run, supply often tends to be ....
6 If costs of production rise, what will happen to supply?

7 Given an inelastic demand a rise in price will lead to .... in total revenue.

8 Suggest the reasons why a supply curve might shift to the right.

9 Following a reduction in the basic rate of income tax, the demand curve for a normal good will shift to the ....

10 What does a January sale of goods indicate?

11 Define equilibrium.

12 The shape of the demand curve is its ....

13 The formula $\dfrac{\% \text{ change in quantity supplied}}{\% \text{ change in price}}$ enables the calculation of ....

14 What sort of good has an Ed of between 1 and infinity and give an example.

15 If the price of eggs doubles and quantities demanded fall by half calculate the Ed of eggs.

16 As you move up a straight line demand curve, what happens to its elasticity?

17 If a product has many substitutes and a lot of income is spent on it, its demand will tend to be ....

18 Draw a unit elastic supply curve.

19 Supply will tend to be more elastic when ....

20 What does a negative income elasticity of demand indicate?

In questions **21** and **22**, the following code applies **(a)** 1 only   **(b)** 1+2   **(c)** 1,2,3   **(d)** 2 only   **(e)** 2+3.

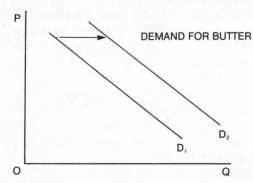

21 In the diagram, the shift in the demand for butter from D_1 to D_2 could have been caused by:
   (a) A reduction in the price of bread
   (b) An increase in the price of margarine
   (c) A pay rise for dairy workers.

22 Which of the following is/are conditions of the supply for home computers?
   (a) Technological developments
   (b) Changes in the cost of raw materials
   (c) Climatic conditions.

23 Price £   Quantity Demand (000's per month)
      10   50
      11   40

In the above demand schedule for Blodgetts, when price rises from £10 to £11, elasticity is measured at **(a)** +2 **(b)** −2 **(c)** −½ **(d)** +½ **(e)** 1.

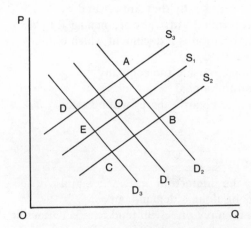

Questions **24** and **25** refer to the diagram above, showing the supply and demand for private houses. Indicate the letter which represents the equilibrium price after the following changes.

24 An increase in tax relief on mortgage repayments and an improvement in prefabrication techniques.

25 A government subsidy to builders on each new home started and a government subsidy on council house rents.

Unit 5 Production

1 In the diagram, name B and D types of integration.

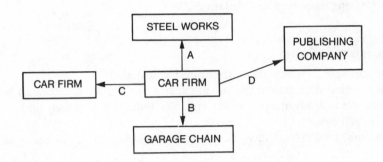

2 Primary, Secondary and .... are the three types of production.

3 The fall in manufacturing output in Britain and the closure of factories has been termed ....

4 A human resource which earns profit for risk-bearing is called ....

5 List the advantages of division of labour to a firm. Remember to 'post me'.

6 Standardized products and the loss of individual craftsmanship is a disadvantage of specialization to ....

7 Define the 'short run'.

8 What is the relationship between marginal cost and average cost?

9 Where does profit maximization occur?

10 Why did large-scale production develop?

11 How are internal economies of scale different from external?

12 Name two trading economies.

13 The mnemonic **'SWIRL'** gives what?

14 The social costs of industrial decline in a local area may be a feature of ....

15 What is the difference between a merger and a takeover?

16 Who vets mergers?

17 The most common type of integration nowadays is ....

18 What is the definition of a small manufacturing firm?

19 How many liquidations occur annually?

20 What is the Loan Guarantee Scheme?

21 Marginal cost is the cost of production:
   (a) at which minimum profit is obtained
   (b) of the most inefficient firm in an industry
   (c) of the most efficient firm in an industry
   (d) of one extra unit of production by a firm.

22 An internal economy of scale is **not** illustrated by:
   (a) a 'day release' course at local technical college
   (b) a research and development unit
   (c) specialization among management
   (d) the bulk buying of raw materials.

23 If a potato crisp manufacturer took over a farm producing potatoes, this would be an example of:
   (a) backward vertical integration   (c) horizontal rational integration
   (b) forward horizontal integration   (d) vertical diversification.

24 An example of capital intensive production is:
   (a) a department store;   (b) a fruit shop;   (c) an oil refinery;   (d) the Post Office.

25 The extraction of raw materials from the earth is:
   (a) commercial production;   (b) primary production;   (c) secondary production;
   (d) tertiary production.

26 The only natural resource amongst the factors of production is:
   (a) capital;   (b) enterprise;   (c) labour;   (d) land.

27 In the long run, all costs of production are:
   (a) constant;   (b) falling;   (c) fixed;   (d) variable.

28 When information is shared among firms in one industry this could be classified as an:
(a) external diseconomy; (b) external economy; (c) internal diseconomy; (d) external diseconomy.

29 The growth of a firm may be limited by all of the following **except**:
(a) available finance; (b) owner's preference; (c) size of the market; (d) transport costs.

30 The Government has helped small firms by:
(a) increasing income tax; (b) prohibiting competition; (c) raising capital transfer tax; (d) relaxing employment regulations.

Unit 6 Location of industry

1 Name one example of a heavily concentrated industry.

2 Individual location decisions in the private sector are usually determined by ....

3 Name three natural advantages which crucially influence location, and give one actual example in each case.

4 Many new industrial estates have developed alongside .... in order to benefit from ....

5 How much does the Government spend per annum on regional policy?

6 Goods made from raw materials which lose weight during production tend to be located ....

7 What were the main factors influencing the location of the Aluminium Smelter at Lyneworth?

8 Name two towns in Assisted Areas.

9 What is the main locating influence for modern industries and the service sector?

10 Name two declining industries which have created localized unemployment.

11 In what ways does congestion cause economic inefficiency?

12 Explain how a social problem can have an economic cost.

13 How does government try to encourage Capital Mobility?

14 Why were New Towns set up? Name one example.

15 What are Enterprise Zones?

16 Why is assessment of regional policy difficult?

17 Suggest one benefit of regional policy.

18 How has the EEC helped regions?

19 Why is the steel industry in decline?

20 Who sets BSC's 'financial target'?

21 The most dispersed industry out of the following is:
(a) brewing; (b) coal mining; (c) iron and steel; (d) shipbuilding.

22 Industries which are declining in importance will tend to:
(a) apply for an Industrial Development Certificate
(b) move closer to their markets
(c) open new branch factories
(d) remain in their original location.

23 Footloose industries are influenced, in their location, by:
(a) economies of scale; (b) markets; (c) power; (d) raw materials.

24 The source of power which has contributed the least pull in locating factories is:
(a) coal; (b) oil; (c) steam; (d) water.

25 Consumer durables that are assembled from many parts usually require:
(a) Government Grants; (b) local suppliers; (c) natural advantages; (d) skilled labour.

26 The regional problems facing Britain include all of the following **except**:
(a) congestion; (b) industrial mobility; (c) localized unemployment; (d) urban decay.

27 The free market approach to regional problems ignores:
(a) long term profits; (b) private costs; (c) private benefits; (d) social costs.

28 The area in Britain with the highest level of unemployment is:
(a) East Anglia; (b) North East; (c) Northern Ireland; (d) Scotland.

29 The Government encourages labour mobility by all of the following **except**:
(a) available housing; (b) movement grants; (c) retraining; (d) tax allowances.

30 The development of the North Sea Oil and Gas resources has caused Peterhead to suffer from:
(a) greater employment; (b) increased house prices; (c) more local demand;
(d) quicker communications.

Unit 7 Markets

1 What is the difference between a retail and a wholesale market?
2 Name one commodity market.
3 Why is Perfect Competition an unrealistic market structure?
4 How are average revenue and marginal revenue related in perfect competition?
5 What shape is demand curve in perfect competition and why?
6 Suggest two advantages of Perfect Competition.
7 Define monopoly.
8 Suggest two causes of monopoly.
9 What is a 'cartel'?
10 What control has a monopolist over price and quantity?
11 Why do abnormal profits remain in the long run for the monopolist?
12 Outline two advantages of monopoly.
13 Why is optimum output not achieved in a monopoly?
14 Suggest two ways in which the Government can control monopoly.
15 Give main details of 1976 Restrictive Trade Practices Act.
16 What power has Director General of OFT?
17 Who can prevent takeovers?
18 What was Hoffman La Roche an example of?
19 Give three characteristics of Monopolistic Competition.
20 The tendency to collusion between firms occurs in ....
21 An industry dominated by a few large firms is called a/an:
   (a) duopoly; (b) monopoly; (c) oligopoly; (d) free market.
22 According to an economist, the place where goods are bought and sold is a/an:
   (a) exchange; (b) market; (c) shop; (d) state.
23 The Stock Exchange is an example of:
   (a) duopoly; (b) monopoly; (c) oligopoly; (d) perfect competition.
24 All of the following are features of Perfect Competition **except**:
   (a) a large number of sellers; (b) homogeneous products; (c) many buyers; (d) restricted entry.
25

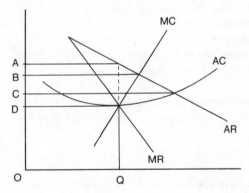

On the above diagram, the abnormal profit per unit of output is represented by:
(a) AB; (b) AD; (c) BC; (d) CD.

Unit 8 Money

1 Before money was invented, trade was by ....
2 Borrowing money usually requires the borrower to pay ....
3 Give a definition of money.
4 The functions of money can be remembered by the mnemonic **'SUMS'** which stands for ....
5 Why are perishables not very good as money?
6 What % of the adult population have current accounts?
7 Which quality of money is undermined by inflation?
8 Explain what is meant by the 'uniformity' quality of money.
9 Which type of money is most portable?
10 What were the three main problems with barter?
11 Name three early forms of money.
12 Paper money developed as a result of receipts issued by ....
13 The 1844 Bank Charter Act gave the .... the sole right of note issue.

14 The instruction 'to pay a named sum to a particular person' is the basis of a ....
15 Define 'legal tender'.
16 The limit on a cheque guarantee card is ....
17 Coins are classed as 'token money' because the .... value is worth more than the .... value.
18 Describe two disadvantages of a credit card to a bank customer.
19 Name a credit card designed for businessmen.
20 How often is a credit card stolen in Britain?
21 Money is at its most liquid in the form of:
    (a) a current account bank balance   (b) a building society subscription account
    (c) a Post Office Savings account   (d) a £5 Premium Bond holding.
22 A fiduciary issue of money means that the:
    (a) coins are made of gold   (c) issue is only temporary
    (b) coins are only token   (d) issue is not backed by gold.
23 The main form of money used in the UK in the 1980s is:
    (a) bank deposits;   (b) cheques;   (c) coins;   (d) notes.
24 The most important characteristic of money is its:
    (a) acceptability;   (b) homogeneity;   (c) liquidity;   (d) stability.
25 Money does **not** perform the function of a:
    (a) medium of exchange;   (b) measure of credit;   (c) store of value;   (d) unit of account.
26 Barter declined as a result of:
    (a) banks developing;   (b) gold being found;   (c) paper money being invented;
    (d) trade expanding.
27 'A written instruction' to pay a named sum to a named person from out of a bank account is a definition of:
    (a) a bank note;   (b) a cheque;   (c) a credit card;   (d) legal tender.
28 The main problem facing credit card companies is:
    (a) the high interest rates;   (b) increased demand for cards;   (c) loss through fraud;
    (d) low rate of profit.
29 The measure of money stock M3 is composed of:
    (a) cash and current accounts
    (b) cash, current accounts and deposit accounts
    (c) cash, current accounts, deposit accounts and money market bills.
    (d) cash, current accounts, deposit accounts, money market bills, Gilts and other accessible savings.
30 Credit cards are not included in the official money definitions because they are not:
    (a) a medium of exchange;   (b) a store of value;   (c) held by private sector;   (d) issued by the banks.

Unit 9 Inflation

1 The figures below represent the February retail prices of a new retail price index started in January.

Item	Weight	Index of current price
1	10	110
2	30	100
3	60	90

Calculate the February retail price index.
2 How did Britain's inflation 1951–1982 compare with that of her main industrial competitors?
3 Define inflation.
4 Name three types of inflation which apply to Britain.
5 Suggest two reasons why inflation cannot be measured accurately.
6 How is calculation of RPI useful?
7 Name (a) the largest, (b) the newest, weight in RPI.
8 When looking at RPI characteristics, for what does **'WEBB'** stand?
9 What is a base year?
10 How does inflation affect business confidence?
11 Outline three problems of RPI measurement.
12 What % of dishwashers sold in Britain are imported? What does this show?
13 Inflation discourages .... and encourages ....
14 Which type of inflation is likely to be caused by:
    (a) increases in the money supply;   (b) tax reductions.

15 In the following diagram, which price above the initial equilibrium price (P) is likely to be caused by cost push factors?

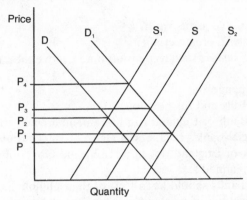

16 Why is Britain particularly vulnerable to inflation caused by raw material prices?
17 How might trade unions cause inflation?
18 If wage increases are matched by ………… the cost per unit of output need not rise.
19 Suggest two reasons why the Government's influence over inflation is limited.
20 Why might incomes policy be introduced?
21 Creeping inflation is a rate of inflation which is:
   (a) continually high; **(b)** short lived and high; **(c)** slowly accelerating and fairly low; **(d)** very low and steady.
22 The RPI basket of goods needs to be **all** of the following **except**:
   (a) accurately recorded; **(b)** collected daily; **(c)** consistently applied; **(d)** representatively sampled.
23 The following are all categories in RPI **except**:
   (a) food; **(b)** luxuries; **(c)** services; **(d)** transport.
24 RPI is calculated by:
   (a) price × weight divided by total weight **(b)** total weight divided by price × weight
   (c) prices divided by weights **(d)** weights divided by prices.
25 RPI becomes less accurate when:
   (a) a new base year is chosen **(b)** goods and services change in quality
   (c) more households are surveyed **(d)** spending patterns are stable.
26 During times of inflation, gains are made by:
   (a) exporters; **(b)** powerful trade unions; **(c)** savers; **(d)** those on fixed incomes.
27 Demand pull inflation is likely to be caused by:
   (a) a fall in the value of the currency
   (b) a rise in the price of imported raw materials
   (c) increases in basic rate income tax
   (d) increasingly large budget deficits.
28 RP Index

	Year 1	Year 2	Year 3
	100	110	112

   From the above data, it can be deduced that:
   (a) the cost of living has fallen **(b)** the cost of living has increased
   (c) the standard of living has fallen **(d)** the standard of living has increased.
29 Cost push inflation can be caused by:
   (a) high wage claims; **(b)** increased credit; **(c)** lower raw material prices; **(d)** rising value of pound.
30 Rising costs can be passed on by manufacturers in the form of higher prices, without a loss of income: if –
   (a) supply is relatively inelastic **(c)** demand is relatively inelastic
   (b) supply is relatively elastic **(d)** demand is relatively elastic.

Unit 10 Banking

1 What did the 1979 Banking Act achieve?
2 Name one merchant bank.
3 How is the National Girobank different from a commercial bank?
4 Describe the clearing system for cheques.
5 Suggest three differences between a loan and an overdraft.
6 How many people hold just current accounts?
7 How do banks make profits?

 8 What is a liability on a bank balance sheet?
 9 The banks' assets which are most liquid are generally .... profitable. Give one example.
10 What is the current reserve assets ratio?
11 Why are the banks able to create credit?
12 Why do institutional investors such as pension funds, move their money between different financial institutions?
13 What is a 'Bill of Exchange'?
14 Who issues Treasury Bills and for how long?
15 The functions of the Bank of England can be remembered by the word ....
16 How are the commercial bank's balances at Bank of England useful?
17 What would the Bank of England do, in assisting the Government's monetary policy, if credit expansion was planned?
18 The present rule that banks should keep ½% of their eligible liabilities in a non-interest-bearing account at the Bank of England is the essential part of the ....
19 Funding is the selling of more .... dated stock and less .... dated stock.
20 An instruction by the Bank of England to banks telling them to lend more to exporters and less to their personal customers is an example of ....
21 The most liquid asset of a commercial bank is/are:
    (a) an advance;   (b) cash in hand;   (c) money at call;   (d) Treasury Bills.
22 The Bank of England:
    (a) fixes interest rates;   (b) issues notes and coins;   (c) regulates public expenditure;   (d) underwrites new share issues.
23 The lender of last resort in the British banking system is the:
    (a) Bank of England;   (b) Government;   (c) Royal Mint;   (d) Treasury.
24 A 12% Treasury loan is an example of a:
    (a) Bill of Exchange;   (b) gilt edged stock;   (c) preference share: (d) premium bond.
25 The banks which act as wholesalers of money are known as:
    (a) commercial banks;   (b) discount houses;   (c) merchant banks;   (d) savings banks.
26 A deposit account does **not**:
    (a) give interest;   (b) make charges;   (c) provide statements;   (d) take savings.
27 The following commercial bank services are all mainly for traders **except**:
    (a) business references;   (b) bills of exchange;   (c) mortgages;   (d) night safe facilities.
28 If a bank's base rate is 10%, it is likely to pay interest to depositors of:
    (a) nothing;   (b) less than 10%;   (c) 10%;   (d) more than 10%.
29 'Discounting' means that a bill is:
    (a) bought for less than its face value   (c) paid for in cash immediately
    (b) credited to someone's account   (d) sold to the highest bidder.
30 Credit can be curtailed if the Government:
    (a) buys stocks on the open market   (b) increases the amount of special deposits
    (c) lowers the assets ratio   (d) raises the rate of interest.

Unit 11 Savings and investment

 1 For whom does the Capital Market cater?
 2 What are the five methods of issuing new shares? Remember **'POPIT'**.
 3 Explain how the Government sells its bonds by tender.
 4 Describe what unit trusts do.
 5 What % of adults have a building society account?
 6 The main building society asset is its ....
 7 In what ways have trustee savings banks diversified from their original function (savings)?
 8 Most Stock Exchange firms are partnerships with .... liability.
 9 Describe the work of a stockbroker.
10 Explain the term 'My word is my Bond'.
11 Suggest why the Stock Exchange is given as an example of a perfect market.
12 What effect would a general election victory by the Labour Party probably have on the FT Index?
13 What is a capital gain?
14 Investors who buy new issues expecting an immediate price increase are known as ....
15 What are the functions of the Stock Exchange? Remember **'MINGS'**.
16 What % of personal savings are held in banks?

17 The Stock Exchange is criticized for its failure to produce beneficial investment in the British economy. Explain this argument.

18 What is 'single capacity'?

19 Suggest four general factors influencing how you save. Remember **'MURT'**.

20 What are the advantages and disadvantages of saving through life assurance?

21 A company which has issued one million ordinary shares, with a nominal value of £1 each, announces a dividend of 10% to the shareholders. If the current share price is £2, the yield will be:
(a) 2% (b) 5% (c) 10% (d) 20%.

22 Among the following, the most liquid is a/an:
(a) building society account; (b) insurance policy; (c) national savings certificate;
(d) premium bond.

23 The supply of long-term loans on the security of private dwelling houses purchased for owner occupation is by:
(a) building societies; (b) finance companies;
(c) investment trusts; (d) savings banks.

24 Investment to the economist means:
(a) buying stocks and shares (c) saving money
(b) earning a rate of interest (d) using capital goods.

25 The Stock Exchange does **not**:
(a) enable the valuation of paper assets (b) issue new shares for companies
(c) make existing securities liquid (d) provide a market in government stock.

26 A 'bull' speculates in
(a) falling prices; (b) Government stock; (c) New issues; (d) rising prices.

27 An example of a private sector non-profit maker is:
(a) a commercial bank; (b) a building society; (c) an insurance company; (d) an investment trust.

28 The Government is involved with all of the following savings schemes **except**:
(a) National Savings Bank; (b) Savings Certificates; (c) Trustee Savings Banks;
(d) Unit Trusts.

29 Jobbers dealing in stocks and shares act as:
(a) general retailers; (b) general wholesalers; (c) specialist retailers; (d) specialist wholesalers.

30 When the interest received on savings is 'tax paid', the money will be in:
(a) a building society; (b) a commercial bank; (c) a finance house; (d) a local authority.

Unit 12 Population

1 Population is a major .... of an economy.

2 Suggest two questions which should appear on a census form, apart from name, address, age and sex.

3 Why did British population grow only slowly before 1801?

4 Why have children become an economic liability to parents?

5 Suggest three causes of population increase.

6 Define the term 'birth rate'.

7 How does attitude to marriage affect the birth rate?

8 How has China tried to reduce her birth rate?

9 What is the average life expectancy in Britain?

10 What is meant by the term 'natural increase in population'?

11 Name one overpopulated nation.

12 What did Malthus predict?

13 In terms of age how is the population classified?

14 'Those inhabitants at work, or available for work, usually between ages of 16–65' is a definition of ....

15 Suggest four economic effects of Britain's ageing population.

16 Why are there more women in Britain than men?

17 Which nation within the UK has the least dense(!) population?

18 How has the Government tried to increase occupational mobility of labour?

19 List the obstacles to geographical mobility. (**'FIBPEA'** helps)

20 What is the poverty trap which affects world population growth?

21 The next year for a full population census will be:
(a) 1986; (b) 1988; (c) 1990; (d) 1991.

22 The dependency ratio in the population shows the proportion of:
   (a) births to deaths;   (b) men to women;   (c) unemployed to employed;   (d) workers to non-workers.

23 The British population increased most in size between:
   (a) 1701–1801;   (b) 1801–1851;   (c) 1851–1901;   (d) 1901–1951.

24 The decline in the birth rate in Britain since 1901 can be explained by all of the following **except**:
   (a) better methods of birth control   (b) children being cheaper to look after
   (c) higher living standards   (d) more women going out to work.

25 Net immigration into Britain occurred during the period:
   (a) 1871–1900;   (b) 1901–1930;   (c) 1931–1960;   (d) 1961–1984.

26 When a nation is making the fullest and best use of its resources it is said to be at its:
   (a) distribution;   (b) maximum;   (c) minimum;   (d) optimum.

27 Since 1971 the density of population has increased in:
   (a) E. Anglia;   (b) Industrial Lancashire;   (c) Inner London;   (d) Tyneside.

28 In post-war Britain employment has increased in:
   (a) manufacturing;   (b) primary production;   (c) secondary production;   (d) services.

29 If a person changes to a new type of job in the same organization without moving home, this is an example of:
   (a) geographical mobility;   (b) immobility of labour;   (c) industrial mobility;   (d) occupational mobility.

30 Industrial mobility is mainly induced by:
   (a) general economic expansion;   (b) Government retraining schemes;   (c) longer apprenticeships;   (d) more job centres.

Unit 13 Trade unions and wages

1 Wages are the .... of labour.
2 Name two deductions taken from gross wage.
3 Suggest three disadvantages of piece-work.
4 Define the marginal physical productivity.
5 The demand for labour is a .... demand, based on demand for the final product to which it contributes.
6 'The addition to total revenue resulting from the employment of one extra unit of labour' defines ....
7 List the factors affecting the demand for labour (remember **'SPED'**).
8 How does the supply curve for labour slope?
9 Name the specific factors affecting the supply of labour (remember **'PICTSE'**).
10 What are 'relativities'?
11 If wage costs increase what needs to happen for the unit cost of production to fall?
12 What is the aim behind an incomes policy?
13 How many trade unions and trade union members are there in Britain?
14 What is the main aim of the trade union movement?
15 What are the main functions of the trade unions? (remember **'NIPS'**)
16 Which type of trade union is fastest growing and why?
17 Name the odd one out – local trade union official, shop steward, executive member, general secretary.
18 For what does ACAS stand?
19 What are the main characteristics of **unofficial** strikes?
20 Outline the main features of the 1982 Employment Act.
21 The following table shows the change in a firm's output as the number of workers employed varies, assuming other factors remain constant.

Number of workers	Total output per week
0	0
1	10
2	20
3	34
4	45
5	54

The maximum number of workers which can be employed before diminishing marginal productivity occurs is:
(a) 2;   (b) 3;   (c) 4;   (d) 5.

22 Disposable income is also known as:

(a) gross income; (b) income in kind; (c) net income; (d) total earnings.

23 There will be an increase in the demand for dockers if:

(a) air freight becomes cheaper (b) labour-saving devices become more expensive

(c) tariffs are introduced by the Government (d) they get an increase in basic wages.

24 If the Government introduces a minimum wage in an industry above the existing equilibrium rate then:

(a) the quantity of labour demanded will fall and quantity supplied will fall

(b) the quantity of labour demanded will fall and quantity supplied will increase

(c) the quantity of labour demanded will increase and quantity supplied will fall

(d) the quantity of labour demanded will fall and quantity supplied will increase.

25 In conditions of full employment, a trade union is likely to be successful in obtaining a wage increase when:

(a) the demand for the final product is elastic

(b) the demand for the final product is falling

(c) the labour costs are a small percentage of total cost

(d) the supply of labour-saving equipment is increasing.

26 Consider the following data:

Year	Average wage (£)	Index of Retail Prices
1	100	50
2	120	75
3	150	100
4	200	140

Real wages were highest in:

(a) Year 1; (b) Year 2; (c) Year 3; (d) Year 4.

27 'When employees are paid a certain percentage of the value of their output' they are said to be receiving:

(a) commission; (b) fees; (c) salaries; (d) wages.

28 In comparison with Britain's major European competitors, our economy can be described as:

(a) high wage, high output, high cost (c) low wage, low output, high cost

(b) high wage, high output, low cost (d) low wage, low output, low cost.

29 Incomes policies were *not* used in the period:

(a) 1972–1973; (b) 1973–1974; (c) 1975–1977; (d) 1979–1983.

30 The EEPTU (Electricians and Plumbers) is an example of a:

(a) craft union; (b) general union; (c) industrial union; (d) white collar union.

Unit 14 National income and standard of living

1 Describe the simple model of the circular flow of income.

2 What is a 'leakage' from the circular flow?

3 Define 'investment'.

4 The national income of a country is the .... of all the goods and services produced from a nation's .... in one year.

5 Suggest two problems facing calculation by the Expenditure Method.

6 Name the main sources of income in the national income accounts.

7 What is Stock appreciation?

8 How is GDP calculated by the output method?

9 What adjustment is made to convert **domestic** product into **national** product?

10 Net investment for one year in Britain is the difference between .... and ....

11 What happens to national income in real terms, if income increases by 10% and there is 15% inflation?

12 What adjustments have to made to get from real income per head to disposable income per head?

13 How will a reduction in the working week from forty-three hours affect national income?

14 What problems are faced when making inter-country comparisons of living standards?

15 In 1982, what was the average net wealth in Britain?

16 What do you understand by the phrase 'the quality of life'?

17 Define economic growth.

18 Give three arguments against economic growth.

19 Name an example of well marketed British technology.

20 How much has North Sea oil contributed to British growth?

21 The table below shows the population and gross national product for four imaginary countries:

Country	A	B	C	D
Population (*millions*)	200	55	300	70
GNP (*£m*)	8	275	9	280

Assuming the price levels and other factors are similar in each country, the country with the largest per capita real income is:

(a) A; (b) B; (c) C; (d) D.

22 During the period 1980–85 this nation's land, capital and prices were unchanged but population and output fell as shown:

Year	Output units	Population
1980	1080	120
1981	990	110
1982	945	100
1983	900	90
1984	720	80

The population was at an optimum in:

(a) 1981; (b) 1982; (c) 1983; (d) 1984.

23 In calculating national income, transfer payments such as pensions are:

(a) added to consumer spending in the expenditure method

(b) added to wages in the income method

(c) deleted from government spending in the expenditure method

(d) deleted from residual error in the income method.

24 The depreciation of productive assets in the creation of national income is known as:

(a) capital consumption; (b) double counting; (c) economic growth; (d) stock appreciation.

25 The use of value-added calculations in national income accounting occurs in:

(a) all three methods; (b) the expenditure method; (c) the income method; (d) the output method.

26 Assuming nothing else changes, real national income per head will increase if:

(a) free services are dropped; (b) income tax increases; (c) inflation increases; (d) population falls.

27 Economic growth can be supported for the following reasons **except** that:

(a) it encourages efficiency (b) it enables the reduction of poverty

(c) it improves living standards (d) it widens wealth inequality.

28 The difference between total domestic expenditure and gross domestic product at market prices is obtained by:

(a) adding exports and subtracting imports (b) adding subsidies and subtracting taxes

(c) adjusting for property income from abroad (d) deducting capital consumption.

29 An example of injections into the circular flow of income would be:

(a) imports; (b) savings; (c) taxes; (d) transfer of payments.

30 Britain's rate of economic growth since 1970 has averaged approximately:

(a) 2% (b) 4% (c) 7% (d) 12%.

Unit 15 Public finance

1 Define public spending and give one example.

2 What effect has the ageing population had on public spending?

3 Name one 'transfer income'.

4 Merit goods are provided by the State at .... price.

5 How much does the Government spend annually?

6 List the main aims of taxation – **'MARS'**.

7 What % of a packet of cigarettes goes in tax?

8 Adam Smith's canons included certainty, convenience ...., ...

9 Distinguish between direct and indirect taxation.

10 A tax whose payment falls as income increases is described as ....

11 Most levels of National Insurance contribution are an example of .... taxation.

12 Define marginal rate of tax.

13 List the advantages of income tax – have a 'fayre' guess!

14 Distinguish between tax evasion and tax avoidance.

15 The current standard rate of VAT is ......%.

16 List the disadvantages of VAT – there are 'dire' consequences if you cannot remember them.

17 Distinguish between protective and excise duties.

18 Which tax has been levied on North Sea oil profits?
19 How does the elasticity of demand influence the real incidence of expenditure taxes?
20 What is PSBR?
21 Corporation tax is:
   (a) a direct proportional tax on sellers
   (b) a direct regressive tax on consumers
   (c) an indirect regressive tax on sellers
   (d) an indirect progressive tax on consumers.
22 The Government gains the largest proportion of its annual revenue from:
   (a) borrowing; (b) income tax; (c) national insurance; (d) value added tax.
23 The National Debt includes all of the following **except**:
   (a) gilt-edged stocks; (b) local authority loans; (c) National Savings Certificates;
   (d) war loans.
24 A tax will have the effect of automatically stabilizing the economy if its yield:
   (a) falls with a rise in income (b) increases with a rise in income
   (c) increases with a fall in income (d) remains constant as income changes.
25 If a tax is placed on a good, the market price of the good will not change if:
   (a) demand is fairly elastic (b) demand is fairly inelastic
   (c) demand is perfectly elastic (d) demand is perfectly inelastic.
26

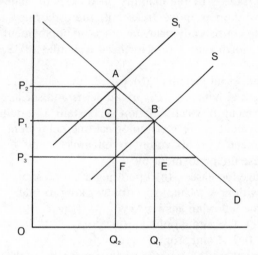

   In the diagram, the burden of taxation falling upon the consumer is shown by the area:
   (a) $P_1 P_2$ AC; (b) $P_1 P_3$ FC; (c) P_3 E Q_1O; (d) $P_3 P_2$ AF.
27 All of the following are public goods **except**
   (a) defence; (b) education; (c) roads; (d) street lighting.

28

Income per annum £	Amount of tax paid £
2000	800
3000	900
4000	1000

   In the above table, the tax is:
   (a) incidental; (b) progressive; (c) proportional; (d) regressive.
29 A criticism of a high marginal rate of income tax is that it:
   (a) can be passed on to the consumer
   (b) makes the distribution of income more unequal
   (c) may be a disincentive to effort
   (d) will raise the public sector borrowing required.
30 An example of an indirect and regressive tax would be:
   (a) capital transfer tax; (b) national insurance; (c) rates; (d) valued added tax.

Unit 16 Unemployment

1 When, after 1945, did unemployment become a major problem in Britain?
2 Suggest one major difference between British unemployment in the 1930s and the 1980s.
3 Which groups of people are particularly susceptible to unemployment? (Remember **'YOU'**
   and **'ME'**.)
4 Why are young workers more likely to be made redundant than middle-aged employees?
5 Which ethnic group has largest % male unemployment?

6 Name two declining industries which have created unemployment.

7 Describe the costs of unemployment. (**'DESTITUTES'**)

8 How much does each unemployed person cost the State per year?

9 How is unemployment measured?

10 Name one government scheme to alleviate unemployment.

11 Figure 16.4 shows that in 1976 there were 1.35 million unemployed and 150 000 vacancies. If there had been perfect mobility of labour then, how many people would have been unemployed?

12 Which type of unemployment is closely linked with structural unemployment?

13 What effect does technology have on employment in the long run?

14 What is the difference between Voluntary and Involuntary unemployment?

15 How did 1979 Conservative Government's inflation control policies affect unemployment?

16 What is meant by the term 'replacement rate'? What is the average rate?

17 Suggest two general measures to minimize frictional unemployment.

18 Name three types of unemployment which might be alleviated by rapid economic growth.

19 List three arguments for and three arguments against the Youth Training Scheme (and similar Government schemes).

20 How has the Government influenced the labour market to reduce the supply of labour?

21 Cyclical unemployment was caused by:
   (**a**) a decline in world trade   (**b**) the inability of workers to change occupations
   (**c**) the reluctance of workers to move areas   (**d**) the use of new technology.

22 An area in Britain with consistently **below** average unemployment is:
   (**a**) East Anglia;   (**b**) North East;   (**c**) Northern Ireland;   (**d**) Scotland.

23 Unemployment creates:
   (**a**) private benefits and social benefits   (**b**) private benefits and social costs
   (**c**) private costs and social benefits   (**d**) private costs and social costs.

24 'The rate of unemployment at which inflation is constant' is a definition of:
   (**a**) frictional unemployment   (**c**) technological unemployment
   (**b**) natural unemployment   (**d**) voluntary unemployment.

25 Trade unions may cause unemployment by:
   (**a**) obtaining large wage increases   (**b**) operating a closed shop
   (**c**) refusing to work with new technology   (**d**) working to rule.

Questions 26–30 all use the following answer key:
   (**a**) 1 and 3 only   (**c**) 1, 3 and 4 only   (**e**) 5 only.
   (**b**) 2 and 4 only   (**d**) 2, 4 and 5 only

26 Registered unemployment may underestimate the true extent of the problem because one or more of the following groups is/are omitted from the total figure:
   (**1**) members of the armed forces   (**3**) university students   (**5**) the disabled.
   (**2**) people seeking part time work   (**4**) teenagers on YTS

27 Which of the following policies is/are **inappropriate** in dealing specifically with Structural unemployment?
   (**1**) increased government spending   (**4**) reduced welfare benefits
   (**2**) improved retraining facilities   (**5**) selective import controls.
   (**3**) reduced income tax

28 Which of the following policies is/are **appropriate** to reduce 'search' unemployment?
   (**1**) import controls introduced   (**4**) school leaving age increased
   (**2**) income tax lowered   (**5**) welfare benefits lowered.
   (**3**) public spending raised

29 Which of the following are said to be consequences of unemployment?
   (**1**) a fall in tax revenue
   (**2**) an increase in spending on imports
   (**3**) increased expenditure on welfare benefits
   (**4**) physical deterioration of land, labour and capital
   (**5**) technology used more widely.

30 In which group/s is/are above average unemployment found:
   (**1**) females 16–24 age group   (**4**) males 25–54 age group
   (**2**) females plus 55 age group   (**5**) skilled workers.
   (**3**) males 16–24 age group

Unit 17 International trade

1 International trade differs from domestic trade in that .... are used.

2 List the advantages of international trade – remember to **'SMILE'**

3 Distinguish between Comparative Advantage and Absolute Advantage.

4 Construct an example to show how specialization can help trade and benefit two countries.

5 Name one example of a British industry which has experienced great import penetration.

6 Name one product over which Britain and France have clashed.

7 Britain needs to import ....

8 The comparative advantage which Britain has in trade, lies in .... now rather than manufactured goods.

9 What effect has EEC entry had on British trading patterns?

10 Define the Terms of Trade.

11 Suggest two causes of export price increases.

12 Give four reasons why governments seek to control trade. (Remember **'BRIDES'**)

13 Name one British industry protected by the government.

14 Explain how dumping works.

15 Describe two ways in which trade became free between 1945–72.

16 What is the difference between *ad valorem* and 'specific'?

17 Name two administrative controls used to restrict trade.

18 What are the disadvantages of import controls?

19 What is the difference between a free trade area and a customs union?

20 Outline the main economic features of EEC.

21 An adverse movement in a country's terms of trade means that:
   (a) prices of exports have risen relative to prices of imports
   (b) prices of exports have fallen relative to prices of imports
   (c) volume of exports has risen relative to volume of imports
   (d) volume of exports has fallen relative to volume of imports.

22 An example of a customs union is:
   (a) EEC; **(b)** EFTA; **(c)** IMF; **(d)** LAFTA.

23 The possible gains from international trade include all of the following **except**:
   (a) economies of scale; **(b)** greater specialization; **(c)** increased competition; **(d)** self sufficiency.

24–25 Tradeland has the following indices for export prices and import prices:

	Export Index	Import Index
1982	100	100
1983	121	110
1984	126	120
1985	130	130

24 The Terms of Trade index in 1983 for Tradeland was:
   (a) 91; **(b)** 110; **(c)** 111; **(d)** 121.

25 The Terms of Trade index for Tradeland moved favourably in:
   (a) 1982; **(b)** 1983; **(c)** 1984; **(d)** 1985.

26 The organization set up to reduce trade barriers throughout the world was:
   (a) Comecon; **(b)** EEC; **(c)** OPEC; **(d)** GATT.

27 An **invalid** reason for imposing import controls is to:
   (a) improve the efficiency of resource allocation
   (b) maintain employment in an industry
   (c) protect an infant industry
   (d) raise revenue for the Treasury

28

OUTPUT UNITS

	Good X	Good Y
Country A	10	5
Country B	6	4

From this data to benefit from international trade:
   (a) Country A should specialize in the production of good Y.
   (b) Country A should produce both good X and good Y.
   (c) Country B should use its absolute advantage in producing Y.
   (d) Country B should produce none of good X and import it from A.

29–30 The following answer key applies:

	Assertion	Reason	Explanation
(a)	TRUE	TRUE	The reason correctly explains the assertion.
(b)	TRUE	TRUE	The reason does **not** correctly explain the assertion.
(c)	TRUE	FALSE	
(d)	FALSE	TRUE	
(e)	FALSE	FALSE	

29	*Assertion*	*Reason*
	Manufactured imports have become an important part of United Kingdom imports.	Countries such as Japan and West Germany are more efficient than we are in producing manufactured goods.
30	Other things being equal, inflation in the United Kingdom will lead to a deterioration in the terms of trade.	The economic effects of movements in the terms of trade are influenced by demand elasticities.

Unit 18 Balance of payments

1 What is the difference between visible and invisible trade?

2 Suggest three reasons why Britain's balance of trade moved into surplus in 1980.

3 Give one example of an invisible earning.

4 What does a deficit on the current account indicate?

5 The expenditure by Britain's residents on foreign shares is classed as ....

6 Explain three reasons why investment into Britain has substantially increased since mid-1970s.

7 How does inward investment help **and** hinder the Balance of Payments?

8 What does a positive figure on Official Financing show?

9 When a balance of payments has persistent imbalances this indicates that it is in ....

10 When was £ sterling floated?

11 Suggest three possible disadvantages to having an overall balance of payments surplus.

12 How is 'depreciation' different from 'devaluation'?

13 What determines the effectiveness of devaluation/depreciation as a policy to improve balance of payments?

14 How can deflation be criticized as a policy to deal with a balance of payments problem?

15 How are British exports subsidized?

16 Define 'exchange rate'.

17 Suggest two advantages of floating exchange rates.

18 Why did the system of managed exchange rates end?

19 How has the International Monetary Fund tried to increase international liquidity?

20 Who provides aid for capital projects in developing countries?

21 The balance of trade is the difference between imports and exports of:
(a) assets;   (b) capital;   (c) goods;   (d) services.

22 Invisible trade includes:
(a) food and drink;   (b) portfolio investment;   (c) raw materials;   (d) tourism and transport.

23 A depreciation of the £ makes:
(a) exports cheaper and imports cheaper   (b) exports cheaper and imports dearer
(c) exports dearer and imports cheaper   (d) exports dearer and imports dearer.

24 'A national account which shows the financial transactions of one nation with the rest of the world over a period of time' is a definition of the:
(a) Balance for Official Financing   (c) Balance of Trade
(b) Balance of Payments   (d) Current Account

25 The major deficit item on the British invisibles account is:
(a) government expenditure;   (b) interest, profit, dividends;   (c) other financial services;   (d) private transfers.

26 The section of the Balance of Payments helped by a depreciating £ is:
(a) capital inflows because £ becomes more desirable
(b) invisible earnings because they are inelastic in demand
(c) official financing because loans become cheaper
(d) visible receipts because their demand is elastic.

27 Official Financing is achieved through all of the following **except**:
(a) borrowing from IMF;   (b) borrowing from other central banks;   (c) raising taxes;   (d) using reserves.

28 Exchange control attempts to limit:
(a) expensive imports;   (b) government overseas aid;   (c) overseas investment;   (d) subsidized exports.

29 Floating exchange rates have been favoured because they encourage:
(a) automatic adjustments;   (b) business uncertainty;   (c) currency speculation;   (d) government interventions.

30 The supervision and surveillance of exchange rates is a function of:
(a) GATT;   (b) IMF;   (c) SDR;   (d) World Bank.

Unit 19 Government policy

1 In a mixed economy, the major parties disagree over ....
2 Name four aims of the Government.
3 What is meant by an economic 'target'?
4 Give one example of the conflict between government aims.
5 In what sense is Britain's economy 'open'?
6 What is a 'siege economy'?
7 What % of public expenditure each year is subject to government manipulation?
8 Suggest two problems that a government finds with the information which it receives.
9 How long do income tax changes take to implement?
10 What actions can the government take to change the economy? Beware **'LEST'** you forget!
11 What policies has the government used to encourage competition in the economy?
12 Give one example to explain how social policies can have economic implications.
13 Suggest two policies to improve the balance of payments.
14 What might the creation of more credit and expansion in the money supply cause?
15 How many people does local government employ?
16 What is the 'rate support grant'?
17 Since 1981 what has happened to councils which overspend?
18 What is the 'rate poundage'?
19 Suggest three disadvantages of the rating system.
20 Name two alternatives to rates.
21 A reduction in unemployment could be achieved by all of the following policies **except**:
   (a) lower interest rates; **(b)** lower money supply; **(c)** lower taxes; **(d)** increased public spending.
22 Tax changes would be an example of:
   (a) fiscal policy; **(b)** manpower policy; **(c)** monetary policy; **(d)** trading policy.
23 Out of the working population, the % employed by the Government is:
   (a) 5%; **(b)** 15%; **(c)** 30%; **(d)** 45%.
24 If the prices of goods were rising quickly and employment was at a high level, a government would be most likely to:
   (a) increase taxation without raising government spending
   (b) lower the rate of interest
   (c) lower the value of the pound
   (d) raise the supply of money.
25 The main source of local government revenue is:
   (a) income from local services   **(c)** rates from local residents
   (b) loans from the stock market   **(d)** rate support grant from the central government.

Unit 20 Consumption and distribution

1 Describe the normal chain of distribution.
2 Why are some wholesalers being omitted from this chain?
3 Give one example of the government acting as a wholesaler.
4 Name three services provided by wholesaler for a manufacturer.
5 Suggest two services which supermarkets do **not** provide for consumers.
6 List four services performed by a retailer for a consumer.
7 Name two large retail organizations which benefit from economies of scale.
8 Which types of retail outlet are moving downmarket?
9 How does persuasive advertising differ from generic advertising?
10 How much would a 30-second TV advert cost?
11 Name one advertising agency.
12 What do the initials ASA mean?
13 What is market research?
14 What effect did the advent of self-service have on packaging?
15 List the three main details of 1893 Sale of Goods Act.
16 Which Act makes it illegal for sellers to offer for sale food which is unfit for human consumption?
17 What rights has a householder under the Unsolicited Goods and Services Act?
18 What is a credit reference agency?
19 Name one Trade Association and say what it does.
20 Suggest two advantages of buying on credit.
21 All of the following are 'producers', except:
   (a) consumer; **(b)** retailer; **(c)** manufacturer; **(d)** wholesaler.

22 The form of retailing which enables you to shop from home, often on credit, is known as:
   (a) discount selling; **(b)** mail order; **(c)** vending; **(d)** voluntary trading.
23 Woolworth's is an example of a:
   (a) department store; **(b)** hypermarket; **(c)** variety chain store; **(d)** voluntary group.
24 The enforcing of certain consumer protection legislation is done by the:
   (a) Advertising Standards Authority
   (b) Consumer Association
   (c) Citizens Advice Bureau
   (d) Trading Standards Department.
25 A disadvantage of advertizing to the consumer is that it:
   (a) creates employment
   (b) gives necessary information
   (c) raises a product's price
   (d) subsidizes the price of newspapers.
26 When a company advertises its brand it is seeking to:
   (a) gain consumer loyalty   **(c)** increase its prices
   (b) help the whole industry   **(d)** omit the wholesaler.
27 The scrutiny and testing of manufactured products is done by:
   (a) British Standards Institute   **(c)** Design Centre
   (b) Citizens Advice Bureau   **(d)** Trade Associations
Questions 28–30 For each of these questions select from the list (a) to (e) below the most appropriate Act which gives the consumer certain rights in the situations described:
   (a) Consumer Credit Act   **(d)** Trade Descriptions Acts
   (b) Food and Drugs Act   **(e)** Weights and Measures Act.
   (c) Sale of Goods Act
28 A dissatisfied customer finds that his watch is not 'waterproof' as the seller claimed it to be.
29 A seller tries to repossess, without a court order, some goods bought on hire purchase when more than a third of the price has been paid.
30 A shopkeeper refuses to give a customer either a repair, a refund or a replacement when his newly-bought shoes leak in the rain.

Answers to self-test questions

Unit 1 Economic ideas and concepts

1 No – it costs money to produce the school meal, even though it may not have to be paid for by a child. It is 'free' because it has been subsidized.
2 Yes – there is no cost of production involved.
3 Leasing a vehicle and renting property
4 Fixed capital, such as a factory, is unchanged in use from year to year, whereas working capital, such as raw materials, is the stock of resources ready for use and sale and these change daily.
5 Social capital consists of man-made resources which are produced for the benefit of the whole community *e.g.* a motorway.
6 A market.
7 Opportunity costs.
8 People act as producers, citizens, consumers.
9 £4500
10 A nation where most people's basic needs are not met and average income per head is very low.
11 No-one is self sufficient, we all specialize and use our income to buy the goods and services of other specialists. This makes people dependent on one another.

12 The most effective usage of resources in solving a problem of scarcity.
13 The economic problem is how to use the available resources in a community to meet the existing needs of society.
14 For whom to produce? What to produce? Where to produce? How to produce?
15 Inflation reduces the value of real income, because rising prices mean that a smaller range of goods and services can be bought with the existing income – thus inflation and unchanged income make people worse-off.
16 A consumer good is purchased for its own sake and the benefit which it can give whereas a capital good is bought for its ability to assist in production of consumer goods.
17 It is because of scarcity that choices have to be made. For instance, the Government wants to spend £25 000m on defence, but only have £20 000m available; the scarcity of funds means that some projects have to be scrapped and some retained, thus necessitating a choice.
18 40%
19 Any factor of production.
20 Single-parent families, unemployed, the elderly, the low paid and the disabled/sick.
21 – (c); 22 – (a); 23 – (a); 24 – (c); 25 – (c); 26 – (d); 27 – (b); 28 – (d); 29 – (c); 30 – (c).

Unit 2 Economic systems

1 Capitalist, Collective, Mixed.
2 No government interference in decision-making, private individuals own resources which they sell to highest bidders, maximum profits, labour is perfectly mobile, consumer sovereignty.
3 It stimulates innovation and makes an economy dynamic.
4 It is maximized by the complete absence of government restrictions, both legal and fiscal.
5 Wealth is very unevenly spread because the rich tend to get richer and the poor get poorer.
6 USA
7 40%
8 Its role is one of total control (almost) over the allocation of resources in the system.
9 As the government is in such control, there is little personal freedom and there is a large bureaucracy of planners. In addition, few incentives occur in the production and distribution processes.
10 Special shops, holiday villas, 'thirteenth month' salary.
11 £45.
12 Public sector.
13 Conservative.
14 British Rail.
15 Subsidies are given in order to reduce price. In 1975, the Labour Government subsidized the price of cheese and milk.
16 It participates by providing public goods and services, merit goods, uneconomic goods/services and transfer payments.
17 The function of the subsistence economy was to organize production in order to meet the consumption needs of the people.
18 The subsistence economy provided little choice and tended to underutilize resources.
19 Black.
20 Collective is the odd one out, because the other three all describe the same sort of economy, where there is no government interference.
21 – (a); 22 – (b); 23 – (b); 24 – (a); 25 – (b); 26 – (c); 27 – (d); 28 – (a); 29 – (c); 30 – (a).

Unit 3 Business units

1 Sole trader, partnership, private company, public company.
2 Denationalization or privatization.
3 Labour Party, which believes in more public ownership, set up National Enterprise Board in order to expand State involvement in the private sector.
4 Avoid **W**asteful duplication, achieve **E**conomies of scale, prevent consumer **E**xploitation, provide **S**ufficient capital, provide **U**neconomic service, prolong life of a **D**eclining industry, control industries of **S**trategic importance.
5 Another nationalized industry e.g. coal and gas; imports *e.g.* Australian coal.
6 Investment spending of gas limited, price increases by British Steel.
7 People starting a business have their responsibility for losses (liability) restricted to the amount of money they originally subscribed in shares.

8 This document lays down the rules and regulations governing the internal organization of a company *e.g.* powers of the directors.

9 Public limited company.

10 **D**iseconomies of scale, **I**nterests of management different from shareholders, **S**mall groups may dominate company, **A**ccounts annually submitted, **D**ocumentation is expensive.

11 1½m

12 Partnership **D**eed, **U**nlimited liability, **O**wnership by 2–20 people.

13 A producer co-operative is a group of workers who provide the capital and jointly own a business making goods.

14 Co-operative Movement.

15 A trader receives goods which he may sell before he has paid for them.

16 Savings, loans/overdrafts, trade credit, hire purchase, profits, leasing, share sales.

17 Industrial and Commercial Finance Company provide long-term finance for small- to medium-sized firms; between £5000 to £3m per firm.

18 Rolls-Royce, ICL.

19 The nominal value of share is price paid when it is first issued, whereas the market value is price obtained when the share is resold.

20 Merchant banks known as Issuing Houses.

21 – (b); 22 – (c); 23 – (c); 24 – (a); 25 – (c); 26 – (d); 27 – (a); 28 – (b); 29 – (a); 30 – (b).

Unit 4 Demand and supply

1 Demand and supply.

2 Consumer reaction to **price**.

3 Exceeds. Diagram is D_2 in Figure 4.5.

4 Complements, Income, Substitutes, Tastes and fashions.

5 Very inelastic. It cannot respond quickly to changes in price *e.g.* a field being put to a fixed use such as growing peas.

6 Supply with fall *i.e.* less will be supplied at each price.

7 Increase

8 An innovation will enable goods to be made more cheaply.
Increased production of a good in joint supply.
The price of goods in competitive supply falls.
Government subsidy given.

9 Right

10 It shows that there is excess supply, a glut of unsold goods.

11 The position from which there is no tendency to change.

12 Elasticity

13 Coefficient of elasticity of supply.

14 Relatively elastic good. Normal goods with several substitutes *e.g.* makes of car, beans, bread.

15 $\frac{50}{100}$ = ½ which is relatively inelastic.

16 It becomes more elastic, its elasticity increases.

17 Very elastic.

18 See Figure 4.10. Your curve should be straight line and through the origin.

19 A larger time period is considered and it is easy to obtain and substitute other factors of production.

20 The good is inferior – as income increases, the quantity demanded falls.

21 – (b); 22 – (b); 23 – (b); 24 – (B); 25 – (E).

Unit 5 Production

1 B = forward vertical; D = diversified/lateral;
A = backward vertical; C = horizontal.

2 Tertiary, which can be subdivided commercial and social.

3 De-industrialization

4 Entrepreneurial ability/enterprise

5 **P**ractice makes perfect, **O**utput increases, **S**avings in training, **T**ools/equipment fewer, **M**achinery utilized, **E**fficiency.

6 Customer

7 Period of time in which at least one cost of production is fixed.

8 Marginal cost falls faster than average cost and rises faster. It crosses the AC curve at the lowest point of average cost.

9 Where MC = MR and MC is rising.

10 Larger markets caused by improved transport, communications and technology.

11 Internal economies are specific advantages **within one** firm whereas external economies accrue to **all firms** in an industry.

12 Purchasing, selling, diversifying (see 5.6).

13 The internal diseconomies of scale – **S**tandardized products, **W**asted resources, **I**mpersonal behaviour, **R**ed tape, **L**abour relations poor.

14 External diseconomies of scale.

15 In a merger, two firms join together to form one new organization, whereas with a takeover, one firm buys out another. Thus in a merger A + B = C whereas in a takeover A + B = A.

16 Monopolies Commission if assets exceed £15m, otherwise no one, except perhaps Stock Exchange Council.

17 lateral/conglomerate

18 A firm with less than 200 employees.

19 Currently about 2000.

20 It is a scheme to provide finance for small firms. The Government promises to provide 80% of any loan given by a bank to a firm if the firm goes bust (see Unit 5.8).

21 – (d); 22 – (a); 23 – (a); 24 – (c); 25 – (b); 26 – (d); 27 – (d); 28 – (b); 29 – (a); 30 – (d).

Unit 6 Location of industry

1 Car making (W. Midlands), whisky distilling (S. Scotland).

2 Desire to make a profit.

3 See Unit 6.2 *e.g.* deep water harbour, shipbuilding, Tyneside.

4 Motorways. Better transport/communications.

5 about £750m

6 Near the source of raw materials

7 40% Development Area grant, local coal, imported raw materials, rail links.

8 See Figure 6.3 *e.g.* Glasgow, Newcastle.

9 The market.

10 Coal (S. Yorkshire), shipbuilding (N. East).

11 Congestion increases the time of making a journey. As time = money, then costs are increased.

12 A social problem such as increased crime can lead to:
(a) personal distress which may require health service treatment (at a cost);
(b) more resources devoted to deterrence and detection (which could have been used elsewhere).

13 See Unit 6.4 – creation of Assisted Areas, with special grants and tax allowances.

14 To relieve congestion in large cities *e.g.* Skelmersdale (Liverpool).

15 Small areas in run down inner city areas, which receive special concessions over rates, VAT, industrial training levies etc. They are planned to be growth points.

16 We cannot tell what would have happened if the policies had not been used.

17 New jobs created, foreign investment obtained, gradual industrial decline, humane government approach.

18 Grants up to 40% of capital cost of new investments.

19 See Unit 6.5 – decline for product because of older staple industry's decline, new substitutes, intense foreign competition.

20 The Government has defined their financial target as 'break even'.

21 – (a); 22 – (d); 23 – (b); 24 – (b); 25 – (b); 26 – (b); 27 – (d); 28 – (c); 29 – (d); 30 – (b).

Unit 7 Markets

1 A retail market is where usually single units are sold by the retailer to the final consumer, whereas on a wholesale market, large quantities are sold in bulk by manufacturer to the wholesaler.

2 Tea, coffee, cotton, jute, cocoa, silver.

3 Its assumptions of perfect knowledge, perfect mobility of factors and homogeneous products are unrealistic.

4 They are equal. See Figures 7.3, 7.4, and Unit 7.2.

5 The demand curve for the firm is elastic (horizontal) because each firm must accept the market price. However, the demand curve for the industry is downward sloping left to right.

6 No excessive profits and normal profit in long run. Production is at lowest average cost.

7 In theory – 'supply of a product is controlled by one firm'. In practice, the Government defines it as where a quarter of an industry is controlled by one firm!

8 See Unit 7.3 – legal protection, avoid wastage, supply restrictions, takeovers.

9 A group of firms who agree, arrange and act together in price fixing – market shareouts.

10 He can fix price on quantity supplied, **not** both.

11 The entry of new firms is restricted severely or banned.

12 Economies of scale, wasteful competition is avoided, excess capacity is reduced.

13 Figure 7.8 – Monopolist produces where MC = MR (max. profit) which is different from lowest AC.

14 Nationalization, Ministerial Supervision, Monopolies Commission and Restrictive Practices Court.

15 Regulation of restrictive agreements relating to goods and services and enabling judicial investigations.

16 He can negotiate a voluntary undertaking with a firm or refer the 'uncompetitive practice' to Monopolies and Mergers Commission.

17 Monopolies and Mergers Commission.

18 It exploited its monopoly position in production of drugs for National Health Service, thus MMC ordered it to repay £3m excess profits.

19 Monopolistic competition is characterized by price cutting, non-price competition, packaging and advertising and special services for the consumer.

20 oligopoly

21 – (c); **22** – (b); **23** – (d); **24** – (d); **25** – (b).

Unit 8 Money

1 Barter

2 Interest

3 '. . . what money does' or '. . . anything that is acceptable to its users'.

4 Store of value, Unit of Account, Medium of exchange, Standard for deferred payments.

5 They are not durable so cannot act as a store of value.

6 60%

7 Stability

8 The coins and notes of same denomination (*i.e.* all £1) are of exactly the same size, colour, shape, weight.

9 Cheques are very portable. However, they are rarely used for spending of less than a £, so notes are equally good, in practice. Both notes and cheques are more portable than coins for large amounts. Cheques are clearly the most flexible.

10 Rate of exchange, Indivisibility of goods, Double coincidence of wants.

11 Goods, Rare objects, Precious metals.

12 Goldsmiths.

13 Bank of England

14 Cheque.

15 'The money that a creditor has to accept in settlement of a debt.'

16 £50

17 Face and intrinsic.

18 Need good credit record, interest charged.

19 Diners Club, American Express.

20 Every five minutes on average.

21 – (a); **22** – (d); **23** – (b); **24** – (a); **25** – (b); **26** – (d); **27** – (b); **28** – (c); **29** – (b); **30** – (b).

Unit 9 Inflation

1 Item 1 = 1100

2 = 3000

$3 = \dfrac{5400}{9500} \div 100 = 95$

2 Britain's inflation was consistently higher.

3 A persistent general increase in prices.

4 Creeping, strato, hyper, British in 1960 and 1970s was creeping, but since 1981 it has been falling.

5 The impact of inflation varies between people, places and times.

6 It provides information for government policymaking, it indicates changes in the cost of living and it is a standard for calculation of some government benefits.

7 (a) food (b) meals out.

8 'WEBB' is a mnemonic for Weights, Exclusions, Basket of goods, Base year.

9 The first year of an index, which is hopefully typical.

10 High rates discourage investment as businessmen fear government policy of a deflationary nature to lower demand in the economy.

11 'CRABS' – Changes in nature of goods and services.
  – **R**ange of households covered.
  – **A**verages used.
  – **B**ase year gets out of date.
  – **S**pending patterns change rapidly.

12 99%; competitively priced imports.

13 saving; borrowing.

14 (a) demand pull   (b) demand pull

15 P_2 – cost push will mean less is supplied at each price.

16 Britain imports a lot of raw materials for processing, refining and manufacturing, and this is very susceptible to price increases caused by world shortages.

17 If they claimed and gained wage increases above the level of productivity. However, in the service sector, particularly the public sector, productivity cannot be measured and so wage rises lead to higher prices (or greater government spending and more borrowing which is inflationary).

18 Productivity improvements.

19 It may not wish to suffer the side effects, such as unemployment worsening or economic growth slowing, of inflation control policies.

20 Incomes policy has been introduced to curb wage increases and thus halt cost-push inflation.

21 – (c); 22 – (b); 23 – (b); 24 – (a); 25 – (b); 26 – (b); 27 – (d); 28 – (b); 29 – (a); 30 – (c).

Unit 10 Banking

1 It classified banks into two groups – 'recognized banks' such as Barclays and 'licensed deposit takers' such as the Baptist Union Corporation.

2 Rothschilds, Lazard Bros.

3 National Girobank is owned by the State, whereas commercial banks are owned by their shareholders (*i.e.* public sector and private).

4 See Figure 10.1.

5 A loan is for a set period of time at a fixed rate of interest. It often needs a separate account and collateral. In contrast, an overdraft is often short-term, unspecified with prevailing rate of interest at the time being charged. It usually means that the current account goes into deficit.

6 16m people.

7 They charge higher interest than they pay. They put surplus cash into investments.

8 What the bank owes – the amount credited to people's deposit and current accounts.

9 Least. Money at call can be obtained within 24 hours thus the rate of return on it is very low.

10 There isn't one. It was abolished in 1981.

11 The banks do not have to provide actual cash for all the money in people's accounts. Also, as the amount of cash needed is only a very small proportion of the amount deposited, money can be sent out in the safe knowledge that it will not be needed. There is a fuller explanation in Unit 10.5.

12 They move their money around to gain the benefit of changes in the rate of interest.

13 A Bill of Exchange is a document for which one trader promises to pay another trader a sum of money on a certain date.

14 The government, ninety-one days.

15 'BINGOES': **B**ankers bank, **I**ssue of **N**otes, **G**overnment accounts, **O**perating monetary policy, **E**xternal functions, **S**upervising the monetary system.

16 They are used in clearing to facilitate payment of inter-bank debts.

17 Buy stocks on open market, lower interest rates, repay special deposits, increase the assets ratio.

18 Monetary base (or modified cash ratio).

19 long . . . short

20 A directive.

21 – (b); 22 – (b); 23 – (a); 24 – (b); 25 – (c); 26 – (b); 27 – (c); 28 – (b); 29 – (a); 30 – (d).

Unit 11 Savings and investment

1 Large long-term borrowers, such as PLC, government and local authorities.

2 **P**rospectus, **O**ffer for sale, **P**lacing, **I**ssue to existing shareholders, **T**ender.

3 The government seeks offers for its bonds and sells them to the highest bidders.

4 They sell units of a stated value to small savers. The units are composed of parts of a share portfolio.

5 50%

6 Mortgages.

7 TSB provide current accounts and clear cheques.

8 Unlimited.

9 See Unit 11.4 – buys/sells shares for general public.

10 Deals made on the Stock Exchange are on the basis of word of mouth between trusting people. The 'bargain' is noted by the jobber and broker separately and payment made at the end of the period of account.

11 Both buyers and sellers have nearly perfect knowledge of prices.

12 It would probably lead to a fall as speculators might become more pessimistic (because Labour is less pro-business than the Conservatives and more likely to reduce the size of the private sector).

13 The difference (increase for gain, decrease for loss) between buying price and selling price of shares.

14 Stags.

15 Market for secondhand securities. Indicator of business prospects. New share supervisor. Government funds source. Savings outlet.

16 1978–82 average was 19%. Clearly, this fluctuates with interest rate changes and the differing policies of other financial institutions.

17 It is argued that many 'investors' seek 'capital growth' rather than dividend income. Thus some companies have been taken over and disbanded, so that the assets could be realized to earn a capital gain. The finishing of these companies means less production in the economy.

18 The prevention of stockbrokers doing the jobbing function and vice versa. Britain's is the only stock market which has this distinction.

19 How much **M**oney you have; what to **U**se it for; how willing you are to take a **R**isk; how much **T**ax you pay.

20 Life assurance has the advantages of safety, convenience and no tax liability. It gives a fair long-term return. The main disadvantage is that liquidity is only gained at a large capital loss.

21 – (b); 22 – (a); 23 – (a); 24 – (d); 25 – (b); 26 – (d); 27 – (b); 28 – (d); 29 – (d); 30 – (a).

Unit 12 Population

1 resource

2 Where do you live? What is your job? (see Unit 12.1 Census).

3 Very high death rate (when little hygiene, poor standards of nutrition and food shortages).

4 They have to be looked after, clothed and fed up to age 16, whereas in the past, child labour was allowed and education was not compulsory. This meant that children worked from an early age to supplement the family income.

5 (1) increased birth rate   (2) lower death rate   (3) immigration rise.

6 The ratio of total live births to total population. This is usually expressed in 'births per 1000 of total population' per annum.

7 If marriage becomes less popular, fewer births are likely. In practice, illegitimate births might increase but the total number of births would probably fall. Similarly, if married people put their standard of living above 'having a family' in their scale of values, then birth rates will fall.

8 The Chinese Government restricts the size of families. This indirectly occurs in Britain through the issue of free contraceptives by the NHS to married women.

9 74 years.

10 It is the increase in population where birth rate exceeds death rate. As it excludes migration effects, it just considers natural factors rather than artificial aspects.

11 Mexico, Bangladesh and most other developing nations.

12 He predicted that the supply of food would not increase rapidly enough to meet the needs of the faster growing population. In the long run he may be right!

13 Those up to 16 (school leaving age); those men +65 and women +60 (above retirement age); the rest (those of working age).

14 the working population.

15 changing spending patterns, increased dependence ratio, less labour mobility, less adaptive workforce (12.3).

16 The sex distribution is the result of working habits/patterns exacting a greater toll on men,

net emigration of men, and the death of many men in the two world wars of the twentieth century.

17 Scotland

18 It has set up skill centres, tried to limit closed shops and weaken trade union resistance to retrained workers.

19 **F**amily, **I**gnorance, **B**enefits, **P**rejudice, **E**xpense, **A**vailability of accommodation (Unit 12.4(2)).

20 The high rate of population growth per head in many developing nations leads to lower income per head which creates poverty. Only if economic growth is faster than population growth can income per head be raised and poverty marginally reduced.

21–(d); **22**–(d); **23**–(c); **24**–(b); **25**–(c); **26**–(d); **27**–(a); **28**–(d); **29**–(d); **30**–(a).

Unit 13 Trade unions and wages

1 price

2 Income tax (above a certain minimum amount), national insurance (on earnings +£23/week) and pension contributions.

3 Shoddy workmanship, inspection costs, worker strain, boredom, disputes, (see 13.2).

4 'The addition to total output resulting from the employment of one extra unit of labour.'

5 derived

6 Marginal revenue product.

7 The **S**ubstitution of other factors of production, **P**roductivity, **E**lasticity of demand for the final product, **D**emand for the final product (Unit 13.3).

8 Upward from left to right – see Figure 13.5.

9 **P**ay, **I**ncome in kind, **C**onditions of employment, **T**ype of employment, **S**ecurity, **E**ntry requirements. (Unit 13.4).

10 Differences in wages between similar jobs *e.g.* a cleaner at DHSS may be paid a higher wage rate than a cleaner at a small garage showroom.

11 Productivity (output per man) needs to increase faster than wages so that the overall average cost per unit made falls.

12 To reduce inflation, particularly the cost push type produced by high wage increases.

13 425 trade unions in 1982, 11.3m trade union members in 1982.

14 To improve the terms (including wages) and conditions of their members.

15 **N**egotiation, **I**nformation, **P**ersuasion, **S**upport. (Unit 13.7).

16 White-collar because of increased number of workers in services and less favourable attitude to management.

17 Shop steward – unofficial, works on shop floor and is elected by workers there.

18 Advisory, Conciliation and Arbitration Service (Unit 13.8)

19 They are small scale, brief, unpredictable and usually at one factory.

20 Pickets – maximum of six. New closed shops needed 80% support. Trade unions liable for damages. Individual rights extended. (See Unit 13.9)

21–(b); **22**–(c); **23**–(b); **24**–(b); **25**–(c); **26**–(a); **27**–(a); **28**–(c); **29**–(d); **30**–(a).

Unit 14 National income and standard of living

1 Producers pay income to workers, who as consumers spend that money on the producers' goods and services, thereby giving income to producers. (See Figure 14.1)

2 Spending which is not directly returned to producers *i.e.* taxes, savings, expenditure on imports.

3 Money spent on capital formation.

4 Total value; resources.

5 Transfer payments need to be deducted from Government spending and an adjustment has to be made for taxes and subsidies, because they distort market prices. Taxes are deducted because they artificially raise prices whilst subsidies are added.

6 Wages and salaries 70% of total, rent, profits.

7 The increased (appreciated) value of goods which have not been sold.

8 The values added by each industry are totalled. Allowances are then made for financial services, public services and residual error, as explained in Unit 14.2 (3).

9 Property income from abroad, needs to be added, so that the accounts show the value produced by British-owned resources.

10 Gross capital formation; capital consumption.

11 It falls (by approximately 5%).

12 Deductions have to be made for direction taxation, national insurance and pension contributions.

13 If national output is maintained, this will produce an improvement in the standard of living. It effectively means higher productivity per man hour. However, if national output falls then living standards may fall (but not inevitably as it depends on the rates of change).

14 Spending habits, prices, income distribution, the composition of output, exchange rates, political factors, the accuracy of information, wealth and social indicators all need consideration.

15 £33 000 (£38 000 assets – £5000 liabilities).

16 The quality of life refers to certain general aspects of life which affect everyone but cannot be accurately measured in their impact, unlike national income. For instance, pollution, excessive crime and immorality may be disliked as they make everyday living less enjoyable but we cannot put a negative value on them.

17 Economic growth is the % real increase in total output.

18 Social costs may increase; waste disposal becomes more difficult; complacent attitudes may develop; the divisions in a society may be widened if the benefits of growth are unequally distributed.

19 Sinclair computers.

20 Between 1972 and 1978 it was calculated that it added 0.5% per annum to GDP growth. Since 1979 the figure is likely to be double.

21 – (b); 22 – (c); 23 – (c); 24 – (a); 25 – (d); 26 – (d); 27 – (d); 28 – (b); 29 – (d); 30 – (a).

Unit 15 Public finance

1 Spending by central government *e.g.* paying a soldier's wages.

2 Higher spending on social security, particularly pensions.

3 Any State benefit *e.g.* unemployment pay.

4 Zero (no).

5 1983–4 – at least £135 billion.

6 **M**anagement of the economy. **A**lteration of income distribution. **R**aise revenue. **S**pecific objectives. (See Unit 15.2)

7 70%

8 economy, equality (see Unit 15.2 (2)).

9 With direct taxes the burden of paying the taxes falls upon the income of those from whom the tax is collected. However, when an indirect tax is collected the collectors may not bear the burden (see Unit 15.3).

10 Regressive (Unit 15.3).

11 proportional

12 The % amount of extra income which is paid in tax *e.g.* income increases from £70 to £80/week and tax paid goes up by £8 means a marginal rate of 80% (⁸⁄₁₀).

13 **F**airness, **A**utomatic stabilizer, **Y**ield, **R**edistribution of income, **E**fficiency.

14 Tax evasion is illegal whereas avoidance is legal. Avoidance is using all the loopholes and exemptions to lower the tax bill. Evasion is not declaring income so that the taxmen do not know that it has been earned.

15 15%

16 **D**isliked by business, **I**nflationary, **R**egressive, **E**vasion (15.4 (2)).

17 Protective duties are customs duties on non-EEC goods imported into Britain whereas excise duties are taxes placed on domestic goods.

18 Petroleum Revenue Tax.

19 The more inelastic the demand curve, the greater the percentage of the tax paid by the consumer (and the less that is paid by the producer).

20 Public Sector Borrowing Requirement (see 15.6).

21 – (a); 22 – (b); 23 – (b); 24 – (b); 25 – (c); 26 – (a); 27 – (b); 28 – (d); 29 – (c); 30 – (d).

Unit 16 Unemployment

1 1976, although some economists would argue that it has always been a significant problem in the twentieth century.

2 In the 1930s the per cent unemployment was higher, more regional and more spread across all occupational groups.

3 **Y**oung people (16–24). **O**lder men (+55). **U**nskilled. **M**arried people. **E**thnic minorities.

4 Less experienced, cheaper, fairer (last in, first out) – (see 16.2).

5 West Indians – see Figure 16.3.

6 Shipbuilding, coal, textiles, agriculture.

7 **DE**terioration in skill of worker, fall in **ST**andard of living for the unemployed, lost **I**ncome

Tax revenue for the government, increased Unemployment payments, reduction in Total
Economic activity, Social costs – Unit 16.3.

 8 £5000 approximately (see Unit 16.3 (4)).
 9 Those people claiming unemployment benefit (Unit 16.4).
 10 Youth Training Scheme, Job Release Scheme.
 11 1.2m (1.35 − 0.15)
 12 Regional (because of industrial localization).
 13 It increased employment opportunities on USA and Japanese evidence by improved living
standards, thus creating new demands (*i.e.* Services Sector).
 14 Voluntary = people unwilling to work at present wages.
Involuntary = people wanting to work but no available jobs.
 15 These policies, by limiting public expenditure and the growth of money supply, deflated the
British economy, contributing to higher unemployment.
 16 The amount of income received out of work compared with the amount obtained in
employment – (Unit 16.6).
In the short run 66%, in the long run 50%.
 17 Lower welfare benefits, more efficient job centres.
 18 Demand deficiency, involuntary, structural, technological.
 19 Arguments for – useful training, work habits developed, reduced social costs, employment
afterwards for some, improved quality of workforce.
Arguments against – replace adults, cheap labour, public cost, artificial jobs, lower wages.
 20 Job Release Scheme – encouraging ageing workers to retire early (see Unit 16.7).
21 – (a); **22** – (a); **23** – (d); **24** – (b); **25** – (a); **26** – (b); **27** – (c); **28** – (e); **29** – (c); **30** – (a).

Unit 17 International trade

 1 foreign currencies
 2 Specialization. Monopolies limited. Increased choice. Links with other countries.
Economies of scale.
 3 A country with an absolute advantage is better than another country at producing one good
but worse at producing another (see Figure 17.2). A country has a comparative advantage if
it is worse than another country at producing two goods but in one case it is not quite so
inefficient (see Figure 17.4).
 4 See Figure 17.2 and 17.3, or 17.4 and 17.5.
 5 Motor cars, electrical machinery.
 6 Milk, beef, apples.
 7 food (or raw materials)
 8 oil
 9 We now import and export much more within Europe (see Figures 17.7 and 17.8).
 10 The Terms of Trade show the average change in the price of exports compared with the
average change in the price of imports (see 17.3).
 11 The increase in production costs and a rise in the exchange rate.
 12 Balance of payments. Revenue raising. Infant industries. Dumping. Employment
protection, Strategic reasons.
 13 Textiles (Multi-Fibre Agreement) and cars (VERA with Japan) are best examples.
 14 Excess domestic production is sold abroad at an artificially low price (it is subsidized by vast
profits made at home – see Figure 17.12).
 15 Rounds of tariff cuts, end of quotas, GATT's.
 16 *ad valorem* = tax a % of price
'specific' = tax so much per item (irrespective of price)
 17 Forms, specific customs centres.
 18 Welfare losses, retaliation, inefficiency.
 19 They both allow free trade between members **but** a customs union insists on a **common**
external tariff; whereas in a free trade area each nation can negotiate its own tariffs with
different non-members.
 20 Free trade within, common external tariff, CAP, free movement of labour and capital (see
17.6).
21 – (b); **22** – (a); **23** – (d); **24** – (b); **25** – (b); **26** – (d); **27** – (a); **28** – (d); **29** – (a); **30** – (d).

Unit 18 Balance of payments

 1 Visible trade is trade in goods whereas invisibles refers to services provided.
 2 World depression, destocking in Britain's recession and the change in the oil trade position
(Unit 18.1).

3 American tourist paying hotel bill in Britain; foreign trade using British vessel; profits made by British company in Europe.

4 A deficit on the current account indicates that a nation is spending more than it is earning.

5 capital outflow (portfolio investment).

6 British entry into EEC; North Sea oil; high interest rates; regional aid policies (Unit 18.1 (2)).

7 Inward investment helps in the **short run** because it strengthens the Capital Account and reduces the balance for official financing. However, in the **long run**, when the profits from the investment are remitted, it becomes a deficit item on the invisible part of the current account.

8 A positive figure on Official Financing shows a net inflow of funds into a country.

9 fundamental disequilibrium.

10 1972

11 It may mask underlying weaknesses; it may cause increases in money supply; it may be caused by inward investment; it may cause the appreciation of the exchange rate (Unit 18.2).

12 Devaluation refers to the lowering of one exchange rate from a higher to a lower **fixed** parity. Depreciation is the floating downward of an exchange rate when there are **no** fixed rates.

13 The Balance of Payments only benefits if the demand for exports is relatively elastic and the demand for imports is relatively elastic also. Other significant factors outlined in Unit 18.3.

14 It is too general and may have unfortunate consequences on the domestic economy *i.e.* lower employment and falling output.

15 They are exempt from VAT. To a lesser extent they get subsidized export credits and cheap promotional help.

16 An exchange rate is 'the external value of a currency expressed in another currency' (or as a weighted average of the currencies of its main trading partners).

17 Market prices reflect demand and supply; rates automatically adjust; internal economic policy is freed from external considerations; fewer reserves needed (see Unit 18.4).

18 This system ended because demand for dollar as a reserve currency fell, because it was overvalued and people expected it to be devalued. The fixed rates became unrealistic in light of trading performances (particularly USA's).

19 It allows nations to borrow; it has developed the oil facility; it is expanding the use of special drawing rights (Unit 18.5).

20 The World Bank. Also individual countries donate aid.

21 – (c); 22 – (d); 23 – (b); 24 – (b); 25 – (a); 26 – (b); 27 – (c); 28 – (c); 29 – (a); 30 – (b).

Unit 19 Government policy

1 the size of the public sector.

2 Lower unemployment, low inflation, Balance of Payments surplus, improved economic growth.

3 A specific objective of government policy *e.g.* 5% unemployment.

4 Reducing unemployment by public spending may increase inflation.

5 As a trading nation, Britain has few tariffs and quotas on imports.

6 An economy which is mainly self-dependent, isolated and hidden behind trade barriers.

7 20%.

8 Often it is well out of date. Also, some statistics are estimates *e.g.* monthly invisibles.

9 Three months.

10 Legislation, Employment, Spending, Trouble-shooting as outlined in Unit 19.3.

11 Monopolies legislation (see Unit 7.4), privatization (see Unit 3.1, 3.2 and 2.4), small firms help (see Unit 5.8).

12 The provision of a National Health Service which is free (but provided from tax revenues) is a redistribution of income from taxpayers to those needing medical services. Free treatment probably makes the workforce fitter and more productive than otherwise (leading to economic growth).

13 Higher taxes to deflate and reduce import spending; less credit available and higher interest rates to curtail spending (again) (see Figure 15.2).

14 Possibly: lower unemployment, higher inflation, worsened balance of payments, greater economic growth (see Figure 19.2).

15 2½ million (1984).

16 An annual subsidy by central government to local authorities. It accounts for over 50% of their total spending.

17 They have found that their rate support grant has been cut.

18 The amount of rate needed per pound (of rateable value), to pay for the Council's services in an area.

19 It is unfair because rates are not related to income; it is regressive, bearing hardest on the lowest-income property owners; it is highest in poor areas (see 19.5).

20 A local sales tax, a local income tax.

21 – (b); 22 – (a); 23 – (c); 24 – (a); 25 – (d).

Unit 20 Consumption and distribution

1 Manufacturer – wholesaler – retailer – consumer.

2 Large retailers can perform storage and bulk-breaking functions, some manufacturers prefer to influence retailers directly whilst other manufacturers have their own retail outlets.

3 Milk Marketing Board.

4 Saving manufacturer time/money; warehousing; marketing; risk bearing (see 20.3).

5 Credit (although a cheque usually allows two days before it is cleared), delivery.

6 Variety of goods, local supplies, advice, after sales service (see 20.4).

7 Superstores, hypermarkets.

8 Department stores.

9 Persuasive advertising tries to persuade the consumer to buy one brand instead of another competing brand. In contrast, generic (or collective) advertising promotes **all** the brands of a particular product rather than one specific brand.

10 It depends which ITV region accepts it. A region such as Anglia serving fewer viewers than Thames might charge as little as £1000 (see 20.5).

11 Saatchi & Saatchi.

12 Advertising Standards Authority.

13 The finding out of detailed information about a good and its competitors.

14 Packaging became much more important as a means of persuasion in selling.

15 Goods must be of merchantable quality, as described, and fit for the purpose sold.

16 Food & Drugs Act 1955.

17 He/she has the right to keep goods if not collected within 6 months or within 1 month if he/she writes (asking for them to be collected).

18 An organization keeping a file on someone's credit worthiness.

19 Trade Associations, such as ABTA, were set up to protect and help the traders (and consumers) in an industry. They publish codes of practice, lay down complaints procedures, and investigate/compensate complaints.

20 Immediate use of goods, more expensive goods can be afforded, repayment can be spread out.

21 – (a); 22 – (b); 23 – (c); 24 – (d); 25 – (c); 26 – (a); 27 – (a); 28 – (d); 29 – (a); 30 – (c).

Part IV Essay questions and answers

Essay questions

Unit 1 (Questions 1–3)

1 Show how the economic concepts of 'scarcity' and 'opportunity cost' are involved in the basic economic problem. Why does the price mechanism fail to solve this problem completely?

(*AEB 1981*)

2 (a) Define and give an example of
(i) opportunity cost (3)   (ii) social cost (3)
(b) Explain how each concept would affect the Government's decision to develop a new coalfield

(9)

(*AEB 1982 Nov.*)

3 The information below refers to the national income of a country in two consecutive years. During that period prices rose by 25%.

National Income £b	Year 1	Year 2
	80	120

(a) Calculate the % increase in money national income (1)
(b) Explain the difference between money income and real income (3)
(c) Calculate % change in national income in real terms (5)

(*AEB 1981 Nov.*)

Unit 2 (Questions 4–7)

4 Describe the economic features of a command economy (USSR) and a market economy (USA).

(*Welsh 1981*)

5 What is a mixed economy? (6)
Account for the growth of the size of the public sector? (9)

(*AEB 1982*)

6 List and explain three advantages of the market economy. Under what circumstances might a government intervene in such an economy? (*AEB 1981 Nov.*)

7 (a) Describe some of the ways in which the Government intervenes in the economy today.

(14)

(b) Does this intervention by the Government mean that there is no free market in United Kingdom?

(6)

(*JMB 1980*)

Unit 3 (Questions 8–11)

8 Indicate the differences between a partnership and a public joint stock company from the point of view of:
(a) objectives; (b) ownership; (c) control; (d) finance.   (*London 1982*)

9 What are the differences between NCB (a public corporation) and ICI Ltd., (public limited company) from the points of view of:
(a) ownership; (b) finance; (c) control; (d) objectives.   (*London 1983 Jan.*)

10 Describe the main forms of business organization to be found in the private enterprise sector of the economy of UK.   (*Welsh 1980*)

11 What are the main similarities and differences between a public joint stock company and a nationalized industry.

(20)

(*Oxford 1981*)

Unit 4 (Questions 12–15)

12 (a) By means of a diagram explain how an equilibrium price is determined by the forces of supply and demand.

(b) A situation where there is a shortage of tickets for the FA Cup Final at Wembley represents a position of disequilibrium. How would this disequilibrium be removed by the free operation of the forces of supply and demand? (*CSE Mode 3 1982*)

13 Study the following supply and demand schedule for a commodity in a free market.

Price (p/lb)	Quantity Demanded	Quantity Supplied
	Million lbs	
70	80	230
60	100	210
50	120	180
40	150	150
30	200	120
20	300	80
10	500	40

(a) Calculate:
  (i) the equilibrium market price. (1)
  (ii) the elasticity of demand when price rises from 30p to 40p. (3)
  (iii) the elasticity of supply when price falls from 60p to 50p. (3)
  (iv) the new equilibrium price if a tax of 20p per pound (lb) is placed on the commodity. (3)
(b) Describe the main factors influencing the price of cocoa. (10)
(*CSE Mode 3 1982*)

14 (a) What is the meaning of:
(i) elasticity of supply (3); **(ii)** elasticity of demand (3).
(b) What factors influence the elasticity of:
(i) supply (7); **(ii)** demand (7). (*Oxford 1982*)

15 (a) Distinguish between an extension of demand and an increase in demand.
(b) Indicate the possible effects of:
  (i) an increase in consumer's income on the demand for private transport.
  (ii) an increase in the price of iron ore on the demand for steel. (*CSE Mode 3 1983*)

Unit 5 (Questions 16–20)

16 (a) What is meant by 'Economies of Scale'? Illustrate your answer with examples.
(b) How are small firms able to survive? (*London 1983*)

17 (a) Why do firms integrate vertically?
(b) What advantages can be gained by a firm from the growth in size of the industry? (*AEB 1981*)

18 What are the main costs involved in the production of a motor car? Show how costs can change in **(a)** short run **(b)** long run? (6, 7, 7) (*Oxford 1980*)

19 With regard to small businesses,
(a) discuss obstacles to their establishment and growth. (10)
(b) explain why it is thought to be so important for the Government to assist them. (6)
(c) describe two measures by which the Government assists them. (4) (*JMB 1982*)

20 What is specialization? Explain and comment on the suggestion that specialization is limited by the extent of the market. (*Cambridge 1983*)

Unit 6 (Questions 21–24)

21 Explain how each of the following may influence the location of a manufacturing industry:
(a) availability of raw materials   **(c)** government policy
(b) nearness to a market
Illustrate your answer by reference to specific examples. (*London 1983 Jan.*)
22 (a) Why is the level of unemployment higher in some areas of Britain than in others? (6)
(b) How does the Government assist these areas? (9) (*AEB 1982*)

23 What factors influence the location of manufacturing industry? (*Welsh 1980*)
24 (a) Describe the factors influencing the location of any one major UK industry. (10)
(b) Describe briefly the recent history of your chosen industry. (10) (*Oxford 1981*)

Unit 7 (Questions 25–26)

25 What is a monopoly? How might a firm obtain monopoly power? (5, 15) (*Oxford 1982*)

26 Why might the Government be concerned to prevent the growth of a monopoly in an industry? *(CSE Mode 3 1983)*

Unit 8 (Questions 27–30)

27 Explain the meaning of the statement 'money is a medium of exchange, a standard for deferred payments, a measure and a store of value'. *(Cambridge 1983)*
28 **(a)** Describe the functions of money.
   (b) What are the main causes of a fall in the value of money? *(AEB 1982)*
29 **(a)** What are the functions of money? (12)
   (b) Why would each of the following be inadequate as a basis for our monetary system: **(i)** cigarettes (2); **(ii)** gold (2); **(iii)** coal (2); **(iv)** cattle (2)? *(Oxford 1982)*
30 **(a)** What are the main forms of money in the UK today? (5)
   (b) Explain how the commercial banks can create money. (15)
   (Oxford 1981)

Unit 9 (Questions 31–34)

31 **(a)** Define inflation. (4)
   (b) Why is it thought to be so important to control the rate of inflation? Relate your answer to the experience of UK in recent years. (16)
   (JMB 1982)
32 **(a)** What are the major difficulties associated with the construction of RPI?
   (b) What purposes do index numbers serve? *(AEB 1979)*
33 **(a)** Define **(i)** wage rate; **(ii)** money wages; **(iii)** real wages. (2, 2, 2)
   (b) How is each affected by inflation? (9)
   (AEB 1982)
34 **(a)** What are the causes of **(i)** cost push inflation (5); **(ii)** demand pull inflation (5).
   (b) How has the Government tried to control inflation in recent years? (10)
   (Oxford 1982)

Unit 10 (Questions 35–38)

35 How does a joint stock bank seek to satisfy the interests of **(a)** its depositors **(b)** its shareholders **(c)** the central bank? *(London 1983)*
36 Figure 10.2.
   (a) List three reserve assets shown in the Balance Sheet. (3)
   (b) Calculate the reserve assets ratio. (3)
   (c) If the reserve assets ratio changed to 20% and banks keep the same quantity of reserve assets, what would be the maximum amount of deposits that the banking system could maintain? (4)
   (AEB 1981)
37 Examine the main functions of a commercial bank. *(JMB 1982)*
38 Show how a banker, through arranging his assets, makes a compromise between the conflicting aims of profitability, security and liquidity. *(Oxford 1982)*

Unit 11 (Questions 39–42)

39 **(a)** What does the economist mean by 'saving' and 'investment'? (6)
   (b) Under what circumstances should the Government encourage saving? (9)
   (AEB 1982)
40 **(a)** Distinguish between the type of securities which are available on the Stock Exchange.
   (b) How does the Stock Exchange operate as a market? *(London 1982)*
41 **(a)** What are the differences between a Stockbroker and a Stock jobber?
   (b) Outline the main functions of the London Stock Exchange. *(Welsh 1981)*
42 You have been left £6000 by an Aunt, on condition that you save it for at least five years before beginning to spend it.
   (a) Give three forms in which you could save the money? (6)
   (b) For each of the three ways, give their respective merits and weaknesses. (30)
   (c) Explain why saving the money instead of spending it straight away might be disadvantageous. (14)
   (London 1983 (Econ. Principles))

Unit 12 (Questions 43–47)

43 How has the population changed in the last fifty years in its – **(a)** age distribution **(b)** geographical distribution and **(c)** size?

Indicate the economic consequences of the changes in age distribution and in size.
(*CSE Mode 3 1983*)

44 (a) What is the 'working population'? (3)
(b) Describe the factors that would lead to an increase in the supply of labour. (12)
(*AEB 1982*)

45 (a) Define 'birth rate'.
(b) Explore the possible economic effects of a fall in the population caused by a long-term reduction in birth rate. (*London 1983*)
46 (a) Distinguish between geographical mobility of labour and the geographical distribution of population.
(b) Outline the factors which influence the geographical mobility of labour.
(*London 1982*)

47 Describe the geographical distribution of the population in United Kingdom. Account for the variations in the density of population. (20)
(*Oxford 1982*)

Unit 13 (Questions 48–52)

48 Why do wages vary between occupations? (*Cambridge 1981*)
49 (a) Why have agricultural workers always tended to be among the lowest-paid workers in the United Kingdom? (12)
(b) What are the arguments for and against a national minimum wage? (8)
(*JMB 1980*)

50 Explain each of the following trade union terms:
(a) closed shop **(b)** collective bargaining **(c)** picketing **(d)** arbitration. (*Welsh 1982*)
51 When you begin work you may join a trade union.
(a) In what ways might you expect it to help you? (20)
(b) How could you influence its decisions? (15)
(c) Are there any disadvantages in joining? Explain your views. (15)
(*London 1983 (Econ. Principles)*)

52 Define three types of industrial action undertaken by trade unions. Examine the arguments used by trade unions in support of wage claims made on behalf of their members.
(*AEB 1981*)

Unit 14 (Questions 53–56)

53 Distinguish between consumption and investment. Explain how an increase in the production of investment goods might affect–
(a) current living standards **(b)** future living standards. (*AEB 1980*)
54 (a) Give four reasons why it is worth while to calculate the National Income. (8)
(b) Explain the difference between Gross Domestic Product at market prices and Net National Product at factor cost. (4)
(c) What factors could lead to an increase in real national income? (8)
(*JMB 1980*)

55 What do you understand by the 'Standard of living'? How do you account for the difference between the Standard of living in India and United Kingdom? (4, 16)
(*Oxford 1982*)

56 Define **(a)** National income **(b)** National debt
Explain why national income figures may give a false impression of a country's living standards. (*AEB 1981*)

Unit 15 (Questions 57–60)

57 Explain what is meant by:
(a) a progressive tax and **(b)** a regressive tax. Give an example of each. Why do governments use both types of taxes? (*Cambridge 1981*)
58 Discuss how the taxation system of the United Kingdom may affect:
(a) an income earner **(b)** a consumer and **(c)** a producer. (20)
(*JMB 1980*)

59 Explain what is meant by the Budget in the United Kingdom. Discuss the objectives of the Budget. (*Welsh 1982*)
60 (a) What is meant by 'the incidence of taxation'?
(b) How is the incidence of income tax likely to differ from that of value added tax?
(*London Jan. 1983*)

Unit 16 (Questions 61–65)

61 **(a)** Define and give an example of:
  (i) technological unemployment   (3)
  (ii) seasonal unemployment   (3)
  (b) Explain how the Government can use fiscal policy to reduce the general level of unemployment.   (9)
                                                                        (*CSE Mode 3 1983*)

62 Explain the meaning of each of the following types of unemployment:
  (a) cyclical; **(b)** structural **(c)** regional.   (*London Jan. 1983*)

63 Indicate briefly the main causes of unemployment. How, if at all, would unemployment be affected if the Government **(a)** raised the school leaving age to 17, and **(b)** encouraged emigration?   (10, 5, 5)
                                                                            (*Oxford 1980*)

64 Examine the present day unemployment situation in the United Kingdom, making reference to variations in its level between different industries and different regions.   (*Welsh 1982*)

65 **(a)** Identify the main types of unemployment.
  (b) Discuss policies which a government may adopt to reduce unemployment.
                                                                           (*AEB Nov. 1981*)

Unit 17 (Questions 66–69)

66 **(a)** Why do governments place restrictions on international trade?
  (b) Outline the methods by which governments may regulate international trade.
                                                                            (*London 1982*)

67 **(a)** What are a country's 'terms of trade'?   (3)
  (b) How are they calculated?   (3)
  (c) What will be the effects of an unfavourable movement in the terms of trade?   (9)
                                                                           (*AEB Nov. 1982*)

68 Why do countries trade with one another?   (*Welsh 1980*)

69 Describe the activities of each of the following: **(a)** GATT **(b)** IMF **(c)** EEC.
                                                                        (*CSE Mode 3 1983*)

Unit 18 (Questions 70–74)

70 **(a)** How is it possible to have a Balance of Payments surplus and a Balance of Trade deficit at the same time?
  (b) Why might countries seek to have a surplus on the current account of the Balance of Payments?   (*London Jan. 1983*)

71 What are the likely effects on Britain's Balance of Payments of the following:
  (a) an increase in the number of cars imported from Europe.
  (b) the building in Scotland of a large German-owned factory.
  (c) the sinking of several supertankers in a hurricane.
  (d) a sharp deterioration in the value of sterling.   (4 × 5)
                                                                            (*Oxford 1981*)

72 'Whereas the Balance of Payments must balance, the Balance of Trade need not.' Explain and comment on this statement.   (*Welsh 1982*)

73 Read the tables below and then answer the following questions.

United Kingdom Tourist Expenditure £ billion at 1979 prices:

	1972	1974	1976	1978	1980
Expenditure by United Kingdom residents abroad	1.6	1.5	1.2	1.6	2.4
Expenditure by foreigners in the United Kingdom	1.6	1.9	2.7	3.0	2.6
Expenditure by United Kingdom residents in the United Kingdom	3.9	3.8	3.7	3.7	3.8

	1972	1974	1976	1978	1980
Average exchange rate of £ sterling	$2.40	$2.35	$2.00	$1.95	$2.30

(Source: *Lloyds Bank Economic Bulletin*)

Answer *all* the questions. Marks for each question are shown in brackets.
  (a) Clearly showing your workings, calculate the net earnings of tourism on the invisible account in 1976.   (2)

(b) Name the year and the amount when the total receipts of the United Kingdom tourist industry were greatest. (2)

(c) Describe the relationship between the exchange rate of sterling and the pattern of tourist expenditure. (4)

(d) What factors would promote an increase in foreign travel by United Kingdom residents? (3)

(e) How will improvements in the United Kingdom transport system be beneficial to tourist areas and to the economy as a whole? (4)

(AEB June 1982)

74 Study the following table of the Balance of Payments for a certain country in a recent year.

	£m
Exports	20 121
Imports	26 157
Government services (net)	−1684
Private transfers (net)	+2677
Interest, profits and dividends (net)	+1418
Shipping (net)	+ 12
Investment and other capital flows (net)	−2886
Balancing item	+ 410

(a) On the basis of the above information only calculate:
 (i) the visible trade balance (1)
 (ii) the invisible trade balance (2)
 (iii) the balance of payments on current account (2)
 (iv) the balance for official financing (3)
(b) Comment on the state of this particular country's balance of payments and suggest what policies the government might have adopted to deal with it. (12)

(Oxford 1982)

Unit 19 (Questions 75–76)

75 In what ways do local authorities obtain their revenue?
Can you suggest any alternative sources of revenue which might be made available to local authorities?
What are their main items of expenditure? (10, 5, 5)

(Oxford 1980)

76 What are their main methods of obtaining revenue adopted by
 (i) the central government, and
 (ii) local authorities (14, 6)

(Oxford 1981)

Unit 20 (Questions 77–80)

77 (a) What are the major changes which have occurred in the retail trade over the last 20 years?
 (b) Outline the advantages and disadvantages of these changes for consumers.

(London Jan. 1983)

78 Compare the functions of a wholesaler with those of a retailer. Is the specialized role of the wholesaler disappearing? *(Cambridge Nov. 1982)*

79 In each of the following cases, name the Act which was designed to protect the consumer and has been broken. State – how the Act was broken, what the consumer's rights are and what you would do:
 (a) You buy a brand new pair of shoes. After two weeks the soles come loose. You take them back to the shop and complain. The manager offers you a credit note. (4)
 (b) You are in a restaurant and enjoying your meal until you discover a small dead mouse on the spoon. You point this out to the owner who apologises. (4)
 (c) You receive an expensive book through the post, although you did not order it. Two weeks later you get a letter asking for payment. (4)

(CSE Mode 3 1983)

80 (a) Define the term 'credit' and give one example of a credit card. (3)
 (b) Explain two advantages and two disadvantages to a customer of using credit cards. (4)
 (c) Describe two differences between a bank loan and a bank overdraft. (2)
 (d) Explain the differences between APR (annual percentage rate) and flat rate interest.

(CSE Commerce 1984)

Essay answers

Unit 1 Answers

1 The basic economic problem is obtaining the most efficient allocation of resources. This allocation will be in order to meet the consumption needs and wants of the community. These demands are infinite whereas the supply of resources is limited. For instance, there is not sufficient usable agricultural land in Britain to meet the food needs of the people. Thus land is **scarce**. However, not all of the available land for food production is used for that purpose. Much of it is used for manufacturing because land may have several profitable uses.

When a choice is made between alternative uses, then the uses not adopted are the opportunity costs involved. Thus one opportunity cost of using a 5-acre field for agricultural production might be a golf course which cannot now be developed.

The allocation of resources can be done in two ways – by government decision or by price. The way used depends on the economic system which has been developed. In all countries today, there is a market sector and a State-controlled sector. In the market sector, those with wealth allocate resources towards profitable production *e.g.* food production. They charge prices to maximize their profits, in theory.

However, not all goods and services can be supplied in this way, because:
(a) Uncivilized inequalities of income and wealth might result.
(b) The consumer would not pay for services which give no tangible benefit *e.g.* defence.
(c) Producers would not provide services which allow free riders (people receiving without paying).
(d) Producers would not make goods/services which do not yield an income.
(e) Non-economic values, such as justice, often need consideration.

The allocation of resources via the price mechanism means that owners of resources are influenced by the demands of producers. The saying 'every man has his price' is relevant here because it implies that the owner of a resource will be prepared to give it up, if a high enough price is bid for it. The producers, in turn, are influenced by the market prices of goods/services when they decide what to produce. The prices determine which goods consumers will buy and who will be able to buy.

2 (a) (i) Opportunity cost refers to the alternatives foregone when an economic decision is made. For instance, a local council can spend £3m on a new hospital, a new school or a leisure centre. If the hospital is built its opportunity cost is all the other things that could be built for £3m.

(ii) Social cost is the cost to society of an individual's economic actions. For example noisy low-flying aircraft may disturb a person's sleep and affect a cow's milk production. If the person who causes it pays the cost then it is a private cost. However, if others suffer and the instigator does not pay, society bears the cost.

(b) The development of a new coalfield requires a large capital outlay. If the funds for NCB come from government spending, then the opportunity cost is what else could have been done with the money used *i.e.* new schools, roads, hospitals, weapons, etc.

The social costs of the enterprise may be widespread. If the land used was formerly peaceful, then any extra noise, and lower property values for the local residents, are social costs. If the land provided recreational activities, then their replacement by an industrial complex would be a costly loss of amenity. The existence of a new factory usually produces extra traffic and more pollution, both of which affect the local people. Because of these costs the local people might object to a coal mine development, although there are many possible benefits such as increased trade and increased employment.

3 (a) $\dfrac{40}{80} = \dfrac{\text{(increase National Income)}}{\text{(original National Income)}}$ 50% increase

(b) Money income refers to the current value of income. It takes no account of inflation.

Real income, on the other hand, indicates the value of the income in real terms; it allows for price changes. Thus if money income rises 10% and prices increase by 20%, the recipient of the income is worse off in real terms (by about 10%). This means that his income will not buy as many goods and services now, as it did before.

(c) National income has increased in money by 50%. As prices have risen by only 25%, national income has increased in real terms by 25%. However, this assumes that other things such as working hours and conditions have not changed. Adverse movements in them could offset the real increase in National Income.

Unit 2 Answers

4 The brackets in the question are to indicate that the question refers to practical reality, rather than theory. The essential features of a command economy are government control; State planning; little individual economic freedom; no unemployment; wide provision of basic services; price fixing; lack of competition. (See Unit 2.3.)

In contrast the market economy is characterized by the price mechanism; large extremes of wealth and poverty; maximum economic freedom; possible under-utilization of resources, little state influence in society, flexible prices, plenty of choice. (See Unit 2.2.)

5 A mixed economy is an economic system featuring a significant proportion of public and private sector production. The public sector is provided by the government whilst the private sector is composed of individuals and firms. The former aims mainly to provide services whilst the latter is profit-orientated. (See Unit 2.4.)

The growth of the public sector in UK is such that 60% of national income is now under direct government influence. A large and expanding public sector usually indicates a highly-developed nation with high living standards. The State sector is responsible for providing merit goods, public goods, certain uneconomic goods/services and transfer payments. In Britain, Labour and Conservative governments agree over the need for the first two but disagree over the last two. So the rate of public sector growth in United Kingdom varies with the political party in power.

The general reasons for the growth of the public sector are the increased realization that basic standards in some areas have to be set by the State: the provision of basic living conditions for unfortunate people in society; State control of monopolies; longer living population needing Welfare State services; increased complexity of modern society which needs government regulation and supervision.

6 (1) Efficiency **(2)** Economic freedom **(3)** Innovation

(1) The allocation of scarce factors using the price mechanism ensures the most efficient use of resources. This arises because resources are moved to produce goods/services upon which an entrepreneur can make a profit; and they are moved away from unprofitable markets.

(2) The individual's economic freedom is maximized because there is no government interference in the economy. There are no restrictions on consumption and no taxation, thus allowing consumers to spend all their income as they wish.

(3) Innovation is more likely in a market economy because each producer is trying to outdo his competitors. Thus new ideas are continually sought, as it is a question of the 'survival of the fittest'.

Government intervention in a market economy will be to minimize the disadvantages which are likely to arise. The main disadvantages are outlined in Unit 2.2. They are–over concentration on luxury goods, neglect of basic needs, extremes of wealth and poverty, wasteful competition and unfair trading.

7 (a) Government intervention in Britain's mixed economy today is substantial. The State attempts to control and regulate the economy in a variety of ways: nationalization (see Unit 3), fiscal policy (see Unit 15), monetary policy (see Unit 10), wage policies (see Unit 13), trade policies (see Unit 17), industrial location (see Unit 6).

The government is responsible for the activities of nationalized industries and certain nationalized firms (*e.g.* British Leyland). By its imposition of financial limits on their borrowing powers, it can influence the general policy of each industry. Such controls would be set down in the Budget which has many other effects. Changes in taxes and their rates can influence the level of consumption and investment and thus general economic activity. For instance, lowering VAT cuts prices and encourages consumption.

The government's influence in other areas tends to be less direct. Monetary policy is administered via the Bank of England who influence commercial banks. For example, the increased amount of special deposits curtails the clearing banks' liquid assets and thus limits credit creation in theory. In practice, though, banks have avoided this, indicating the need to act indirectly. Trade can also be influenced by government policies *e.g.* interest-rate falls can lower the value of the £ and thereby make imports more expensive. Also, protective tariffs could be introduced to reduce the quantity of imports.

Domestically, the government can also affect wages and industrial location. Incomes policies and reduced public expenditure tend to depress wages. Regional incentives may be used to encourage industrial development in areas of high unemployment and urban decay. Both types of policy can have specific effects, although they are often indiscriminate.

(b) Government intervention distorts the market mechanism and thus the free market does not operate. For instance, grants to development areas make some sites marginally more attractive than otherwise. Thus a firm may develop and utilize resources in a place which it would not naturally have chosen. The subsidy which has lowered a firm's costs means that most economic location has not been selected. Political and social factors have been allowed to impurify economic forces.

Unit 3 Answers

8 (a) The objectives of a partnership and a public joint stock company are broadly the same – to make a profit. However, in the short term a large public company may be prepared to make a loss in order to secure its market. Furthermore, the directors may occasionally pursue other motives such as maximizing sales.
(b) Partnerships are owned by between two and twenty people, except in the case of solicitors and accountants. Between them they provide the capital and share the profits. As they have unlimited liability, the owners may be responsible for all debts, even if it means selling their own assets. In contrast, public limited companies often have millions of owners, or shareholders. There are Ordinary shareholders who have more influence, but get less reward, than Preference shareholders.
(c) Partners control the business directly between them. Their influence will be determined by the Deed of Covenant. Decisions usually require unanimity.
A Board of Directors controls a PLC. They are elected in theory by shareholders at the Annual General Meeting and usually have shares in the company. They decide on general policy and may be called to explain their decisions at the AGM.
(d) Partnerships raise capital from amongst their partners, and they secure bank loans. Their sources of finance are essentially limited, being of small amounts. On the other hand, PLCs have access to more capital through the Stock Market, specialist suppliers such as Finance for Industry and government agencies. They usually receive privileged treatment at the banks.
9 (a) NCB is owned by the nation as a whole (56m people) whereas ICI is owned by its shareholders – all half million of them.
(b) NCB raises finance by selling its products and borrowing from the Treasury. Each year the Government sets external financing limits in order to prevent excessive borrowing. ICI does not obtain central government finance unless it sets up in a development area or maintains employment when it might otherwise make redundancies. The main sources of funds are outlined in Unit 3.7.
(c) NCB is controlled by a Board, accountable to a Government Minister who in turn is responsible to Parliament. This is detailed in Unit 3.2. In contrast, ICI is run by a Board of Directors which delegates daily decision-making to factory managers. The Board is elected at the AGM. However, in practice the institutional investors influence who is chosen.
(d) ICI's main aim is to maximize profits or minimize losses. However, this aim may be relegated to second place by the Government. It may wish to cut public spending (Cons. 1982), keep open uneconomic pits (Cons. 1981), or enforce prices and incomes policies (1967–70, 1976–78 Labour Govt.). In doing so, the government may over-ride the aims of the NCB.
10 The main forms of organization in the private sector are sole traders, partnerships, companies and co-operatives. They are outlined in Units 3.5, 3.4, 3.3 and 3.6 respectively.
11 The similarities between companies and nationalized industries are:
(a) Operation in market place selling goods/services
(b) Large scale enterprises
(c) Control by a Board
(d) Both strive for efficiency (and at least minimizing losses).
The main differences are outlined in **Answer 9 – (a)**, **(b)**, **(c)**, **(d)**, above.

Unit 4 Answers

12 (a) The three concepts – Equilibrium price (see Unit 4.4), Supply (see Unit 4.3), Demand (see Unit 4.2) should be accurately defined. Figure 4.7, showing equilibrium price and quantity, needs drawing as you are specifically asked to use diagrams in the question. The equilibrium is achieved, as explained in Unit 4.
(b) It is assumed that all Cup Final tickets are the same price, although in practice ticket prices vary with the position of the seats in the stadium. In the case of Cup Final tickets it is reasonable to regard Supply as fixed *i.e.* supply is perfectly inelastic. Similarly, it is likely that demand will be highly, though not perfectly, inelastic. This can be represented by the following diagram. There is an excess demand ($Q_D - Q_S$) at the market price which has been fixed. Q_D quantity want tickets but only Q_S are available, creating a shortage. If a free market was allowed to

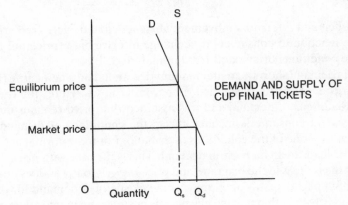

DEMAND AND SUPPLY OF
CUP FINAL TICKETS

operate price would rise to eliminate the excess demand (as explained in Unit 4.4). As demand is inelastic, price will have to rise considerably, as shown in practice by black market prices. As the Football Association wishes to maintain prices at face value, the excess demand continues to exist and some supporters go without tickets.

13 (a) (i) 40p per lb.

(ii) $Ed = \dfrac{\% \text{ change in Quantity demanded}}{\% \text{ change in price}} = \dfrac{-\frac{1}{4}}{+\frac{1}{3}} = -0.75$

(iii) $Es = \dfrac{\% \text{ change in Quantity supplied}}{\% \text{ change in price}} = \dfrac{-\frac{1}{7}}{-\frac{1}{6}} = +0.87$

(iv) the imposition of a tax means that the supply schedule will change. Firms will need to obtain an additional 20p per lb to continue to supply at each level of output. Thus:

Price	Qu. supplied	Qu. supplied after tax	Qu. demanded
70	230	180	80
60	210	150	100
50	180	120	120
40	150	80	150
30	120	40	200
20	80	—	
10	40	—	

The new equilibrium price will be 50p per pound.

(b) Changes in the conditions of demand and changes in the conditions of supply will influence the price of cocoa. Unit 4.2 lists the **Conditions of Demand** which are remembered by **'CIST'**. 4.3(2) lists the conditions of supply which are remembered by **'COPING'**. These factors should be related to cocoa, as follows, for demand:

In the case of cocoa, if complementary goods, like milk and sugar, increase in price, the demand for cocoa may well fall. Income is a major influence on the demand for many products; however, it seems unlikely that there will be a significant change in the demand for cocoa following a change in income because it is only a small proportion of income which is spent on it.

The price of substitute goods such as Horlicks or even tea or coffee may have a considerable impact. A rise in the price of these substitutes may cause an increase in demand for cocoa. Similarly, a positive movement in taste may cause an increase in demand. This could be provoked by favourable medical reports or effective advertising.

14 (a) Unit 4.5 – the responsiveness of supply (or demand) to a given change in price. Measurement formula.

(b) (i) Unit 4.5(4) Time and Factors of Production

   (ii) Unit 4.5(2) **'THIS'** – Time, Habit, Income and **Substitutes**.

15 (a) This important distinction is best illustrated with a diagram.

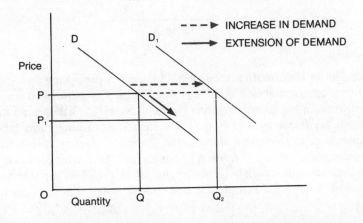

An extension of demand refers to a movement **along** a demand curve (red arrow on diagram) and it shows the reaction of consumers to a change in **price** only (price fall from P to P_1). It assumes that the conditions of demand remain unaltered.

An increase in demand shows a greater amount demanded on a **new curve** (D_1) at each price level. Thus at price P, quantity demanded rises from Q to Q_2. Here, the consumers react to changes in the **conditions** of demand and it is assumed that price remains unaltered (at P).

(b) (i) An increase in consumer's income affects the **conditions of demand**, not the price. Changes in income are one of the conditions of demand. For most normal and luxury goods an increase in income leads to an **increase in demand**. This is the case with private transport. Thus demand shifts to the right as in the diagram, and price rises (P to P_1) as does quantity (Q to Q_1).

The degree of impact depends upon the income elasticity of demand for private transport. Empirical evidence suggests that income elasticity is positive and greater than one. Thus a small increase in income will produce a greater surge in demand. The demand for private transport is thus income elastic.

We assume that the **supply curve** is unchanged. However, its shape (Elasticity) will determine the effect of changes in the conditions of demand on price. The more elastic the supply curve is, the lower will be the price increase when demand increases. As there are many imports, the supply curve for private transport in Britain is probably fairly elastic as shown in the diagram below.

PRIVATE MOTORING

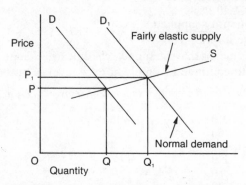

(ii) The increase in the price of iron ore will affect the **conditions of supply**. It will raise the costs of production per unit of steel made, because iron ore is a necessary raw material for steel production. The impact of these higher costs of production will be to shift the supply of steel to the left. **Each supplier** will **produce less** at **existing prices**. The extent of this shift will depend on what % of total cost is accounted for by iron ore. If the % is small then the shift in supply may be slight. Again, it is assumed that the price and other factors influencing supply do not change.

The effect on the price of steel will also depend on the elasticity of demand for steel. If the demand for steel is elastic (which is likely, given the number of substitutes available for it today) then the price increase, resulting from a fall in supply, will be small. Thus in the diagram below price increases slightly from P to P_1 whilst demand falls substantially from Q to Q_1.

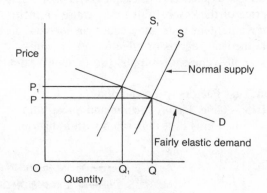

Unit 5 Answers

16 (a) Economies of scale are the advantages obtained by producing on a large scale. They can be either internal or external (see Unit 5.6). For instance, one financial economy is easier and cheaper borrowing for big companies than for small ones. The other main internal advantages are managerial, technical and trading. The external advantages are labour, information, concentration and education. You should give examples of each as in Unit 5.6.

(b) Firstly, you need to give a definition of 'small firm' (see Unit 5.8). Their survival can be explained by **their strengths**, such as flexibility, industrial relations and transport costs. Also, the disadvantages of large-scale production can enable small firms to operate. Standardized products, impersonal attitudes and market size all give openings which small firms can occupy and exploit. The information and examples are in Unit 5.6.

17 (a) Vertical integration refers to the **joining** of firms at different stages of production. It may be **forward** or **backward** as illustrated in Figure 5.10 and explained in Unit 5.7. The main reasons usually given are – to increase efficiency, safeguard sources of supply and/or outlets, increase barriers to entry, improve research, gain better access to markets and make fuller use of by-products.

(b) The advantages to a firm when an industry grows are firstly a **larger** market and secondly certain **external economies of scale**. The bigger market will mean more production, assuming the firm has the capacity and also retains (or increases) its market share. This should lead to **internal** economies of scale (as outlined in Unit 5.6). Similarly, a growing industry may benefit from external economies, particularly concentration, education and training. Examples from expanding new industries such as video entertainment would be useful.

18 The main costs involved in the production of cars can be subdivided between **fixed** and **variable** costs. Fixed costs refer to those which do not change with the level of production. Variable costs alter with changes in production. For example, a **robot** would be classified as a fixed cost because it is capital equipment and is available, whatever the level of production. On the other hand, **paint** would be described as a variable cost, as the amount bought and used depends on the number of cars produced.

(a) In the short run, in Economics, it is assumed that at least **one factor** of production is **fixed**. In practice, this is usually land. The result of this assumption is that the average cost of production falls up to a point, called the **optimum** output. Beyond that point, **diminishing** returns set in and so average cost rises – see Figure 5.4. In the car industry, labour and capital are probably the most variable factors in the short run, as labour can be laid off and made redundant and borrowing can be reduced if sales fall.

(b) In the long run, it is assumed that **all costs** of production are variable. This means that the quantity of each factor of production, which can be used, is able to be changed to suit the needs of the market. This allows the average cost of production to **fall**, **rise** or remain **constant**. Clearly in efficient firms average cost is likely to fall in the long run.

19 (a) The establishment of small firms in Britain is handicapped by a lack of capital, a lack of knowledge, and personal preferences. The **lack of capital** is explained in Units 5.8 and 3.7. The **shortage** of **knowledge** about market opportunities is inevitable in a large modern society, whilst government help has only recently taken off. The causes are probably the tradition of employment, the educational system, lack of State funding and the relative indifference of the banks. The importance of **personal preference** applies rather more to growth than to the starting up of a small firm; but it covers aspects such as excessive administration and tax disincentives which are outlined in Unit 5.8(2). Fewer new firms start each year in Britain than in USA and West Germany.

(b) The reasons for government assistance to small firms are because of the value they see in the small firm sector of the economy, *i.e.* innovation, competition, employment, efficiency, and the seedbed function. These are explained in Unit 5.8(5).

(c) The Business Start up Scheme ⎱
Loan Guarantee Scheme ⎰ Unit 5.8(4).

20 Specialization is the performance of a certain individual task which makes one dependent on another. This may refer to an individual, a factory, a firm, an industry, a town, a region or a country. Specialization involves the **division of labour** – the advantages and disadvantages are outlined in Unit 5.4.

The extent of the market determines the capacity for specialization. A very small market may require just enough production for one man *e.g.* Prime Minister's speech writer! Conversely, a large market will be too much for one man and so several may concentrate on different aspects. For instance, newspaper journalists specialize in sport, features, fashion, news, etc. Generally, the larger the market, the greater the scope for the division of labour. An international market such as motor cars has more potential for specialization than Royal Crown making!

However, as no one in modern society is totally self sufficient, everyone specializes to some extent. Some markets may facilitate greater specialization than others which could be limited by factors such as the available raw materials, demand, transport costs and perishability. These are explained with examples in 5.8(3).

Unit 6 Answers

21 (a) The importance of available raw materials varies between different types of manufacturing industry. Those industries that **lose weight** in production tend to be located near their raw materials *e.g.* coal mining. This is so that they do not have to bear the cost of transporting some raw materials, which will be waste. Thus, the new coalfield at Selby is located above the seams!

When raw materials are **bulky**, the tendency is also to locate near the source of supply *e.g.* car maker within easy reach of components. If the raw materials are **imported** then a port would be a good location *e.g.* furniture maker using imported wood. If the raw materials are **perishable** then the industry is likely to be situated nearby *e.g.* cheese and milk products.

Conversely, if the raw materials are light and easy to transport *e.g.* television parts and the final products gain weight in production *e.g.* beer brewing, then the raw materials do not pull the industry to their location.

(b) The market is becoming increasingly influential in making location decisions. Modern **consumer durables** *e.g.* video recorders are manufactured near their market. The raw materials are collected and assembled close to large centres of population. Where the final product is particularly **bulky** or **fragile** and may cause problems in transport *e.g.* glass, or lemonade, then it is made near large towns. For instance, caravans are manufactured near the seaside.

(c) There has been little new manufacturing in Britain, as the industrial base has declined and **services** have expanded. Governments have tried to push new firms to development areas *e.g.* British Aluminium smelter at Lynemouth (Figure 6.1); ICL to Wales; BL cars to Linwood.

The government influences location in several ways. It may decide where it is the **employer** (*e.g.* Driver & Vehicle Licensing Centre, Swansea – a government department) and strongly persuade where it is the **provider** of funds (ICL – £50m subsidy dependent on Welsh Location, 1981). When dealing with the private sector, the government gives incentives and imposes deterrents. These are outlined in Unit 6.4 (2) and (3). The current levels of grants are shown in Figure 6.4.

22 (a) The areas of highest unemployment are N. Ireland, North Wales, Scotland, N. West and W. Midlands. They are shown in Figure 6.2. The general **causes** are fourfold.

(i) Lack of employment with insufficient new jobs to replace disappearing old ones. Firms are not attracted to these regions, as they have few advantages.

(ii) Relatively immobile population in these regions, often for cultural reasons.

(iii) The declining industries (coal, ships, etc.) are located there and are shedding labour. Often the employees have spent a lifetime in one industry and are not occupationally mobile. Many are too old for retraining. For instance, 75% of miners made redundant in the 1970s were aged over fifty.

(iv) The distance of the region from the main markets was/is a handicap. The pull of the market which attracts modern footloose firms to the main centres of population makes these regions relatively unattractive. London with its range of expert commercial services which are increasingly necessary in international trade has accentuated this pull. Britain's entry into the EEC has made the Midlands and South East more attractive to firms exporting to Europe because they have better access through the motorway network and SE ports.

(b) Government assistance is outlined in 6.4 and Figure 6.4.

23 The factors influencing the location of manufacturing industry vary in importance between **industries**. Certain factors have declined over the years whilst others have become more significant. For instance power and raw materials have become less of an attraction to engineering with the development of the National Grid and a nationwide transport network. As heavy industry has declined, so **light** industry has grown. It is **less dependent** on a **specific** location for power. Also, assembly industries such as many consumer durables are not tied to raw materials which need processing.

The main factors are explained in Unit 6.2. They are power, natural advantages, transport and communications, the supplies of raw materials, components and water, government policy, labour, external economies, markets.

24 (a) See Unit 6.5 (1). This is a study of the steel industry's initial and recent locational factors.
(b) See Unit 6.5 (2) and 6.5 (3).

Unit 7 Answers

25 Monopoly is defined in two different ways. A **pure** monopoly in which one firm = the industry, which rarely occurs in practice, even with nationalized industries. The **official** government **definition** of monopoly is any firm which controls at least a quarter of the industry's market share.

The gaining of monopoly power occurs through nationalization, cartels, trade associations and informal and formal agreements. These **forms** of monopoly are outlined in Unit 7.3. The **reasons** for the creation of monopolies are legal and economic, such as restrictions on supply, usage of resources, general advantages and takeovers. These are explained and illustrated in Unit 3.2 and Unit 7.3.

26 The government may consider certain monopolies to be '**against** the **public interest**' because of their power. For instance, the Conservative Government, 1984, selling off parts of British Telecom, a nationalized industry, to 'break' its monopoly. Monopoly power allows firms to fix either its price or its output (see Figures 7.5 and 7.6). Such action can lead to consumer exploitation in particular and the other **disadvantages** of **monopoly** in general: high prices in long run, not producing at the optimum, lower quality goods, diseconomies of scale, little public control, political interference (Unit 7.3 and Unit 3.2).

By preventing the growth of a monopoly, the government wish to encourage competition. In practice, this will mean **imperfect** competition rather than **perfect** competition. However, some of the advantages of the 'free' market may result: new entrants, competing products, rewards to enterprise, price competition, many sellers (Unit 7.2).

Unit 8 Answers

27 The functions of money are explained in Unit 8.3. You should devote equal space to each function and give suitable examples.

28 (a) See Unit 8.3.

(b) This part is really saying what are the causes of **inflation** – when inflation occurs money becomes less valuable as it will not buy as much. The causes of inflation are explained in Unit 9.7.

29 (a) The information to answer this is in Unit 8.3. This question is slightly more difficult than Question 27, in that you need to remember the functions – '**SUMS**'! As the Oxford Board shows the marks for each part, allocation of time to each function is straightforward. It appears that each function receives 3 marks and this part should take about 15–20 minutes of writing.

(b) This part requires you to apply the qualities of each money substitute to the functions of money in a modern world. You should concentrate on the defects of each because the question seeks their **inadequacy**.

(i) Cigarettes – poor medium of exchange as lack of **uniformity** (different brands) and not divisible. Limited as a store of value because they are not very durable. However, they are used in prisons as money.

(ii) Gold – the main weakness is its scarcity – it is not plentiful enough to be a medium of exchange in a modern society. Its value means that it is not very portable without great precautions. Furthermore, it is not homogeneous as there are differences in carat value which are not easily identified without expert help. However, it is an excellent 'store of value' because of its intrinsic value.

(iii) Coal – as coal is not divisible easily, not portable in a convenient way and lacks uniformity, it would be a poor medium of exchange. It could be a store of value because of its durability but its declining economic importance might reduce its acceptability.

(iv) Cattle – as they lack portability, divisibility and homogeneity they could not function as a medium of exchange. Their changing nature (ageing) and lack of durability make them poor performers of the 'standard for deferred payments' and 'store of value' functions.

30 (a) The main forms of money are explained in Unit 8.5(3). A form of money which is used for small amounts is the postal order and this does not appear there. It is not very important and is rapidly being replaced by the cheque.

The 5 marks given for this part thus require one sentence on each of the forms.

(b) Credit creation is dealt with under the topic of banking and explained in Unit 10.5.

Unit 9 Answers

31 (a) A persistent general increase in prices. This means that the value of money is falling. There are three types of inflation – creeping, hyper and strato – which reflect different speeds and severity of increase.

(b) Inflation needs controlling because of its undesirable effects – businessmen become pessimistic and investment is unlikely to be forthcoming; exports become uncompetitive which may lead to balance of payments problems; income tends to be redistributed because some people (weakly unionized, savers, those on fixed incomes) suffer more than others.

'Recent years' refers to the postwar period during which British inflation has exceeded that of her rivals (see Unit 9.1). This has international and domestic effects.

In international trade, British goods became relatively dearer – this increased imports and reduced exports, both of which made the **balance of trade in deficit**. Domestically, the lack of investment, because of business pessimism and the high wage claims to compensate for the inflation, meant that British costs/unit compared unfavourably with most industrial nations *e.g.* British cars.

The policies adopted by the governments in 1960s and 1970s to deal with inflation also had unfortunate effects on the UK economy. Bouts of deflation, as part of demand-management policies to reduce inflation, led to **'stop-go' policies** which harmed Britain's economic growth but maintained low levels of unemployment. The 'stop' was the government restraint on the economy by less spending, tax increases and credit restrictions to limit consumption. This usually cut import demand and therefore eased balance of payments problems, as well as inflation. The 'go' aspect of the policy was deficit budgeting, and money supply expansion to encourage consumption. Such switchbacks in the economy tended to damage business confidence and inhibited investment.

The use of **incomes policy** to control the main domestic cost of wages worked for brief periods *e.g.* 1975–77. However, they seriously distorted pay differentials and stimulated evasion during their operation. In addition, when controls were relaxed trade unions pushed for big increases to restore living standards, and seemingly undid any good that had been done.

The advent of the **1979 Conservative Government** with a different policy, namely tight monetary control, had other consequences. The raising of interest rates and cuts in government spending were aimed at limiting money supply increases. The resultant fall in consumption and increased unemployment made workers fear for their jobs and led to the moderation of trade union claims and attitudes. By 1984, this strategy had caused inflation to fall to tolerable levels (less than 6%) but at the expense of high and rising unemployment (+3m from 1982).

32 (a) The retail price index is constructed by the government in order to measure increases in retail prices *i.e.* inflation. There are many **problems** in doing this – spending patterns change frequently; prices vary between retailers; incomes differ enormously; averages have to be used; time is taken in collecting and assembling the data. In addition, it is **costly** to compile. These problems mean that certain groups are excluded from the construction, weights have to be used, a representative basket of goods is devised and a base year needs setting. (See Units 9.4 and 9.5).

(b) As the quantity of information is vast, averages have to be used to **simplify** the complexity of real world. A meaningful measure would be difficult to devise without index numbers. Starting from 100 in the base year, increases in inflation can be fairly **easily calculated** and understood. Unless the base year is changed, index numbers are capable of only **one interpretation**. For instance they are not revised like balance of payments figures. Furthermore, they are **up to date**, being compiled monthly.

The RPI is just one index number. There are others, for example the volume of output and wholesale prices. This facilitates some **comparison** between different economic indicators. For instance, large increases in the wholesale prices index in one month usually presage spurts in the RPI as goods feed through the distribution network. Similarly, international comparisons of inflation can be made, despite dissimilar currencies, spending habits, incomes, taxes and prices.

Possible marks **(a)** (10) **(b)** (5).

33 (a) (i) a rate of pay for doing a job over a period of time, usually calculated per hour.
(ii) the wages received by workers in money, based on the wage rate and hours worked.
(iii) the purchasing power of money wages *i.e.* what they will buy.
(b) Inflation makes wages rates less valuable. Thus to maintain his **standard of living** the worker needs to gain a higher rate per hour, as his existing hours' labour will not earn him enough to buy the same amount of goods and services as before inflation.

Real wages show the relationship between money wages and prices. If prices rise and money wages are unchanged, real wages fall. Conversely, if prices rise more slowly than money wages, real wages have increased and the standard of living has improved. There may also be indirect effects. For instance, inflation may stimulate high wage claims which may succeed in raising wage rates and thus money wages.

34 (a) See Unit 9.7.
(b) See Unit 9.8 and Essay Answers 31(b) above.

Unit 10 Answers

35 (a) A bank's depositors usually require three things. Firstly, they want their money to be kept **safely** until they need it. There is no danger of bank failures today, unlike the nineteenth century, because of the Bank of England's supervision and the self-discipline of the banks (who do not overlend).

Depositors also require **access** to their money. Banks provide current account holders with cheque books to enable easy payment and withdrawal. With a deposit account the intention is saving, so money is not often withdrawn. Seven days notice may be required if a large sum is withdrawn.

Depositors who intend saving expect **interest**. This is usually paid twice yearly. The banks try to compete with the interest rates of other savings institutions.

(b) The shareholders of a joint stock bank expect a **dividend** on their investment. In order to pay high dividends, a bank needs to make big profits. Furthermore, shareholders probably wish to see their **share price increase** (capital growth) as a result of prudent banking and good profits.

The interests of shareholders may differ according to the **type** of share they hold. For instance, preference shareholders are less dependent on big profits than ordinary shareholders who get the last cut out of the profits. The banks will try to keep both groups of shareholders happy, particularly prominent ordinary shareholders such as institutional investors (see Unit 11.3) who may have some influence at the AGM.

(c) The Central Bank tries to implement government **monetary policy** and this may involve pulling joint stock banks into line. For instance, banks may be expanding credit creation when the government wants to be restrained. The Central Bank can act directly, by issuing **directives** or calling for **special deposits**. Also, in theory, the Central Bank can indirectly force banks to co-operate through **open market operations** (using this method in this case the Bank of England would sell more Treasury Bills than it buys, creating a cash shortage and reduced balances at the Bank of England). These weapons and their effectiveness are discussed in detail in Unit 10.8.

36 (a) Treasury bills, balance at Bank of England, money at call.

(b) $8/50 = 16\%$

(c) If 8m in reserve assets and this is to be 20% of the total, the total assets will be 40m ($8m = \frac{1}{5}$). As total assets = total deposits, then the banks would have to reduce their investment and advances by 10m (50 − 40).

37 See Unit 10.3

38 This essay can be approached in one of two ways: either by explaining the assets and referring to the profitability, security and liquidity of each **or** by looking at the three aspects and in each case relating the relevant assets. I will illustrate the latter as it is probably the more difficult approach.

A bank seeks profitability in order to pay **dividends** to its shareholders. Thus it desires the maximum return possible on its lending. The main assets contributing to profitability are **advances** (*i.e.* loans and overdrafts). Customers are charged at least 2% over **base rate** on these. The bank will also hold a portfolio of **investments**, which should yield regular income. This may be from interest on Treasury, commercial and other bills or dividends from shareholdings. Generally, the shorter the period for which the asset is held, the lower the rate of interest received. See Units 10.4 (2) and (3).

However, the most profitable items are generally the most **illiquid**. The assets bearing high interest do so because they cannot be redeemed quickly *e.g.* 20-year loan to government. A company overdraft can probably be slightly lowered in short terms but not called in without a lot of notice, because it might dislocate a company's production. Conversely, **money at call and short notice** is very liquid being retrievable overnight. However, it does not earn much interest.

The security of an asset may determine its profitability. For instance, personal loans are often charged at a higher rate to more **risky** and less credit-worthy customers. The higher rate of interest will mean more profit, unless the borrower defaults. The security of an asset is usually determined by the **credit status** of the borrower. Thus loans to the **government** (stocks) are more secure than shares in public companies which may go bankrupt.

Unit 11 Answers

39 (a) Saving is **not spending** *i.e.* putting off consumption to a later date. It usually takes the form of unused money placed into various financial institutions. This money may earn a return, or rate of interest. In so doing it is popularly called 'investment' or buying a 'claim for money'.

To the economist, investment means **buying capital goods** *e.g.* machinery. These goods can be used to make consumer goods or provide consumer services. Also capital goods may be used to make other capital goods *e.g.* large machinery makes part of smaller machine.

(b) As savings are used by financial institutions as funds for **lending** they perform an important role in an economy. More lending is possible when savings increase and this may increase investment. However, the extra funds available will only be taken up if businessmen are **optimistic**. If the government wishes to increase private sector investment it should encourage more saving.

If extra saving goes to government sources, then it provides funds for public expenditure. In recent years, national savings have been encouraged in order to finance government spending.

But much of this goes in current consumption through transfer payments rather than into investment projects.

However, increased saving means less consumption, assuming incomes do not change. This means **less demand** in the economy. Lower demand means fewer sales and this may cause business pessimism. So the extra funds (the savings) may not be taken up for investment. Also, lower demand may mean **more unemployment**.

If inflation is caused by 'too much money chasing too few goods' (see Unit 9.7 and Unit 9.8) then extra savings will tend to lower inflation. This might be what the government wants in certain circumstances. Alternatively, if unemployment is high, extra savings will depress demand and make the problem worse.

Generally, the government encourages saving because thrift is thought to be a 'good thing'. It teaches self-discipline and **sacrifice**. Furthermore, people can use savings in later life to provide **extra income** (from the interest received) and thus the government may need to provide less income support in some cases.

40 (a) The securities available on the Stock Exchange are mainly ordinary shares, Preference shares and Government Stocks. These are described in Unit 3.8.

(b) The Stock market is a market in **second-hand shares**. It is a place where buyers and sellers of shares meet, through their representatives (brokers). There are many buyers and many sellers, although the transactions are largely done through a few stockbroking and jobbing firms.

Some of the features of perfect competition are revealed by the Stock Market. The buyers can obtain **perfect knowledge** of all prices because there are so few jobbers. So they can react quickly to **price changes**. The sellers can also react immediately to market demand. The goods or shares are **homogeneous** *i.e.* 150 ICI shares are the same as any other 150 ICI shares. These characteristics mean that shares at the lowest price are bought. Also jobbers holding over-priced shares are faced with the choice of price reductions or no sales.

41 (a) Stockbrokers and stockjobbers both operate on the Stock Exchange. Stockbrokers act on behalf of **clients** whilst jobbers act for themselves (as principals). Stockbrokers deal **directly** with the general public and institutional investors whilst jobbers deal with stockbrokers. Stockbrokers get paid **commission** whilst jobbers earn profit through buying and selling shares. Stockbroking is less **risky** than jobbing because there are minimum commission rules and they do not put their capital at risk. Alternatively, jobbers speculate in the market.

Stockbrokers are usually prepared to buy/sell any type of share for their clients, whereas jobbers are specialists.

(b) The main functions of the Stock Exchange are outlined in detail in Unit 11.4(5). Briefly they are a market for second-hand shares, an indicator of business prospects, supervision of new issues, for obtaining government funds, and savings outlet.

Possible marks divided – (8) for **(a)**, (12) for **(b)**.

42 (a) This question refers to medium and long term savings. You could choose three from the following – Government Savings Certificates, Local Authority Loans, building society term shares, unit trusts, life assurance, government stocks. You might also mention bank deposit accounts. $(3 \times 2$ marks each.)

(b) You need to choose three **contrasting** types of saving institution *e.g.* building society shares, unit trusts and a government scheme.

A building society share account is safe, convenient, and gives a good rate of interest, on which basic rate income tax has already been deducted and paid to the Inland Revenue. This is only a disadvantage to non-taxpayers, since the tax cannot be reclaimed.

A unit trust is rather more risky because the money is put into stocks and shares whose value may fluctuate. Thus a return cannot be predicted and any capital gain is taxable. However, they are fairly liquid, although the owner may need to redeem them when the Stock Market is doing badly.

Government schemes are totally safe and very convenient (through any Post Office). However, the rate of return varies. It is usually in the form of a lump sum at the end of a time period. Liquidity is possible but it is at the expense of earning (because lower interest is given for early withdrawal). For instance, SAYE Index Linked, allows the 'cashing in' of certificates but only a low rate of interest (6%) is given. However, if the certificates are kept for the full period, savers receive interest equivalent to the rate of inflation.

(c) The decision to save or spend depends upon a person's view of the future and his/her circumstances. If you expect **inflation** to be higher than the rate of interest received then you will be worse off by saving. Your money will have lost its value in **real** terms. The savings, even with interest added, will be of lower value at the end of the period than that at the beginning because of the inflation.

Spending rather than saving may be preferential if it is possible to buy an **appreciating asset** which can be utilized. For instance, buying a house (or putting down a deposit on one) may be better than saving, for several reasons: **house prices** usually rise at a faster rate than inflation in general, the asset can be used, it gives security (which cannot be measured in economic terms) and it enables ownership. The monthly **mortgage** repayment pays off the loan over a period of time. In contrast, rent payments on a hired property are 'dead money' and do not contribute towards ownership, only temporary use.

Unit 12 Answers

43 (a) The average age of United Kingdom population has increased. This means that people are living longer due to improvements in medical science, fewer wars recently, and better living standards. The average life expectancy has increased by thirteen years since 1931.

The economic effects of an ageing population are: changed spending patterns (*e.g.* increased sales of thermal underwear), more State spending, more dependence on the working population and a less mobile and less adaptable workforce. These are explained in Unit 12.3 (1).

(b) Britain's geographical distribution is still heavily concentrated in urban areas. However, since the mid-1960s the big city areas have lost population to the rural areas. The inner city districts have decayed and some of the people there have moved to the suburbs. Commuter towns and villages have developed outside most towns with the spread of private road transport. (See Figure 12.2.)

The population of Britain is becoming more dispersed, as is its industry. There is greater geographical mobility in the 1980s than in the 1930s which reflects changes in transport and improvements in the standard of living.

(c) In the last fifty years Britain's population has increased slowly. For instance between 1971 and 1981 the population was stable. There was a small growth due to natural factors (birth rate and death rate) which was balanced by outward migration. (See Figure 12.1.)

Population stability should be advantageous because there is no pressure on food resources. Therefore any increase in productivity should lead to greater welfare per head. However, the distribution within the total size is vital. For instance, an increased dependency ratio will cause problems because there will be fewer workers and more non-workers. So each worker will have to raise his output and face a higher tax burden to help pay for the increased number of dependants.

44 (a) The working population is the total number of inhabitants at work, or available for work, in the population. It usually covers men between 16 and 65, women from 16 to 60.

(b) The supply of labour in the **long term** is determined by population trends. It will increase, other things being equal, if the birth rate rises (and more male births occur) and the death rate falls (more old people dying, leaving more middle aged). It will also increase if immigration exceeds emigration and the inflow are mainly from 16 to 64 and male, *i.e.* prospective workers. Natural disasters, *e.g.* wars, distort these natural factors.

In the **short term**, it could be increased by lowering the age of school leaving and raising the retirement age, by law. Higher incentives to work rather than study; and work rather than remain unemployed, will probably increase the supply of labour. For instance, reductions in Supplementary Benefit may encourage some of the unemployed to seek work. In addition, easier immigration laws and harder emigration rules may increase the supply of labour.

45 (a) Ratio of total live births to the total population, usually expressed in 'live births per 1000 of total population' per annum.

(b) A fall in the population caused by a dropping birth rate could lead to **under** population *i.e.* not enough population to exploit the resources of a nation. In answering the question we must **assume** that other things do not change.

In the long term, there will probably be a decline in the **demand** for certain products/services *e.g.* maternity units, midwives. The government may have to spend **money** to encourage immigration. There could be a shortage of **key workers**, affecting wages differentials. Total output would fall unless there was in increase in productivity.

The effects of a fall in birth rate may depend on the specific cause. If a fall in family size is produced by **working wives** and a more negative attitude to **child** rearing, then more jobs will be demanded. Women, who would otherwise be parents, seek jobs and this could cause a short-term rise in unemployment.

46 (a) Geographical mobility of population refers to the extent to which the population is prepared to move between areas to find jobs. The geographical distribution of population shows how the population is concentrated and dispersed around the country. Heavily concentrated areas have high densities. If a population is geographically mobile then the geographical distribution will change more markedly more often.

(b) The geographical mobility of population is determined by two factors: the obstacles to movement (**'FIBPEA'** – 12.4 (2)) and the inducements to move.

The obstacles to movement are family, ignorance, benefits, prejudice, expense, and availability of accommodation. These are explained in full in Unit 12.4.

The desire to move depends on an individual's attitude to work (and life in general) if a person does not want to leave an area where he was brought up then no amount of government influence will persuade him. This is often the case with the middle aged unemployed.

The government encourages movement by providing information at job centres and by subsidizing employers who move key workers. The 1979 Conservative Government sought to induce movement indirectly by reducing supplementary benefit in real terms (thereby making the difference between work income and unemployment income greater).

47 Geographical distribution of population – Unit 12.3 (3). The main factors determining the density of population are geographical, historical and economic. The geographical factors revolve round land use, terrain and communications. Generally, flat agricultural land has few inhabitants. Some land, such as 'green belt', is restricted from building (and thus habitation) by law.

In the past, population concentrated in certain key places *e.g.* York for defensive fortifications, Crewe as a railway intersection, Liverpool as a port and Irish refugee centre and London as a capital city. In the case of York, for religious reasons, and London, for political reasons, the populations grew. **New Town** legislation since 1946 (see Unit 6.4) has led to the creation of over thirty new towns.

However, the geographical and historical factors are less important than the economic ones. The growth of the population since the **Industrial Revolution** (and because of it) has affected the density. Population density in several urban areas has grown markedly *i.e.* Greater London, Greater Manchester, South Yorkshire, West Midlands, East Midlands, Tyne and Wear. These were created as **Metropolitan** counties in 1972 because of their heavy concentration of population. In each case the rapid industrialization of the nineteenth century attracted population. The factors determining the location of industry (and thus their workers and dependants) are described in Unit 6.2.

Unit 13 Answers

48 This question could be answered with a **demand** and **supply** analysis to show how wages are determined and changed. This approach is featured in Units 13.3 and 13.4. The demand for labour is determined by the possibilities of substitution of factors of production, productivity, elasticity for factors, and demand for the final product. The supply of labour is affected by general factors such as population structure and the laws relating to work and immigration and several specific factors. The latter include pay, income in kind, the conditions of employment, security and entry requirements. Changes in either demand or supply will cause wages to vary.

A practical **example** should be used to illustrate the reasons for wage differentials. The main explanations of wage variation between jobs are the **industry**, job **requirements** and **trade union** power (Unit 13.5). These causes include demand and supply elements. For instance, the wage differences between oil engineers and building labourers can be explained by changes in demand and the elasticity of supply.

In the case of oil, demand for engineers has boomed (derived demand) and supply is relatively inelastic (because of the lack of available skilled labour and the time needed for training). Conversely, for building labourers, the **demand** has **fallen** with the decline of the construction industry and a weakly organized general trade union. The **supply** curve is fairly **elastic** because people can easily be recruited quickly, since no specialist skills and qualifications are needed.

49 (a) Agricultural workers' wages are low for many reasons. They are represented by a fairly **weak union** and protected by a **wages council**. In contrast most of their employers are rich and powerful. Traditionally, their wages have been low because they have also received **payments** in kind, such as housing (tied farm cottage) and food (free farm produce).

With the growth of larger-sized farms, **mechanization** has increased, with capital replacing labour. This has meant less demand for agricultural labour. The union representing agricultural workers is at a disadvantage because its membership is so dispersed. The supply of labour is fairly elastic because **few skills** are needed for most jobs and the quantity of **unemployment** in the last five years is a large potential source of supply. These factors have kept wages relatively low. (The example given of building workers in Question 48 is relevant).

(b) There are two main arguments for minimum wages. Firstly, they would raise the wages of many low paid workers *e.g.* in catering. This would make many people **better off** as their income will have increased. Secondly, assuming higher wages do not rise dramatically then increased wages for the poor will slightly **reduce inequality** in society. This assumes that the minimum wages are fixed above current wage levels.

The adverse effects of minimum wages, fixed above the equilibrium rate, start with **unemployment**. Further – the higher wages may raise the **costs** of production as each worker would be paid more (assuming the same quantity are employed). This might lead to cost push **inflation** (Unit 9.7). Minimum wage legislation could also reduce **wage differentials**, as more skilled workers will not receive quite as much more than unskilled (lower paid) workers as they did before.

50 (a) Employment is dependent upon being a trade union member. Thus the 'shop' floor is closed to a prospective employee who will not join the relevant trade union. A few jobs have a **pre-entry closed shop** which means that only people who are already members of a certain union can apply for the job. Most of the 5 million closed shop jobs are post entry which means the employee must join the union when he starts the job.

(b) 13.8 (2) (a) bargaining.

(c) Picketing is done by strikers. They try to persuade workers who wish to work (called 'blacklegs') during the strike not to do so. Since the 1982 Act, a maximum of **six pickets** is allowed at each entrance to their work place and those other firms who are directly involved with the firm in the dispute.

(d) When an employer and a union cannot solve an industrial dispute they occasionally get an independent third party to settle it. This person (it may be a group) is known as an arbitrator. ACAS is a Government backed body which performs this function (Unit 13.8 (2)). In some cases an arbitrator's decision is binding, which means that both sides have to accept it.

51 (a) Trade union aims and functions 13.7 (1) and (2).

(b) Influence is obtained by being an active member or shop steward. The structure of organization is outlined in Unit 13.8 (1).

(c) Paying a membership subscription could be seen as a disadvantage, as it is a payment which reduces disposable income. The subscription goes into the union funds. For most trade unions, a proportion of this money becomes a **political levy** to the Labour Party. A Conservative supporter (and many trade unionists are) may not agree with this. However because at present (1984) people 'contract out', it is more inconvenient to avoid this payment.

If the trade union has a **closed shop** and you do not want to join (but have to, or else no job) then you would resent having to make these payments. Since 1982 workers have been given more freedom not to join unions. The Conservative Government (1984) seeks to reduce the number of closed shops and make the creation of new closed shops more difficult.

Another disadvantage could be the union's activities. It might decide on industrial action, which you do not want but have to accept (since you are in the minority). If you object and don't wish to strike, then you might be picketed and accused of black legging. When the dispute is settled you could be victimized *i.e.* treated with hostility by fellow workers and perhaps even by the management (under pressure from the union). Activities such as 'working to rule', banning overtime, and striking could lead to **lower earnings** in the short term.

52 Industrial action – 13.8 (2). There are several arguments used by trade unions to justify their wage claims.

(a) The union may argue that **inflation** has eroded the real value of their wages, making them worse off. However, unless the workers increase output the cost of production will rise. This will probably produce further inflation which could undermine the wage increase. It all depends on the relevant per cent changes. Clearly, increasing wages are less dangerous in a capital-intensive industry.

(b) A trade union may claim wage increases on the basis of **increased productivity** or the ending of **restrictive practices**. Such an argument is credible but it only applies in a few cases. Most employment is in the service sector today and production is difficult to measure. This limits the extent of the argument.

(c) A claim may be based on **comparability**. The usual argument is that people doing a similar job in a different firm or industry are paid more, and thus the claim is to raise wages to make them equal. The argument is based on the notion of **fairness**. However, the capacity of different firms and industries to reward similar workers varies. For instance a clerk in a declining industry would be unlikely to gain as big an increase as a clerk in an expanding industry, perhaps because the fear of unemployment made his union weaker and the management relatively stronger.

(d) A union may seek to maintain or restore a wage **differential**. It might argue that a skilled group needs a certain increase to keep its wages much higher than an unskilled group in a factory *e.g.* fitters v. labourers. If wage differentials are reduced the incentive to study and train is lowered. The general effect of this would probably be the creation of a less efficient workforce and less capacity for **economic growth**. A variation of the general argument is that 'our members have fallen behind in the **Pay League**'. The miners used this tactic successfully in 1972.

Unit 14 Answers

53 Consumption is the expenditure by people, companies and the government on consumer goods and services. This spending is to satisfy current needs *e.g.* man buys petrol for car, council pays dustman wages for refuse collection. **Investment** is spending money on creating capital goods *e.g.* Ministry of Transport spends £30m on new motorway, ICI build a new factory. **National income** is spent on consumption and investment. In one year, the greater the proportion spent on consumption, the less there is to spend on investment.

(a) Current living standards are determined by **total national income** and the percentage of that income which is spent on consumption. The more that is spent on consumption, the better off is the population as a whole (ignoring the distribution of the income). Thus, if the production of investment goods increases through more spending on investment, there is less to spend on consumption. This means a fall in current living standards. However, if national income is increasing rapidly (economic growth occurring) it is possible to have better living standards and more investment *e.g.*

National income £200m: Consumption £150m, Investment £50m, compared with National income £250m: Consumption £180, Investment £70m.

(b) An increase in investment will usually produce higher future living standards if it is of the right **type** and **quantity**. For instance, it could be argued that the investment in nuclear weapons does not improve the economic potential for growth. However, it could be counter claimed that by increasing security and preventing war it raises the standard of living (in an intangible way).

Most investment should lead to more efficient production of consumer goods so that in the future the **same level of production** (and consumption) can be obtained with **fewer resources**. This would leave more resources available for current consumption or further investment.

54 (a) The main reasons are to provide information for the government, to enable an assessment of the standard of living, to calculate economic growth and to facilitate international comparisons. These are explained in Unit 14.3.

(b) After GDP at market price has been calculated, allowance has to be made for **taxes** and **subsidies**, which distort market prices. Expenditure taxes are deducted from GDP at market prices because they make them artificially high. Conversely, subsidies are added because they keep market prices down. The result of these adjustments is GDP at factor cost. **Net property income** from abroad is added to give gross national product (GNP).

Net national product is arrived at by deducting capital consumption from GNP. **Capital consumption** is the depreciation in the value of the nation's assets over the year. The stages are shown in Figure 14.3.

(c) An increase in real national income means **economic growth**. Economic growth can be achieved through making use of **idle resources** and increasing **productivity**. The latter can be brought about by better quality and greater quantity of investment, by technical progress and by incentives to the labour force. They are illustrated in detail in Unit 14.4 (4).

55 The standard of living shows how well-off a population is in general. It is usually measured as **national income per head**. Such measurement is subject to many limitations (see Unit 14.3 (2)).

The difference between the standard of living in India and the United Kingdom is enormous. There are many explanatory factors.

The population of Britain is much smaller than India's and it is not growing as fast (0.1% compared with 2.2% per annum). Thus the national income is shared among fewer people, giving more to each. India is over-populated. India lacks natural resources which can be exploited. Its largest resource is labour, but it is not renowned for energy and dynamism. This partly results from the climate. The average temperature of 77°F is one of the highest in the world in total contrast to the main industrialized nations of West Europe.

56 (a) The total value of goods and services produced by a country's resources in a year. (See Unit 14.2)

(b) The total amount owed by a nation to its creditors (see Unit 15).

National income figures can be misleading because many qualifications have to be made. These involve taxation, size of population, rate of inflation, regional differences, technical changes, income distribution, State services. (See 14.3 (2).) In addition when making inter-country comparisons certain problems arise: spending habits, the composition of national output, political factors, accuracy of collection, wealth, social factors. (See 14.3 (3).)

Unit 15 Answers

57 (a) and **(b)** see Unit 15.3 and Figure 15.4.

Governments use both types of tax for certain reasons. Income tax which is the main progressive tax has the advantages of efficiency and fairness. It acts also as an automatic stabilizer and produces a high yield, being the biggest single revenue raiser. In addition, Labour governments use it as a means of income redistribution in society. Capital Transfer Tax is similarly used, but to redistribute wealth.

Regressive taxes, such as VAT and rates, also have definite advantages. They are both flexible, cheap to administer and do not affect effort adversely. They also contribute substantially to government revenue and act as automatic stabilizers (this is less true of rates).

58 The taxes levied by the government are not classified in this book along the lines of this question. However, the relevant taxes are illustrated in Figure 15.3 and explained in Units 15.3 and 15.4. They can be applied to each category as follows:

(a) income earner – income tax for individual, corporation tax for companies, capital gains tax for investors, national insurance for employees;

(b) consumer – VAT, excise duties, protective duties (imports), rates (when consuming council services, if a property owner), vehicle licence duty (if motorist);

(c) producer – national insurance as employer, rates, expenditure taxes such as VAT (when goods/services bought) corporation tax, petroleum revenue tax.

59 The Budget is explained in Unit 15.6.

The objectives of a budget generally reflect a government's general economic policy. These are outlined in Unit 20.1.

In addition, a budget may have more **specific aims** *e.g.* cutting PSBR by raising taxes, redistributing wealth more evenly by raising income tax (particularly high marginal rates), lowering inflation immediately by cutting VAT, or controlling nationalized industries' activities by lowering their borrowing (external financing limits). The objectives and use of the budget vary with the government in power.

60 (a) See Unit 15.5 and Figures 15.7 and 15.8.

(b) Incidence of VAT is explained in Unit 15.5. It is occasionally possible, given demand conditions, for a supplier to push the incidence of VAT onto the customer. Generally, the more **inelastic the demand**, the easier it is for the supplier to pass on the tax to the customer.

However, income tax is **direct** and the incidence is difficult to avoid and almost impossible to pass on. When taxpayers have tax deducted from their weekly wages they are paying; some people may **evade** taxation by not declaring their income (but that is illegal).

The only way that income tax incidence can be shifted is if a group of workers, through a trade union, negotiate a pay rise (possibly to compensate for a tax increase). Then the burden could be shifted onto the employer (and perhaps eventually to the consumer) – but this is not very likely.

Unit 16 Answers

61 (a) (i) Unit 16.5. An assembly line worker replaced by a robot.

　　　(ii) Unit 16.5. A Butlin's Redcoat.

(b) Fiscal policy involves changing taxes. The main taxes that influence the **level of demand** (and thus employment) are income tax, national insurance and VAT. You must state the **assumption** that other things do not change.

A fall in the basic rate of **income tax** or a rise in the tax-free threshold will give people more disposable income. Consumers will be able to spend more, raising general demand and causing suppliers to take on more workers. This will lead to lower unemployment. Similarly, a fall in the basic rate **value added tax** will make goods cheaper and hopefully increase quantity demanded.

A drop in **national insurance** contributions for the employer will increase the **supply** of labour, rather than demand. Suppliers will employ more labour, as it will be fractionally cheaper.

62 (a) See Unit 16.5 – demand deficiency

(b) See Unit 16.5

(c) See Unit 16.5 and Unit 6.3

63 The main causes of unemployment are outlined in 16.6.

(a) Raising the school leaving age to 17 would probably **cut the supply** of labour. In the short term there would be a **once-and-for-all fall** in the unemployment figures, as for one year there would be no summer school leavers. The majority of 16-year-olds seek employment but now they would have to endure (!) another year at school.

The **long-term effects** depend upon how children react to another year at school. It might encourage some to leave at 17, who would otherwise have remained until age 18.

A shift in supply could be drawn to show a decreased number of employed.

(b) Inducements to emigrate if successful lead to a **smaller supply** of labour. However, the effect on unemployment depends upon who emigrates.

If existing employed people emigrate then the unemployed total will only be reduced if the unemployed have the qualifications and skills to take their jobs. Most evidence suggests that this is unlikely, as Britain suffers a **'brain drain'** (see Unit 12.2) whilst the bulk of the unemployed are **unskilled** (Unit 16.2 + Figure 16.2).

However, if unemployed people leave the country to find jobs abroad, then the total number unemployed will fall.

64 This question seeks information about the characteristics of the unemployed. The features of Unit 16.2 should be outlined. You should obviously concentrate on the industrial and regional differences – Unit 16.2 (1) (c), (3), (4) and Unit 6.3.

65 (a) See Unit 16.5 – structural, demand deficiency, frictional, natural, technological, voluntary, seasonal. Emphasis should be placed on them in the above order.

(b) Unit 16.7.

Unit 17 Answers

66 (a) This question requires knowledge of the controls introduced by governments to protect their trade. The reasons for intervention (**'BRIDES'**) are Balance of Payments, Revenue raising, protecting Infant industries, preventing Dumping, preserving Employment and Security maintenance – they are further detailed in Unit 17.4 (1).

(b) The methods of control are outlined in 17.5. This is import limitation by 'quotas' and export encouragement by subsidies and cheap credit.

67 (a) 17.3   **(b)** 17.3

(c) The effects of an unfavourable movement in the terms of trade are to make imports relatively more expensive. This requires more exports to pay for each import. The effect of this on the Balance of Payments depends on the relevant demand and supply elasticities.

Figure 17.10 shows that adverse movement will benefit the Balance of Payments if export and import prices are elastic.

Conversely, if they are both inelastic, the Balance of Payments will worsen.

68 In order to answer this question, it is worth distinguishing theory and practice. In theory, the **comparative cost** benefits can be accrued and the benefits of **specialization** obtained. This theory and its assumptions should be outlined with an example as in 17.1. In addition the other benefits of free trade such as increased **choice**, breaking of **monopoly power** and the achievement of **economies of scale** need stressing.

In practice there may be other reasons for trade:

(a) Colonial ties – in Britain's case, trade with the Commonwealth is maintained for traditional reasons, although it is declining.

(b) Aid – loans to underdeveloped countries may be tied *i.e.* they get the aid in return for buying the donor nation's goods.

(c) Political motives – like-minded governments tend to trade together, thus USSR through Comecon encourages other communist states to trade together.

(d) International organizations – bodies such as free trade areas and customs unions influence trade between members.

69 (a) 17.6 (1);   **(b)** 18.5;   **(c)** 17.7.

Unit 18 Answers

70 (a) The Balance of Trade just refers to one part of the Balance of Payments accounts. It is trade in goods and is part of the current account (see Figure 18.1). The British Balance of Trade was regularly in deficit up to 1980.

The Balance of Payments may show a surplus on current account because invisible trade is added to the Balance of Trade. Invisible trade is always a net positive amount for Britain.

When the Capital Account is considered, any deficit on the current account could be compensated for, if there are substantial capital inflows, as in 1979 (see Figure 18.2). The 1979 statistics show a Balance of Payments surplus and Balance of Trade deficit at the same time.

(b) A current account surplus shows successful trading in goods and services. This may be desired for prestige. It usually increases faith in a country's economy, attracting inward **investment** and raising the **exchange rate**. A higher exchange rate makes imports cheaper and so may reduce the cost of living a little. Also, a strong exchange rate may mean less need for high interest rates (to attract foreign capital) and thus domestic investment may be encouraged.

A surplus on the current account may be sought to pay for a **capital account** deficit. The latter may arise through outward investment – the buying of foreign assets (both paper and real) will yield income (invisible earnings) in the **future**.

71 (a) Visible trade will be affected by more imports. This will worsen the Balance of Trade and the overall Balance of Payments. However, if the number of cars increases because price has fallen and demand is fairly elastic then total revenue may fall and the Balance of Trade benefits!

(b) This would be a **capital inflow**. In the short term it would improve the capital account and thus help the Balance of Payments overall. However, in the long run when profits are remitted the invisible surplus will be reduced by the outflow.

(c) The effect depends on certain assumptions. If we assume that the tankers were insured by foreigners at Lloyds then the payment of claims will reduce profits from insurance broking. This will reduce the **invisible surplus**. However, if the tankers were bringing goods *e.g.* oil to Britain then imports would temporarily fall, helping the Balance of Trade.

(d) This would make **imports dearer** and **exports cheaper**. The impact depends on the relative demand elasticities. In the short run, imports are likely to increase in value and exports decrease in value (because demand is relatively inelastic), both weakening the Balance of Trade. In the long run, in theory, they should help the Balance of Trade.

72 The overall Balance of Payments **must** balance because of the accounting procedure. The **balancing item** is added or subtracted from the combined current account and capital account balances so that this combined total equals the official financing undertaken (see Figure 18.1, Unit 18.1 (D)).

The Balance of Trade is just one part of the whole accounts and so it may be in deficit or surplus. For example – see Figure 18.2.

73 (a) £1.5 billion

(b) 1978, £3.0 billion

(c) A lower exchange rate gives more £ for each unit of currency held by a foreigner. Thus it is an incentive for foreign tourists to come to Britain. Conversely, it deters British tourists from going abroad.

(d) A higher standard of living at home would allow more saving and thus people could better afford foreign travel. An appreciation in the £ would give more of a foreign currency for the £ and so encourage tourism abroad.

(e) Transport improvements would help tourism by making beauty spots and historical places more accessible. If they speeded up journeys they might enable tourists to see more and spend more. Generally, the economy would benefit from lower transport costs/unit which should reduce prices (other things being equal). They might enable goods to compete better at home and abroad.

74 (a) (i) Exports – imports = £−6036m.

(ii) Government services, private transfers, interest, profits and dividends and shipping £+4207 − £1684 = £+2523m.

(iii) £−6036 + £2523 = £−3513m.

(iv) Capital account items (investment + balancing item = £−2476) thus Balance of Payments current account and capital account = balance for official financing (£−2476 + £−3513 = £−5989m).

(b) There is a Balance of Payments deficit which needs remedying. The main general measures usually proposed are Depreciation, Deflation, Control of Money Supply – see Unit 18.3.

In addition, certain specific policies could be suggested such as trade controls on imports (which are the main cause in this case), higher interest rates (to attract capital) and reduced government overseas spending (which is a significant deficit in the invisibles account).

Unit 19 Answers

75 Local authorities obtain revenue from government grants, rates, other income and loans – see Unit 19.5 and Figure 19.3.

Possible alternatives are local sales tax, local income tax, assigned revenues and reformed rates.

The main items of expenditure are education, social services, housing, leisure, recreational services.

76 (i) Unit 15.4   **(ii)** Unit 19.5.

Unit 20 Answers

77 (a) The main trends in retailing have been the development of large-scale outlets (*i.e.* supermarkets, superstores and hypermarkets), increased competition (*e.g.* supermarkets v.

corner shop; discount stores v. department stores and specialist multiples) and diversification. They are examined in Unit 20.4. In addition, new technology has been applied: refrigerated equipment, computerized stock control, convenience foods (*e.g.* packet mixes), forklift trucks etc., have all speeded up retail 'production'.

(b) Customers have benefited through: lower prices as a result of competition; easier shopping because of diversification leading to one-stop shopping; quicker shopping (working wives required this); self-selection of goods.

On the other hand consumers have faced the disadvantages of: more speed/pressure in shopping; less contact/more impersonal atmosphere; little advice/service; fewer shops, particularly locally; the need for mobility – *i.e.* transport own goods away from supermarket.
78 The functions of a wholesaler are outlined in Unit 20.3. The functions of a retailer are outlined in Unit 20.4.

The wholesaler has been replaced in certain patterns of distribution as shown in Figure 20.1. When the wholesaler is eliminated his functions still need performing. They may be performed either by the retailer, as in the case of supermarkets, or by the manufacturer, as in the case of many consumer durables. The trend towards larger-scale retailing has worked against the wholesaler because large retailers have bigger premises, faster turnover and more stock. Similarly, the increase in forward vertical integration has meant more manufacturers owning retail outlets and so not needing a wholesaler as a middleman. Undoubtedly general improvements in transport and technology are a threat to the wholesaler.

However, in some markets, particularly agricultural goods, the wholesaler will remain, because his functions are vital and cannot be performed by farmers or retailers. It seems that the smaller, cheaper, and more perishable the final product, the greater the need for wholesalers.
79 (a) The Sale of Goods Act has been broken, because the goods were not of merchantable quality. The consumer has the right to a refund, replacement or repair. You need **not** accept the credit note.

(b) The Food and Drugs Act has been infringed, because the food is not fit for human consumption and not been hygienically prepared. The consumer should not pay for the meal and might report the matter to Trading Standards Officer.

(c) This method of selling breaks the Unsolicited Goods Act. The consumer need not pay for the book but should keep it safe. If it is not collected within six months it is yours!
80 (a) Credit is obtaining goods legally without paying for them at the time they are 'bought'. Access, Visa, American Express are examples.

(b) The advantages are easier, safer shopping and immediate use of something which perhaps could not otherwise be afforded. The main disadvantages are usually interest charges and a limited number of shops allow credit.

(c) See Unit 10.3.

(d) APR is the 'true' rate of interest which lenders have to quote by law. The flat rate is based on the total amount borrowed whereas APR is calculated on the average amount owed.

Part V

Examination hints and techniques

This section is divided into four parts:

1 The general aims of studying Economics
2 The specific objectives which are assessed in examinations
3 Techniques of assessment
4 Examination day

1 The general aims of Economics study

The broad ideas behind an Economics course were identified by the 16+ National Criteria working parties. They suggested that the course should be in part descriptive but also an introduction to elementary economic concepts and theories. Thus, economics up to age 16 should seek:

(a) To provide students with knowledge and skills which enable them to better understand the world in which they live.

(b) To develop a critical understanding of the main economic forces and institutions.

(c) To enable students to participate more fully in decision-making as consumers, producers and citizens.

2 Specific objectives

Examination syllabuses at O level and CSE attempt to assess certain objectives. Candidates are expected to show:

(a) Recall of economics knowledge.

(b) Application of economics knowledge, terminology, concepts and theories in verbal, numerical and graphical form.

(c) Analysis and interpretation of data.

(d) Judgement between evidence and opinion.

The importance (weight) attached to each of these objectives varies between examination boards and levels. For instance, the Welsh Board has an examination requiring 5 essays which does not allow data interpretation ((c) above) to be assessed. Conversely, AEB paper has data analysis questions which cannot be avoided. Generally recall and application of economics content and concepts (a) and (b), above, constitute the bulk of O-level assessment. To gain a high grade at O level, some evidence of judgement, as well as thorough and literate basic understanding, would be sought.

As CSE was aimed at different calibre students (those beneath top 20% and above bottom 40%) to O level, its weightings given to objectives differ a little. There tends to be a greater emphasis on interpreting data in CSE examinations, particularly at Mode 3 (school based assessment). The examinations are also less essay-orientated, with essays rarely accounting for more than two-thirds of the total marks.

The 16+ National Criteria recommended the following mark allocation limits:

(a) recall	30–50%	
(b) application	20–40%	
(c) analysis	10–20%	
(d) judgement	10–20%	

They also suggested that at least 50% of the marks must be available for candidates to demonstrate abilities other than factual recall.

'Social Economics' courses are becoming more popular at both O and CSE level. They emphasize the applied and practical aspects of economics, relating the subject more directly to the economic decisions which individuals take in society. Such courses try to mix theory with practice. They are likely to become more widely taught when 16+ is introduced in 1988.

3 Techniques of assessment

There are three techniques applied to assessing examinations in Economics at O level and CSE level:

(a) Objective questions *e.g.* short answer, multiple choice. These are found much more at CSE than O level but rarely account for more than 30% of the total mark allocation.

(b) Essays/continuous writing questions. O-level exams are still dominated by this means of assessment. However, in recent years the essays have become more structured into separate parts, and other types of assessment have been introduced.

(c) Data response questions. Following the A level trend towards interpretation of economics information, many CSE examinations devised by teachers (Mode 3) incorporate this type of question. The extracts used can be diagrammatical, graphical, tabular, written or informational. However, few O-level Economics examinations currently use this technique of assessment. When used, it usually accounts for 25% (or less) of the total marks.

Objective questions

The main feature of such questions is that there is only **one** correct **answer**. Thus, they do not require personal judgement by the examiner. If there is room for disagreement over the answer then the question is not objective. Generally, most objective questions are brief and specific. As a result often only **one mark** is given to each. For instance, Cambridge O-level Economics Paper One has 40 questions for 30% of the marks.

Objective questions are of two main types:

(a) short answer – a **word**, **phrase** or **sentence** is needed to answer the question. For example
 (i) Name one source of local authority finance – rates.
 (ii) What do the letters ACAS stand for? Advisory, Conciliation and Arbitration Service.
(iii) What is a Demarcation Dispute? – a disagreement between two trade unions over which type of worker should perform a certain job.

Questions **(i)** and **(ii)** test the recall of factual knowledge. Question **(iii)** assesses the ability to explain an idea (*i.e.* demarcation) which is probably more difficult.

Sometimes a **calculation** is required. For instance, from a list of taxes and the amount collected for each, a candidate might be asked to calculate 'how much direct taxation is collected?' Such questions require the application of understanding to a simple problem. There is just one correct answer.

(b) Multiple Choice In Economics at O level, the main types of multiple choice question used are: **(i)** simple completion, **(ii)** multiple completion and **(iii)** matched response.

(i) simple completion The most common objective test item asks for the candidate to select **one** from several possible responses in order to correctly finish a statement. For example:
The most liquid of a commercial bank's assets is/are:
(*a*) advances to customers
(*b*) commercial bills
(*c*) Government bonds
(*d*) money at call
  The correct answer is (*d*).

(ii) multiple completion Candidates select **one** or **more** statements which may 'correctly' answer a question. They then select a code letter for the 'correct' pattern of responses from a table of directions as illustrated below:

Directions Summarized				
A	B	C	D	E
1 only correct	1 & 2 only correct	3 & 4 only correct	2, 3 & 4 correct	1, 2, 3, 4 correct

For example:
Which of the following is/are most likely to cause cost push inflation?
 1 An increase in supplementary benefit payments
 2 An increase in VAT
 3 A rise in wage rates
 4 A rise in raw material prices
  As 1 is inappropriate and 2, 3, 4 may cause cost push inflation then D is the answer.

(iii) matched responses This type of question requires a candidate to match the correct answer from a list against a question. Often, as below, a list of words is given and a candidate chooses the correct definition from another list. Some CSE Boards require that the number of words given should exceed the number of definitions.

Match the following explanations about industrial location to the correct description below:

Bulk increasing, enterprise zones, industrial inertia, bulk decreasing, intermediate areas.

A An industry which tends to locate near its raw materials

....

B The original reasons which established the industry in a place having disappeared

....

C An industry locating near its market

....

D Certain areas such as inner city areas chosen by the government for aid

....

E Areas that do not qualify for the full range of government assistance

....

This is a popular type of question to test understanding, particularly at CSE level.

As Multiple Choice questions give candidates a chance of guessing the correct alternative they have been criticized. However, it is argued that their use enables a wider coverage of the syllabus in an examination, particularly when a wide choice is allowed in essay sections.

In a five option multiple choice question, a candidate with no idea has a 20% chance of guessing correctly (*i.e.* 1 in 5 chance). A candidate's chances can be improved if he can discount one or more of the alternatives as definitely wrong. Thus, if a candidate can definitely eliminate 2 options as wrong, he can improve his chances to 33% by guessing (*i.e.* he guesses between 1 in 3, with 2 options definitely wrong). The best chance is 50% (*i.e.* 1 in 2) with 3 alternatives being excluded from the guess. Some examination boards have banned true/false questions because there is a 50% chance of success.

In the multiple completion type question, the elimination of 'wrong' alternatives is more crucial. For instance in example **(ii)**, the knowledge that 1 is not appropriate immediately eliminates answers A, B and E leaving a choice between C and D. Notice that if the candidate 'knows' that 2 applies he can select answer D, even though he may not 'know' that 3 and 4 statements answer the question. Thus, this type of question may reward intelligent deduction as well as understanding of Economics.

Extracts

The broad category 'extract' covers any type of information or illustration, in the question which needs to be explained in order to answer the question. The extract may be narrative, statistical or diagrammatic.

(a) Narrative This type of extract tests the economic literacy of the candidate. It is used as a peg upon which several questions are hung. The example below seeks certain knowledge, understanding and judgement about the Stock Exchange.

Spurs Share Issue

There was a big rush to buy shares in Tottenham Hotspur FC. The club issues 3.8 million new shares of £1 each. Sheppard and Chase, the club's stockbrokers, reported that the issue was 4½ times over-subscribed. They now have the problem of allocating the 3.8 million shares amongst 12 859 people and institutions who applied to buy shares in the football club. It seems likely that all those who applied will receive the minimum subscription of 100 shares and that above this everyone will receive 15 per cent of the shares they applied for.

Experts think that the large number of applicants was not just made up of Spurs supporters, but that 'stags' who speculate in the new issue market were well represented among the applicants. The 'stags' will probably make a 'killing' because stockbrokers expect the £1 shares to kick-off at £1.20 each when dealing starts on the Stock Exchange next Thursday.

1 What type of business can sell shares through the Stock Exchange? (1)
2 How much money will the club raise through making the share issue? (1)
3 Suggest two reasons why Tottenham Hotspur might be making the share issue (2)
4 What evidence is there to show that the club could have sold more shares? (2)
5 Name two 'institutions' which buy shares through the Stock Exchange and explain where they obtain their funds from. (4)

6 (a) What are 'stags'?   (1)
   (b) Why might they be expected to make a 'killing' on Spurs shares in the following week?
                                                                                                  (3)
7 On what grounds do people often criticize the Stock Exchange?   (6)

This type of question usually has an incline of difficulty. Marks are often given in brackets after each sub-section of a question. The opening questions are relatively easy for single marks and the last question demands more thought and organization which is rewarded with more marks. However, a well-prepared student who has thoroughly revised has no need to fear such questions.

(b) Statistical Figures can be presented in various ways *i.e.* pie charts, histograms, tables, lists, etc. They are given as data which needs interpreting. The interpretation is usually done in a structured way through several questions.

With such questions it is very important to look at the scale of measurement, particularly where official statistics on trade, inflation and unemployment are presented. Thus if a calculation is required, then the answer which you will give will be in the correct measure *i.e.* millions not thousands or billions! You should also examine the data to see if a source is given. This might help you if the data's accuracy needs discussing. In the example below the information is hypothetical.

Workers Employed	Units of output per week			
	Firm A	Firm B	Firm C	Firm D
1	5	50	2	8
2	12	100	12	18
3	26	150	26	29
4	47	200	42	41
5	75	250	57	54
6	110	300	71	68

(i) The table above shows how the output of four firms would vary as the number of employees increases, other factors being constant.
(a) Calculate the marginal product for Firm B when a fifth worker is employed.   (2)
(b) Which firm experiences diminishing returns to labour? At what level of employment does this occur?   (3)
(c) Explain why diminishing returns takes place.   (5)

(Part question Oxford 1981)

The question seeks application of the concept of marginal product (*a*), interpretation of the data to identify the onset of diminishing returns (*b*), and general explanation of the idea of diminishing returns (*c*).

Generally, when data has to be interpreted in order to identify trends, it is sensible to look **along and down** the information. The headings to columns may be important, particularly when making comparisons. You should also remember the difference between **absolute** changes and **relative** changes.

For instance, if the index of industrial rates was as below:

1979 – 100
1980 – 125
1981 – 152

The largest absolute change was 1980 to 1981 (27 points) but the greatest relative change was 1979 to 1980 (25%). Note the % change 1980 to 1981 was 21.6% $\left(\frac{27}{125} \times 100 \right)$.

(c) Diagrammatic Diagrams are a distinctive feature of Economics. Occasionally they are used in examination questions, as below:

The diagram indicates the original demand and supply curves (D and S) for a particular Commodity X, which is complementary to another Commodity Y.
(i) What is a complementary good? Give two examples of pairs of complementary goods.   (4)

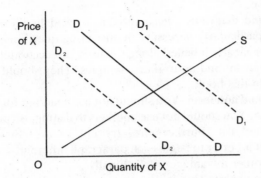

(ii) Assume there is an increase in the supply of good Y, other things being equal. Starting from the original demand and supply curves for Commodity X, which curve best illustrates the new situation? Explain your answer.   (6)

(*AEB 1980*)

Part **(i)** of this question can be answered without the diagram. Part **(ii)** gives a choice between D1 (correct) and D2. It requires understanding of the relationship between complementary goods, knowledge of certain economic assumptions, and application of a concept.

Some economic questions seek the construction of demand and supply diagrams from given data. For example:

The information below refers to the demand and supply schedules for potatoes:

Price (P)	Amount demanded (m tons/week)	Amount supplied (m tons/week)
15	30	62
14	35	60
13	41	57
12	45	53
11	49	49
10	53	45
9	57	41

(i) On the graph paper provided, draw the demand and supply curves for potatoes.   (4)
(ii) What would be the equilibrium price?   (1)
(iii) What would be the effect of the Government fixing a price of 10p per lb?   (2)
(iv) Assuming demand remains unchanged, what effects will a 2p per lb tax on supply have?   (3)

In this question part **(i)** requires accurate drawing and labelling of the demand and supply curves. They could be used to confirm the equilibrium price of 11p (part **(ii)**). On the diagram, the fixed price could be shown. This would make part **(iii)** easier to visualize and describe. Similarly, the fall in supply caused by the tax could be illustrated on the diagram. It would show the increase in price and fall in quantity demanded vividly (part **(iv)**).

Essays

These are still the most popular and widely used method of assessment in Economics. The analysis of syllabuses and examinations shows that for most O levels over 70% of the final marks are gained on essay questions. This is less than in the past. Also, increasingly the essays are subdivided and structured, so that the 'art' of essay-writing is now less important. However, the subdividing of questions has tended to increase the reliability of the marking, which is to the student's benefit.

The main tips which I would give you are:

(a) Only answer questions on topics which you have revised. If you don't do much revision your choice, and therefore your chances, will be limited.

(b) Briefly plan your answer For instance, if a question seeks the advantages and disadvantages of large-scale production, and why small firms manage to survive, jot down the relevant mnemonics – 'MATEFIT', 'LICE, 'SWIRL' and 'FIT'.

(c) Include relevant points and facts It is no good writing down information which you have learned if it does not answer the question. I know that it is galling to spend time revising and not be able to use the knowledge to impress the examiner. However, you just have to accept that this happens. For example, in the question above, it is no good writing about the limitations on small firm expansion because it is not needed. Examiners are looking for relevant information. They also seek some **balance**. If a question specifies advantages and disadvantages, then each should be treated fairly equally. Thus, by over-concentration on one part of a question, to the detriment of the rest, you will be limiting the number of marks which you will receive.

(d) Include examples and diagrams These should be used to illustrate and enhance your answer. Diagrams are particularly necessary in answering questions on Demand/Supply and markets. They should be clearly labelled along the axes and accurately drawn. Examiners are usually impressed by relevant and up-to-date examples. They should be learned beforehand. There are many given in this book.

(e) Do not use headings and noteform You should not use headings for sections, but you should write in continuous prose. You should not use numbers to distinguish points as it is bad style and looks like a remembered list. Furthermore, try not to use 'Firstly . . .' 'Secondly . . .' 'Thirdly . . .'. Instead, it is better to begin each paragraph differently such as – 'Firstly . . .'; 'A second point . . .'; 'Another advantage . . .'; 'Finally . . .'.

(f) Do not write long sentences This is a very common fault with many students. In long sentences, separate points get amalgamated and credit is lost. Short sentences make the points better.

4 Examination day

The amount of **revision** done on examination day depends on the thoroughness with which you have prepared yourself for the examination and the time of day when the examination is sat. If the examination is in the **morning** there will be little time for revision, anyway. If the examination is in the **afternoon** then some time might be usefully spent revising in the morning. This is particularly necessary if you have done less than six hours in total, because you will not have covered enough of the syllabus adequately. In this case last minute revision will be useful, although you should probably not do more than two hours. This will give you enough time to have a substantial break before the afternoon session, so that you can start the examination in a fresh state of mind. The message with regard to last minute revision is therefore – do sufficient to reduce your worries but not too much that you are mentally exhausted.

Half an hour before the examination you should check your equipment to make sure that it is working. Always have a spare pen and pencil available. It is often a good idea to get physically prepared by going to the toilet!

On receiving the paper, **read the questions carefully** and check the **rubric** (instructions on the number of questions to answer). Some examinations, particularly CSE, allow reading time, usually ten minutes. When you have a choice of questions, **tick** those which you know something about. Then answer the question which you think you know **most** about first. After that, decide the order in which you are going to tackle the other questions.

It is usually advisable to **divide your time** equally between the questions. On a typical O-level paper there may be 5 questions to answer in 2½ hours. This means 5 essays of roughly 30 minutes each. In general, try to leave 5 minutes at the end for reading through your answers.

If it is possible, start each question, particularly essays, on a **separate sheet of paper**. This enables you to return to a question if you have some spare time at the end and possibly add extra information.

Try to write **legibly** – it helps the examiner and YOU! Markers aim to give credit for information. Thus neat writing enables them to spot the points more easily. You should write down as much as you can in the time available as it will increase your chances of passing. However, in doing so make your information relevant to the question set.

Index